MW01627379

Surrealism and Animation

TRANSNATIONAL SURREALISM

Series Editors

Abigail Susik, Willamette University, USA

Krzysztof Fijalkowski, Norwich University of the Arts, UK

Exploring all aspects of the Surrealist movement since its establishment in Europe in the 1920s, Transnational Surrealism places particular emphasis on the international scope of the movement and on the long history of Surrealism, extending up to the present day. The series is a venue for scholars from multiple fields to engage with Surrealist history, with a particular focus on themes and concepts from the 1940s onwards, or on the activities of Surrealist groups in areas of the world that lie beyond the usual reach of studies of Surrealism such as Africa, China, Japan, Latin America, Romania and the USA. Monographic studies of individual groups, artists and writers are welcome, especially those that promise to uncover new or relatively overlooked areas of Surrealist activity. Proposals that promote gender and racial diversity in Surrealism studies are particularly encouraged given the fundamental aims of the series.

Previously Published:

Robert Rauschenberg and Surrealism: Art, 'Sensibility' and War, Gavin Parkinson

Surrealist Sorcery: Objects, Theories, and Practices of Magic in the Surrealist Movement, Will Atkin

Duchamp Accelerated: Contemporary Perspectives, ed. Julian Jason Haladyn

Surrealism and Animation

Transnational Connections, 1920–Present

Edited by Abigail Susik

BLOOMSBURY VISUAL ARTS
LONDON • NEW YORK • OXFORD • NEW DELHI • SYDNEY

BLOOMSBURY VISUAL ARTS
Bloomsbury Publishing Plc, 50 Bedford Square, London, WC1B 3DP, UK
Bloomsbury Publishing Inc, 1359 Broadway, New York, NY 10018, USA
Bloomsbury Publishing Ireland, 29 Earlsfort Terrace, Dublin 2, D02 AY28, Ireland

BLOOMSBURY, BLOOMSBURY VISUAL ARTS and the Diana logo are
trademarks of Bloomsbury Publishing Plc

First published in Great Britain 2025
Reprinted 2025

Cover design: Elena Durey
Cover image: LA PLANETE SAUVAGE directed by René Laloux
© 1973 Les Films Armorial – Argos Films
Photo credit : Screenshot of the Film

A catalogue record for this book is available from the British Library.

Library of Congress Cataloging-in-Publication Data
Names: Susik, Abigail, 1977- editor.
Title: Surrealism and animation : transnational connections, 1920-present / edited by Abigail Susik.
Description: London, UK ; New York, NY, USA : Bloomsbury Visual Arts, Blomsbury Publishing Plc, 2025. |
Series: Transnational surrealism | Includes bibliographical references and index. | Summary: "The first book
devoted to surrealism's vivid engagement with the history,
theory, and medium of animation on a transnational basis. Featuring seventeen essays by leading and
emerging scholars, as well as interviews with contemporary artists Penny
Slinger and Jacolby Satterwhite, this collection investigates a shimmering range of
topics on animated surrealism, including black humor, queer subjectivities, ecofeminism, Afrosurrealism,
and more"– Provided by publisher.
Identifiers: LCCN 2024050805 (print) | LCCN 2024050806 (ebook) |
ISBN 9781350475908 (paperback) | ISBN 9781350475915 (HB) |
ISBN 9781350475922 (eBook) | ISBN 9781350475939 (ePDF)
Subjects: LCSH: Surrealism in motion pictures–History. |
Animation (Cinematography)–History. | Surrealism–History.
Classification: LCC PN1995.9.S85 S79 2025 (print) | LCC PN1995.9.S85 (ebook) |
DDC 791.43/61163–dc23/eng/20250131
LC record available at https://lccn.loc.gov/2024050805
LC ebook record available at https://lccn.loc.gov/2024050806

ISBN: HB: 978-1-3504-7591-5
ePDF: 978-1-3504-7593-9
eBook: 978-1-3504-7592-2

Typeset by Integra Software Services Pvt. Ltd.
Printed and bound in Great Britain

Series: Transnational Surrealism

For product safety related questions contact productsafety@bloomsbury.com.

To find out more about our authors and books visit www.bloomsbury.com
and sign up for our newsletters.

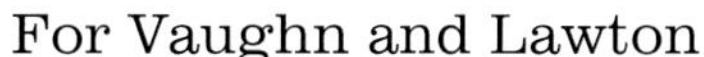

For Vaughn and Lawton

~ I walked with you once upon a dream ~

Contents

Illustrations

The Editor

Abigail Susik is Associate Professor of Art History at Willamette University, USA, and joint editor of the Transnational Surrealism series. She is the author of *Surrealist Sabotage and the War on Work* (2021), editor of *Resurgence! Jonathan Leake, Radical Surrealism, and the Resurgence Youth Movement, 1964–1967* (2023), and co-editor of the volumes *Surrealism and Film after 1945: Absolutely Modern Mysteries* (2021) and *Radical Dreams: Surrealism, Counterculture, Resistance* (2022). She has published widely on the intersection of surrealism, radicalism, and protest.

Notes on Contributors

Paulina Caro Troncoso is a Leverhulme Trust Fellow at Bibliotheca Hertziana – Max Planck Institute for Art History. She recently completed her PhD on Roberto Matta and has published in the *Bulletin of Latin American Research* and the *Journal of Surrealism and the Americas*.

Cheri Donaldson taught art history at UniSA and has written articles and essays on Australian and Czech Surrealism. Her forthcoming biography of Marek, *Dušan Marek: 'The Nature' of Surrealism and its Spell*, is based on her doctoral research and her research into surrealism and ecological philosophy.

Ken Eisenstein is an Associate Professor in Bucknell University's Film/Media Studies Program, USA. His writing, mainly on Ernie Gehr and Hollis Frampton, hopes to soon branch out toward Stan Brakhage.

Krzysztof Fijalkowski is Professor of Visual Culture at the Fine Art programme at Norwich University of the Arts, UK. His research explores the history, theory and cross-media practices of international surrealism.

Catherine L. Hansen is Assistant Professor by Special Appointment at the Centre for Global Education, University of Tokyo, Japan. She writes on surrealism, practices and politics of attention and media/game studies.

David Hopkins is Professor Emeritus and Professorial Research Fellow in Art History at the University of Glasgow, UK. The latest of his many books on dada and surrealism is *Dark Toys: Surrealism and the Culture of Childhood* (2021).

Catriona McAra is Lecturer in Art History, University of Aberdeen, UK. She is author of *A Surrealist Stratigraphy of Dorothea Tanning's Chasm* (2017) and *The Medium of Leonora Carrington* (2022).

Judith Noble is Professor of Film and the Occult at Arts University Plymouth, UK. She writes about film, surrealism, the occult and women artists, Maya Deren, Derek Jarman and Kenneth Anger.

Kristoffer Noheden is Reader and Research Fellow in Cinema Studies at Stockholm University, Sweden. He has published widely on surrealism across the art forms, in relation to ecology, esotericism and documentary.

Jorgelina Orfila and **Francisco Ortega** are Associated Professors at Texas Tech University, USA. They form the collective of animation scholars, AnimationDuo, which explores the intersections and diffractions between animation and modern and contemporary art.

Gavin Parkinson is Professor of European Modernism at The Courtauld Institute of Art, London, UK, and author of *Robert Rauschenberg and Surrealism* (2023), *Surrealism, Art and Modern Science* (2008) and several other books on surrealism.

Ann Reynolds teaches Art History at the University of Texas at Austin, USA. She is currently completing a book entitled *Imagining an Altogether: Cinema, Surrealism, and New York 1940–1970*.

Michael Richardson is Visiting Fellow at Goldsmiths, University of London. He has published widely on different aspects of surrealism.

Marie Arleth Skov is a Danish art historian living in Berlin and currently working on an exhibition on the topic of the body in punk culture for ARoS Aarhus Art Museum.

Raymond Spiteri teaches Art History at Victoria University of Wellington, New Zealand. His research and publications are focused on the culture and politics of surrealism.

Ian Walker was Professor of Photography at the University of South Wales until 2013. He has written extensively about surrealism and photography, including the book *City Gorged with Dreams* (2002).

Alex Zivkovic is a PhD candidate at Columbia University writing a dissertation on the history of greenhouses, aquariums, and colonial gardens built at world's fairs in Paris (c.1860–1940). He recently contributed catalogue entries for *Manet: A Model Family* (The Isabella Stewart Gardner Museum, 2024) and wrote two catalogue essays for *Remedios Varo: Science Fictions* (Art Institute of Chicago, 2023).

Acknowledgements

For supportive collaboration, I extend sincere thanks to editor Ross Fraser-Smith, my Bloomsbury Transnational Surrealism Series co-editor Krzysztof Fijalkowski and all of the contributors. My four-part introduction was written during an Allen W. Clowes Fellowship during the spring of 2024 at the National Humanities Center, and my chapter on Borowczyk, Laloux and Topor was commenced during a City of Vienna fellowship in winter of 2022–3 at the IFK International Research Center for Cultural Studies in Austria. Thanks go to Kristoffer Noheden, who contributed valuable insights, and to Lea Petrikova, for sharing her expertise on films by Éric Duvivier. We are fortunate to have been granted rights for a cover image by artists Nathalie Djurberg and Hans Berg. Artists Kim L. Pace, Jacolby Satterwhite and Penny Slinger generously provided images. I am also grateful to Aube Elléouët Breton and Constance Krebs at the Association Atelier André Breton for their assistance with images. Thanks to the generous support of Ann May Greene and the Norman Rubington Foundation, we have been able to provide images from this artist's rare films. I appreciate Daniel Bird's assistance with my chapter on Borowczyk. Michael Vandelaar applied his keen eye and quick wit to the proofs.

Introduction: 'Beyond Disorientation': Surrealism, Animation and the Hidden World

Abigail Susik

Surrealism and the phoenix of animation

Given surrealism's transnational character as an epochal sociocultural movement, the surrealist engagement with cinema encompasses a vast and varied history.[1] Yet, what can be said about surrealism's profound investment in what Morocco-born film critic and director Robert Benayoun called in 1963 'the phoenix of animation'?[2] Moreover, how does surrealism's extensive engagement with animation relate to its overarching struggle since 1924 to transform human life in revolutionary ways?

Even though many international surrealists have considered animation to be uniquely tied to the movement's aims, surrealism's attraction to the medium of animation has never been addressed extensively in scholarship, perhaps partly because the field of Film Studies itself has often marginalized animation.[3] When Benayoun, a queer member of the Paris Surrealist Group, called animation a 'phoenix', he referred in part to the rapid development of this medium and its technological supports since the turn of the twentieth century – characteristics he thought contributed to its critical neglect. Conceptualizing animation's changeability, Benayoun defined animation as a cinematic approach to diverse experiments with the simulation of 'movement', in which various film-making techniques using images, photographs or objects – ever advancing into more sophisticated methods over time – create the illusion of dynamism out of static materials.[4]

Benayoun's flexible terms for animation, which also inform the working definition used in this volume, presage Maureen Furniss' recent argument for framing animation as a continuum between the polarities of abstraction and mimesis.[5] Yet, although such descriptions of animation reveal much of the medium's quintessentially cinematic essence, Benayoun complained that animation's cinematic status remained ever in question. 'They [critics] treat the genre [animation] as if it were a kind of annex to the beaux-arts, an after-dinner amusement', he said, adding that, 'over the years, film critics have refused to take notice of what they consider a puerile sop on the weekly theater programmes'.[6] In this regard, Benayoun recalled the words of his friend Ado Kyrou, another surrealist film critic and film-maker, who opined a decade earlier in the first edition of his book, *Le Surréalisme au cinéma* (1953), that animation should not be limited by such compartmentalizations or considered a separate genre. Kyrou agreed with Benayoun that animation had almost always been neglected in the realm of cinema, which caused animation to generate its own trajectory and 'myths'.[7]

Contemporary theoreticians such as Lev Manovich have echoed Benayoun and Kyrou in their assessment of the aporias within animation discourse. Because animation accentuates the illusionistic nature of its techniques rather than following in the footsteps of live-action cinema and attempting to suspend disbelief through attempted realism, it became, in Manovich's words, the 'supplement and shadow' of cinema and a 'depository' for outmoded modalities.[8] But, as Alan Cholodenko has shown, since the 1990s, this marginalization of animation for both popular and scholarly audiences has diminished as a result of the mass popularity of feature-length animation and the digitalization of animation processes, which has supported a re-theorization of film itself as just one form of animation, rather than the other way around.[9]

Following such prescient assessments of animation's essence and status by surrealist theoreticians such as Benayoun and Kyrou, this volume calls for the repositioning of animation as a central and vital aspect of surrealism's investment in cinema. In support of such an endeavour, this introduction undertakes a partial overview of select moments in the surrealist history and theory of animation from the 1920s to the present, acknowledging in passing the more frequently discussed subjects of surrealism's affinity for black humour, burlesque, comedy, comics, pulp cinema and slapstick – but placing the full force of analysis on the medium of animation itself. In addition, *Surrealism and Animation: Transnational Connections, 1920–Present* is a study grounded first and foremost in the flourishing interdisciplinary field of Surrealism Studies, although its historical approach and methodology are also influenced by Art History, Visual Culture Studies, Popular Culture Studies, comparative Cinema Studies and, of course, Animation Studies. On that note, it is important to clarify that this volume minimizes considerations of animation as superficially 'surreal' or 'surrealistic' in a vague or commercial sense, especially in what Cholodenko has identified as the hackneyed trope that animation is fundamentally akin to the surreal, given its dreamlike or hallucinatory qualities.[10] Although the important question of surrealism's admiration for popular culture and, in turn, popular culture's enthusiastic absorption and recuperation of surrealism is frequently addressed in this book, our investigation follows a historically specific definition of surrealism. This is an understanding of surrealism rooted in the still-unfolding and enormously varied panorama of the International Surrealist movement (c.1920s to the present), as lived by members and close associates of its disparate but often connected groups around the world over the last century. With that said, it is important to clarify that surrealism is neither an artistic style nor a rigid set of ideas and formal approaches, and so the matter of surrealism's engagement with animation, a subject which we only just begin to address in a comprehensive way in this volume, is one of dizzying diversity.

With a purview that includes the geographic contexts of Asia, Europe, North and South America, with glimpses of African and Oceanic contexts, the contents of this book fall into three categories, providing a selective view of a much larger subject that requires further attention in future studies by other scholars: (1) specific cases of the *influence* of animation-related subjects (directors, studios, techniques, characters, individual films, theories, pre-cinematic devices, optical illusions, special effects, etc.) upon *members of the International Surrealist movement*; (2) examples of *contributions by members of the International Surrealist movement* to animated film production, animated film sequences, or animation history, theory and criticism; and (3) instances of practitioners, institutions, films and techniques in the field of animation evincing *indirect but substantial* ties to the *Surrealist movement*, as determined either by surrealists or non-surrealists with adjacent interests. Furthermore, the bulk of the volume focuses on special effects and animation techniques such as clay, collage (found images and photographs), cut-out, direct on celluloid, drawn/cel, puppet and stop-motion animation, but substantial attention is also devoted to contemporary animation and techniques, living animators and – to some degree – digital forms of animation. Nineteen chapters expand upon my introductory statements prefacing each of the book's three chronologically ordered sections: (1) the early twentieth century to mid-century; (2) post-Second World War; (3) the contemporary period.

From surrealist animated paintings to a surrealist theory of cinematic animation, c.1920s–1930s

Surrealist writer and theoretician André Breton grew up as the medium of cinema itself matured and cinematographic animation developed. Then, as now, animation included a dynamic range of film-making techniques from hand-drawn cartoons to stop-motion sequences, all of which transformed still images into moving pictures. Breton and his cinephile friends began enthusiastically writing and theorizing about cinema during the First World War, well before surrealism became a movement in 1924.[11] Yet, the theory and mechanics of cinematic animation were just as central to the formation and development of surrealism as were live-action films. Indeed, they saw film itself as a form of animation, especially when augmented by special effects that stretched the human perception of time and movement.[12] In a general sense, then, cinematic animation was a way for surrealists to penetrate the depths of unknown experiences and augur an endlessly astonishing future of expanding consciousness, as related to their call for a surrealist societal revolution.

Breton recognized that the 'marvelous invention of cinema' was a form of animation creating a mimicry of continuous movement through the acceleration of still pictures or image frames. Even so, animation as such held a unique place in his conceptualization of surrealism.[13] By 1920–1, Breton became fascinated with the recent developments of slow-motion (*le ralenti*) and time-lapse film (*l'accéléré*) and other cinematic special effects that had developed since the turn of the century. In a short essay written for Max Ernst's first exhibition in Paris in May 1921, he compared the German artist's photomontages, collages and overpaintings to these cinematic special effects whereby 'oak trees surge up', 'antelopes soar' and locomotives '*arrive* on canvas'.[14] According to Breton, Ernst's mixed-media works engaged deeply with the type of spatiotemporal disorientation or *dépaysement* made possible by decelerated and accelerated animation effects in cinema, as well as stop tricks or substitution splices wherein subtle transformations take place between shots retaining the same *mise en scène*. For Breton, Ernst was a magician who at long last killed the already-dead tradition of *nature morte*, or still life.[15]

Breton's friend Louis Aragon echoed these sentiments in his 1923 text 'Max Ernst, Painter of Illusions', in which he argues that Ernst employs a sleight of hand that, while stabilizing the original context of an image, diverts (*détourner*) its associations from within through subtle substitutions and displacements, awakening the image to a new reality.[16] Informing such assessments of Ernst's montage and collage as a form of prestidigitation was the surrealist admiration for turn-of-the-century trick films by auteurs such as the *cinémagician* Georges Méliès, the legendary innovator of stop-motion animation and other special effects that transformed live-action scenarios into phantasmagorias of the *féerique* (fairytale-esque; fantasy).[17] Before his death in 1918, poet and surrealist mentor Guillaume Apollinaire had claimed his affinity with Méliès based on their mutual enchantment of 'vulgar matter', and this parallel was maintained by the surrealists thereafter.[18]

Breton continued to develop his ideas about the revelatory power of animated images following the inception of surrealism as an organized movement in autumn 1924, when he published the first instalment of his essay 'Surrealism and Painting' in the fourth issue of the group's journal *La Révolution surréaliste* in July 1925. For Breton, the human eye and mind retain a state of 'integral primitivism' and untamed wildness, allowing humans to manipulate the world around them in a virtual and quasi-magical way through interventions in perception and consciousness.[19] His example is the prehistoric paintings of animals in the Lascaux caves. Painting, drawing and other forms of mark-making extend this innate

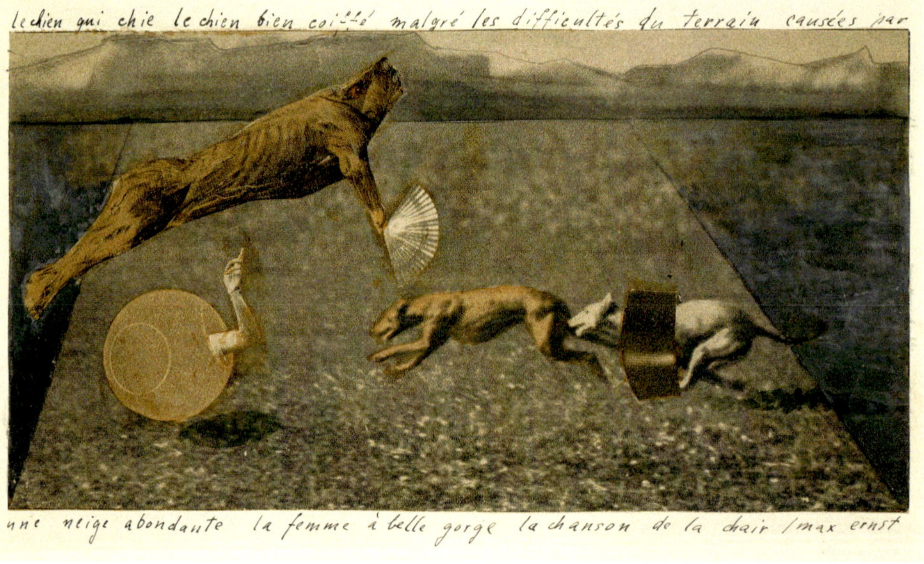

Figure 0.1 Max Ernst, *La Chanson de la chair*, 1920. Collage: gouache, graphite pencil and magazine illustrations cut and pasted on paper, 15 × 20.8 cm. The Centre Pompidou. Digital image © CNAC/MNAM, Dist. RMN-Grand Palais/Art Resource, NY © 2024 Artists Rights Society (ARS), New York/ADAGP, Paris.

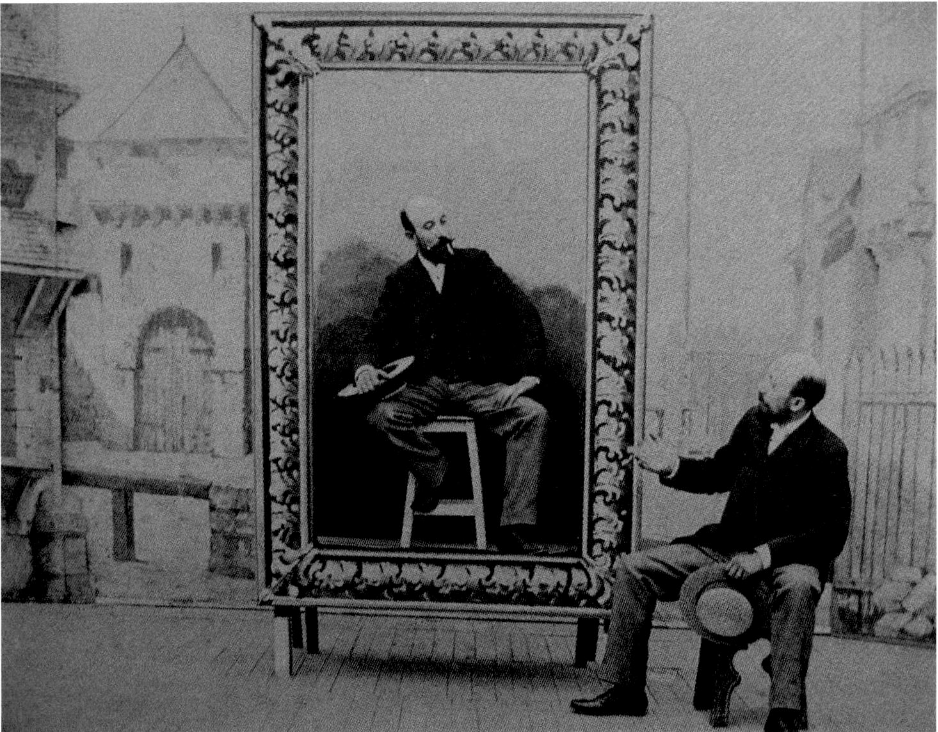

Figure 0.2 Georges Méliès, dir., *A Mysterious Portrait*, 1899.

human ability to alter the perception of reality, which is why any art that reconnects with this integral primitivism possesses a social and political revolutionary function for Breton.[20] In the fourth instalment of 'Surrealism and Painting', from *La Révolution surréaliste* 9–10 in 1927, Breton's discussion of the role of '*mediation*', 'virtual images' and 'hypnagogic visions' in Ernst's work extends his notion of an animated type of plastic artwork sought by surrealism.[21] Breton relates that Ernst believes that the figures he depicts have the independent power of animation, or autokinesis, as if they could 'step down from the frame' and reorganize the composition to their liking in a virtual form of *tableau vivant*.[22] As if echoing Breton's commentary, in the same double issue of *La Révolution surréaliste*, Ernst describes a boyhood reverie he had when suspended between sleep and wakefulness, in which his father created a disturbing animated drawing on a wooden panel depicting a vase that morphs into a spinning top and jumps off the panel into the room when whipped by a soft, phallic pencil pulled from his pocket.[23]

The surrealist concept of an animated, living painting filled with dynamic forms that could break through the fourth wall of the picture plane and invade both psychic and physical space continued to be developed in the early 1930s in connection with Spanish artists Salvador Dalí and Óscar Domínguez, as well as other surrealists.[24] Surrealist animated painting was a speculative type of simulacral representation with virtual aspects that hovered somewhere between erotic dream, transgressive fantasy and disturbing hallucination. As a psychoanalytic–cinematographic theory that preceded any extended discussions of animation in surrealism, the surrealists' exploration of the idea of animated painting in the 1920s laid the groundwork for increasingly explicit attention given to the history of animation by surrealists in the 1930s and beyond.

Breton's 'La Peinture animée' (c.1936–7)

Many surrealist films were made during the 1930s, some of which included animated sequences of different kinds, but it is arguably in Breton's writings that we find surrealism's most extended engagement with animation in the years before the Second World War. The most important and yet frequently overlooked example of this surrealist discourse on theories of animation from the interwar period is an extraordinary unpublished essay by Breton written sometime between the spring of 1936 and the first months of 1937 called 'La Peinture animée' (Animated painting). This essay was written (but never finished) during a period reorientation for surrealism in the wake of the Paris Group's break with the Stalinist French Communist Party a year earlier. The editors of Breton's *Œuvres completes* conjecture that Breton prepared his essay on animation theory for a never-realized volume edited by Paul Éluard. Éluard's book had been planned for the International Surrealist Exhibition in London during June and July of 1936. More recently, Dawn Ades has surmised that Breton instead may have written the essay for Alfred H. Barr's sprawling exhibition *Fantastic Art, Dada, Surrealism* at the Museum of Modern Art in New York in late 1936–early 1937, but that his text arrived too late for publication.[25] Barr included Disney drawings in the 'commercial and journalistic art' section of the exhibition and also screened a Disney animated short alongside trick film reels by Méliès and two 'animated cartoons' by Émile Cohl, so an essay by Breton on related subjects makes sense in the broader context of the American recuperation of surrealism on an institutional and commercial basis.[26] Whatever the case, Breton's 'La Peinture animée' is one of the earliest extended discussions of cinematic animation in the history of surrealism.

After briefly mentioning the cartoon characters Betty Boop (Max Fleischer) and Mickey Mouse (Walt Disney), 'La Peinture animée' invokes Breton's 1921 essay on Ernst, slow-motion and time-lapse cinematography.[27] Breton then proceeds to praise animation for its ever-evolving technologies, which have challenged human vision and quickly accustomed us to novel forms of acute and rapid apperception. He questions when animation will become dissociated from humorous genres associated with childhood and contemplates a future of animation rooted in drama rather than comedy. Breton also declares that animation led to the discovery of a new system of temporal perspective, as opposed to Renaissance one-point perspective, resulting in a radical transformation in the ontological properties of objects depicted in hand-drawn or painted animation. Animated objects, such as weeping pianos and elephants prancing under 'fixed stars', are 'distracted from their usefulness' and 'granted full license' to participate in an 'entirely imaginary life'.[28] This amounts to nothing less than a renewal of both the sense perception of vision and the production of art, because, in the wake of inventions such as animation, authentic creation must henceforth always be oriented toward a future experience of the unknown.[29] Ades points out that Breton invokes the Bergsonian term *durée* to describe this new form of spatiotemporal perspective.[30] As part of a larger shift in human consciousness, animation is for Breton part of the surrealist zeitgeist that surpassed mediums such as painting and sculpture, just as the stereoscope and the flipbook had been displaced by the movie camera.[31] In opposition to the artist of the past, the surrealist, seated at a 'coral desk', must continually go beyond the kind of disorientation (*dépaysement*) stimulated by the vertigo of time-based media such as animation, continually seeking the shock of exposure to previously hidden 'underground paths of penetration' (*voies souterraines de pénétration*).[32]

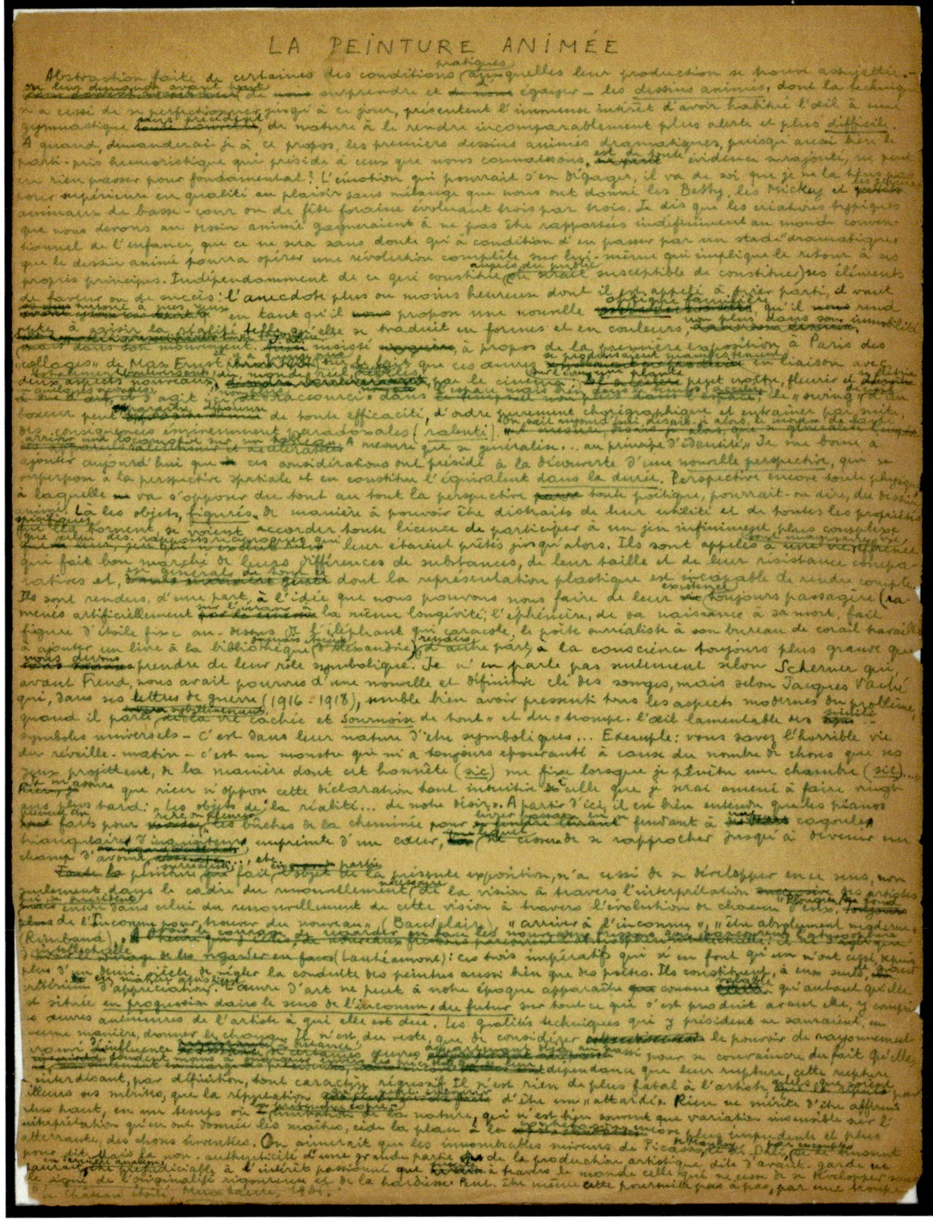

LA PEINTURE ANIMÉE

Figure 0.3 André Breton, 'La Peinture animée', c.1936–7. Unpublished manuscript. Atelier André Breton. https://www.andrebreton.fr/. © 2024 Artists Rights Society (ARS), New York/ADAGP, Paris.

The 1937 debut of the first American animated feature, Walt Disney Productions' *Snow White and the Seven Dwarfs*, may have played a role in Breton's delay in completing and publishing his essay, given the unprecedented international success of this cel animated, Technicolor movie made using a multiplane camera and released with an accompanying musical soundtrack. The revolutionary potential of animation as a critical medium may have receded for Breton in that particular moment of animation's spectacular commercial denouement. However, a more likely cause was the simultaneous embrace of Disney in a surrealist context by Dalí and Alfred Barr at MoMA.[33] Writing to Breton from the United States in 1936–7, Dalí related that 'the creators of animated cartoons are proud to call themselves Surrealists' and Disney was an 'American surrealist'.[34] Whereas for Dalí, surrealism had no limits in Hollywood, Breton surely recoiled at this presumed alliance of anti-capitalist surrealism with the nascent blockbuster cartoon industry. Even though Breton mentioned Mickey Mouse in passing in 'La Peinture animée', he would have abhorred the claim from the MoMA press release for Barr's *Fantastic Art* exhibition later that year that Mickey was 'the world's best loved Surrealist'.[35]

Breton may have sought to counteract the Dalí–Disney showdown looming over surrealism's engagement with animation, and, if that was the case, his answer was recourse to Eros. Perhaps responding to the development of Dalí's theory of concrete irrationality and his paranoiac–critical method in the early 1930s, which was accompanied by the elaboration of the Spanish artist's sexually explicit hypnagogic visions, Breton published his own account of an erotic animated painting in 1938.[36] As had been the case with Ernst and Dalí's accounts of dream visions as animated tableaus relating the tactility of artistic mark-making to the spasmodic or pulsatile movements of sex acts, particularly in the case of Ernst's deployment of surface rubbings or frottage, Breton's dream partly concerned the transfer technique of decalcomania developed by Óscar Domínguez in the 1930s. Breton's 'Oneiric Genesis and Execution of an Animated Painting' recounted like a film scenario a dream he had about Domínguez in February 1937, in which a painting-in-progress by the artist – not unlike Méliès' *fin de siècle* lightning sketch films – became virtually animated with a vision of animal fellatio. In the first portion of the dream, Breton had stopped to watch Domínguez paint, realizing that what he assumed were a series of knots arranged in a grid structure in the work were actually the hindquarters of several lions who were aggressively licking each other's genitalia in real time. The hindquarters of the lions were aligned with the sun and thus created a luminous and gradually morphing spectacle like the aurora borealis: animal as animation. The analysis of the dream that follows in Breton's essay marvels at how the raw information delivered by the dream, stemming from a wellspring of psychological and erotic content, can become a form of knowledge about the force of human desire. This network of ideas related to the surrealist notions of objective chance and the *trouvaille* (gifted or found object) had also been highlighted in Breton's essay 'Le Château étoilé', which was published around the same time that 'La Peinture animée' was drafted and is also quoted therein.[37] Breton ponders the potential for augury or omen-casting abilities of the '*riddle-image*' and the textured 'grid' or screen of unmotivated but deeply personal associations humans form in relation to the objective and phenomenal world, as in the case of pareidolia – the experience of seeing shapes or patterns in ambiguous images.[38] When human sense perception and cognition combine with subjective processes to alter the shape of the world in acts of either detached or paranoiac observation, a metamorphosis of the real occurs, '*riddle-images*' or '*optical remainders*' are produced and reality is animated with our desires.[39]

Breton does not shy away from characterizing both general animation theories and cinematic animation as having the potential to be a unified surrealist means to a psychocultural revolutionary end, the long-envisioned surrealist revolution of the mind that might foster the conditions for future collective sociopolitical revolutionary change. For Breton, animation held great promise for revolutionizing not only art and popular forms of entertainment, but human consciousness itself.

Notes

1 For an overview of surrealist writings on cinema, see Abigail Susik and Kristoffer Noheden, 'Introduction: Absolutely Modern Mysteries', in *Surrealism and Film after 1945: Absolutely Modern Mysteries*, eds. Kristoffer Noheden and Abigail Susik (Manchester: Manchester University Press, 2021).

2 Robert Benayoun, 'Le Phénix de l'Animation', *Positif*, nos. 54/55 (July–August 1963): 1–14.

3 Donald Crafton, *Before Mickey: The Animated Film 1898–1928* (Cambridge, MA: The MIT Press, 1982), 258, 348–9.

4 Robert Benayoun, 'The Phoenix and the Road-Runner' [1963], *Film Quarterly*, 17, no. 3 (Spring 1964): 18–19.

5 Maureen Furniss, *Art in Motion: Animation Aesthetic*, 2nd edn (Eastleigh: John Libbey Publishing, 2007), 4–7.

6 Benayoun, 'The Phoenix', 18.

7 Ado Kyrou, *Le Surréalisme au cinéma* (Paris: Arcanes, 1953), 107–8.

8 Lev Manovich, *The Language of New Media* (Boston, MA: MIT Press, 2001), 298.

9 Alan Cholodenko, 'Introduction', in *Illusion of Life 2: More Essays on Animation*, ed. Alan Cholodenko (Sydney: Power Publications, 2007), 15, 23–9, 34–5.

10 Cholodenko, 'Introduction', 45.

11 Georges Sebbag, *Breton et le cinéma* (Paris: Jean-Michel Place, 2016).

12 Karen Beckman, 'Animating Film Theory: An Introduction', in *Animating Film Theory*, ed. Karen Beckman (Durham, NC: Duke University Press, 2014), 1–22.

13 André Breton, *Lettres à Simone Kahn: 1920–1960*, ed. Jean-Michel Goutier (Paris: Gallimard, 2016), 113.

14 André Breton, 'Max Ernst', in *The Lost Steps* [1996], trans. Mark Polizzotti (Lincoln: University of Nebraska Press, 2010), 61; emphasis in original. Also see Yvan Goll, 'Exemple du surréalisme: le cinéma', *Surréalisme*, 1 (1924): 3.

15 Abigail Susik, '"The Man of these Infinite Possibilities": Max Ernst's Cinematic Collages', *Contemporaneity: Historical Presence in Visual Culture*, 1 (2011): 61–87.

16 'Max Ernst, peintre des illusions' is unedited and is part of a letter to Jacques Doucet dated 18 August 1923. It is reprinted in Aragon, *Les Collages* (Paris: Hermann, 1980), 27–34.

17 Susik, 'The Man of these Infinite Possibilities', 61–87. Paul Hammond, *Marvellous Méliès* (New York: St. Martin's Press, 1975). Aragon and Breton were probably aware that Méliès' office was formerly located in the Passage de l'Opéra, and that he gave pre-cinematic performances at the

Théâtre Grévin in the Passage Jouffroy (where, between 1892 and 1900, Émile Reynaud also projected the earliest animated films, *Pantomimes Lumineuses*, with his Théâtre Optique system; these locations are mentioned in books such as Aragon's *Paris Peasant* (1926) and Breton's *Nadja* (1928)). For an early surrealist reference to Méliès, see Salvador Dalí's 1932 essay, 'Abstract of a Critical History of the Cinema'. See also Paul Hammond, ed., *The Shadow and Its Shadow: Surrealist Writings on the Cinema*, 3rd edn (San Francisco, CA: City Lights Books, 2000), 63. Animator Paul Grimault and former surrealist Jacques Prévert interacted extensively with the elder auteur before his death in 1938. Former surrealist Georges Sadoul encountered the auteur in the late 1920s and started writing about his films in the mid-1940s. Georges Sadoul, *Georges Méliès* (Paris: Éditions Seghers, 1961), 9–10, 83, 232. The chronophotography of Étienne-Jules Marey and Eadweard Muybridge is also relevant to surrealist animation theory.

18 Marcel L'Herbier, *Intelligence du cinématographe* (Paris: Éditions Corréa, 1946), 16.

19 André Breton, 'Le Surréalisme et la peinture', *La Révolution surréaliste* 4 (July 1925): 27. For a translation of this text, see André Breton, *Surrealism and Painting* (1928), trans. Simon Watson Taylor (Boston, MA: MFA Publications, 2002), 1–48.

20 Breton, 'Le Surréalisme et la peinture (1925)', 27–8.

21 André Breton, 'Le Surréalisme et la peinture', *La Révolution surréaliste* 9–10 (1 October 1927): 39, 40, 42; emphasis in original.

22 Breton, 'Le Surréalisme et la peinture (1927)', 38.

23 Max Ernst, 'Visions de demi-sommeil', *La Révolution surréaliste*, 9–10 (October 1927): 7.

24 Georges Sebbag, 'The *Animated Painting* of the Surrealist Dreamer', in *Surrealism and the Dream*, by José Jiménez, Georges Sebbag and Dawn Ades (Madrid: Museo Thyssen-Bornemisza, 2013), 55–73. See also Sebbag, *Breton et le cinéma*, 79–88; Georges Sebbag, *Foucault Deleuze: Nouvelles impressions du surréalisme* (Paris: Hermann, 2015), 29–63.

25 Dawn Ades, 'Surrealism and Fantastic Art', in *Endless Enigma: Eight Centuries of Fantastic Art*, eds. Nicholas Hall et al. (New York: David Zwirner Books, 2019), 28–9.

26 Alfred H. Barr, ed., *Fantastic Art, Dada, Surrealism* (New York: Museum of Modern Art, 1936), 233, 241–2.

27 André Breton, 'La Peinture animée', in *Œuvres complètes*, eds. Marguerite Bonnet et al. (Paris: Gallimard, 1992), 2: 1253. Also see the notes for this entry: 1825–6.

28 Breton, 'La Peinture animée', 1254–5.

29 Breton, 'La Peinture animée', 1255–6.

30 Ades, 'Surrealism and Fantastic Art', 28.

31 Breton, 'La Peinture animée', 1257.

32 Breton, 'La Peinture animée' 1255, 1258. Breton's theorization of the cognition of animation prefigures Torre's application of process philosophies to animation. See Dan Torre, *Animation: Process, Cognition and Actuality* (London: Bloomsbury Academic, 2017).

33 Salvador Dalí, 'Surrealism in Hollywood' [1937], trans. George Davis, in *Dalí & Film*, ed. Matthew Gale (London: Tate Publishing, 2007), 154–6.

34 Dalí on American animators: Letter from Dalí to Breton, 28 December 1936, quoted in Mark Polizzotti, *Revolution of the Mind: The Life of André Breton* (London: Bloomsbury,1995), 439; Dalí on Disney: postcard to André Breton, Feb.–March 1937, Bibliothèque Littéraire Jacques Doucet, Paris.

35 MoMA, 'The Exhibition of Fantastic Art … ', [press release] n.d. MoMA Library. Quoted in Jorgelina Orfila and Francisco Ortega Grimaldo, 'Fantasyland or Wackyland?: Animation and Surrealism in 1930s America', *Journal of Surrealism and the Americas*, 11, no. 1 (20 September 2020): 2. For Eisenstein's 1940s essay comparing Dalí with Disney in terms of protoplasmic *anima* (lifeforce, soul), see Sergei Eisenstein, *Eisenstein on Disney*, ed. Jay Leyda, trans. Alan Upchurch (Calcutta: Seagull Books, 1986), 70. Also see Keith L. Eggener, '"An Amusing Lack of Logic": Surrealism and Popular Entertainment', *American Art*, 7, no. 4 (1993): 31–45.

36 Salvador Dalí, 'Rêverie', *Le Surréalisme au service de la révolution* 4 (December 1931): 31–6. André Breton, 'Accomplissement onirique et genèse d'un tableau animé', *Cahiers G.L.M.* 7 (March 1938): 53–9.

37 André Breton, 'Le Château étoilé', *Minotaure* 8 (June 1936): 25–39. This text was incorporated into Part 5 of Breton's book *L'Amour fou* (1937). On this subject, see Georges Sebbag, 'Breton rêve de Domínguez', in *La Part du jeu et du rêve: Óscar Domínguez et le surréalisme, 1906–1957: exposition au Musée Cantini de Marseille du 25 juin au 2 octobre 2005* (Paris: Hazan, 2005), 65–75. Also relevant is Breton's discussion of the fixed-explosive and convulsive beauty in *L'Amour fou*. See Ramona Fotiade, *Pictures of the Mind: Surrealist Photography and Film* (Oxford: Peter Lang, 2018), 225–9, 251; Darren Thomas, '(Found) Object Lessons: Dalí, Cornell, and Convulsive Cinema', *Journal of Surrealism in the Americas*, 13, no. 1 (2022): 36–7.

38 André Breton, *Mad Love = L'amour fou*, trans. Mary Ann Caws (Lincoln: University of Nebraska Press, 1987), 86, 88; emphasis in original.

39 Breton, *Mad Love = L'amour fou*, 87–8. Here I am influenced by my correspondence with Arnaud Maillet.

PART ONE

Activating Still Life and Materializing Dreams: Surrealism and Animation from the 1920s to Mid-century

Introduction to Part One

Abigail Susik

Part One pursues André Breton's suggestion about the overarching surrealist affinities with animation by exploring the initial decades of surrealism's burgeoning engagement with animation in a transnational context, moving between North American, European and Oceanic continental contexts. By the 1930s, animation had become a key part of Breton's developing theory about the revolutionary capabilities of objective chance, objective humour, black humour and slapstick cinema via directors such as Charlie Chaplin. Breton's 1936 essay 'La Peinture animée', explored previously in the general introduction, briefly mentions the Fleischers' Betty Boop, a cartoon character discussed from a surrealist perspective in this initial part by Michael Richardson, who demonstrates broad surrealist affinities with her libertine tendencies.

A year later, as Krzysztof Fijalkowski explores in this part, Breton lauded Charley Bowers' combination stop-motion and live-action film *It's a Bird* (1930), in an essay from *Minotaure* 10 (1937). Fijalkowski points out that Breton credits Bowers' film as thrusting the viewer into the 'heart of the black star' between 'the real and the fabulous', a statement that was probably an allusion to Georges Méliès' Star Films company. Or, it is possible that Breton was recalling a drawing featuring a black star representing 'the idea' by the artist Nadja that he had published in his 1928 book of that name.[1] Two large film stills demonstrating subtle movement from *It's a Bird* were reproduced alongside Breton's short text *Minotaure*, amplifying the importance of the stop-motion scenario in a surrealist context.

Connecting all of these ideas about surrealism and animation was the surrealist practice and theory of automatism, a critical method for the liberation of the mind under capitalism, in which the movement and content of thought became independent of any regulation or evaluation. Surrealist psychic automatism required that the body of the surrealist be pacified into an inert automatic state, like a robotic automaton. This permitted the stream of thought to become unusually lively, animated and autonomous in comparison. In his chapter in Part One devoted to the New Zealand-born, England-based animator Len Lye, Raymond Spiteri argues that the mechanical nature of cinematic animation resonates with surrealist automatism. Lye's animations made using various techniques starting in 1929 can be considered some of the earliest, if not the earliest, surrealist-adjacent animated films. In animation, technological apparatuses appear to give vital *anima* (lifeforce; soul)

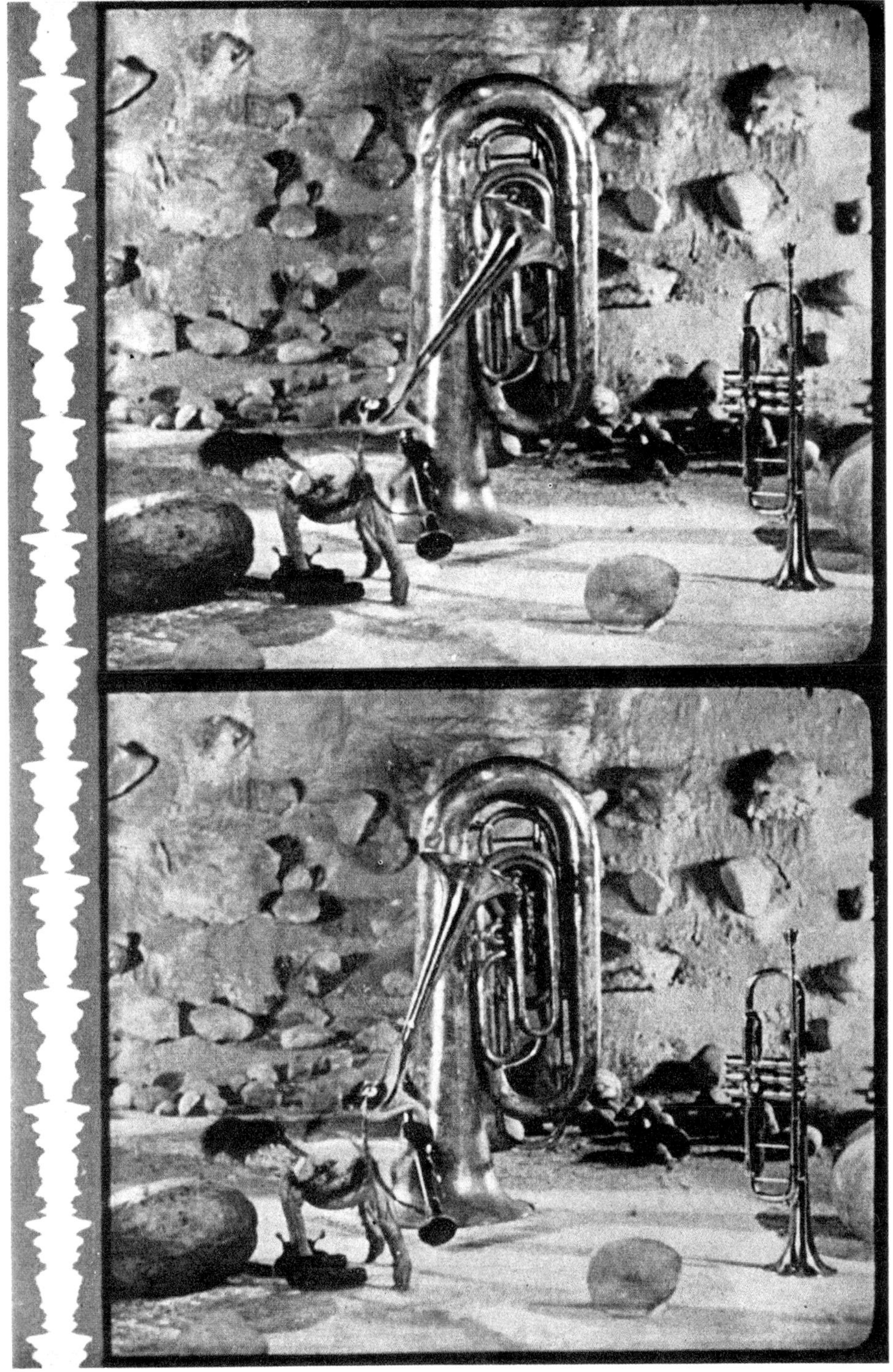

Figure I.1 Film stills from Harold Muller, dir., *It's a Bird*, 1930. Animated by Charley Bowers. Published in: André Breton, Untitled text ['It's a Bird – Harold Muller'], *Minotaure*, 10 (Winter 1937): 2.

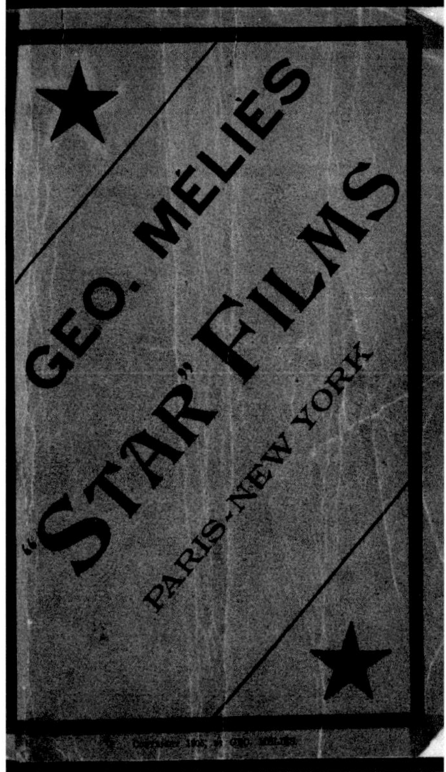

Figure I.2 Cover, *Complete Catalogue of Genuine and Original 'Star' Films* (Paris and New York: G. Méliès, 1905).

to inanimate entities. This resonated with surrealist automatism precisely because it emphasized the uncanny liminality of binary distinctions between sentient being and machine, body and commodity, subject and object, or life and death. Via the devices of the camera and projector, and by other means, cartoons become automatons that nevertheless mutate into chaotic entities capable of defying all limitations and control. Their magical animism is subversive because it defamiliarizes the foundations of so-called capitalist–modernist reality, which, in the name of accumulation, values commodities as much as life forms.[2]

As Alex Zivkovic discusses, Salvador Dalí was a leader in surrealist animation theories and became interested in pre-cinematic and cinematic modes of animation at least as early as the late 1920s. In the film *Un Chien andalou* (1929), Dalí and his co-director Luis Buñuel featured slow-motion and other special effects such as dissolves, multiple exposure and superimposed shots, some of which appeared to reference Méliès' trick films.[3] If it had been completed, Dalí's documentary film *Cinq minutes à propos du surréalisme* (c.1931–4) would probably have incorporated animated sequences of a tree and composite images of a woman–horse–lion. Likewise, during the second half of the 1920s, several films made by surrealists or artists closely associated with surrealism

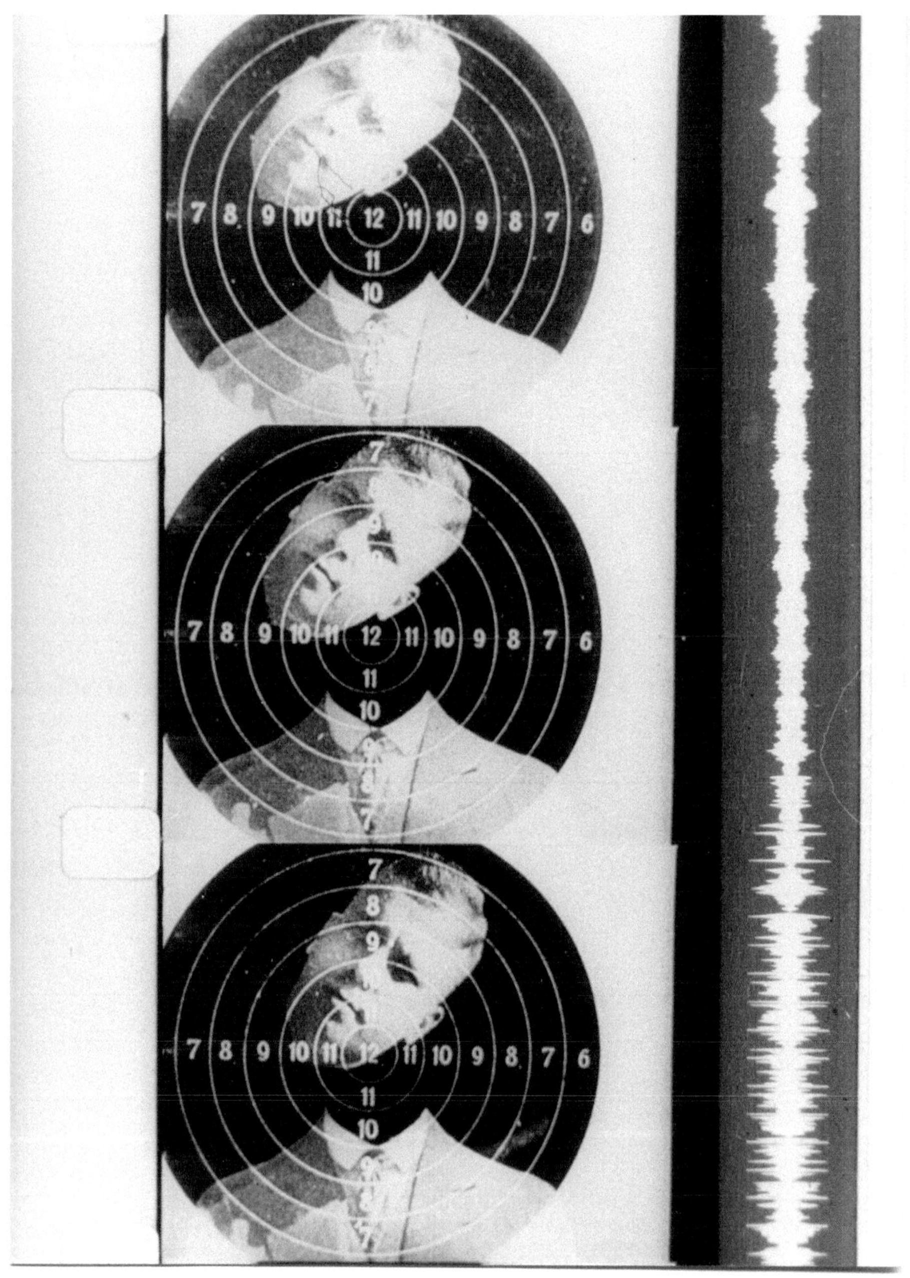

Figure I.3 Hans Richter, dir., *Vormittagsspuk*, 1928. © Estate of Hans Richter, courtesy of Re:Voir.

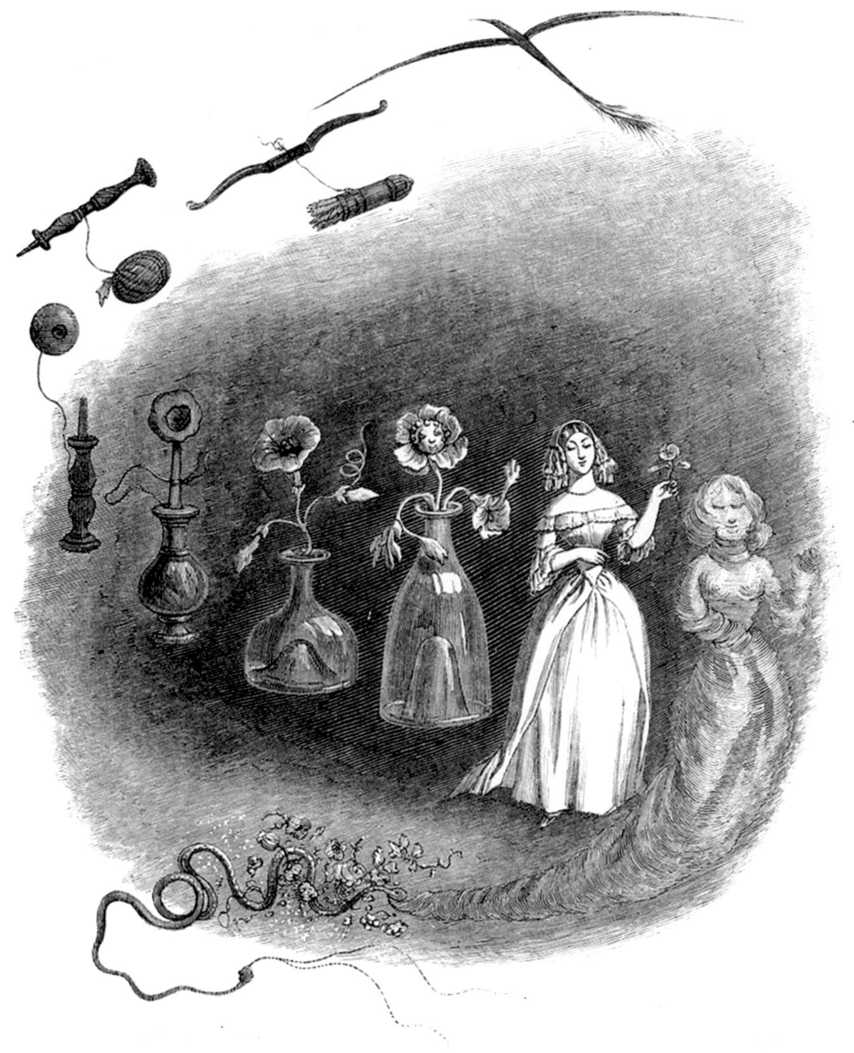

Figure I.4 J. J. Grandville, 'Du sommeil', *Un Autre monde* (Paris: Henri Fournier, 1844), 243.

featured either animation techniques or animation-adjacent special effects, such as stop-, slow- or reverse-motion and time-lapse sequences. One prominent example is Hans Richter's short *Ghosts Before Breakfast* (1928), which used cut-out animation techniques.[4] But other surrealist or para-surrealist films from the 1920s also flirted with manipulations of live-action cinema beyond experimental montage techniques and associative editing, such as René Clair's *Entr'acte* (1924; stop, slow and reverse motion), Germaine Dulac's *La Coquille et le clergyman* (1928; slow and reverse motion) and Man Ray's *Emak Bakia* (1926; stop motion) and *L'Étoile de mer* (1928; slow motion).[5]

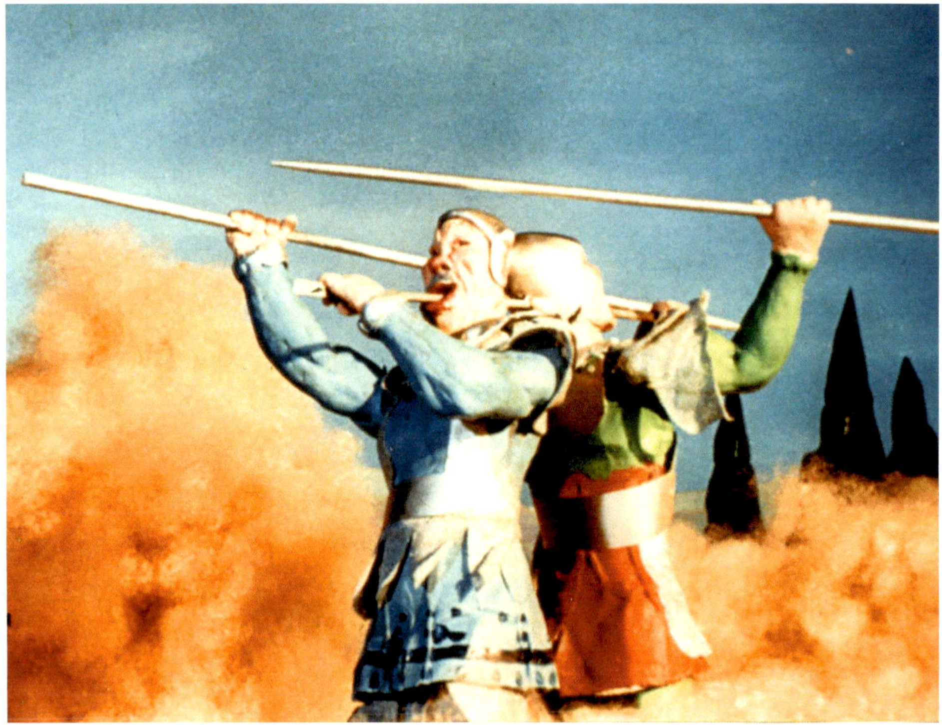

Figure I.5 Jean Painlevé, dir., *Barbe-Bleue*, 1936–8.

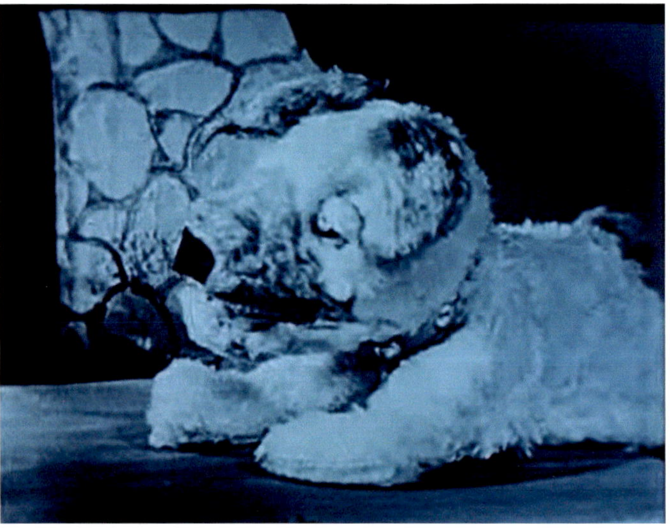

Figure I.6 Joseph Cornell, dir., *Jack's Dream*, c.1938–40.

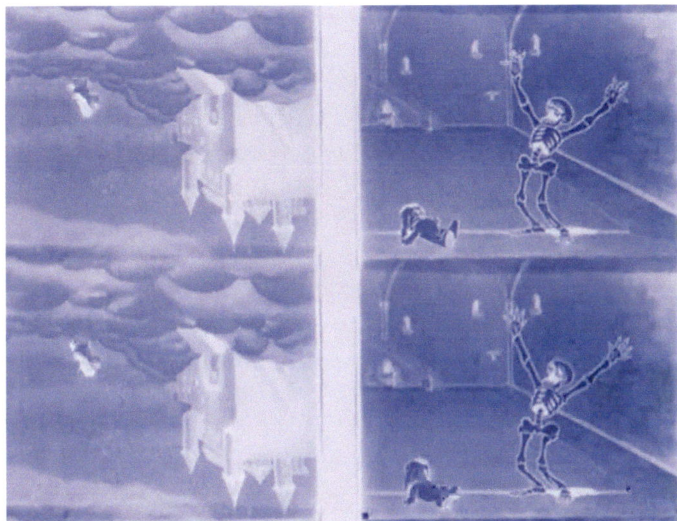

Figure I.7 Joseph Cornell, dir., *Thimble Theater*, c.1938–40.

By the end of the decade following the armistice, some critics were already awakening to the synergies between surrealism and animation, such as the French writer Marcel Brion, who likened surrealism's interest in oneirism and the inner life of the object to the development of cartoons such as Pat Sullivan and Otto Messmer's Felix the Cat (created in 1919), whom Brion called a 'sur-chat'.[6] A few years later, in 1934, the French writer Pierre Mac Orlan, an enthusiast of surrealism and theorist of the 'social fantastic', wrote an important essay about the nineteenth-century illustrator J. J. Grandville as a key precursor for surrealism's penchant for the vernacular marvellous in a tradition that also included Méliès' 'plastic fantastic' animation and recent *Silly Symphony* cartoons from the Disney animation studio.[7] However, as David Hopkins demonstrates ahead in his essay devoted to the iconography of Donald Duck, certain surrealists, such as Max Ernst, were invested in a more nuanced attitude towards the kind of vernacular–spectacular juvenilia offered by Dalí and Disney.[8]

During the interwar period, artists working in the orbit of surrealism, with or without the support of specific surrealist groups, began to contemplate the avant-garde potential of drawn and other forms of animation. For instance, Jean Cocteau's 1932 film *The Blood of a Poet*, featuring surrealist photographer Lee Miller as an actor, was originally commissioned by Charles and Marie-Laure de Noailles as a scenario for a feature-length cartoon.[9] Meanwhile, the prolific French *cinéaste* Jean Painlevé, who was closely connected to surrealism starting in the mid-1920s but never officially joined the Paris Group, was immensely interested in animation and used time-lapse cinematography in his nature documentaries.[10] Working with a team to laboriously mould plasteline figures over two years, he made the thirteen-minute para-surrealist animated film *Barbe-Bleue* [Bluebeard] between 1936 and 1938, a stop-motion animated short in Gasparcolor.[11] Georges Sadoul, a film historian and critic who was a surrealist between 1925 and 1932, when he broke with the Paris Group to become a communist apparatchik, wrote a review of Painlevé's *Barbe-Bleue*, claiming that its clay animation technique recalled the work of trail-blazing French animator Émile Cohl and made Disney's 1937 blockbuster *Snow White* look simplistic in comparison.[12] Then, circa 1938–40, the American artist Joseph Cornell started work on a trilogy of shorts that were later completed in 1968 by West Coast animator Lawrence Jordan, whose own work has extensive ties to surrealism. Two of the films in Cornell's trilogy deploy animation in connection with their exploration of themes related to childhood and toys: *Jack's Dream* combines stop-motion sequences with puppetry and inserted found footage, while *Thimble Theater* includes a reverse double projection of an extended found footage clip from a black-and-white Jack and the beanstalk cartoon.[13]

This initial part of *Surrealism and Animation* concludes with a chapter by Gavin Parkinson that excavates the surrealist obsession with American animator Tex Avery, whose cartoons were first shown in postwar Europe in the late 1940s. Parkinson's chapter serves as a bridge between Parts One, Two and Three of the book, in that the surrealist passion for Avery continues to develop between the late 1940s and the present day.

Notes

1 André Breton, Untitled text ['It's a Bird – Harold Muller'], *Minotaure*, 10 (Winter 1937): 2. Also see André Breton, *Anthologie de l'humour noir* (Paris: Pauvert, 1966); André Breton, *Nadja*, trans. Richard Howard (New York: Grove Press, 1960), 105.

2 On this subject see Scott Bukatman, *The Poetics of Slumberland: Animated Spirits and the Animating Spirit* (Berkeley: University of California Press, 2012), 20–1; Kristoffer Noheden, 'Animation and/as Surrealism', forthcoming in *Encyclopedia of Animation Studies*, eds. Eric Herhuth and Annabelle Honess Roe, 4 vols (London: Bloomsbury, 2025); and Paul Wells, *Understanding Animation* (London: Routledge, 1998), 10–11, 48–9.

3 Elza Adamowicz, *Un Chien andalou: (Luis Buñuel and Salvador Dalí, 1929)* (London: I.B. Tauris, 2010), 14, 40, 78–9.

4 Abigail Susik, 'Animistic Time in Hans Richter's *Vormittagsspuk* (1927–1928)', in *Time and Temporality in Literary Modernism (1900–1950)*, eds. Jan Baetens et al. (Leuven: Peeters, 2016), 243–58.

5 Although Dulac was not a surrealist, and *La Coquille et le clergyman* provoked the wrath of several surrealists, her collaboration with Artaud on the scenario merits a mention of her own theories of cinematic animation here, in texts such as 'Aesthetics, Obstacles, Integral Cinégraphie' (1926). This essay is discussed in Karen Beckman, 'Animating Film Theory: An Introduction', in *Animating Film Theory*, ed. Karen Beckman (Durham, NC: Duke University Press, 2014), 8–10.

6 Marcel Brion, 'Félix le chat ou la poésie créatice', *Le Rouge et le noir* (July 1928): 163–6. See also Esther Leslie, *Hollywood Flatlands: Animation, Critical Theory, and the Avant-Garde* (London: Verso, 2002), 22; Gus Bofa, 'The Animated Cartoon (and, More Generally, the Cinema Envisaged as a Mobilization of the Absurd) (1925)', trans. Richard George Elliott, *Art in Translation*, 8, no. 1 (2016): 62–8. For an example of the American reception of surrealism in relation to animation, see Leo. T. Hurwitz, 'Mice and Things: Notes on Pierre Roy and Walt Disney', *Creative Art* (May 1931): 358–65.

7 Pierre Mac Orlan, 'Grandville the Precursor' (1934), trans. Richard George Elliott, *Art in Translation*, 8, no. 1 (2016): 78.

8 See also David Hopkins, *Dark Toys: Surrealism and the Culture of Childhood* (New Haven, CT: Yale University Press, 2021), 57–64.

9 Annette Schandler Levitt, 'The Cinematic Magic of Jean Cocteau', in *Reviewing Orpheus: Essays on the Cinema and Art of Jean Cocteau*, ed. Cornelia A. Tsakiridou (Lewisburg, PA: Bucknell University Press, 1997), 42–3. In 1965, Philippe Soupault clarified that he considered *The Blood of a Poet* to be the kind of 'fake' surrealism that contributed to the surrealists' increasing distance from cinema. Jean-Marie Mabire, 'Entretien avec Philippe Soupault', in 'Surréalisme et cinéma', special issue, *Études cinématographiques*, 38–39 (Spring 1965): 31–2.

10 Richard Neupert recalls that Painlevé helped provide the ants needed for special effects in Dalí and Buñuel's film *Un Chien andalou* (1929). Richard Neupert, *French Animation History* (Chichester: Wiley-Blackwell, 2011), 79.

11 James Leo Cahill, *Zoological Surrealism: The Nonhuman Cinema of Jean Painlevé* (Minneapolis: University of Minnesota Press, 2019), 96, 142, 149, 152–7.

12 Georges Sadoul, '*Barbe-Bleue*', *Regards* 226 (16 February 1939): 18. In 1947, Sadoul wrote a chapter on the history of animation. Georges Sadoul, 'Découverte du dessin animé', in *Histoire générale du cinéma II, Les Pionniers du cinéma: 1897–1909 (de Méliès à Pathé)* (Paris: Denoël, 1947), 477–88.

13 By the end of the 1930s Cornell had assembled a large collection of early cartoons and trick films. Matthew Affron and Tom Gunning have shown that in the early 1930s Cornell was making or altering commercially available thaumatropes and other optical toys as part of his interest in cinematic animation. Matthew Affron, 'Joseph Cornell's Optical Toys', in *Joseph Cornell and Surrealism*, eds. Matthew Affron and Sylvie Ramond (University Park, PA: Penn State University Press, 2015), 104–21. Also see: Tom Gunning, 'Joseph Cornell's American Appropriation of Surrealism by Means of Cinema', in *Surrealism and Film After 1945: Absolutely Modern Mysteries*, eds. Kristoffer Noheden and Abigail Susik (Manchester: Manchester University Press, 2021), 60–5.

Chapter 1

It's a Bird: Animation, Objective Humour and the Heart of the Black Star

Krzysztof Fijalkowski

It appears that André Breton, for whom the encounter between surrealism and cinema represented a complex but passionate relationship, only devoted a single sentence of his writings to the question of animated film. But this sole reference, in issue 10 of *Minotaure*, to the obscure stop-motion comedy *It's a Bird* (1930; 14 minutes; USA) could hardly be more laudatory. Surveying the collision between film and humour in an untitled note – effectively an extended caption beneath a generous double still from the film – that would later form a paragraph of the preface to his *Anthology of Black Humour* (1940), Breton gives a roll call of comedy prodigies – Mack Sennett, Charlie Chaplin, W. C. Fields, the Marx Brothers – and connects them to the films of Luis Buñuel and Salvador Dalí. Then comes this fleeting but powerful claim, omitted from the *Anthology*: 'But in 1937 it is thanks to *It's a Bird* that we are projected for the first time, our eyes opened wide onto the blandly sensory distinction between the real and the fabulous, into the very heart of the black star.'[1] Subsequently acknowledged in passing references by surrealists as a classic, a deeper awareness of *It's a Bird* and the remarkable work of its maker would not emerge for another three decades, thanks again to research close to and within surrealist circles.

Minotaure credits *It's a Bird* to its director, Harold Muller (1893–1955), but at its heart is actor and animator Charles ('Charley') Bowers (1889–1946), the genius behind a string of forgotten miniature masterpieces. Bowers' filmography features plentiful live-action slapstick comedy in the great American silent short tradition, but it is for combining live action and stop motion – the 'Bowers Process' – that he deserves recognition, putting him in the company of animation innovators such as Willis O'Brien. Released in 1930, *It's a Bird* is a typically raucous and technically brilliant example of Bowers' work.[2] It spins the yarn of enterprising rascal Charley Chucklehead, who finds a legendary metal-eating bird, a genial (and English-speaking: this is among the earliest animated talkies) creature that consumes all kinds of items before laying an egg that hatches into a car. Bowers' animations, as we shall see, stage explosions of absurd humour and extraordinary morphologies within everyday situations that make their appeal to surrealists easy to grasp. This chapter aims to introduce this missing member of the surrealist cinematic pantheon, explore the animation of *It's a Bird*, and see how its relationship to the critical

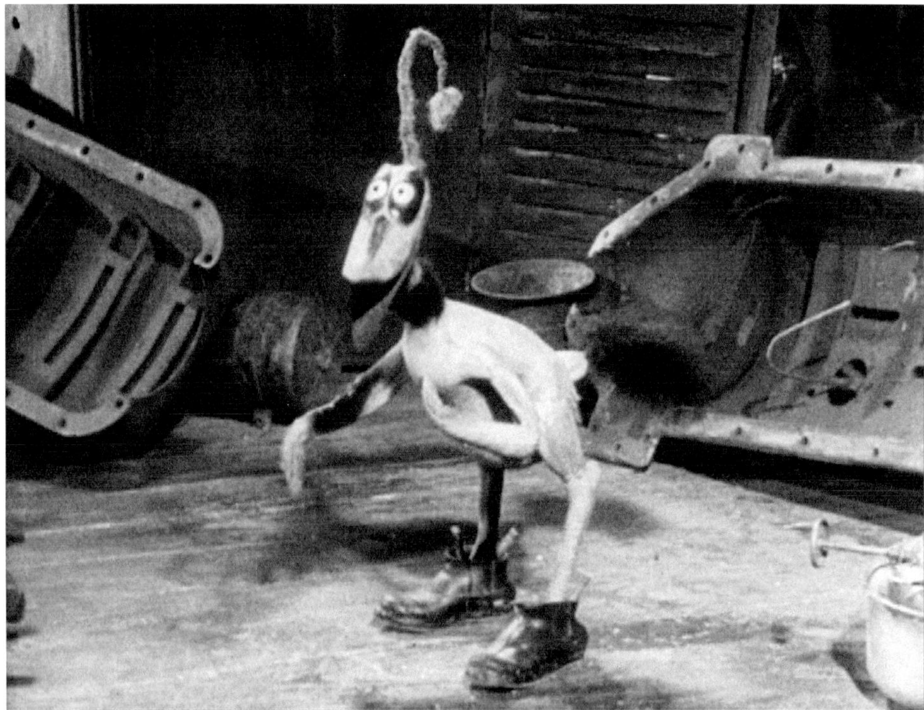

Figure 1.1 Harold Muller, dir., *It's a Bird*, 1930. Animated by Charley Bowers.

perspectives of 1930s surrealism around objects and humour make it such a prize for surrealist formulations of these concepts.

Breton's brief but prominent note encouraged other surrealists to acknowledge *It's a Bird*'s credentials, but often in ways that betrayed their scant knowledge of it. While a chronology in the *Almanach surréaliste du demi-siècle* (1950) cites the film erroneously as a key work from 1937, *Le Surréalisme au cinéma*'s author Ado Kyrou claims it 'among the pinnacles of surrealist film', but apologizes for never having seen it.[3] Breton presumably saw *It's a Bird* as a short before a main feature, and one gets the sense that it was a revelation ('projected for the first time, our eyes opened wide'). Other evidence shows contemporary surrealists already knew of Bowers. There's an account of watching one of his best films, *Now You Tell One* (1926; 22 minutes; USA), in New York in 1927 in the autobiography of Marcel Duhamel, resident of the celebrated surrealist enclave at 54, rue du Château with Yves Tanguy and the Prévert brothers; but Duhamel was also involved in dubbing *It's a Bird* into French – a film of 'pure poetry', in his estimation.[4] Meanwhile, Spanish poet Rafaël Alberti, friend of Federico García Lorca, Dalí and Buñuel, published his poem 'Charles Bowers, Inventor' in 1929: 'Mechanics / Love / Poetry / Oh!'[5]

The first informed perspective on the film within a surrealist forum would not come until 1989, in the Chicago group's journal *Arsenal* – a natural habitat for this acknowledgement given the group's unparalleled knowledge of surrealist eruptions in North American popular culture. Hal Rammel's short article 'Stop Motion Marvellous' pays homage to the film and companion instances of these 'exemplary tales of marvelous poetic humour', giving equal authorship to Bowers and Muller.[6] But the most significant endeavour to resurrect the work – this time with sole credit to Charley Bowers and involving painstaking recovery of his films, most of which had disappeared – was sparked by the research by author and film-maker Raymond Borde from the late 1960s onwards, helping locate a significant proportion of Bowers' output that Borde and others promoted through writings and screenings.[7] Although the first outcome of this investigation, an article in the film journal *Midi/Minuit Fantastique*, appeared not long before Borde parted company with the Surrealist movement, he had been a participant – albeit largely at a distance – in surrealist activities since the 1950s, and his future work as a film critic and promoter continued to be informed by surrealist perspectives.[8] Further discoveries, notably by Serge Bromberg, continued from the 1970s onwards; by the early 2000s, their legacy allowed the current accessibility of Bowers' work through DVD anthologies, some scholarly writing and informed online discussion.[9] Although he remains an obscure figure, rarely discussed in the literature, it is at least possible to acknowledge Bowers' status as a pioneer and neglected master of animation.

Charley Bowers: Bricolo

If there is still some debate about the authorship of *It's a Bird* and other comedies made by its studio during the 1920s, it seems clear that although Muller (about whom little is known) was assigned as director, the responsibility for their animation techniques – the 'Bowers process' explicitly credited for the films – was Bowers', not to mention that he often worked as their scriptwriter, cameraman and producer as well as lead actor.[10] This list suggests a surprising diversity of talents, but the man himself appears no less extravagant: Bromberg describes him admiringly as 'wily, a braggart, a prankster and weirdo, a fantasist at the borders of mythomania'.[11] Born in 1889 in Iowa, according to Bowers himself – a source most commentators treat with understandable scepticism – the son of an Irish doctor and a French countess, kindergarten was his sole education: taught to walk the tightrope by a tramp at the age of five, he was abducted by a circus for two years at age six. Accounts of his early years have him as an elevator attendant, shop salesman, jockey, clown, vaudeville performer, set designer … and eventually cartoonist.[12]

Whatever the truth, by 1916 he had joined an animation studio producing hundreds of short, generally unsophisticated *Mutt and Jeff* cartoons.[13] When this venture foundered, he set up his own studio in 1920, and developed his skills in stop-motion animation – the Bowers process – whose most innovative and distinctive feature would be a seamless integration of live action and animation for the 'Whirlwind Comedies' shorts produced between 1926 and 1930 – sixteen in all, of which seven are lost and some are only partially extant.[14] This gives them a unique character, in which the line between (more or less) believable dramatic action within comedy narratives featuring human performers and a fabulous domain of animated creatures, materials and objects (for the most part items that might plausibly also belong to the first realm but are normally considered bereft of sentient life) is constantly crossed, back and forth. All of this is presented in the framework

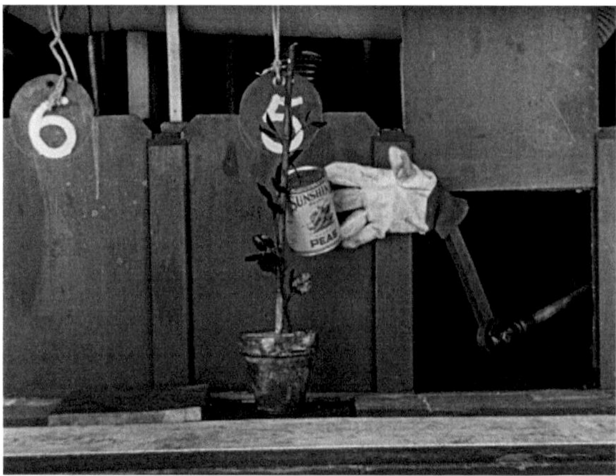

Figure 1.2 Harold Muller, dir., *He Done His Best*, 1926. Animated by Charley Bowers.

of a familiar silent slapstick genre tinged with elements from Bowers' vaudeville and circus background. Many of the gags are anarchic, straining logic and veering from the silly to the sublime. In concert with the animated elements, at their best this lends the films a dreamlike quality, untethered from conventional reality, and closer to the madcap world of cartoon animation than to contemporary puppet animation or film comedy.

In the 'Whirlwind Comedies', animation typically appears on the scene sporadically and late in the day, but its arrival signals a change in gear, a twist in the plot. Often marshalled around ingenious and extravagant inventions, it enacts radical solutions to everyday problems. In *He Done His Best* (1926; 23 minutes; USA), a series of hapless antics leads to the destruction of a restaurant and the loss of its staff, but Bowers' character has a plan: an immense food preparation and serving machine. Ungainly pipes above the diners' heads deliver tablecloths and dinner services laid neatly in place. Food is prepared by mechanized hands and gadgets: for soup, an oyster obligingly crawls out of its shell and into a bowl of water; a hammer smashes potatoes to mash, and for the finishing touch a pea planted in a flowerpot flourishes into a plant that sprouts a tin of peas. *Egged On* from the same year (24 minutes; USA) features another crackpot invention, a barn-sized contraption to produce unbreakable eggs. When Bowers' character steals eggs from another farm and brings them back under the bonnet of a car, the result is a vivid, strangely touching sequence. Incubated on the Model T Ford's engine, the eggs hatch not into chicks but miniature Model T's, unfolding and then racing in their dozens across the floor past the astonished Charley before scurrying back under their mother, who obligingly folds her wheels and snuggles down to protect them.

The list of wonderful springings to life in the films is long: shellfish scuttle across the floor; living shoelaces thread their way into boots; cats grow on trees; a painted seascape pours rain into a bedroom; a toy monkey grows a beard … Admittedly, there is also a tendency to recycle ideas, some of which crop up repeatedly. This is particularly the case for Bowers' animation-only films of the 1930s; his work did not adapt well to the advent of sound, and these later examples feel less spontaneous and independent, despite their technical prowess. Severe illness, leading to Bowers' death in 1946, and the fact that the majority of his films had been silent shorts meant that his early popularity was soon forgotten, not helped by the fact that animation would not receive the same scholarly attention as mainstream film for several decades.

It is significant that Bowers' eventual rediscovery happened in France, where his films had been widely distributed and appreciated, not only in conventional cinema programmes but also by travelling carnivals and entertainers.[15] Here, his character was known as 'Bricolo' – in homage to his inventor's prowess, a diminutive of *bricoleur*: someone who creates and mends things using available resources. It would be years before Claude Lévi-Strauss, in his study of structures of knowledge and thought, *La Pensée sauvage* (1962), identified *bricolage* as the principle of mythopoetic thinking in Indigenous cultures, gathering and adapting whatever elements lie at hand (in contrast to the engineer's reliance on specialist technical skills and tools in industrial societies). In many ways, however, Bowers' French nickname anticipates Lévi-Strauss' proposal admirably. As Rob King observes in a study of Bowers' films as exemplary of slapstick's anti-modernity, Bricolo's obsession with extraordinary inventions, shared with contemporaries such as Buster Keaton, owes less to modernizing visions of progress than to an earlier tradition of 'showmen and hucksters', wherein novelty, imagination, spectacle and hokum come together in 'vestiges of magical thinking', while the natural environment of Bricolo's experiments is not the factory or laboratory but the barn.[16] As King argues persuasively, the trick processes of early cinema, especially early stop-motion animation, are themselves part of this nexus of adaptive innovation sparking between invention and magic, subject to the same aura of secrecy and inside knowledge pertaining to *bricoleurs*, magicians and showmen.[17]

Bowers' connections to strands of magic, spectacle and *bricolage* also have one clear precedent from the perspective of surrealism's engagement with cinema history: the work of Georges Méliès. Often mythologized as one half of a foundational dichotomy within cinematic practice – where the Lumière brothers' invention of film spawned realism and documentary, the work of Méliès opens onto fiction and the fantastic – during the postwar era in particular surrealists would claim Méliès as the first to initiate cinema as the proper domain of the marvellous.[18] Author of over 500 films (the majority now lost) between 1896 and 1912, in an era when an international industry was challenging the artisanal modes of early cinema to which his works belong, Méliès had multiple roles as director, writer, producer, designer and often lead actor, just like Bowers two decades later. As with Bricolo's miniature treasures, Méliès' films, all very short by today's standards, were as likely to be encountered in fairgrounds as in cinema theatres. For this reason as well as the failure of his Star Films studio in the face of aggressive business practices, by the First World War cosmopolitan audiences, including first-generation surrealists, would have been forgiven for missing the brief moment when the works were in circulation.[19]

Significantly, just like Bowers, and a central motive for surrealist enthusiasm for his works, Méliès' career was notable for its origins and engagement in popular entertainment, theatrical phantasmagoria, stage magic and automata.[20] Made in a custom-built studio complex just outside Paris, the majority of Méliès' films were fictional dramas in which themes such as fairy tales, incredible journeys in the tradition of Jules Verne like the celebrated *Voyage dans la lune* (*A Trip to the Moon*; 1902; 18 minutes; France) and demonstrations of illusions and magic feats took centre stage. Like Bowers yet again, extraordinary mechanisms and imaginary technologies are juxtaposed with a certain cynicism about modernity, as for instance in *Le Raid Paris–Monte-Carlo en automobile* (*An Adventurous Automobile Trip*; 1905; 12 minutes; France), portraying the car as an instrument of mayhem. Nearly all the works are essentially comedies, although this categorization covers not only pratfalls, mishaps and staged explosions but also outbursts of anarchy and the absurd. Kyrou notes the 'absolute freedom' of Méliès' scripts, the destructive poetry of an 'avalanche of gratuitous acts' in his stories: his work is revolutionary 'because his frantic fantasies went against the habits established by society'.[21] Claimed by Kyrou as the first instalment of a surrealist history of cinema exemplifying emanations of the marvellous in film, Méliès is the founding master of a realm in which film, rather than reflecting the world as it appears, assumes its autonomous potential to construct and reveal a hidden kingdom of its own.

Crucially in our context here, what Méliès particularly bestowed upon film – origins soon forgotten and claimed by others – was a panoply of cinematographic 'tricks': in Jacques Brunius' list, 'fading, dissolving, masking, superimpositions, slow motion, quick motion, parallel action, close-ups',[22] deployed not as formal experiments but as a means to draw in audiences and make the incredible credible. Above all, Méliès is credited with inventing the very principle of stop motion – or rather, in classic surrealist mode, falling upon it by chance, when a jammed camera mechanism produced an accidental jump cut and turned one moving object into another, a technique his films would exploit extensively.[23] It is for this reason that, even if Méliès makes only occasional use of animation in the narrow sense of the term, and does so as just one tool in a whole box of them, he could be seen as the grandfather of animation, in which every decor, object and actor is set in motion, as the raw material of an animate world in which everything is liable to be transported into new forms and meanings.[24]

It's a Bird: animation versus modernity

But what of *It's a Bird*, and how might we view it to understand Breton's exceptional enthusiasm? Drawing upon several recurring themes from Bowers' 1920s comedies, as though to rephrase them for fresh audiences now that this was a talkie, in fact this would be his last film using the Bowers process (later works being pure animation). Like many of his previous films, the first half is live action, presented as a narrative within a narrative. Opening credits proclaim 'Charley Bowers in a Lowell Thomas Tall Story: *It's a Bird*', and an announcer introduces the host of a broadcast of 'Great American whoppers': Thomas, a real-life broadcaster, adventurer and travel writer who specialized in far-fetched comedy narratives and indeed would edit a book of *Tall Stories* in 1931.[25] Thomas invites Charley Chucklehead of Chattanooga (played by Bowers) to tell his story. Working in a breakers' yard, Charley's task is to dispose of scrap metal, which we see him do to comic effect, always at the expense of ruling class or authority figures: replacing antiques from a removal van with old fenders and boilers, attaching unwanted wheels to a fancy automobile, or assembling car components around a cop dozing on a park bench. At the Natural History Museum, Professor Diterhoffer tells him of a legendary metal-eating bird; Charley launches a ramshackle expedition to find it. This segment features two concerning moments: a poster in Diterhoffer's office with plainly racist caricatures of 'natives' feeding tin cans to the metal-eating bird, and the map of the expedition that eventually tracks it to the Belgian Congo (scene of some of the most iniquitous colonial repressions of the nineteenth and twentieth centuries). Did Breton, a vigorous anticolonial activist, miss these very brief moments, or choose to overlook them?[26]

If the film has been entertaining enough so far, now it shifts gear as live action is infiltrated by animation in a series of sequences in the vanguard of contemporary techniques.[27] Charley captures the metal-eating bird, resembling a plucked chicken in boots, tufted tail, ruff and top-knot, bicycles back to New York and puts her in a shed to devour scrap metal. We have already seen her eat a whole trombone; now she consumes the chassis, fenders, licence plate and wheel of a car, as easily as if they were biscuits. 'Can you lay eggs?', asks Charley; 'Sure, and I can hatch 'em too!' comes the reply. The bird obligingly lays an egg and pops it on a paraffin stove to incubate. Seconds later, the egg rolls around on the floor, and we hear cheeping: but in a *tour de force* of animation, what hatches out is not another bird, but an entire Model A Ford, unfurling from a smut of black fabric that grows first to a deflated rubber bag, then into a hood, radiator and cab that soon sits up on its fenders and wheels, finally growing a steering wheel, windscreen, roof and headlights.

The sequence takes all of forty seconds, and was presumably made by slowly dismantling an actual car, then reversing the film.[28] The Model A only entered production at the very end of 1927, so Bowers must have broken up a new or nearly new car, no doubt at some expense. Notwithstanding its slapstick genre, some deft critical messages are being proposed here. King notes how Bowers draws upon a fascination for technical invention as entertainment, using his films to create a 'delirious *mise-en-abyme* of mechanical spectacle'.[29] Whereas the animated car is the latest model, for Bowers it is pre-modern or (as King argues) antimodern magical thinking rather than the rhythms of the contemporary assembly line that hold sway. In the context of Breton's response to *It's a Bird*, Bowers' heady mixture of subverted technology, poetic imagination and brazen

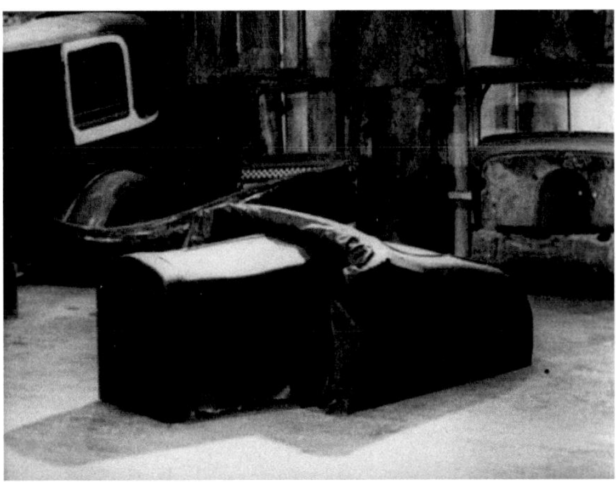

Figure 1.3 Harold Muller, dir., *It's a Bird*, 1930. Animated by Charley Bowers.

imposture can be linked both to surrealism's radical political critiques and its recurring fascination with crackpot inventions. In the very first issue of *La Révolution surréaliste*, Louis Aragon reported on the Concours Lepine – an annual Paris trade fair showcasing innovations and gizmos – enthused by its display of poetic–philosophical thinking, pure invention proposing 'a novel relationship between materials' in a dialectic that generates the surreal and propagates social change: 'invention is summarized by the establishment of a surreal relationship between concrete elements whose mechanism is inspiration'.[30]

For Charley, the metal-eating bird is a chance to use poetic inspiration to switch the polarity of progress, transforming grifting into a full-scale takeover of industrial production: 'I've got a great idea!', he announces, 'We'll start a flivver factory' (a 'flivver' is a cheap, poorly produced car). The bird laughs uproariously and dashes Charley's hopes at the film's close: 'We metal birds only lay one egg every hundred years!' But the storyline of a hybrid reality connecting nature and machine, (African) wildness and 'civilized' progress and economy is one Bowers also explored in previous works. When he animated an ostrich egg in *Say Ah-h* (1928; 14 minutes; USA), it had hatched into a *bricolage* ostrich made from the random found materials Charley grinds for bird feed at his farm – a pillow, broom, shoes, trousers and feather duster. This object-bird again eats metal, dances to the gramophone and lays eggs that produce more hybrid hatchlings, turning the farm's production principle on its head. It's an attitude that by 1937 would have chimed well with surrealists in France who, as Abigail Susik has shown, were producing artworks and texts that not only staged a complex critique of labour, capitalism and economy in contemporary society, but often did so specifically through the vehicle of hybridized forms that problematized bodies and machines, nature and artifice in ways that could be poetic and political at the same time.[31]

Between humour, object and myth

1937: the date of Breton's discovery and enthused reception of *It's a Bird* is significant, dropping Bowers' film precisely at a turning point in European history and a moment of intersection between two major conceptual currents for Breton and his colleagues: one a predominant focus for surrealist research and practice throughout the 1930s that would come to a head in the 1938 International Surrealist Exhibition in Paris, the object; the other that for Breton was just coming into focus, humour. These twin poles of attraction, humour and the object seem to have been activated in Breton's viewing of *It's a Bird*, and they offer the dynamic for a surrealist reading of this film (and of Bowers' work more generally).

With its choreography of perverted material relations and morphologies, *It's a Bird*'s animation parallels surrealism's attention to found and created objects from the early 1930s onwards. As the decade progressed, this theme produced some of surrealism's most familiar and enduring works, expanding into the stunning installations and environments of its later exhibitions.[32] The determining spark for this collective research, however, was a game of 'Symbolically Functioning Objects', devised by Dalí in 1931, in which participants concocted spontaneous assemblages from found materials before subjecting them to analytical readings, in a playful dialogue between *bricolage* and psychoanalysis.[33] Significantly, movement was a notable feature of the resulting constructions, and indeed Dalí's proposal was prompted by a work that fascinated the group, powered by the ambivalent motion of an object: Alberto Giacometti's *Suspended Ball* (1930–1). Giacometti's category of 'mobile and mute' objects – carved sculptures the audience was invited to manipulate or activate in a zone between desire and anxiety – seemed to promise that objects springing from the unconscious or seen in dreams (as Breton had suggested as early as 1925) could indeed be made tangible and animate, forcing their way into the everyday realm.

Breton's own forays into sculpture from the mid-1930s onwards, his *poèmes-objets*, also sometimes featured moving parts, such as *Rêve-objet* of 1935 which staged a model hotel corridor whose doors opened to reveal objects, images and messages. Taken together, one senses that an actual or latent animation lies behind many of surrealism's object experiments of the 1930s. This argument gains traction when we notice that, as Georges Sebbag points out, the theme of 'animated painting' – the idea that painted images (especially images of objects) would also imply their motion and development over time – preoccupied Breton around the same period he saw *It's a Bird*, specifically in recounting a dream about the work of surrealist painter Óscar Domínguez from February 1937.[34] We might thus agree with Sebbag that the projection of *It's a Bird* some months later chimed with Breton not just as a revelation but as a culmination of his recent thinking about the animation of the object and image realms.

If *It's a Bird* speaks to the fascination of the object, its framing within slapstick – with ancestry going back to Méliès' showmanship – situates it at the same time in the midst of the category of humour, a central concept for surrealism. As we have seen, with the exception of its final sentence, Breton's note in *Minotaure* is a paragraph about film comedy from the preface to his *Anthologie de l'humour noir* – six sections from the forthcoming book were laid out on the following pages. This work, gathering extracts from forty-five writers (some of them surrealists, the majority precursors) with brief introductory texts and a preface that laid claim to black humour as a sublime and liberating explosion, 'a superior revolt of the mind', had a long gestation; in particular, a version of its preface seems to have been drafted for some time. This might explain why Breton's comment on *It's a Bird* is missing from the eventual book: that it was added to an already existing paragraph, so as to complement the image in *Minotaure*. Finally published in 1940 (although censorship delayed distribution until 1945), the project was first mooted in 1935 and largely completed by the end of the following year. The central specific term and idea of 'black humour', however, asserted itself more gradually, and indeed seems to have crystallized around the very period in 1937 when Breton encountered *It's a Bird*.[35]

We might object that the sovereign qualities Breton claims for black humour feel a considerable distance from the anarchic world of Bowers' animated comedy, to which the viewer's response is more likely glee than *gravitas*. The answer is partly that Breton's is a capacious category, with space aplenty for ridicule, nonsense or dada facetiousness – not to mention that of course cinematic humour, represented by silent comedy, is invoked in his preface. Not enough has been said about Breton's own capacity for humour and laughter – Breton whose writings and thought can be solemn and demanding, but of whom Robert Benayoun (a surrealist colleague as well as specialist in cinema, comedy and animation) would say that he laughed 'with all of his being'.[36] But it perhaps also lies in the backstory for his thinking about humour, which during the mid-1930s drew upon the specifically Hegelian concept of 'objective humour' – thus aligning it not only with objects but also with another key idea from this era, and placing both under the sign of material but imaginative forms in the dialectic connecting inner and outer realms: objective chance: 'these, strictly speaking, are the two poles between which surrealism trusts it can generate the brightest sparks'.[37]

Among the least understood of his theoretical proposals – in part because the term 'black humour' passed into popular parlance with almost no reference to its original context – *humour noir* does not simply concern comedy and laughter: it is a profoundly ethical concept, flooded with pessimism and intensity, marshalled at moments of crisis but also capable of resolving or sublimating them: a kind of 'lightning rod' of the mind, as Breton would title his preface. The quality of blackness has particular resonance here, shadowed no doubt by the impending sense, as Breton's project trailed on through the decade, of looming political and moral catastrophe, but also with shades of night and occult revelation. This is the sense of gravity and dark illumination Breton identifies with *It's a Bird*: transporting the viewer 'into the very heart of the black star'. As Sebbag observes, for Breton the figure of the black star aligns with the tragic euphoria of Friedrich Nietzsche's last letters, but it is also associated with the zone of dream, where the 'Jeu de Marseille' card deck of 1941 designed by surrealists gathered at the Villa Air-Bel in Marseilles featured one suit allocated to Dream whose emblem would be a black star.[38] For Breton, as his note on *It's a Bird* concludes, this black star shines its penetrating but hermetic light at the precise confluence – and reconciliation – of the realms of 'the real and the fabulous', in other words where the everyday material world meets the domain of myth.[39]

Surveying the condition of animation in 1963, surrealist film critic Robert Benayoun reached for an avian metaphor to best sum up its mercurial state: part roadrunner (in homage to Chuck Jones), part owl, above all phoenix, he emphasized its will to activate the forms of the everyday realm in an 'irresistible delirium of movement', and its essence as an explosion of 'gags'.[40] In this light, then, animation stages its encounter between the given realm of things as they appear, and the insurgent possibilities of humour, personified as an emanation of protean nature, soaring above the world we know. Breton's keynote text of 1937, 'Limites non-frontières du surréalisme', had defined objective humour as 'a synthesis of the imitation of nature in its accidental forms on the one hand, and humour on the other. Humour, as the paradoxical triumph of the pleasure principle over real conditions at the moment when these are judged to be least favourable'.[41] It is in this sense that at a turning point in history Breton reads *It's a Bird* across a web of tensions and communications between material, myth and poetry, between tangible and psychic or imaginative zones, in which objectifying humour and subjectivized objects might align, and to which Charley Bowers' work gives privileged access. For a moment, in Breton's gamble on an alignment of humour and the object, at the fulcrum that is 1937, animation is an exemplary surrealist practice.

Notes

1 André Breton, Untitled text ['It's a Bird – Harold Muller'], *Minotaure*, 10 (Winter 1937): 2; all translations are by the author. Aside from this final sentence, the text is repeated verbatim in the preface to his *Anthologie de l'humour noir* (Paris: Pauvert, 1966), 19.

2 Although several DVD compilations are available, the one used here is the Lobster Films anthology *Charley Bowers: Un génie à redécouvrir* (2014), containing the complete extant works and a booklet by Serge Bromberg. Bowers' films are also readily accessible online.

3 'Panorama du demi-siècle', *Almanach surréaliste du demi-siècle*, *La Nef*, nos. 63–64 (March 1950): 207–23 (18); Ado Kyrou, *Le Surréalisme au cinéma* (Paris: Ramsay, 1985), 190.

4 Marcel Duhamel, *Raconte pas ta vie* (Paris: Mercure de France, 1972), 232 and 327–8. See also Louise Beaudet and Raymond Borde, *Charles R. Bowers ou le mariage du slapstick et de l'animation. Les Dossiers de la Cinémathèque*, 8 (Toulouse and Montreal: Le Cinémathèque de Toulouse/La Cinémathèque Québécoise, 1980), 41–2; Louise Beaudet and Raymond Borde, *Du nouveau sur Charley Bowers*, *Archives*, 3 (January–February 1987), 6. These two sources are the most extensive publications on Bowers' life and work.

5 Beaudet and Borde, *Bowers ou le mariage*, 39–41.

6 Hal Rammel, 'Stop Motion Marvellous', *Arsenal; Surrealist Subversion*, 4 (1989): 97.

7 For an overview of this rediscovery, see Beaudet and Borde, *Du nouveau sur Bowers*, 1–2, and the documentary by Christophe Coutens, *À la recherche de Charley Bowers*, 2003, in Lobster Films, *Charley Bowers*.

8 Raymond Borde, 'Le film retrouvé: le mystère Bricolo', *Midi/Minuit Fantastique*, 17 (June 1967): 62–5.

9 A notable contribution is Rob King's 'The Art of Diddling: Slapstick, Science and Antimodernism in the Films of Charley Bowers', in *Funny Pictures: Animation and Comedy in Studio-Era Hollywood*, eds. Daniel Goldmark, et al. (Berkeley, Los Angeles and London: University of California Press, 2011), 191–210. (Page references below are for the e-book version.)

10 Bromberg, leaflet for Lobster Films, *Charley Bowers*, 7. On the authorship question see King, 'Art of Diddling', 3 and note 8.

11 Bromberg, leaflet for Lobster Films *Charley Bowers*, 4; King, 'Art of Diddling', 3.

12 James Quirk, 'An Impression of Charley Bowers', *Photoplay Magazine* (February 1928): 13; Bromberg, leaflet for Lobster Films, *Charley Bowers*, 4–5; Beaudet and Borde, *Du nouveau sur Bowers*, 6–7.

13 Beaudet and Borde, *Du nouveau sur Bowers*, 8–11.

14 Bromberg, leaflet for Lobster Films, *Charley Bowers*, 4.

15 Coutens, *A la recherche de Bowers*, in which Borde recalls that the first reels he rescued came from a *gitan* (gypsy).

16 King, 'Art of Diddling', 2–4. On Bowers' films as critique of technology, see also Beaudet and Borde, *Du nouveau sur Bowers*, 4.

17 King, 'Art of Diddling', 9.

18 For example Kyrou, *Le Surréalisme au cinéma*, 60 ff.

19 Méliès' film output began in 1896, the year of Breton's birth (most of his early colleagues were around the same age or younger); because prints soon went out of circulation, it could have been hard for surrealists to see them until the rise of the French ciné-clubs in the 1920s began to revisit film histories. Jacques Brunius notes how Méliès' innovations were 'already

half-forgotten' by 1918 ('Experimental Film in France', in *Experiment in the Film*, ed. Roger Manvell (London: Grey Walls Press, 1949), 60–112 (65)). An early Méliès retrospective was held in 1929 at Studio 28, close to Breton's home and the opening venue for *L'Âge d'or* the following year. (La Belle Équipe, 2016, https://www.la-belle-equipe.fr/2016/12/29/apres-gala-georges-melies-a-salle-pleyel-decembre-1929-nouvel-art-cinematographique-1930/).

20 The best introduction remains Paul Hammond's *Marvellous Méliès* (London: Gordon Fraser, 1974). Méliès' interest in magic also includes allusions to alchemy, another factor likely to arouse surrealist attention. On the prehistory of animation in technologies of automata, another surrealist fascination also related to Bowers' works, see Siegfrid Zielinski, 'Expanded Animation: A Short Genealogy in Words and Images', in *Pervasive Animation*, ed. Suzanne Buchan (New York and London: Routledge, 2013), 25–51.

21 Kyrou, *Le Surréalisme au cinéma*, 70 and 134.

22 Brunius, 'Experiment', 65–6.

23 Hammond, *Méliès*, 34 and 90. Historians have located earlier instances of stop motion, but Méliès was the first to proliferate the technique.

24 See for example Ray Harryhausen and Ray Dalton's *A Century of Model Animation: From Méliès to Aardman* (London: Aurum, 2008), which begins its history with Méliès (38). Hammond notes the morphology of forms in Méliès' world, his 'willingness to grant objects complete semantic liberty in ceaselessly transforming them into other objects', and his tendency to treat actors like puppets (*Méliès*, 89 and 128). An instance of 'conventional' animation is discussed on page 97.

25 This framing has led to suggestions that Lowell was the author of *It's a Bird*. The continuity between the film and previous Bowers/Muller works makes this seem unlikely, although there are intimations that the film was originally planned as the first in a sequence of 'Tall Stories' under the umbrella of Lowell's brand (see King, 'Art of Diddling', 3 and note 9). The book, in print for many years, includes stories such as 'The Wooden-Legged Cat', 'The Convivial Snake' or 'The Frostbitten Car' that echo themes in *It's a Bird*.

26 These problems also chime with the less savoury aspects of Thomas' views, which included recurring racist tropes in his adventure tales. See Juli Kearns, 'It's a Bird', Letterboxd.com, May 2021, https://letterboxd.com/idyllopus/film/its-a-bird/. Put together, these serious reservations might also account for Breton's omission of his comment about *It's a Bird* from the preface to the *Anthology of Black Humour*.

27 For comparison, consider the celebrated stop-motion work by O'Brien, whose first forays dated from 1915 but whose major successes came only with sequences for *The Lost World* (1925) and *King Kong* (1933). The animation in these films, however, strives for a credible realism, whereas Bowers' world is anything but. For an overview of this early history, see Harryhausen and Dalton, *Century of Model Animation*, chapters 2 and 3.

28 If *It's a Bird* lampoons mechanization, such animation demands serious effort. Joseph Losey, who worked with Bowers towards the end of his life, remembered him as 'a tireless worker and obviously a first-rate technician … His work seemed like endless labour' (in Coutens, *A la recherche de Bowers*).

29 King, 'Art of Diddling', 2.

30 Louis Aragon, 'L'Ombre de l'inventeur', *La Révolution surréaliste*, 1 (December 1924): 22–4. Inventions are a theme of Jacques Brunius' surrealist documentary about inspired amateurs, *Violons d'Ingres* (1939; 32 minutes; France), which features an appearance from Méliès and closes with a brief animated sequence about astronomy.

31 Abigail Susik, *Surrealist Sabotage and the War on Work* (Manchester: Manchester University Press, 2021), for example chapter 3. One direction to take this might be Bowers' interest in staging mechanical animals, as an emanation of animation's powers to instil a vital life force in the inanimate: see Zielinski, 'Expanded Animation', 26–7 and 31–2.

32 The 1938 International Exhibition famously featured Dalí's *Rainy Taxi* installation, made from an actual car, extending the recurring theme of amorphous automobiles in his contemporary work; did Dalí see *It's a Bird*?

33 Salvador Dalí, 'Objets surréalistes', *Le Surréalisme au service de la révolution*, 3 (December 1931): 16–17.

34 Georges Sebbag, *Breton et le cinéma* (Paris: Jean-Michel Place, 2016), 79–88. As Sebbag details (80–2), Breton wrote an unpublished text, 'La Peinture animée', the previous summer. We might also recall that the dialectic between movement and rest (the category of the 'explosive-fixed') is embedded in another of Breton's defining concepts of the 1930s, convulsive beauty.

35 For an overview of the book's publishing history see Étienne-Alain Hubert's presentation in André Breton, *Œuvres complètes*, vol. 2 I, eds. Marguerite Bonnet et al. (Paris: Gallimard, 1992), 1745–70. In a letter to his publisher in September 1936 (1761) Breton mentions *humour noir* as one of several possible title options, but the decision to organize the project around this term, and develop its concept, only emerged later.

36 Robert Benayoun, *Le Rire des surrealists* (Paris: La Bougie du Sapeur, 1988), 13.

37 André Breton, 'Limites non-frontières du surréalisme', in *La Clé des champs* (Paris: Pauvert, 1979), 13–24 (18). This text, first published in February 1937, does not yet specify the category of *humour noir*, which Breton presumably decided upon later that year; the idea of objective humour, and its relation to objective chance, had already been presented in his 1935 lecture 'Surrealist Situation of the Object'.

38 Georges Sebbag, 'The *Animated Painting* of the Surrealist Dreamer', in *Surrealism and the Dream*, ed. José Jimenés (Madrid: Museo Tyssen-Bornemisza, 2013), 55–74 (72). Kyrou (*Le Surréalisme au cinéma*, 70) would demand to view authentic films by Méliès, 'the ones that in a corner of the set bear the most marvellous trademark: a black star' (a reference to the logo for Star Films).

39 Here we might note once again the resonance – in terms of Lévi-Strauss' formulation – of the animated marvellous of Bricolo's world as mythopoetic *bricolage.*

40 Robert Benayoun, 'Le Phénix de l'Animation', *Positif*, nos. 54–55 (July–August 1963): 1–14.

41 Breton, 'Limites non-frontières', 17.

Chapter 2

Len Lye: Animation, Automatism and Surrealism

Raymond Spiteri

In January 1937 two of Len Lye's experimental films, *A Colour Box* and *Rainbow Dance*, were included in a programme of surrealist and avant-garde films shown at the Everyman Cinema in Hampstead.[1] Although the programme did not include any films closely associated with the French surrealist group, many of the newspaper reviews focused on the term surrealism, reflecting the movement's high public profile in Britain after the 1936 International Exhibition of Surrealism in London. This chapter considers the relation of Lye's experimental film practice to surrealism. Rather than arguing that Lye was a surrealist, it suggests that his practice offers a simulacrum of surrealism, an amalgam of techniques that appeared to echo surrealist practices and ideas yet carefully maintained a modicum of distance.[2] This distance is exemplified by a distinction between *animation* and *automatism*: on one hand, the animation of static images to produce the illusion of movement, a process central to cinema; on the other hand, the principle of psychic automatism that, according to André Breton, remained a touchstone of surrealist practice, albeit one rarely attained.[3]

Breton based his definition of surrealism as 'psychic automatism in its pure state' on the example of automatic writing as 'a monologue spoken as rapidly as possible'.[4] This model of 'spoken *thought*' unfolding in time as a dynamic flux accorded well with the coincidence of conception and expression in verbal forms of automatism. In the visual arts, however, conception and expression rarely coincide. Indeed, when Max Morise attempted to address this problem in the first issue of *La Révolution surréaliste*, along with collage he proposed cinema as a possible solution, 'a sophisticated cinema which would rid us of technical formalities'.[5]

In many ways the distinction between animation and automatism resides in these 'technical formalities'. Morise's ideal of overcoming technical difficulties so that the cinematic image is an immediate trace of mental processes – a dream, no less – discounted the artifice of cinema, the carefully arranged montage of images that produces the illusion of movement. Animation makes visible the blind spot in Morise's argument: rather than a direct trace of the unconscious, animation employs the 'technical formalities' of cinema to transform a series of static images into a dynamic flux capable of evoking the non-rational source of the artistic imagination. This is certainly the case with Lye, whose direct films employed the technical formalities of animation to produce filmic experiences close to automatism. Yet this automatism was qualitatively different from the 'psychic automatism' of surrealism, based more on an experience of movement in time than a trace of psychic processes.[6]

It is important to remember that surrealism was not limited to a single movement with clear membership or shared ideas. Although André Breton sought to annex the definition of surrealism in France, the term *surrealism* goes back to Guillaume Apollinaire, whose more expansive definition is useful to describe neo-romantic cultural practices during the interwar period that drew on similar sources to the 'official' Surrealist group, such as the interest in depth psychology, modernist primitivism, and a deep dissatisfaction with reason and European civilization – tendencies close to Lye's own interests.[7] Indeed, rather than focusing on links to the Surrealist group, Lye's surrealism is best understood as part of a broader cultural current that is closer to Apollinaire than Breton. The work that comes closest to a surrealist mode – the 1929 film *Tusalava*, photographs and drawings circa 1930 – precedes the emergence of an organized Surrealist movement in Britain. By the time the British Surrealist movement emerges in the mid-1930s, Lye's work, particularly his experimental films, is already moving beyond key surrealism concerns, at least in a doctrinaire sense. He appears to anticipate the advent of surrealism in Britain; yet once it finally arrives, he has already moved beyond it.[8]

***

Lye initially encountered surrealism in the review *transition*, a context that diluted the doctrinaire character of French surrealism. Established in 1927 by Eugene Jolas and Eliot Paul, *transition* was an important clearinghouse for international Modernism during the interwar years.[9] Its editorial policy supported the principles of experimentation and innovation without any preconceived artistic bias, drawing on expressionism and surrealism, the irrational and the unconscious. As Céline Mansanti has noted, *transition* was closer to the 'internationalist brand of Surrealism' espoused by Ivan Goll, seeking to 'absorb all the isms dividing Europe'.[10] Although *transition*'s outlook was broader, it nonetheless published English translations of writings by leading French surrealists, and reproduced paintings, drawings, photographs and objects by Man Ray, Max Ernst, Joan Miró and André Masson.[11] In this context, it represented an important conduit between surrealism in France and Anglo-American modernism.

Lye was undoubtedly aware of *transition* through his friendship with Laura Riding and Robert Graves, whom he met soon after moving to London in 1926. Riding was an early contributor, publishing eleven poems plus essays on Gertrude Stein, Hart Crane and Edgar Allan Poe between June 1927 and the summer of 1928. She ceased contributing in June 1928, after falling-out with Jolas over his continuing support for surrealism and expressionism.[12] Any attraction Lye may have felt to surrealism was counterbalanced by Riding's rejection of key tenets of the movement. In *A Survey of Modernist Poetry*, published in 1927, Riding and Graves defended the independent existence of the poem, separate from both the poet and the reader, 'a new and self-explanatory creature' that possessed its own 'personality'.[13] In this light, they were critical of the surrealist principle of automatic writing:

> The policy of leaving the poem to write itself makes it only a form of automatic writing which inevitably leads to the over-emphasis on the dream element in the writing of poetry. It is true that dreams seem to exercise the same kind of control over the mind as the poem does over the poet. But in dreams we have thought in an uncreative state running itself out to a solution out of sheer inertia, unrefreshed by any volitional criticism of it; a solution which is like a negative image of the solution which thought would arrive at in a creative, waking state, refreshed by volitional criticism.[14]

Although Riding and Graves were critical of the dream element in poetry, they did not completely dismiss automatism, which returned through the example of Gertrude Stein, who they discussed in the book's conclusion. Riding developed these ideas in *Contemporaries and Snobs* (1928), arguing that poetry had lost contact with its origins in the absolute.[15] To recover a sense of the poetic absolute required a 'new barbarism' that would purify poetic experience of the accretion of history, knowledge and literary tradition. In advocating for a 'new barbarism', Riding was responding to T. S. Eliot's recent review of Stein's *Composition as Explanation*, where he dismissed the 'peculiar hypnotic power' of Stein's rhythms and their 'kinship with the saxophone' as a herald of impending barbarism.[16] Where Eliot aligned Stein with forms of mass entertainment that threatened to undermine high culture – criticism that betrayed class, race and gender bias – Riding characterized Stein's writing as an effort to renew language, a renewal modelled on modernist primitivism in the visual arts, where 'painting and sculpture merely had to revert to barbaric modes – negroid, Oceanic, Aztec, Egyptian, Chinese, archaic Greek – creating modern forms as if in primitive times'. Poets, however, faced a greater challenge, because language had been 'intrinsically affected' by both the history of literature and the non-poetic uses of language. Language 'had to be reorganized, used as if afresh, cleansed of its experience' so that it could become 'as "pure" and "abstract" as colour or stone'.[17]

Gertrude Stein came closest to this ideal; Riding described her as 'the only artisan of language who … succeeded in practising scientific barbarism literally', using repetition to strip words of literary associations to become 'primitive in the sense that they are bare, immobile, mathematically placed, abstract'.[18] Whereas critics like Eliot dismissed Stein's writing as 'romantic vulgar barbarism', Riding recognized its originality not in some personal eccentricity, but in her use of ordinary language 'automatically', making it 'capable of direct communication not by caricaturing contemporary language – attacking decadence with decadence – but by purging it completely of its false experiences'.[19] Unlike the 'dream elements' of surrealist automatism, this automatic character of Stein's use of words purified language of history and restored it to a pristine, primitive state.

The other significant aspect of Stein's writing was the use of the 'continuous present', the role of which Stein discussed in *Composition as Explanation*, a lecture given in June 1926, and subsequently published.[20] The continuous present allowed the writer to access the absolute by creating a singular duration in which no events occur: it is 'always beginning again, for this keeps everything different and everything the same'.[21] This automatism emerged from language itself, rediscovered in a primitive state by neutralizing its narrative function. As such, it bore slim resemblance to the flickering play of subjectivity evident in surrealist automatism.[22]

Two elements of Riding's critique are relevant to Lye's practice. First, the rhetoric of primitivism, which allowed visual artists to strip the artifice of convention to create 'modern forms as if in primitive times'. Lye had a longstanding interest in Indigenous and prehistoric art: his first film, *Tusalava*, was inspired by reading about Australian Aboriginal culture, while his study of Palaeolithic and African rock art contributed to the development of the direct film technique – a point I will discuss shortly. Second, an understanding of aesthetic experience being tied to a singular temporality outside history and tradition, which for Lye was manifested in the phenomenology of movement exhibited in non-narrative cinema and kinetic sculpture – what he would call 'figures of motion'.[23]

***

Lye's first film was the hand-drawn animation *Tusalava*, completed in 1929. The advantage of animation was that it offered a way to incorporate movement as an artistic element. Lye later noted his lifelong interest in movement, which he traced back to his student days in Wellington, when he first acknowledged his goal 'to compose movement as movement' and to 'create a shape, compose its motion, and keep it going as a figure of motion'.[24] Lye learned the principles of animation in Sydney during the early 1920s while working at Filmads Ltd, which produced animated cinema advertisements.[25] Although his contributions were minimal due to his junior status, he experimented with animating sketches and the effect of scratching filmstock during his spare time. Lye commenced work on *Tusalava* after he moved to London in 1926. He found part-time work at another company producing animated commercials, Hopkins and Weir, where he learned to use a rostrum camera.[26]

The completion of a hand-drawn animation film was a time-consuming process. According to Roger Horrocks, *Tusalava* required over 4000 drawings, which Lye completed at the rate of eight drawings per day, allowing him to complete one minute of film every two months.[27] Jack Ellitt, a musician friend from Sydney, helped by filling in Lye's line drawings.[28] Ellitt also composed an original score for two pianos to accompany *Tusalava*. This score has not survived, and for later screenings Lye substituted a piece for two pianos by Eugene Goossens, *Rhythmic Dance*.[29] Ellitt also helped Lye with music for later films, providing charts to coordinate visuals with the soundtrack music. *Tusalava* was approximately 10 minutes in length (at 16 fps), and its final production costs were covered by Robert Graves and the London Film Society, where it premièred on 1 December 1929.[30]

While the technique of hand-drawn animation required careful planning, the imagery of *Tusalava* was closer to surrealism, depicting a type of primal scene dealing with 'the beginnings of organic life up to development of an anxiety all human'.[31] The imagery and themes were loosely based on ideas derived from Australian Aboriginal art, although Lye later claimed his goal was to capture its 'feeling', not copy its forms.[32] A key source was the account of the Witchetty Grub totem in *The Native Tribes of Central Australia* (1889), in which a large quartzite block hidden in a cave represented the *Maegwa* or adult insect, surrounded by smaller stones representing the insect's eggs; later in the ceremony the participants visit several places where stones symbolize the chrysalis and egg of the witchetty grub.[33] The book included numerous photographs depicting sacred rock drawings, specific ceremonial sites and the different stages of the ceremony.

Lye described *Tusalava* as 'a drawn film relying on the intrinsic form to convey the meaning': 'the form is developed continually from the original motif, *i.e.*, dots, without the motif leaving the screen', evolving into 'an attacking element which annihilates a "self" shape but in so doing is itself annihilated'.[34] In *No Trouble* (1930), Lye claimed the film's title was based on a 'circumspect Polynesian word inferring that eventually everything is just the same', and that 'dots are used to convey organic life in a primary stage'.[35] The film opens with two vertical black and grey strips on the screen, dots moving up the black strip, while a black cog-chain slowly moves up the grey strip. A series of dots then flow through an arch formed by two cog-chains. Next, a 'cocoon or core shape' appears, out of which emerges a long black cog-chain which divides into 'two grubs or microbes or whatever, one grey and the other black, with dots as vertebrae'. The cog-chain develops into a 'monstrous python shape' that menaces the cocoon core shape, which is now 'a sort of mummified human shape'.[36] The focus of the film becomes the conflict between the python shape and the core shape: the python develops into a 'grotesque octopus head with two blinking eyes', its extremities 'two hunchbacked straddled arms with channels as veins', which obliterate the 'human core shape' with ink. 'Mr. Octopus then darts out a blunt tongue and licks all black away

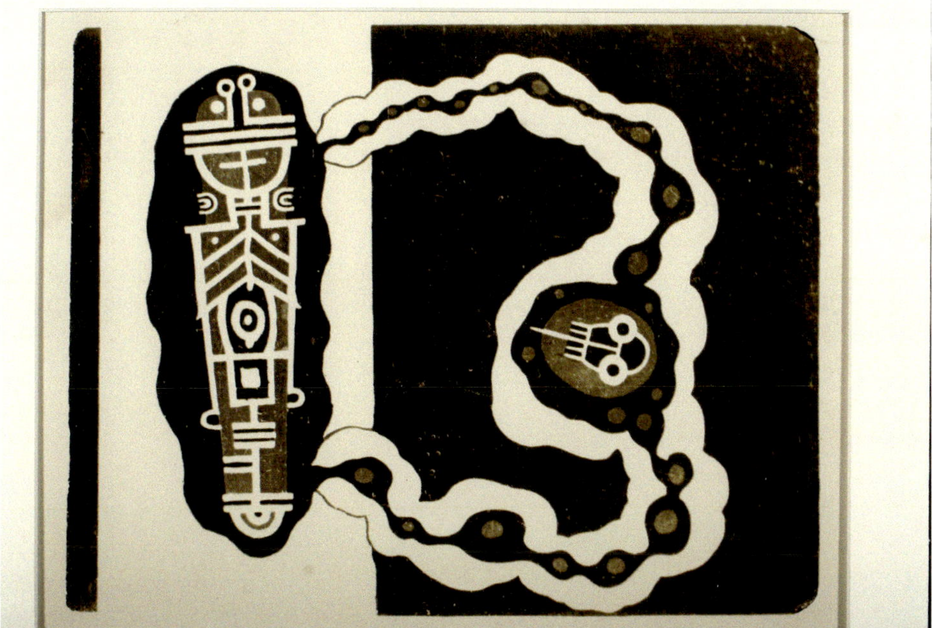

Figure 2.1 Len Lye, dir., *Tusalava* (showing 'Mr. Octopus' and totemic 'core shape'), 1929. Film still from material preserved and made available by Ngā Taonga Sound & Vision. Courtesy the Len Lye Foundation and British Postal Museum and Archive.

leaving core shape grey and soft and ready for mastication', which he swallows with 'great gusto'.[37] As this description makes clear, *Tusalava* was not an exercise in non-figurative abstraction, but possessed an implicit narrative depicting the development of life into antagonistic elemental forces.[38]

Lye conceived *Tusalava* as the first section in a trilogy of films. The writer and film-maker Oswell Blakeston described Lye's original plan for the unfinished second and third sections:

> The second section … deals with earth and sea figures. Layer upon layer the earth builds up, and the sea corrodes, washes away. The earth figures become palpitating light, recessed circles of vibrations; the sea figure forms a contact, and, again, there is annihilation in a series of electric sparks.[39]
>
> The third section, a ballet movement, deals with more humanized shapes and 'the human "self" attached to its leanings to live only to die to start again'. The film ends with a shot of two stones thrown into rippled water; the camera dives down under the water to take a shot of nebulous dots and flickering lights – the completed circle![40]

The trilogy of films describes the evolution of life forms, starting with the simple forms in the 1929 film, then becoming more complex in subsequent sections, with the repetition of themes to give the cycle coherence. However, the cycle also signalled Lye's growing technical ambition, moving beyond hand-drawn animation to incorporate three-dimensional space and camera movement. This interest in the origins of life, whether on an individual or collective scale, was consonant with aspects of surrealism, such as Max Ernst's frottage cycle, *Histoires naturelle* (1926) or Miró's *Birth of the World* (1925).[41] Blakeston also described Lye as 'the most serious and original FILMTHINKER still *thinking*' and noted: 'Since filming the first section of *Tusalava* … Len Lye has created hundreds of plans, diagrams, photograms, batiks, all relating to the other sections of his film. Alas! economic problems have not, so far, allowed him to transfer these moments to celluloid'.[42]

While working on the drawings for *Tusalava*, Lye began doodling as a strategy to unlearn his earlier artistic training. 'Doodling', according to Horrocks, 'involved learning to trust the hand to think for itself'.[43] This strategy would be central to the next stage in Lye's practice. He abandoned the hard-edged drawing style used in *Tusalava* 'as too conventional in the totemic sense' in favour of a mode of drawing that 'enabled him to record the actual activity of sensation in pictorial form'.[44]

Lye's doodling would converge with a growing interest in Palaeolithic cave art. After *Tusalava*, Lye moved away from the ethnographic sources that he had studied during the 1920s to seek inspiration in Palaeolithic cave art, graffiti and cracked surfaces – interests that paralleled contemporary developments in the practice of Miró and Brassaï.[45] Lye first explored the creative possibilities of natural and found textures in photographs of a series of constructions circa 1930.[46] Lye frequently visited the library of the Victoria and Albert Museum to study illustrations in books on European and African Palaeolithic cave art, copying designs on 11 × 17 cm catalogue cards.[47] Lye disregarded the figurative images

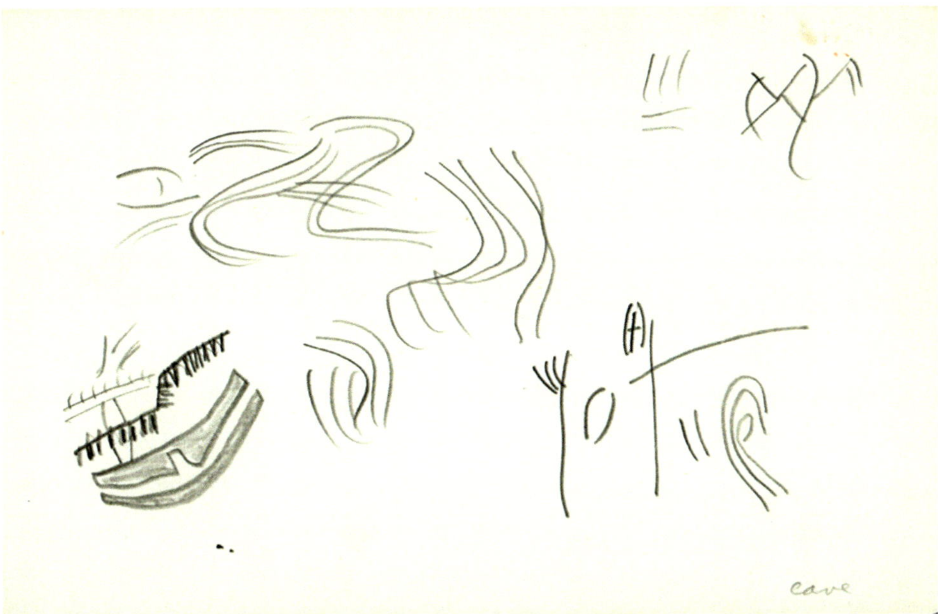

Figure 2.2 Len Lye, *Drawing (Cave Mine Card)*, c.1933. Pencil on paper, 11.5 × 17.3 cm. Len Lye Foundation Collection, Govett-Brewster Art Gallery, New Plymouth, New Zealand. Accession no. 1774. © Len Lye Foundation.

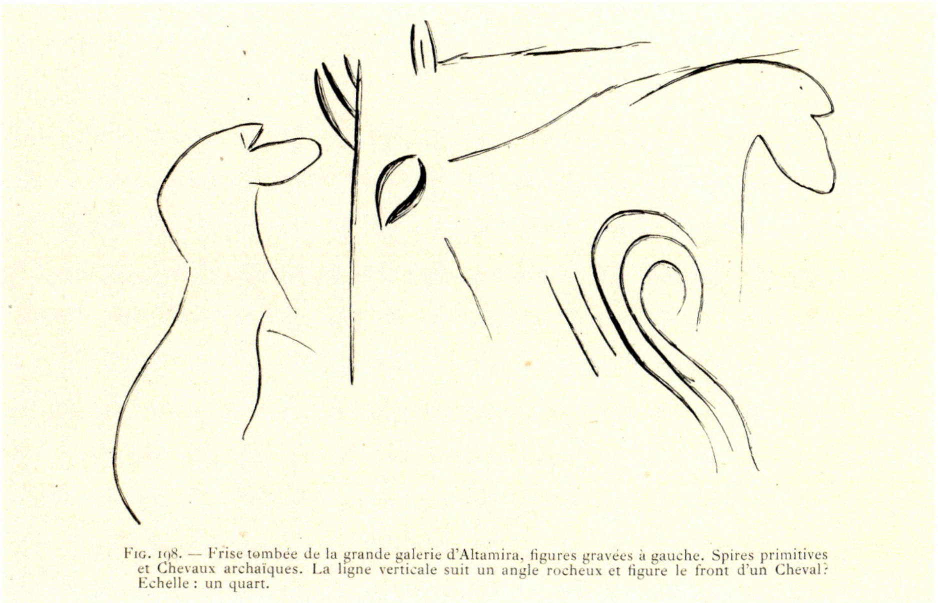

Figure 2.3 'Frise tombée de la grande galerie d'Altimira', in Hermilio Alcalde del Rio, Henri Breuil and Lorenzo Sierra, *Les Cavernes de la région cantabrique* (Monaco: Chêne, 1911), 194. Digital image KB Nationale Bibliotheek, The Hague.

of bison, ibex, horses and other animals that populate cave art; rather, he focused on the non-figurative designs carefully recorded in publications on Palaeolithic art. An example of this can be seen in a *Drawing (Cave Mine Card)* (c.1933), which reproduced four drawings by Henri Breuil in *Les Cavernes de la région cantabrique*; three drawings are non-figurative, while Lye has suppressed the outlines of two horses in the fourth drawing to retain non-figurative elements.[48] In focusing on these designs, Lye was returning to the prelapsarian moment before the emergence of figuration, the immediacy of gesture that communicated feeling without representation. This was a version of automatism purged of 'dream elements', closer to Riding's account of Stein 'always beginning again' than the psychic automatism of surrealism.

For Lye these non-figurative designs were records of bodily sensations that would be lost once figuration emerged as the goal of painting.[49] Primitivism here served to recover a stratum of experience repressed through civilization. In Lye's case, this primitivism was framed by cultural assumptions typical of the time, which regarded Indigenous and prehistoric art as the product of cultures outside history and untouched by 'civilization'. As he noted in *No Trouble*:

> I'm through with talking about art: after all the fuss and when the art critics have stopped making history there's nothing left but a few designs by Aus., Af., Am., or Ocean Is. aboriginals, designs complete in themselves, unattached to history or sentiment; done because they were feeling good and not goofy. They remain what they are, a record of well-being, unspiritual.[50]

The value of Indigenous art, for Lye, was not its endogenous cultural significance, but as a record of 'well-being' that was absent from European 'civilization'. Although Lye was aware of the negative effects of colonialization – he was born in the settler-colonial society of Aotearoa New Zealand, lived in Australia during the early 1920s and spent several months in Samoa in 1924 – his attitude to Indigenous artforms reflected many of the biased cultural and racial preconceptions of modernist primitivism. Unlike the Paris surrealists, he did not articulate an explicit critique of European colonialism in his work.[51]

Shortly after completing *Tusalava*, Lye travelled to Mallorca, where he began to experiment with photograms and assemble constructions that he recorded in photographs.[52] Lye's interest in photograms was probably initiated by articles on Man Ray and László Moholy-Nagy in *transition*.[53] In *Self-Planting at Night* (1930), Lye used plasticine to create a hybrid form combining a tree with a monoped, reminiscent of some of Miró's pictures of the late 1920s.[54] He was also commissioned to design book covers for Graves and Riding's Seizen Press and Nancy Cunard's Hours Press.[55] These experiments, particularly the photograms, would contribute to development of the direct film technique, suggesting ways to produce photographic images without the use of a camera.

***

Lye's experiments with photograms and drawings would converge in the direct film technique. Unlike the time-consuming technique of traditional hand-drawn animation,

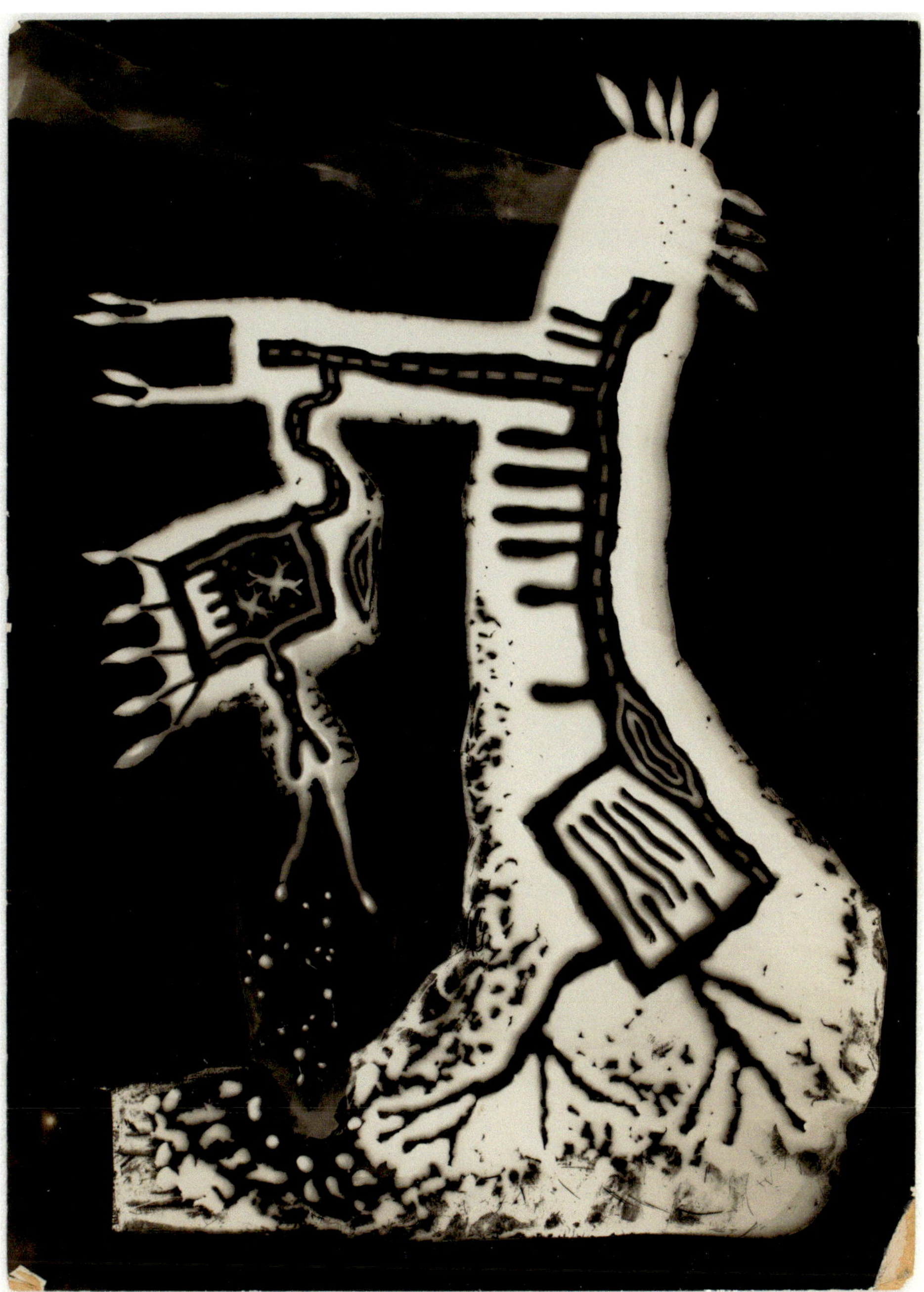

Figure 2.4 Len Lye, *Self-Planting at Night (Night Tree)*, 1930. Photogram, 50 × 30 cm. Len Lye Foundation Collection, Govett-Brewster Art Gallery, New Plymouth, New Zealand. © Len Lye Foundation.

where carefully planned drawings were photographed using a rostrum camera, or stop-action animation, which he explored in *Experimental Animation (The Peanut Vendor)* (1933), the direct film technique was camera-less, applying paint directly to 35-mm celluloid filmstock. The technique also allowed Lye to animate movement without relying on recognizable figurative imagery. Lye was already sensitive to the motion implied in static images through his study of ethnographic and archaeological illustrations, so the direct film technique allowed him to translate bodily sensations into a dynamic flux of graphic marks. Lye soon developed a repertoire of techniques, using combs or similar implements to create a series of parallel marks, and stencils to create regular dot patterns or to animate shapes. These techniques are evident in *A Colour Box* (1935), but Lye expanded on the use of stencils in *Kaleidoscope* (1935) and later films. The technique also allowed Lye to work in colour, placing him at the forefront of innovation in film-making during the 1930s.

Lye's technical efforts attracted the attention of other experimental film-makers. His first direct film (now lost) was *Full Fathom Five*, based on the 'Chant of Ariel' from Shakespeare's *The Tempest*.[56] Albert Cavalcanti encouraged Lye to show *Full Fathom Five* to John Grierson, the director of the recently established GPO Film Unit; suitably impressed, Grierson commissioned *A Colour Box*, devising the plan of including text advertising the Post Office's parcel service to justify spending government money on an experimental film.

Another key aspect of the direct films was the combination of sound and visual images, which were coordinated with soundtracks of jazz music. Financial constraints meant Lye could not commission original music or use recordings by well-known performers. For *A Colour Box*, Lye and Ellitt listened to hundreds of recordings before selecting a *beguine* by Don Baretto and His Cuban Orchestra. Ellitt prepared a chart of the music, which allowed Lye to synchronize visual sequences with the music, using a comb to create parallel lines that varied in colour and rhythm to match the soundtrack.[57] In contrast to the flat, two-dimensional drawing in *Tusalava*, the direct films create a more complex pictorial space, where Lye superimposed layers of marks by varying the direction of lines, the transparency of the colour, and using screens or stencils to repeat images across frames.

The immediate effect of the direct film technique was to produce a dynamic stream of non-figurative imagery in vivid colour. The effect was both dramatic and hypnotic, an outcome enhanced by the rhythmic soundtrack. Lye largely avoided figurative images in his experimental films, although *Rainbow Dance* incorporated a dancing figure performed by Rupert Doone, who was transformed into a coloured silhouette, while *Colour Flight* (1938), a film commissioned by Imperial Airways, incorporated the company's logo as a recurring motif. Lye would explore new possibilities of the film language he had invented in each new film, although an understanding of animation, particularly how to control movement within the film frame through the repetition of images, remained at the heart of the direct film technique.

Because the freehand application of paint often produced erratic movement in the projected film, Lye employed etched zinc or cardboard stencils to produce the illusion of a shape's smooth movement through the film frame.[58] These stencils were based on a sequence of 24 film frames, and Lye could incrementally adjust the position or

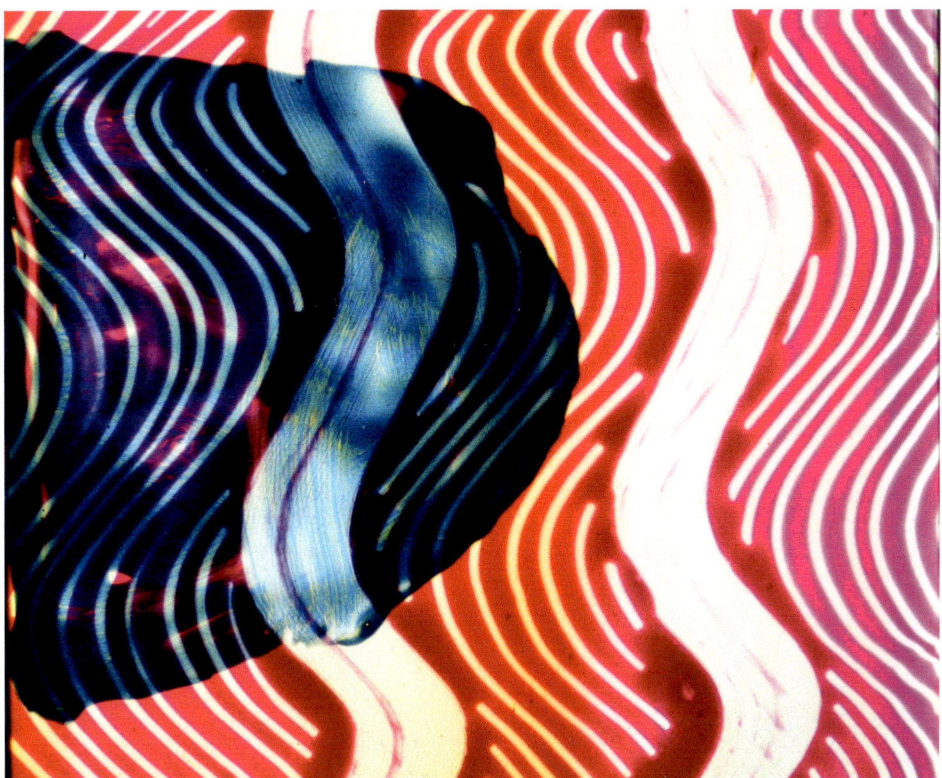

Figure 2.5 Len Lye, dir., *A Colour Box*, 1935. Digital image, Stills collection, Ngā Taonga Sound & Vision. Courtesy the Len Lye Foundation and British Postal Museum and Archive.

orientation of a shape in each frame to produce the illusion of fluid movement. This technique allowed Lye to automate parts of the animation process. Lye used perforated screens to create a grid of regularly spaced dots or shapes, etched zinc for text or intricate shapes, or thin cardboard for less complex shapes. He applied paint with an airbrush, allowing him to produce translucent layers of colour. This working method is evident in some stencils: in this example, from *Musical Poster*, the position of each cut-out diamond shape has been calculated using a grid of diagonal lines; once the stencil has been placed over the filmstock, Lye then placed a perforated screen over the stencil, and used an airbrush to apply paint to the filmstock, leaving an imprint of the screen on the cardboard stencil.

***

In 1935 Lye collaborated with Riding on 'Film-Making'. This essay addressed the theoretical implications of *A Colour Box* and *Kaleidoscope*, focusing on what the authors called 'movement-compositions': 'the total effect of accidental design created by cross-movements, perspective movements, timing, accenting'.[59] Movement allowed access to a stratum of 'living' experience otherwise obscured by the conceptual categories of shape

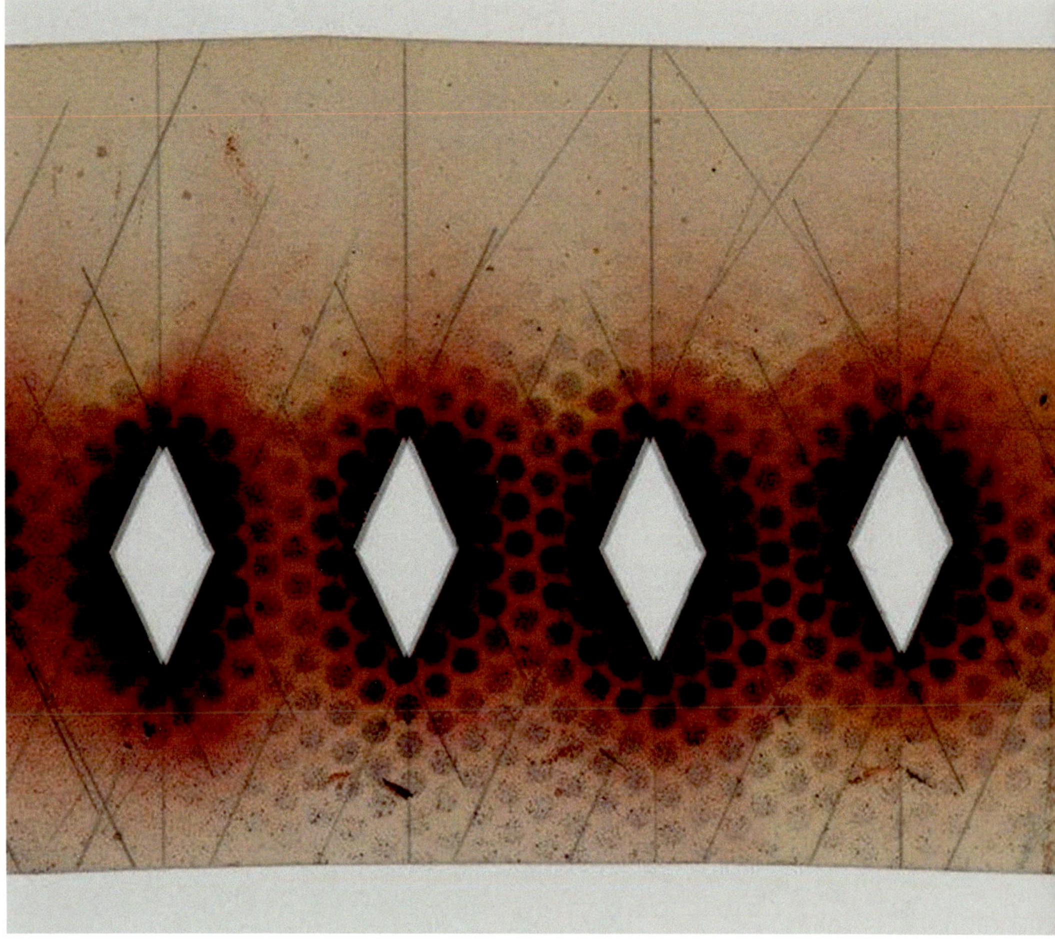

Figure 2.6 Len Lye, Detail of stencil used in the direct film process, c.1940. Paper card, 6 × 57 cm. Len Lye Studio Box 55: Film stencils for *Musical Poster*, accession no. 6702. Len Lye Foundation Archive, Govett-Brewster Art Gallery, New Plymouth, New Zealand. © Len Lye Foundation.

and form: when conscious of movement, the mind is 'conscious of nothing else', liberating it from the 'finalities or shapes', and allowing it to 'translate the memory of time back into time again – to relive experience instead of merely remembering it'.[60] Rather than succumb to the 'literary temptation' of narrative, movement is 'unpremeditated being', the 'uncritical expression of life': 'Movement is strictly the language of life … the earliest language'.[61] Here the authors establish a distinction between movement as a sign of vital life and form as a quality of the conscious mind. This distinction served to define cinema specifically as a language of movement:

> The cinema can visualize only movement; it cannot visualize meaning – meaning, or explanatory sense, is not visualizable. The language of the cinema is movement. When it attempts to make of movement a literary language the result is a physical-intellectual caricature-language which furnishes stories of life as something half-true, half-ridiculous.[62]

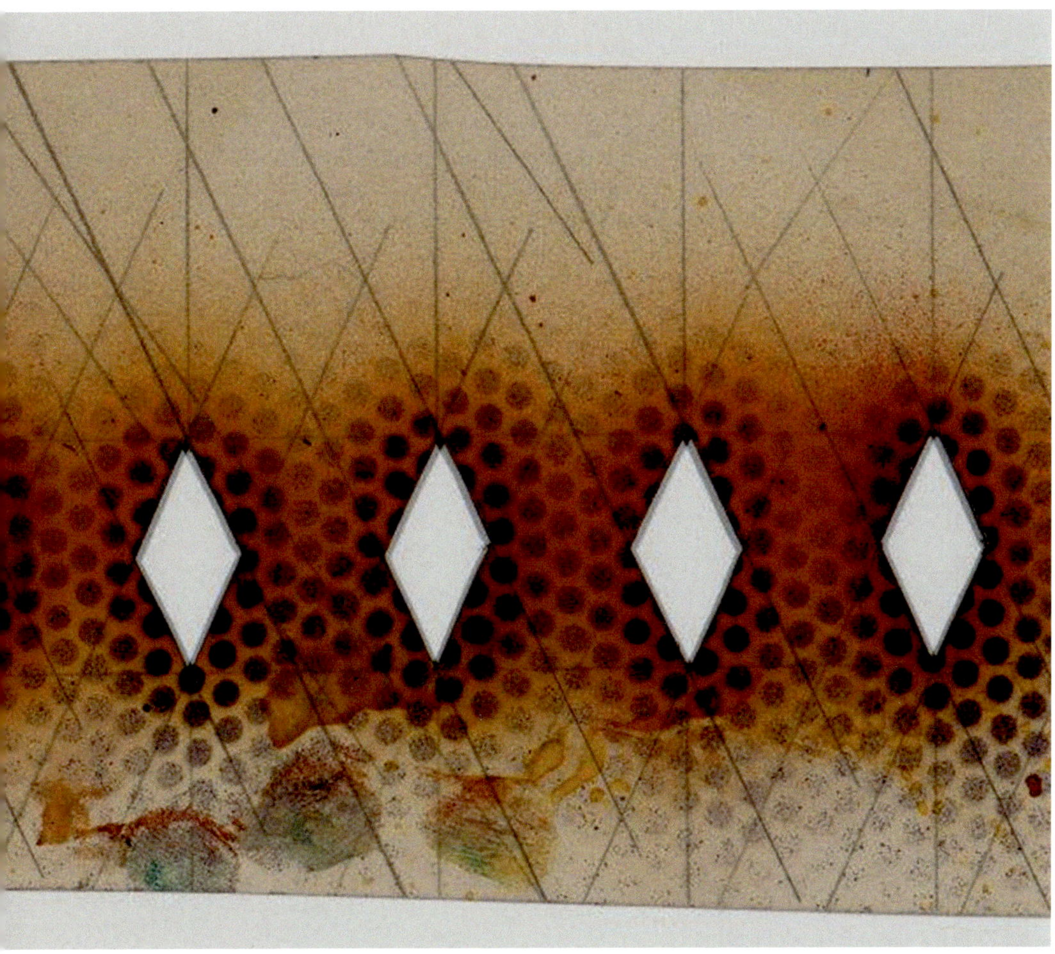

In this context, the direct film technique was part of Lye's effort to establish a cinematic language of movement, in opposition to conventional narrative cinema (as well as the implied narrative in *Tusalava*). The goal was an 'absolute consciousness of life', a paradoxical prelapsarian state prior to the intervention of conscious volition.[63] As a 'language of movement' cinema evoked emptiness more than the 'murmur' that Breton associated with automatism.[64]

The argument in 'Film-Making' relates back to Riding's earlier critique of surrealism and promotion of Stein's 'barbarism'. First, the desire to promote an absolute aesthetic experience that was outside history and literary tradition, an experience that could be found in the 'continuous present' so as to 'relive experience instead of merely remembering it'; and second, the belief that this experience could also be found in 'primitive' artforms: both contemporary Indigenous art and prehistoric art. The 'continuous present' of the direct films not only refused the literary distortion of narrative film, but sought to recover a primordial experience outside of history – a goal typical of modernist primitivism. Indeed, Lye cites the example of prehistoric rock art in 'Film-Making':

> For examples of movement in shapes we might use paleolithic [*sic*] paintings; but marks just as good as cave marks can be found on walls or pavements if one can be bothered to sort them out from civilized vision. Such marks are the nearest visual contact with moving life: things in themselves extricated from mental after-life – early realities. The mind gives the shape, the definition as something, but it is the geometric nothings and dots and lines in the relative perspective of movement that are the physical content of the shape – and which come before shape.[65]

The authors contrast civilized vision, where the mind imposes shape and form on a configuration of marks, to the sense of movement they perceived in Palaeolithic painting and random marks upon walls and pavements, the 'nearest visual contact with moving life'. Although the direct films abandoned the narrative of *Tusalava*, they shared an interest in movement as 'the simple compulsion to live'.[66]

***

The development of the direct film technique coincided with the establishment of the British surrealism movement. Lye contributed two photograms, *Self-Planting at Night* (1930) and *Watershed* (1930), and a painting, *King of Plants Meets First Man* (1936), to the 1936 International Surrealist Exhibition in London.[67] Yet Lye had misgivings over participating in the exhibition; as he wrote to John Aldridge:

> The international surrealists (Mr Roland Penrose and Herbert Read) came down this evening to look at my paintings and didn't like them … I nearly got angry with them but why should I educate utter know-all surrealiste strangers, so avoided all art talk rather than risk it. Thinking about it later it was simple to solace my penchant for painting by thinking, well, I know of no one except myself who has an understanding of my line. Similar kinks are only in Papuan or early paleolithic cave stuff, only in a few African bushman cave things. All other people's visual kinks, except in pattern stuff, are derivative from realism in various degrees of distortion, and in surrealism there is literary distortion galore.[68]

However, given the notoriety of surrealism after the 1936 exhibition, it is not surprising that experimental films like *A Colour Box*, *Kaleidoscope*, or *Rainbow Dance* were associated with surrealism, particularly by the general public. Lye was undoubtedly aware of this risk, and he was careful in his public statements not to align his film-making with surrealism. In 'Notes on a Short Colour Film', an article published several months after the 1936 International Surrealist Exhibition, Lye would reiterate Riding's earlier critique of the 'dream elements' associated with surrealism. Here Lye described his goal in terms of 'colour sensation' as 'a direct and immediate impulse-feeling', which he opposed to 'literary feeling'.[69] Although he does not address surrealism by name, he alludes to it when he states:

> In contemporary art, intelligent people have been influenced by psycho-analysis to exploit the literary content of the dream element in our mentality. They particularly liked

> the subconscious displacement of polarities, in particular the dream-trick of realistic image-displacement – the accenting of the significance of a literary idea by investing an object with false scale or relationship to the conscious order of realistic objects.[70]

Here Lye alluded to the juxtaposition of images evident in the work of Giorgio de Chirico, René Magritte or Salvador Dalí, where the literary quality of surrealist dream imagery eclipsed its value as 'colour sensation'. Lye then contrasted the state of contemporary art to present-day jazz dance music:

> Yet in western civilization sensation form is widely evident, for instance in good swing dance music. And with primitive races, who have little conscious literary crust on their minds, this sensation form is their emotional bread and butter. Their use not only of sound but also of colour and imagery depart at times completely from literary realism. And the music and dance of their rituals result from, and also convey, pure sensation stimuli. In these rituals the literary content is definitely an adjunct to the sensation stimuli.[71]

Although conflating jazz and Indigenous music is questionable, films like *A Colour Box* and *Kaleidoscope* exemplified Lye's primitivism, rejecting the 'literary crust' of western civilization to use sound, colour and imagery to express 'colour sensation'. This sensation revolved around a phenomenology of visual and aural movement, an absorption in the singularity of a moment analogous to the 'continuous present' in Stein's writing.

However, Lye's relation to surrealism remains ambiguous. *Tusalava* was consonant with many aspects of surrealism on a thematic level, yet the development of the direct film practice strayed from the central concerns of surrealism. Although the flux of 'colour sensation' appeared to approximate a type of automatism, the films themselves were not the product of an automatic technique. Their originality lay in their singular temporality, neutralizing narrative in favour of a dynamic flux of 'colour sensation', which served to 'relive experience instead of merely remembering it'. In place of psychic automatism, Lye substituted a kinetic and somatic automatism that he associated with the primordial states he saw manifested in Palaeolithic rock art, Indigenous art, dance and ritual, and contemporary jazz music. It is in this sense that Lye's direct film practice offered a simulacrum of surrealism. Although the films themselves were not a product of surrealist techniques like automatic writing or drawing, they did evoke an experience that resonated with the immediacy of automatism, an immediacy attained through the animation process.

Notes

1 See the news clippings for January 1937, Newspaper Cuttings, 55–60. Len Lye Archive, Len Lye Centre, New Plymouth, New Zealand. The programme included Jean Vigo's *Zéro de conduite* and short films by Lye, Alexandre Alexeïeff, Oscar Fischinger, Anthony Gross and Walt Disney.

2 On simulation see David Lomas and Jeremy Stubbs, *Simulating the Marvellous: Psychology, Surrealism, Postmodernism* (Manchester: Manchester University Press, 2013).

3 On cinema's relation to animation, see Alan Cholodenko, 'Introduction', in *The Illusion of Life: Essays on Animation* (Sydney: Power Publications, 1991), 9–36.

4 André Breton, 'Manifesto of Surrealism', in *Manifestoes of Surrealism*, trans. Richard Seaver and Helen R. Lane (Ann Arbor: University of Michigan Press, 1969), 26, 23.

5 Max Morise, 'Enchanted Eyes', in *The Sources of Surrealism*, ed. Neil Matheson (Aldershot: Lund Humphries, 2006), 325.

6 On surrealist attitudes to automatism see Jacqueline Chénieux-Gendron, *Surrealism*, trans. Vivian Folkenflik (New York: Columbia University Press, 1990), 47–60; Lomas and Stubbs, *Simulating the Marvellous*, 181–212.

7 Willard Bohn, 'From Surrealism to Surrealism: Apollinaire and Breton', *Journal of Aesthetics and Art Criticism*, 36, no. 2 (1977): 197–210; Marguerite Bonnet, *André Breton: Naissance de l'aventure surréaliste* (Paris: José Corti, 1975).

8 On Lye and surrealism see Michel Remy, *Surrealism in Britain* (Aldershot: Ashgate, 1999), 49–62; Roger Horrocks, *Len Lye: A Biography* (Auckland: Auckland University Press, 2001), 159–62; Tyler Cann, 'Surreal Sight Seer? Len Lye, Mind, Self, and Time', in *Len Lye*, eds. Tyler Cann and Wystan Curnow (New Plymouth: Govett-Brewster Art Gallery, 2009), 61–84.

9 On *transition* see Céline Mansanti, 'Between Modernisms: *transition* (1927–38)', in *The Oxford Critical and Cultural History of Modernists Magazines*, eds. Peter Brooker and Andrew Thacker, 3 vols (Oxford: Oxford University Press, 2012), 2: 718–36.

10 Mansanti, 'Between Modernism', 731–32. Goll had launched the review *Surréalisme* in October 1924.

11 In August 1927 *transition* published Breton's 'Introduction Discourse on the Dearth of Reality' (his first major statement on surrealism published in English), and in March 1928 it published the first section of *Nadja*.

12 Deborah Baker, *In Extremis: The Life of Laura Riding* (London: Hamish Hamilton, 1993), 182.

13 Laura Riding and Robert Graves, *A Survey of Modernist Poetry* (London: Heinemann, 1927), 124.

14 Riding and Graves, *Survey*, 129–30.

15 Riding revised the conclusion to *A Survey of Modernist Poetry* as 'T.E. Hulme, the New Barbarism, and Gertrude Stein', in *Contemporaries and Snobs* (London: Heinemann, 1927), 123–99; also see 'The New Barbarism, and Gertrude Stein', *transition*, 3 (June 1927): 153–68.

16 T. S. Eliot, 'Charleston, Hey! Hey!', in *The Complete Prose of T. S. Eliot: The Critical Edition*, eds. Frances Dickey, Jennifer Formichelli and Ronald Schuchard (Baltimore, MD: Johns Hopkins University Press, 2015), 3:27.

17 Riding and Graves, *Survey*, 273–4.

18 Riding and Graves, *Survey*, 274.

19 Riding and Graves, *Survey*, 280–1.

20 Gertrude Stein, *Composition as Explanation* (London: Hogarth Press, 1926).

21 Riding and Graves, *Survey*, 285.

22 According to Lisi Schoenbach, Stein's understanding of automatism was different from surrealism, being based on the role of habit in the pragmatic psychology of William James. *Pragmatic Modernism* (Oxford: Oxford University Press, 2012).

23 Roger Horrocks, *Art That Moves: The Work of Len Lye* (Auckland: Auckland University Press, 2009), 40–2, 89–99.

24 Len Lye, ‘Inspiration’, in *Happy Moments*, ed. Roger Horrocks (Auckland: Holloway Press, 2002), 29–30.

25 Horrocks, *Len Lye*, 55. Lye worked on storyboards at Filmads, but was able to observe the animators at work. Wystan Curnow, ‘An Interview with Len Lye’, *Art New Zealand*, 17 (Spring 1980): 54.

26 Horrocks, *Len Lye*, 91.

27 The drawings were photographed twice at 16 fps. Horrocks, *Len Lye*, 91.

28 Jack Ellitt, *Homage to Rachel Carson #2*, 1987, audio recording, 16:26 min., available at https://shamefilemusic.com/jack-ellitt (accessed 29 February 2024).

29 Roger Horrocks, ‘Tusalava’, in *Colour Box: 19 Films by Len Lye* (New Plymouth: Len Lye Foundation/Govett-Brewster Gallery, 2016). DVD.

30 *Tusalava* is now projected at 24 fps, reducing its length to 6:39 mins.

31 Len Lye, *No Trouble* (Mallorca: Seizen Press, 1930), reprinted as ‘No Trouble’, in *Figures of Motion: Selected Writings*, eds. Wystan Curnow and Roger Horrocks (Auckland: Auckland University Press, 1984), 105.

32 Curnow, ‘An Interview with Len Lye’, 54.

33 Baldwin Spencer and F. J. Gillen, *The Native Tribes of Central Australia* (London: Macmillan, 1899), 172–4. On the influence of Spencer and Gillen see Anne Kirker, ‘The Early Years in London’, *Art New Zealand*, 17 (Spring 1980): 53; Ann Stephen, ‘The Oceanic Primitivism of Len Lye’s Animation *Tusalava*’, *Art History*, 40, no. 3 (June 2017): 612–33.

34 London Film Society, ‘Programme, Fifth Season, Sunday, December 1, 1929’, in *The Film Society Programmes, 1925–1939* (New York: Arno Press, 1972), 133–4.

35 See Lye’s account of *Tusalava* in ‘No Trouble’, 105.

36 Lye,‘No Trouble’, 105–6.

37 Lye, ‘No Trouble’, 106.

38 The London Film Society screened abstract experimental films by Hans Richter and Viking Eggeling in its programme of 16 October 1927; Eggeling’s work was also mentioned in the programme introduction for *Tusalava*. London Film Society, *The Film Society Programmes*, 66, 134.

39 Oswell Blakeston, ‘Sketches by Len Lye’, *Close Up*, 6, no. 2 (February 1930): 156. Also see Oswell Blakeston, ‘Len Lye’s Visuals’, *Architectural Review*, 72, no. 428 (July 1932): 25. Blakeston’s description is partly based on Lye’s account in *No Trouble*.

40 Blakeston, ‘Len Lye’s Visuals’, 25.

41 Max Ernst, *Histoire Naturelle* (Paris: Éditions Jeanne Bucher, 1926); Joan Miró, *The Birth of the World*, 1925, oil on canvas, 250.8 × 200 cm, Museum of Modern Art, New York.

42 Blakeston, ‘Len Lye’s Visuals’, 25.

43 Horrocks, *Len Lye*, 104.

44 Laura Riding, *Len Lye and the Problem of Popular Film* (London: Seizen Press, 1938), 39; Horrocks, *Art That Moves*, 53–4.

45 Elke Seibert, Agathe Cabau and Markus A. Castor, eds., *Discovering/Uncovering the Modernity of Prehistory* (Heidelberg: arthistoricum.net, 2020). https://doi.org/10.11588/arthistoricum.613 (accessed 29 February 2024).

46 Lye used a photographed construction for the cover of Robert Graves, *Ten Poems More* (Paris: Hours Press, 1930). Also see Lye's description of a construction in 'No Trouble', 110–13.

47 The Len Lye Archive preserves approximately twenty-five library slips from the Victoria and Albert Museum between August 1933 and October 1936, as well as library slips from the British Museum dating from 1940, and Lye's application for a library card, dated 18 October 1933, suggesting the archive only retains a partial record of Lye's reading (Len Lye Archive, fol. 2146). On Lye's drawings see Len Lye, *Motion Sketch*, eds. Gregory Burke and Tyler Cann (New York: Drawing Center, 2014).

48 Hermilio Alcalde del Rio, Henri Breuil and Lorenzo Sierra, *Les Cavernes de la région cantabrique* (Monaco: Chêne, 1911); see illustrations on 180, 188, 194, 196.

49 There are parallels here with Georges Bataille's interest in Palaeolithic art, but, whereas Bataille saw the alteration of the figure as evidence of destructive impulses, Lye considered it more as prefigurations than disfigurations. Georges Bataille, 'Primitive Art', in *The Cradle of Humanity: Prehistoric Art and Culture*, ed. Stewart Kendall, trans. Michelle Kendall and Stewart Kendall (New York: Zone Books, 2005), 35–44.

50 Lye, 'No Trouble', 107.

51 Lye's uncritical attitude to colonialism is evident in his films *Experimental Animation (Peanut Vendor)* (1933) and *The Birth of the Robot* (1936.) On surrealism and anticolonialism see Sophie Leclercq, *La raçon du colonialisme: Les surréalistes face aux mythes de la France coloniale (1919–1962)* (Dijon: Presses du réel, 2010).

52 Lye executed several photograms in 1930 while staying with Graves and Riding in Mallorca, and may have exhibited examples in the 1931 Seven and Five Society Exhibition. He discussed these experiments in a letter to Ben Nicholson (TGA 8717.1.2.2722, Tate Archive, London), cited by Paul Brobbel, 'Eighty Years On: Len Lye and the *International Surrealist Exhibition*', *Art New Zealand*, 160 (Summer 2016): 90. There are five extant photograms from this period reproduced in *Len Lye: Shadowgraphs*, ed. Paul Brobbel (New Plymouth: Govett-Brewster Art Gallery, 2016), 17–21.

53 Man Ray, 'Eight Photographic Studies', *transition*, 15 (February 1929): 25–7; L. Moholy-Nagy, 'The Future of the Photographic Process', 289–93. This issue also included Robert Desnos' article, 'The Work of Man Ray', 264–6.

54 For instance, Joan Miró, *Nude*, 1926. Oil on canvas, 92 × 73 cm, Philadelphia Museum of Art, or *Person Throwing a Stone at a Bird*, 1926, oil on canvas, 73 × 92 cm, Museum of Modern Art, New York. *Nude* was reproduced in André Breton, *Le Surréalisme et la peinture* (Paris: Gallimard, 1928), 65; *Person Throwing a Stone at a Bird* was reproduced in *La Révolution surréaliste*, nos. 9–10 (October 1927): 62.

55 Lye reused the plasticine matrix from *Self-Planting at Night* for the cover of John Rodker, *Collected Poems* (Paris: Hours Press, 1930).

56 Horrocks, *Len Lye*, 135.

57 Horrocks, *Len Lye*, 137.

58 On Lye's use of stencils see Alla Gadassik, 'Trade Tattoos: Animation Stencils and Readymade Movement', in *The Long Dream of Waking: New Perspectives on Len Lye*, eds. Paul Brobbel, Wystan Curnow and Roger Horrocks (Christchurch: Canterbury University Press, 2017), 184–203. The use of stencils may have been influenced by tapa cloth from Lye's time in Samoa or his studies in the V&A library. Lye consulted William Tufts Brigham, *Ka Hana Kapa: The Making of Bark-Cloth in Hawaii* (Honolulu: Bishop Museum Press, 1911), which contained colour reproductions of Hawaiian tapa cloth reminiscent of sections of *Kaleidoscope* (1935).

59 Len Lye and Laura Riding, 'Film-Making', in *Figures of Motion*, 41. Originally published as 'Film-Making: Movement as Language/Movement as Medium', *Epilogue*, 1, no. 1 (Autumn 1935): 231–5.

60 Lye and Riding, 'Film-Making', 41.

61 Lye and Riding, 'Film-Making', 39.

62 Lye and Riding, 'Film-Making', 40.

63 Lye and Riding, 'Film-Making', 41.

64 Breton, 'Manifesto of Surrealism', 30. There are parallels here with Michel Leiris' account of Miró's work; see Charles Palermo, *Fixed Ecstasy: Joan Miró in the 1920s* (University Park, PA: Penn State University Press, 2008), 120–3.

65 Lye and Riding, 'Film-Making', 40.

66 Lye and Riding, 'Film-Making', 40.

67 International Surrealist Exhibition, 11 June–4 July 1936, New Burlington Galleries, London. On Lye's participation in the exhibition see Paul Brobbel, 'Eighty Years On', 90–3, 121; *Marks & Spencers in a Japanese Garden* (1930), was reproduced in Herbert Read, ed., *Surrealism* (London: Faber and Faber, 1936).

68 Unpublished 'Note 14 May [1936]', cited in Horrocks, *Len Lye*, 160.

69 Len Lye, 'Notes on a Short Colour Film', in *Figures of Motion*, 49. Originally published in *Life and Letters To-Day*, 15, no. 6 (Winter 1936): 162–4.

70 Lye, 'Notes on a Short Colour Film', 50.

71 Lye, 'Notes on a Short Colour Film', 51.

Chapter 3

Boop-Oop-a-Doop: Betty Boop's Adventures in Surrealism

Michael Richardson

Whoever doesn't expect to find the unexpected will not find it, for it is trackless and unexplored.

HERACLITUS

Betty Boop is a significant figure in the iconography of popular culture and her image has undergone various transformations since she was born in 1930 from out of the inkwell on the desk of film producer Max Fleischer. During the early 1930s she became the most important personage in the animated series of films made by Fleischer in collaboration with his brother Dave and their animators before she had her wings clipped in no uncertain terms due to the rigours of the Hollywood Production Code as it was enforced in mid-1934, after which she became a rather lacklustre and conventional character in the brothers' roster, often playing second fiddle to other characters in her own cartoons, before being dropped altogether in 1939.

Surrealism is an active element not only in the early Betty films, but also in others made by the Fleischer brothers during the 1920s and early 1930s, something recognized both by the surrealists themselves and by critics, although maybe in different ways. This connection is frequently mentioned, but it never appears to have been explored critically, either by surrealists or by critics who have approached the Fleischer's films. Yet, it does appear that the brothers were well aware of surrealism and consciously incorporated elements of it in their films, as Richard Fleischer states in the documentary included on the DVD box set issued by Warners in France in 2005. However, this doesn't explain the remarkable symmetry between the films and surrealism that is apparent not only in the Betty Boop films but in others made by the Fleischer studio.

Max Fleischer himself was an inventor whose initial claim to fame arose from his invention of the rotoscope in 1915, which transformed the nature of animated films. Previously the process of making them had been laborious and the results were disappointing, because it was almost impossible to create a smooth transition from one frame to the next. Fleischer's invention solved the problem of transition, even if the process itself remained painstaking. The Fleischers had started experimenting with films in 1914, but it wasn't until the end of 1918 that their first serious productions began with a series called *Out of the Inkwell*. The earliest examples are now lost; the first to survive dates from early in

1919. This represents some symmetry with our topic, as the early part of 1919 was when surrealism can be said to have been conceived. In January Jacques Vaché, the man who for André Breton had first embodied the attitudes that would come to define surrealism, died. In the same month, first contacts were made with Tristan Tzara and the dadaist movement. It was also the year in which Breton conceived the idea of automatism, which displayed its first result with the publication of *Les champs magnètiques*, written by him in collaboration with Philippe Soupault.

Might there even have been a certain synchronization of thought at work here, as the *Out of the Inkwell* films seem to respond interestingly to what Breton conceived as automatism? At least, it would appear that rather than starting like most film-makers with a preconceived idea about their films' content, the Fleischers worked with the inherent possibilities that film had to generate poetic meaning. Even among later film-makers influenced by surrealism, only perhaps Raúl Ruiz, in some of the films he made in the 1980s, approached film-making with a comparable poetic sense of freedom.

Over the next decade, Fleischer would make more than a hundred short *Out of the Inkwell* films mostly featuring Koko the Clown, a figure either drawn on a board by Max Fleischer or else taken by him out of the inkwell and placed within a frame. Once formed, Koko would come to life, often tormenting or being tormented by his creator. A classic example is *Jumping Beans* from 1922, which actually looks forward to a famous incident in the history of surrealism.[1]

In this film, Max Fleischer first creates a Mexican landscape and then starts to draw Koko, but leaves him tied to the fountain pen, causing Koko to protest as he jumps around while trying to extricate himself. Eventually Max takes pity on him and cuts the ink bond linking Koko to the pen. He then opens a box of (real) Mexican jumping beans and starts throwing them at Koko. Trying to escape the assault, Koko catches one of the beans, which he plants. It soon starts rising high into the sky and Koko begins climbing it, encouraged by Fleischer. It isn't long before he finds himself in outer space, passing by outlandish planets, but Max keeps urging him on until he reaches a legendary city in the sky presided over by an ogre, who chases him until Koko eventually falls back down to Earth. He furiously berates Fleischer, telling him 'I'll get you!' He then proceeds to draw a stamp on which he forms an image of himself. Using the stamp to create clones of himself, he assembles an army and commands them to attack Max, tying him up à la Gulliver. Finally Max manages to find a penknife in one of his pockets and is able to cut himself free. This enables him to tip the army of Kokos into the inkwell, whose top he firmly closes.

This combination of live action and animation characterizes all of the *Out of the Inkwell* films, which display a remarkably consistent level of invention. It is their spontaneity that makes them perhaps the closest examples we have to a process of automatism in the realm of cinema. They even partake of some of the spirit we find in the then contemporary stories of Benjamin Péret, something that will become even more apparent in the Betty Boop films that started to appear at the beginning of 1930.

As the *Out of the Inkwell* films evolved, other characters than Koko started to appear, most notably an anthropomorphic dog initially called Fitz who would soon morph into the character of Bimbo and gain his own series, known as *Talkartoons*.[2] Betty would gradually be introduced into Bimbo's films until she became the central protagonist, with Bimbo and Koko becoming her main companions in the early films.

Betty Boop's character evolved while taking different forms during the course of her first few appearances. In the first, *Dizzy Dishes* (1930), she is an unnamed and rather frumpy torch singer in a café in which Bimbo is the waiter. He lusts after her as she sings 'Oh I can't go on like this / Give me a kiss, huh? / And make me … Poop-Oop-a-Doop-a-Doop!'

In the second, *Barnacle Bill*, Bimbo is a sailor on leave who boasts of having a girl in every port as he loves and leaves Betty much to the disapproval of her catty neighbours. The third sees Bimbo become *Mysterious Mose* and he literally scares the nightshirt off Betty in a ghost story that creates a very chilling atmosphere. Then, in *The Bum Bandit* (the first of 1931), she takes centre stage for the first time as Dangerous Nan McGrew, the sister of Dan, who brings her errant husband Bimbo to heel after he holds up a train: '*My father and brother were tough / But I'm the toughest of the lot*,' she sings.

Although these four films established the basis of an interesting character, she is not yet 'Betty Boop' (she has also not been named as such) and one has the feeling that the studio was experimenting, trying to find an appropriate persona to establish her distinctiveness. Or perhaps even that the character was herself evolving in a way to impose her own personality, as it appears that she was initially conceived merely as one of Bimbo's girlfriends. Had she remained as Dangerous Nan we might have had a completely different but equally fascinating character from the one we know, indeed one that might have been more in tune with the mood of the time, perhaps a cross between Barbara Stanwyck and Mae West. Instead something quite different would emerge over the course of the next few films. Was this the intention of the film-makers, or did Betty impose her own persona on them?

The next film, *Any Little Girl that's a Nice Little Girl* (1931), is a regression after what had come before; indeed, it is among the more forgettable in the series. The jazz babe, flapper-type girl that is the familiarly iconic Betty is yet to appear but starts to take shape in the next two from 1931, *Silly Scandals*, in which she is referred to as

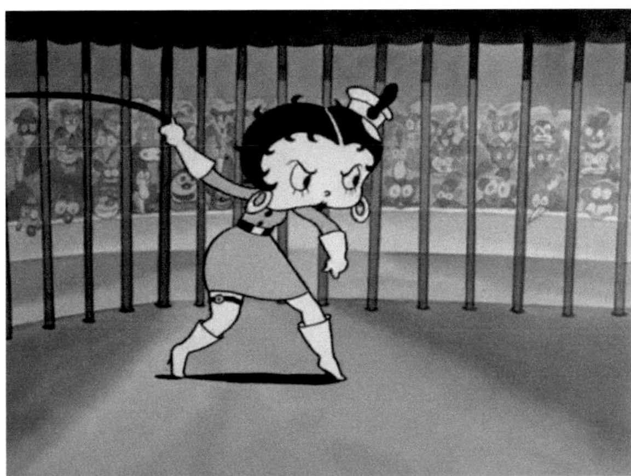

Figure 3.1 Dave Fleischer, dir., *Boop-Oop-a-Doop*. © Fleischer Studios, 1932.

'Betty' for the first time, and most especially in *Bimbo's Initiation*, one of the greatest cartoons of all time and in which, even though she appears only for a few moments, she makes quite a stir. In the latter film, Bimbo is walking along the street without a care in the world when he steps on a manhole cover that opens and casts him into an underworld in which he has to tackle a number of deadly situations and is presented with terrifying challenges. As he survives each one, he is confronted by the robed leader of an apparently secret cult, the 'Mystic Order of the Boom Boom a Hotcha', who asks 'Wanna be a member?' When he refuses, he is faced with the next test. At each juncture he refuses, until the leader takes off the robe and is revealed to be Betty Boop. His attitude changes and he accepts the invitation, when the other members take off their robes and are revealed as clones of Betty. He and Betty end by indulging in a salacious dance. *Bimbo's Initiation* takes him into a world of myth and secret knowledge. Is it an initiation into sex, or something more subversive, a revolutionary group like that of Marx's old mole, working to undermine the foundations of society? Perhaps it is even an initiation into surrealism?

In all of the films so far Betty has largely been playing second fiddle to Bimbo, although increasingly she has been upstaging him. After her remarkable appearance in *Bimbo's Initiation*, the following instalment, *Betty Co-Ed* (1931), which doesn't feature Bimbo, will be the first in which she headlines, even though she hardly features and her appearance is quite unlike that in any of those that came either before or after. A regression to the mode of *Any Little Girl …* it is also one of the least inspired of all the Fleischers' films.

Betty's evolution has therefore been somewhat erratic. Up to this point, she has ostensibly been a dog, although the only dog-like thing about her was her poodle ears. Unlike other animation studios, the Fleischers made little attempt to give their anthropomorphic creatures specifically animal-like qualities, or to play on any ambivalence between human and animal behaviour: their 'animals' all have entirely human qualities.

It should be said that the Fleischers were great plagiarists, as though they had heard Ducasse's assertion of plagiarism's necessity with his rationale that 'progress implies it'.[3] Betty's emerging character was initially built on that of Helen Kane, a minor Paramount star of the time, as well as on flapper girls Clara Bow and Colleen Moore, or even perhaps Louise Brooks, something that would become more pronounced as her character developed. Although her personality may be seen as an amalgam of such actresses, the Fleischers directly appropriated the voice, aspects of her appearance, and the 'boop-oop-a-doop' catchphrase, from Kane (who had also played Dangerous Nan McGrew in a feature film of this title made in 1929). This impelled Kane to sue Fleischer Studios in a legal case that became infamous and may have ruined her career when the judge found against her on the basis that she may have herself plagiarized the voice and catchphrase from a Black child singer called Baby Esther.[4]

However, the Fleischers had few compunctions about appropriating material from a range of sources, acknowledged or not, making their films a cornucopia of the popular culture of the time. Many of the cartoons were built around contemporary popular songs, both tin pan alley and more broadly, and they frequently incorporated jazz directly into them, giving the spotlight to musicians like Cab Calloway, Louis Armstrong, Don Redmond and Duke Ellington. Their engagement with music was not confined to jazz and the American song book, but extended to Indigenous music in *The Bamboo Isle* (1932), which features the Royal Samoan orchestra.

The Fleischers were neither storytellers nor did they have a great ability to forge convincing characters. Their forte was their inventiveness and the fast-moving gag (indeed, some of the films are little more than a succession of gags), qualities that of course contributed to the surrealist quality of their best work. Koko and Bimbo, although memorable in their different ways, were never given consistent personalities but assumed forms contingent with the situation of the particular film. Their only other successful characters, Popeye and Superman, were already existing comic book characters licensed for the films from their creators rather than characters original to the Fleischers. This makes the creation of Betty as their only fully formed original character all the more remarkable, especially as she is the only credible female character anywhere in early animation, challenged only by Tex Avery's Red Hot Riding Hood, although she only survived for three films (1943–5) in contrast to the more than 100 in which Betty features.

Betty didn't lose her doggy ears until the end of 1931, but with each succeeding film even up to this point she is increasingly sexualized and starts to assume a consistent and provocative personality, including a turn as Red Riding Hood (itself a precursor to Avery's later incarnation), the final film of 1931 – one that seems to represent a kind of transition. Setting off to visit her grandmother, she tells Bimbo he cannot go with her, but he surreptitiously follows nevertheless. When the wolf eyes Betty as potential lunch, Bimbo attacks him and divests him of his fur, in which he covers himself and goes ahead of Betty to take a place in Grandma's bed. Betty doesn't seem too surprised to see him and when he kisses her and removes the wolf's fur they are transported to the moon where they rock to and fro in its crescent.

Boop-Oop-a-Doop is the title of one of the early 1932 films. Betty here is a brilliant circus performer, her act including a turn as a fearless lion-tamer. But when her act is finished, she has to resist the insistent sexual advances and threats of her boss. She fights him off helped by Bimbo and Koko, proclaiming at the end, 'No, he couldn't take my boop-oop-a-doop away.' Betty is now a fully formed and independent character,

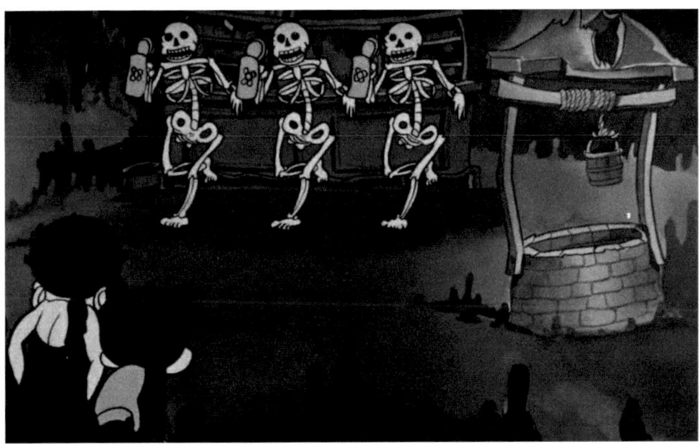

Figure 3.2 Dave Fleischer, dir., *Minnie the Moocher*. © Fleischer Studios, 1932.

provocative and sure of herself. After this, the Fleischers start to up the ante. The first of their jazz collaborations, *Minnie the Moocher*, soon follows, featuring Cab Calloway (Native New Yorkers, the Fleischers were frequent visitors to Harlem and the Cotton Club, and their incorporation of jazz into their films is done with sensitivity and subtlety). Following an argument with her parents, in the film Betty does what all rebellious teenagers contemplate and runs away from home, taking Bimbo with her. Darkness falls, and they take refuge in a cave, encountering Calloway in the form of a walrus singing 'Minnie the Moocher', the tale of a woman who gets involved with a man called Smokey who is 'cokey' and teaches her 'to kick the gong around'. The hallucinatory and fast-running visuals become increasingly nightmarish as the boundaries of life and death break down, skeletons indulge in revelry as they drink to the point of an intoxication that alternately restores them to life and kills them again, ghosts cheerfully allow themselves to be taken to the electric chair and a myriad of ghosts and phantoms transform themselves to the jazz rhythms, finally chasing Betty and Bimbo back home. Betty seeks sanctuary under the covers of her bed, while Bimbo atavistically tries to return to being a real dog by hiding in a kennel, causing the actual dog already in it to run off, taking the kennel with him. Betty's farewell letter to her parents magically tears itself up, leaving only the words 'Home Sweet Home'. The effect is almost that of a Maurice Henry cartoon come to life (although one feels that Henry must have himself been strongly influenced by the Betty cartoons).

In other films of 1932, we even get some political commentary via an ecological theme in *A Hunting We Will Go*, in which Koko and Bimbo vie for Betty's attention after they hear her longing for a fur coat. They go off hunting and bring her back a profusion of animal furs only to be rejected by Betty when she sees the animals themselves freezing without their fur. And, in the year Franklin D. Roosevelt will be elected president, Betty herself stands for president, promising 'a lot of Hi-De-Ho, Boopy Doops, and chocolate ice cream', as well as free 'movies, cabarets and jazz'. Standing against 'Mr Nobody', she is of course duly elected. Louis Armstrong takes a turn in *I'll Be Glad When You're Dead You Rascal You*, which continues some of the motifs of *Minnie the Moocher*, albeit not as successfully.

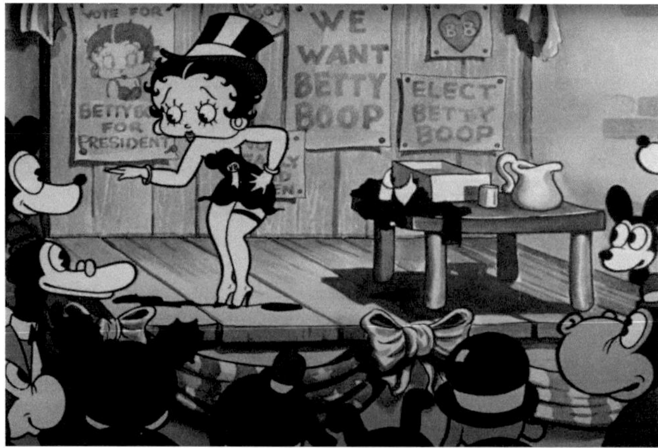

Figure 3.3 Dave Fleischer, dir., *Boop For President*. © Fleischer Studios, 1932.

The year 1933 was marked by a succession of classics. Highlights include *Is My Palm Read*, *Betty Boop's Penthouse*, *The Old Man of the Mountain* and *I Heard*. In *Is My Palm Read* (word-play is another aspect of the Fleischers' surrealist lineage), Bimbo is a dubious fortune-teller with Koko as his assistant. When Betty visits for a consultation, his crystal ball shows her shipwrecked on a desert island where she is attacked by evil spirits. Bimbo saves her and they return to the consultation room, but when they embrace the evil spirits emerge from the crystal ball and chase them back to the desert island. They finally escape by fooling the ghosts into falling off a cliff into the sea. One of the craziest of all the Fleischer films, *Is My Palm Read* dispenses with any sense of logical continuity as it plunges us into a world in which time and space are infinitely mutable and 'reality' is built on shifting sands into which one may sink at any moment.

Betty Boop's Penthouse features Betty atop a penthouse doing her washing and then taking a shower before becoming something of a spoof of *Frankenstein* when mad scientists Bimbo and Koko, working in the opposite skyscraper, are so distracted by seeing Betty showering that they don't realize that a rogue cat has added something to their apparatus. This results in the creation of a monster they cannot control that uses telegraph wires to cross to Betty's penthouse. We fear the worst, but when he appears about to attack Betty he is so entranced by her beauty that he performs a dance for her! In *The Old Man of the Mountains* Betty also tames a monster through song and dance, this time the titular character, a kind of Gilles de Rais figure, who terrorizes the village at the foot of the mountain. When the villagers start fleeing, Betty, in charge of the local tourist shop, fearlessly goes up the mountain to confront him. Another of the Cab Calloway collaborations, here he takes the role of the Old Man whom she engages in a song and dance routine as they sing a duet, *You Gotta Hi-Di-Ho (To Get Along With Me)*, another drug-themed song: *You've gotta learn my song / I gotta learn your song / If you do me wrong / I'm gonna do you wrong / You gotta kick the gong /To get along with me*.

The pinnacle of the films of 1933, however, is without doubt *Snow White*, a retelling of the old story that gives it fresh dimensions. When Betty turns up at her stepmother's castle and the magic mirror declares her to be the fairest in the land (promptly giving her a kiss), the furious stepmother orders her guards, Koko and Bimbo, to execute her. The elements

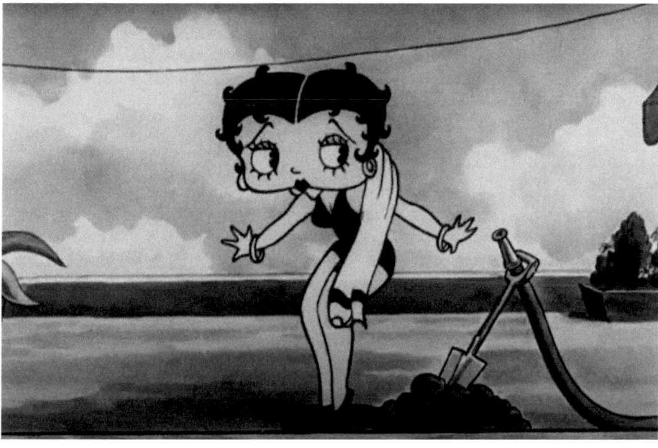

Figure 3.4 Dave Fleischer, dir., *Betty Boop's Penthouse*. © Fleischer Studios, 1933.

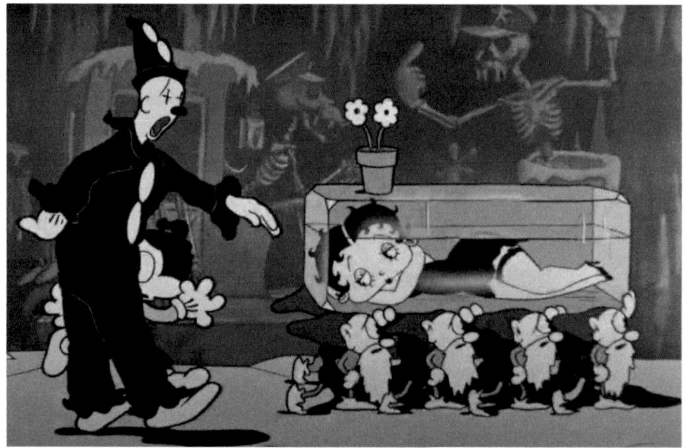

Figure 3.5 Dave Fleischer, dir., *Snow White*. © Fleischer Studios, 1933.

come to her rescue, and the tree on which she has been tied up frees her when Koko and Bimbo neglect their duty, only for her to fall into a snowball which transforms into an ice coffin and slides to the home of the seven dwarfs, who hide her in a mystery cave where she is guarded by Koko and Bimbo. Finding Betty's garter, which she lost after being released by the tree, the stepmother follows, using the magic mirror to transform Koko (played by Cab Calloway) into a ghost, but the magic mirror also melts Betty's coffin and turns the queen into a dragon that pursues the three fugitives until Bimbo is able to save them by grabbing the dragon's tongue to turn it inside out so that it goes off running in the opposite direction. Koko, Bimbo and Betty have a celebratory dance to end the film.

The fateful year of 1934 began with *She Wronged Him Right*, a more conventional damsel-in-distress melodrama, which sees the first appearance of Betty's future, although short-lived, boyfriend Fearless Fred, about more anon. It was followed by *Red Hot Mamma*, another classic that contends with *Snow White* and *Minnie the Moocher* as perhaps the greatest of all Betty's films. In it she wakes up in the middle of the night freezing to death on a snow-filled night. For some reason she has left the windows wide open. She gets up and closes them before lighting a fire and moving her blanket close to it. Before long it becomes so hot that two chickens that have taken roost in the grate get literally roasted. Betty herself finds herself transported through her fireplace, which has transformed into the gates of hell. Here the devil himself and a motley crew of demons try to have their way with her before the icy stare she gives them all literally causes hell to freeze over. She wakes up to find the fire has gone out, but rather than relight it she buries herself under a pile of quilts.

Red Hot Mamma was actually banned in the UK for blasphemy (!) and the next film in the series *Ha! Ha! Ha!* would apparently later be banned from TV for encouraging drug use, although this may be an urban myth as I haven't been able to find any evidence for it, and the drug involved (laughing gas) was not illegal. Be that as it may, the latter film is a return to the *Out of the Inkwell* concept. It begins with Max Fleischer himself saying goodnight to Betty, whom he leaves as a drawing on a canvas sheet. When he has gone, Koko struggles out of the inkwell and eats a chocolate bar Max has left on the desk, giving himself a terrible toothache. Betty steps down from the canvas and tries to help him. She paints a dentist's surgery and forces him into it where she tries to take out the offending tooth. In a scene recalling that in the contemporaneous W. C. Fields film *The Dentist*, the tooth resists and she pulls Bimbo around the surgery, finally resorting to laughing gas to calm him down. The gas escapes into the New York night causing the whole city to succumb to uncontrollable fits of laughter. Betty and Koko escape back into the inkwell, where they presumably spend the night together. This will be the last we shall ever see of Koko the Clown, for by now the storm clouds over the series were looming and would break a few months later.

An *Alice in Wonderland* spoof, *Betty in Blunderland*, followed, and then *Betty Boop's Rise to Fame* would again go back charmingly to the *Out of the Inkwell* format as a (human) journalist interviews Max Fleischer and Betty herself about her career. The next film, *Betty Boop's Trial*, released on 15 June 1934, would be the last before the imposition of the Production Code. Perhaps wanting to raise the bar before the curtain fell, it is the most risqué of all of Betty's adventures. In it, traffic cop Fearless Fred pursues Betty as she passes in her car, forcing her to stop, saying 'Hello cutie, I'd like to know ya!' When he demands her driving licence, which she takes from her garter to hand to him, she describes her profession as 'Boop-Oopy-Doop! Bop'. He continues to harass her. Trying to escape, she breaks the speed limit and Fearless Fred takes her to the court where she is finally found not guilty after flirting outrageously with the judge and jurors.

Although appearing here as a rather lascivious and dodgy officer of the law, Fearless Fred was being prepared in anticipation of the implementation of the Production Code

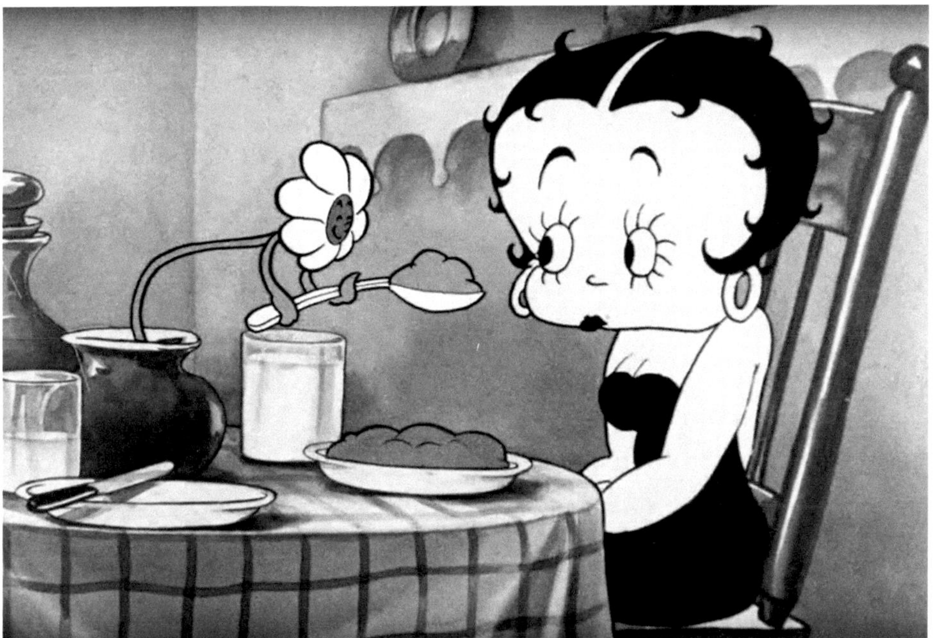

Figure 3.6 Dave Fleischer, dir., *Red Hot Mamma*. © Fleischer Studios, 1934.

as Betty's more wholesome, all-American, Charles Atlas-type boyfriend in contrast to the decidedly ambivalent and sometimes morally dubious Koko and Bimbo, who will henceforth be banished from view. Fred himself will in fact only survive for a further four episodes as the Fleischers no doubt realized that such a character was singularly inappropriate as a companion for Betty. Instead, for the rest of her career she will be a single career woman and housewife whose companions, mainly the crazy Rube Goldberg-style inventor Grampy and an infuriatingly 'cute' doggy called Pudgy, would increasingly upstage her until she sadly faded away from the screen in 1939.

The Production Code was enacted, or rather came to be strictly enforced, from 1 July 1934, after which all Hollywood films had to be submitted to the Production Code Administration (PCA) and could only be released when given its seal of approval. A great deal of mythology has accrued around the code but, as Richard Maltby has shown, its activity was more nuanced than popular discourse would have it. The PCA was a regulatory body.[5] It did not censor films and did not have strict criteria as to what was and was not acceptable. The Code itself was only a set of guidelines and each film was judged on its merits. Maltby shows that there was never a clear distinction between 'pre-code' and 'post-code' as has come to be popularly believed. In the case of Betty Boop's films, however, such a distinction is manifest and there can be no question about the existence of a 'pre' and 'post' code Betty, even if her domestication only occurred gradually.

The first film issued after implementation was *Betty Boop's Life Guard*, in which she goes for a swim in the sea. When she gets into difficulties, Fearless Fred rescues her, but not before she dreams she has fallen to the bottom of the sea, been turned into a mermaid, and is pursued by a killer whale. She wakes to find herself in his arms. In the next, *There's Something about a Soldier*, she is recruiting officer for an army to protect the city from an attack by giant mosquitoes. The soldiers, led by Fearless Fred, are not terribly successful, and Betty has to come to their rescue by gassing the insects.

In these films, and the others issued until the end of 1934, she gets to keep her garter and short skirt and isn't reticent about showing her underwear, albeit not as provocatively as previously. The PCA had, however, ordered the removal of the credits sequence in which Betty's winking and shaking of her hips was considered 'suggestive of immorality'. Already gone, as well, along with Koko and Bimbo, are the friendly anthropomorphic creatures and other aspects of nature coming to life. There will be no more trees coming to save Betty from execution or mischievous chair legs lifting up her skirt.

Henceforth nature will be presented naturalistically as either an irritant or as an actual danger to be overcome. There would be no further collaborations with jazz musicians and no visits to the underworld. Her adventures will be confined to the everyday and the prosaic and if she dreams it will only be to alleviate the irritations of daily life. For instance, in *Judge for a Day*, having been annoyed by various people on her way to work as a court clerk, she imagines assuming the role of the judge and condemning inconsiderate people to cages in a pests zoo where audiences can come to laugh at those who suffer the consequences for their thoughtless actions in, for instance, having blown cigar smoke into people's faces or carelessly disposed of chewing gum so that it sticks to people's clothes.

By 1935, though, the short skirts and garter would be gone and replaced by demure career girl outfits with high collars and long sleeves. Although in the episodes with Fearless Fred one fears that she might be married off and saddled with this characterless dolt, he too had vanished before the end of 1934 and thereafter she would (perhaps unsurprisingly!) show no interest in men and not even the slightest whiff of sexual provocation or innuendo will be found in any of the remaining films. Moreover, Betty was no longer a being 'of pen and ink who will win you with a wink'. From being a fantasy sex symbol, she becomes a 'real' character with ordinary day-to-day concerns, none of which involve sex. There would also be no more occasions when she would step out of the drama and speak directly with Uncle Max. Plays between reality and appearance would cease to occur. The 'animist' elements, in which immaterial things come to life, would also be eliminated. The latter is one of the most significant fractures, because it transformed the very world in which Betty existed. Previously it had been one in which the unexpected was always to be expected, but now everything happens in predictable, or at least banal, ways. Instead of the natural world being in complicity with Betty, often helping her against the evils threatening her, it would now be entirely indifferent to her problems, if not actually their agent.

It seems more likely that these changes were made by the studio itself rather than being specifically imposed by the PCA. Fleischer Studios was a production line in which a vast number of people worked collectively to produce often three or four films every month (one or two of which would feature Betty, at that time their most important 'star'). Not only did each finished film have to be submitted to the PCA; the production process had to be approved at every stage, beginning with the script. Any doubtful material wasn't proscribed but was subject to negotiation as to what would make it acceptable. One imagines that such a process would have made the Fleischers' working methods untenable: having to negotiate the content of each film would have complicated the production process inordinately, besides destroying the spontaneity that had made the imaginative leaps in the material possible. They thus needed to find a *modus vivendi* and may have decided that discretion was the better part of valour and to forestall any PCA intervention by cutting anything they feared might raise objections.[6] Moreover, the fact that the studio was in New York, far from the political intrigues of Hollywood, must have meant they had no chance for day-to-day interaction with the members of the PCA and so were cut off from the possibility of negotiating the content of their films. Whatever the case, Betty Boop was the major casualty of the introduction of the Code, suffering far worse than even Mae West.

Ninety-one official Betty Boop films were made between 1932 and 1939. In addition, she made a further twenty-one appearances in *Talkartoon and Screen Songs* series before being given her own series in 1932. Of this total of 112 films, fifty-two were made prior to the implementation of the Production Code and, rather surprisingly, sixty after it, more than half of which featured the insufferable Pudgy. Betty must therefore have retained some popularity, even if she becomes increasingly marginalized from the action as time went by. Although some of the latter films have moments of interest none can compare with those that came before, not even the prestige Technicolor *Poor Cinderella* (1934), which was already in production prior to the Code, but not released until August.

Although extremely beautiful and technically flawless, it is somewhat bloodless and lacks real invention. It was the only Betty Boop film to be made in colour; no doubt any further experimental incursion became too risky after implementation of the Code. The best of the later films is *A Language of her Own* from 1935, made specifically for a Japanese audience and in which Betty visits the Land of the Rising Sun in her own handmade aeroplane for a concert in which she sings in both English and Japanese, exchanging costumes as she does so in a rare attempt at cultural entente cordiale. It is rumoured that the Fleischers surreptitiously defied the censors by slipping the lines ‘Come to bed with me / And we’ll boop-oop-a-doop’ into the Japanese version, although if they did it hasn’t survived in the prints available today.[7]

Unfortunately the rather colourless character of the later films for a long time came to characterize Betty. She did survive as a more vivacious character in a syndicated comic strip, licensed by the Fleischer studio but in which it appears to have had no direct hand. She assumes yet another persona here, being presented as a star entertainer and having to deal with the tribulations of show business and stardom and there are few flights of imaginative fancy. The series appears not to have been very successful and only ran from 1934 to 1937. Various other attempts have been made over the years to revive her, but none have been successfully realized (perhaps fortunately). In the 1970s her image was sold to a marketing company and she suffered the indignity of being commercialized as a sub-pornographic doll-like image for a range of accoutrements from keyrings to fridge magnets. The latter seems to a great extent to have subsumed the memory of her 1930s film career.

All this means that if we are speaking of Betty Boop in relation to surrealism, we are referring only to her incarnations prior to 1935. Aside from the qualities identified earlier we can specifically point to the ‘automatism’ of the Fleischers’ working methods, already established in the *Out of the Inkwell* films and continued up until this time which, together with the collective environment in which the creators worked, which appears to have responded to the adage of Heraclitus always to ‘expect the unexpected’.

Although critics are agreed on the fact that ‘surrealism’ is one element in the early Betty films, precisely what this surrealism might be is not clear. The box set of Betty films issued by Warners in France, for instance, included a section devoted to ‘surrealism’ consisting of eight apparently rather arbitrarily chosen films, including one, *The Robot* (1932), that doesn’t actually feature Betty at all. In *Betty Boop M.D.* she works with Koko and Bimbo in a travelling medicine show à la W. C. Fields selling a wonder tonic called ‘Jippo’ to a gullible populace. Alongside the classics *Bimbo’s Initiation* and *Red Hot Mamma*, discussed earlier, we are given *Betty Boop’s Ups and Downs*, *Betty Boop’s May Party* and *Crazy Town*. The representations in these three films are less subtle than many of Betty’s other films and tend simply to reverse everyday perceptions rather than challenge the nature of reality itself. In *Crazy Town*, for instance, patrons visit a shop to have their heads replaced, whereas in *Betty Boop’s Ups and Downs* the world, having become bankrupt, is put up for auction by the Moon and bought by Saturn, which decides to remove gravity, causing everything to be pulled up into the sky. Eventually Saturn puts gravity back, and so everything falls back down to Earth.

It is difficult to see why these three or even the others of these eight films might be regarded as 'surrealist' rather than others and the classification appears to arise from an attempt to pin surrealism down to a definition, or at least a category. If we wish to speak of surrealism in relation to the Betty Boop films, however, we need to look at the overall sensibility for its correlation with a surrealist attitude. As we have seen there is a clear correspondence between the Fleischers' working methods and key surrealist ideas. This alone would make the films of interest to the surrealists but does not make them in any way 'surrealist films', nor can particular elements in them be isolated and classified as 'surrealist'. Rather, we might say, as Franklin Rosemont did of Krazy Kat, that she 'was not "conceived", not "born"' but 'jus grew'. 'Wonderfully nonsensical, defiantly poetic, and proceeding unconsciously – or rather *sur*consciously, as if by magic – *Krazy Kat* is one of the triumphs of pure psychic automatism.'[8] Exactly the same thing could be said of Betty Boop.

Moreover, Betty has to be seen as a culture hero, one of those figures we might designate as part of the 'mythology of the modern' of which the surrealists saw the contemporary world as being of so much in need. As a wise woman who doesn't realize she is wise because her wisdom is so integral to her being, Betty stands between the flapper of the twenties and the 'dumb blonde' of the 1950s, as exemplified by Marilyn Monroe or Judy Holliday, whose 'dumbness' is a blind to wrong-foot patriarchal attitudes. With Monroe and Holliday she shares an innate intelligence that comes not from the surface but from deep within her being.

As noted earlier, however, she was modelled on the flapper girls of the late twenties, and as her character evolved it was surely Clara Bow who came to assume ascendancy as her archetype (indeed, Ado Kyrou calls Clara 'the personification of Betty Boop'). In fact, in Clara Bow's most famous film (*It*, 1927) her character is actually called Betty.[9] Like Betty Boop, Clara was 'scandalously beautiful'. From all accounts, she was one of the most unaffected actresses in cinema (perhaps in the whole history of cinema): what you see on screen is what she was in real life. Being so natural, having no 'side', and remaining only what one 'is' may precisely be what the morality police find most difficult to tolerate. But it is also what many people most love. As Clara said, 'I'm reproached for loving life, gaiety and youth. They say I am a danger to men. They relate stupid things, true things and ridiculous things …'[10] And like Betty Boop, Clara's career was brought to a premature end largely because of the attentions of intrusive guardians of morality (not in her case the PCA or the Legion of Decency, but the general media).

In this respect Clara, like Betty, embodies the idea of the *femme-enfant*, the 'child woman' extolled by Breton in *Arcane 17*, one of the most misunderstood notions in surrealism, one with which women drawn to surrealism are often uncomfortable because it may imply a certain infantilization. Although it can be argued that Breton invoked this figure with a certain lack of sensitivity, it should be understood as a myth, not as a female ideal. Indeed, surrealism also extols (perhaps more significantly even if without naming him as such) the *homme-enfant*. Silent comedians like Buster Keaton or more specifically Harry Langdon offer the greatest exemplars of this figure, those who are incapable of attaining 'maturity' but embrace the sort of Sadeian 'indifference'.[11]

Indeed, might we not see Breton himself, especially in *Nadja*, as something of an *homme-enfant*? These figures, whether male or female, represent the surrealist rejection of the Sartrean notion of engagement in which the freedom of human personality lies in the extent to which they have established a *pour-soi* by which they can assume responsibility to act in a predetermined and established world that has preceded us. In contrast, freedom for surrealism lies in availability to the processes of the world and in establishing a harmony between what we are and the challenges the world presents us with.

The character of Betty Boop, whose availability to the world, as developed by Max Fleischer and his studio in the early years of the 1930s, is exemplary, in this respect alone would correlate significantly with surrealism. But it can also be said that their real surrealism remains *to be discovered*.

Notes

1 In 1934, some Mexican jumping beans arrived in Paris and led to a dispute about the nature of surrealism itself. There are various versions of the story, involving André Breton, Roger Caillois and Jacques Lacan. Caillois wanted immediately to cut open one of the beans to examine what caused them to jump; Breton wanted to exhaust all of the imaginative possibilities of their jumping, whereas Lacan apparently thought they should leave the beans alone. For Caillois, Breton's attitude was symptomatic of a lack of scientific seriousness within surrealism. This caused him to withdraw from the surrealist group. See Roger Caillois, 'Lettre à André Breton', in *Approaches de l'Imaginaire* (Paris: Gallimard, 1974), 35–8.

2 In the 1920s 'bimbo' was most often used as slang word for a 'tough guy' with limited intelligence. Initially conceived as an anti-Mickey Mouse, Bimbo's personality changes depending on the situation encountered in a particular film.

3 Lautréamont, *Maldoror*, trans. Paul Knight (Harmondsworth: Penguin Books, 1978), 274.

4 The trial has been extensively documented in James D. Taylor Jr., *Helen Kane and Betty Boop: On Stage and On Trial* (New York: Algora Publishing, 2017).

5 Richard Maltby, 'The Production Code and the Mythologies of "Pre-Code" Hollywood,' in *The Classical Hollywood Reader*, ed. Steve Neale (London: Routledge, 2012), 237–48.

6 The impact of the PCA's work was also strengthened by the activity of censorious religious bodies of the time concerned with the supposedly deleterious effects of the film industry, most notably the Legion of Decency, founded in 1934 by a group of Catholic bishops, which classified films according to their level of moral suitability. I haven't been able to discover whether this body actually had Betty Boop in its sights, but it seems likely.

7 Thanks to Michiyo Miyake for checking this.

8 Franklin Rosemont, 'George Herriman (*Krazy Kat*)' in *Cultural Correspondence, Surrealism and its Popular Accomplices*, nos. 10–11, special double issue (1979): 61.

9 Ado Kyrou, *Amour-érotisme et cinéma* (Paris: Le Terrain Vague, 1957), 447.

10 Kyrou, *Amour*, 448.

11 Petr Král, *Les Burlesques ou Parade des somnambules* (Paris: Stock, 1986), 224–8.

Chapter 4

Animation and Animacy in Salvador Dalí's 1930s Multimedia Projects

Alex Zivkovic

'Animation' is a medium but it is also a state of energetic being. Both senses of the word involve objects or beings that seemingly come to life – whether via sequential images or inner vital forces. Crucially, both definitions play a role in Salvador Dalí's art and writing of the 1930s. Although Dalí never finished an animation project, this sense of objects, bodies and images coming alive is a consistent refrain across his art and writing throughout his career. For example, around 1956, Dalí painted *Nature Morte Vivante (Living Still Life)* – a parody of the still-life genre that shows both inanimate objects and living birds flying around a table. This spontaneous animacy – an inability for objects to remain 'still' (or in French 'morte' or 'dead') – is a frequent characteristic of images and objects that Dalí both made and encountered in his creative work from the outset of his career.

In his writings about art and film, Dalí seems to propose that modern art should not be confined to static forms. Rather, modern art was becoming increasingly unstable and animated – characteristics he admired in optical toys, Art Nouveau, Disney animated films and Italian cinema which he then brought into his art and theory. These same qualities also appear in Dalí's paranoic-critical method – a mode of seeing the world in which images morph between different interpretations. For Dalí, it is not just that a village could be a face – to take one famous example – but that the image always oscillates between the two. The influence of modern art's increasing animacy especially impacts his art of the 1930s, when he experimented across a range of media, including films, sculptures and installations.

In this period, Dalí even directly addressed the medium of animation's early history within his art, as when he incorporated a zoetrope strip into a sculpture or made boxes that recreated nineteenth-century optical toys. These animation-adjacent projects offer a key through which to understand how the rest of his art practice similarly interrogated changing bodies, living forms and other animated effects across a range of media. Whether making his own optical toys, decorating a mannequin, working with live performers, blurring boundaries on façades, or storyboarding animated sequences, Dalí's art uncannily straddles (and often breaks) the stable boundaries of animate and inanimate – a model for an enlivened surrealism.

Painting: from optical toy to three-dimensional painting

Dalí's interest in animation history begins with a primal scene: a childhood encounter with an optical theatre that was repeatedly self-mythologized and subsequently referenced in a variety of scholarship on his relation to early moving image culture.[1] According to his memoirs, this optical theatre from his youth produced both a stereoscopic and moving image effect. Scholars have consequently variously categorized the unknown object as a stroboscope, phenakistoscope, zoetrope or a stereophantoscope – none of which actually capture both qualities he remembered.[2]

In the 1930s, two of Dalí's artworks seemingly attempt to recreate the three-dimensional effect of that semi-forgotten object. The first, *Babaouo* (1932), was composed of seven painted panes of glass: a layered painting that showed several bicyclists with baguettes on their heads, cycling through a landscape of cypresses. Two years later, he made *The Little Theater*, which – across eleven panes of glass – presents a desert landscape, framed by a theatre in the foreground. The handheld nature of *Babaouo* seems to directly reference many optical toys that were often handled kinaesthetically, while the proscenium on the first pane of *The Little Theater* evokes the viewing condition of the praxinoscope, an early projection technology that had a theatrical viewing frame.[3]

In addition to looking back at cinema's prehistory, the structure of these boxes evokes the apparatus of the multiplane camera – inadvertently recreating the cutting-edge of animation technology in Dalí's own time.[4] The compositional logic of painting a scene on multiple panes of glass is the underlying basis for the production of parallax effects in animation of the late 1920s and 1930s.[5] Elements on one pane of the glass can then be moved relative to the other panes – like the way elements in the foreground or background of a landscape seem to move at different speeds from a train or car, for example. Thus, in attempting to recreate the experimental optical toys of his past, Dalí also incidentally invoked experiments in animation from his own time.

Sculpture: surrealism and the frozen past

Around the same time as he made these two pseudo-optical toys, Dalí placed a paper strip from a zoetrope within one of his sculptural assemblies. In *The Retrospective Bust of a Woman* (1933), a mannequin sports a desiccated baguette on her head and is dressed only in two ears of corn and a prominent paper 'necklace'. This necklace is in fact a zoetrope strip that shows a cartoon of a dancing man who rolls his head on and off his shoulders. An early animation technology, the zoetrope was composed of a cylinder with drawings on the inside. When spun, the device produced the effect of animation for a viewer who peered through a series of slits on the device. Without the motion of the original machine, the strip is 'stuck' and the figure's playful action simply shows several states of decapitation. A similar sense of frozen time is in fact prominent throughout the assemblage.

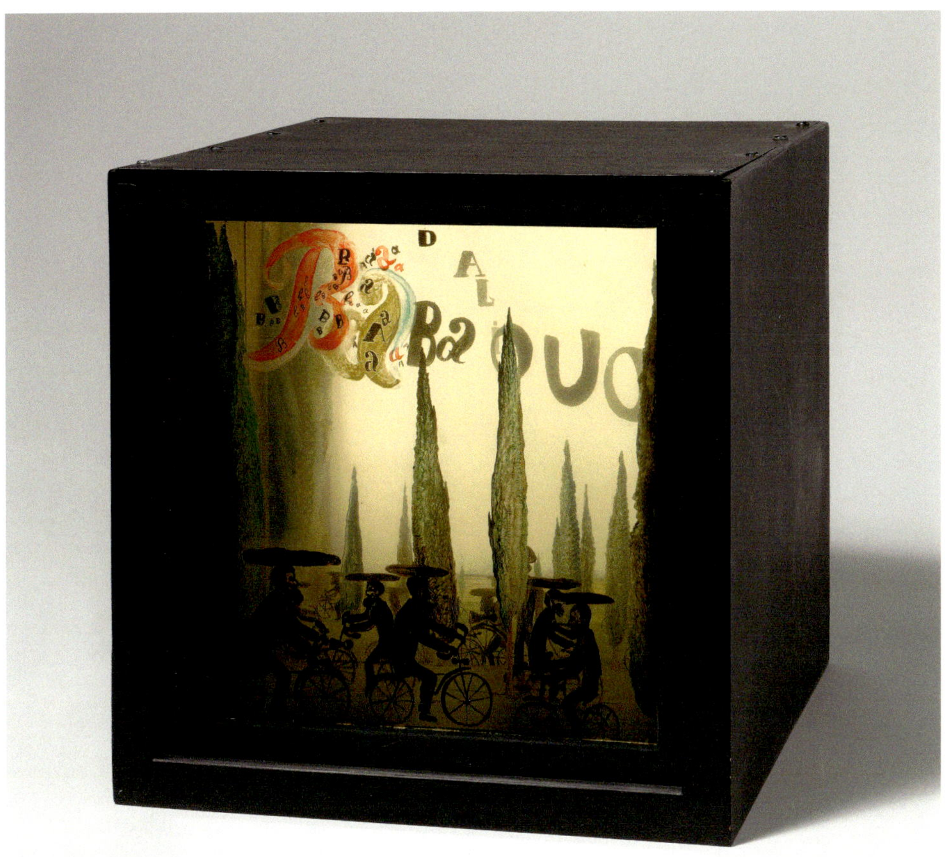

Figure 4.1 Salvador Dalí, *Babaouo*, 1932. Wooden box, sheets of painted glass and light source. © 2024 Salvador Dalí, Fundació Gala-Salvador Dalí, Artists Rights Society.

For example, ants are painted all over the mannequin. Like the figures in the zoetrope, the ants too are in a state of suspended animation. In real life, ants are usually in constant motion – swarming, marching, fleeing. Of course, we do not expect ants in the controlled environment of an art museum today, but approaching the sculpture, there is a moment of confusion while determining the precise nature of the tiny creatures. Are they real or fake? Three-dimensional or painted?

In this indeterminate period, the encounter between the ants and the woman also further heightens the inanimacy of the woman who does not 'react' to the creatures swarming her face. The ants seem to move towards the figure's eyes and one even crawls over and onto her lip. But of course, there are no reactions between them because the ants are (of course) painted on and the mannequin is (of course) not alive. The tension between the bugs and mannequin was perhaps the inspiration for a later installation that amplified that effect. In 1938, Dalí put living snails on a mannequin inside of his *Rainy Taxi*

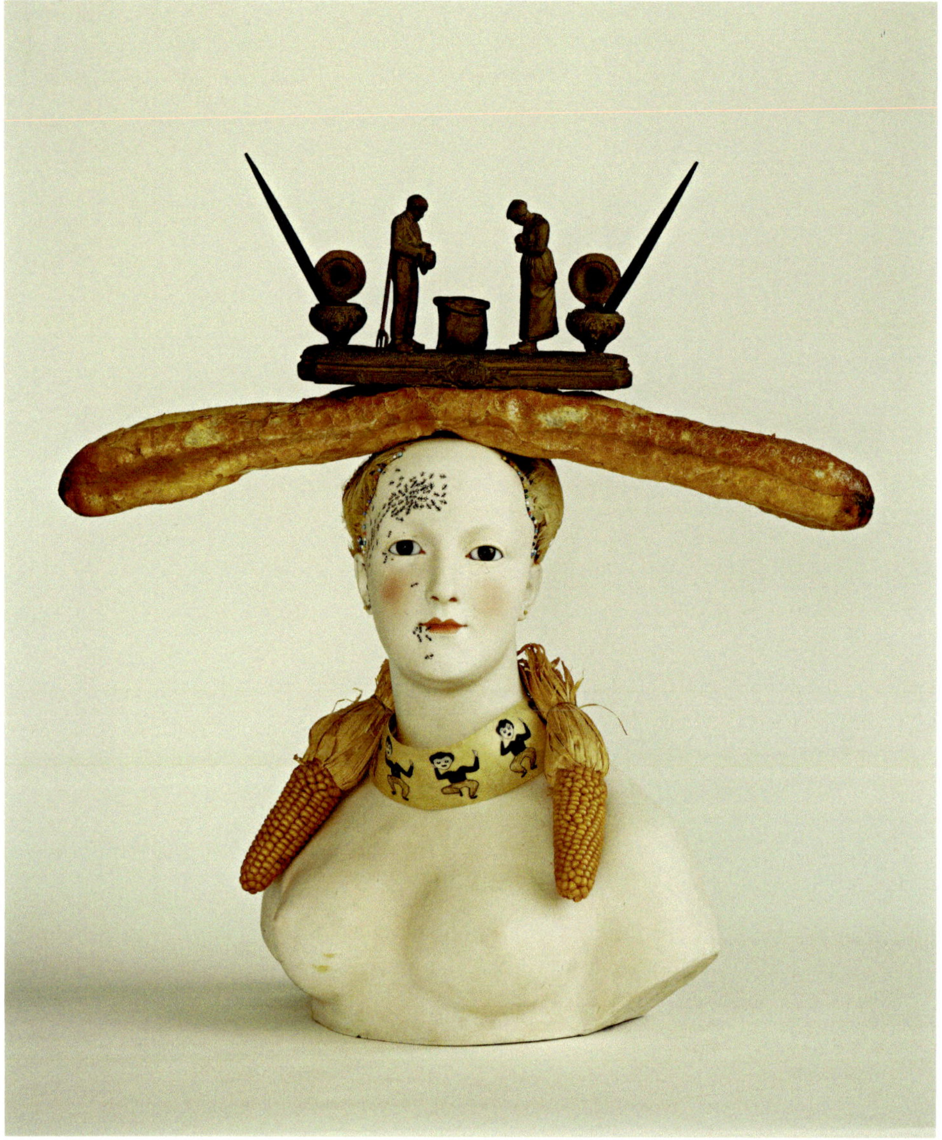

Figure 4.2 Salvador Dalí, *Retrospective Bust of a Woman*, 1933. Painted porcelain, bread, corn, feathers, paint on paper, beads, ink stand, sand and two pens, 73.9 × 69.2 × 32 cm. Museum of Modern Art, New York. Acquired through the Lillie P. Bliss Bequest and gift of Philip Johnson (by exchange). 301.1992. Digital image: The Museum of Modern Art, New York/Scala, Florence © 2024 Salvador Dalí, Fundació Gala-Salvador Dalí, Artists Rights Society.

sculptural installation. The snails there were said to have been induced to move by some means; consequently, their motion produced a heightened contrast between the animate (albeit slow) live snails and the totally inanimate mannequin.[6]

An uncanny sense of inanimacy may be the governing principle of this bust assemblage as well as his three-dimensional painting. It is not just that figures are still – which is of course how the medium of painting and sculpture traditionally operate – but that every figure in these works appears uncannily ready to move. The mannequin should blink, the bicyclists in *Babaouo* should cycle, and the ants should crawl (and, in *Rainy Taxi*, the snails *did* move, although the mannequin – again – did not). Similar ideas of suspension permeated surrealist discourse around Dalí, like the 'film still' effects in Max Ernst's collages or the empty, frozen street photographs of Eugène Atget.[7] Like Dalí, both of these artists not only captured discrete moments in time but, crucially, preserved an outmoded past. The nineteenth-century print material Ernst employed and the *fin de siècle* Paris documented by Atget are records of a bygone era. Brought into the present, they now produce surrealist effects through their invocation – and preservation – of the past as well as their confounding stillness. So too *Retrospective Bust*, which features a fragment of a zoetrope strip, or Dalí's little boxes, which both invoke frozen – thereby, thwarted – variants of the moving figures of his youth.

Installation: animacy, animals and Art Nouveau

Optical toys are part of the vast constellation of animation culture – at the smallest, most intimate scale. *The Little Theater* is on one hand (or rather in one's hands) an imagined world in a box. But it could also be understood as a scalable model for a big theatre somewhere, in which there would not be illustrated figures but real people and creatures that inhabit it.

And indeed this intimate interest in animation 'scaled up' into Dalí's installation design. The same two terms that characterized Dalí's relationship to the optical theatre of his youth – three-dimensional and animated – conspicuously reappear in his *Dream of Venus* pavilion built for the 1939 World's Fair in New York. The original proposal submitted to the World's Fair committee was for a surrealist pavilion featuring multiple artists. Even before Dalí's involvement, the gallerist Julien Levy and others wrote to the fair organizers that 'Exhibits will be designed each by a different artist as if they were paintings in three dimensions, as many as possible animated.'[8] Dalí's project maintained these qualities: 'Populated by girls and mermaids in costumes designed by Dali [*sic*], the Bottom of the Sea is in reality a surrealist drawing in three dimensions and animated besides.'[9]

The three-dimensionality of the installation is obvious. An entire pavilion, the *Dream of Venus*' scale moves beyond surrealist encounters with individual paintings (or even three-dimensional *Little Theaters*) to instead follow a model honed in the immersive surrealist exhibition of 1938 at the Galérie Beaux-Arts in Paris. There, visitors entered a pseudo-grotto, navigating the dark space with flashlights to look upon strange sculptures and paintings. Dalí adopted these immersive exhibition strategies, wielded now to celebrate Dalí's own most recognizable images. Moving through 'dry' and 'wet' tanks, viewers encountered paintings, performers and sculptures that featured Dalí's key motifs, including a flaming giraffe, melting clocks, mermaids, nymphs and desert landscapes.

As to the quality of animation, it was primarily the performers who quite literally brought life to the pavilion. Dalí hired several women who swam inside of aquarium tanks and lounged in a big bed as the dreaming Venus herself. Dalí had also wanted to include a live seal alongside the human performers, but his request was shut down by the city's Deputy Commissioner of Public Health.[10] Following the snails of his *Rainy Taxi* – and this thwarted attempt to feature a seal – his work with live animals nonetheless continued with his 1941 fundraiser at the Del Monte hotel in California where live lions, monkeys and frogs were present for 'A Surrealist's Night in an Enchanted Forest'. In particular, his presentation of frogs straddled the line between animacy and inanimacy. Presented in a covered platter, four frogs initially stood still when the dish's lid was removed. Only when prodded did they leap from the plate, revealing that they were not dinner, but guests.

Enhancing the swimmers in the *Dream of Venus*, the water of the so-called wet tanks produced additional effects of animacy. Water buoyed objects and people – producing slow, sensual movements – while further casting reflections and refractions on surfaces around the tank. Moving through this strange medium, Dalí's mermaids participated in a longer history of surrealist interest in underwater optics, joining the slow-moving figures in Man Ray's *Les Mystères du Château de Dé* (1929) and Rogi André's blurry photographs of Jacqueline Lamba swimming in a glass tank.[11]

Dalí also believed water produced some of Art Nouveau's sense of liveliness – an effect he brought to the pavilion's grotto-like façade. In an essay in *Minotaure* (1933),

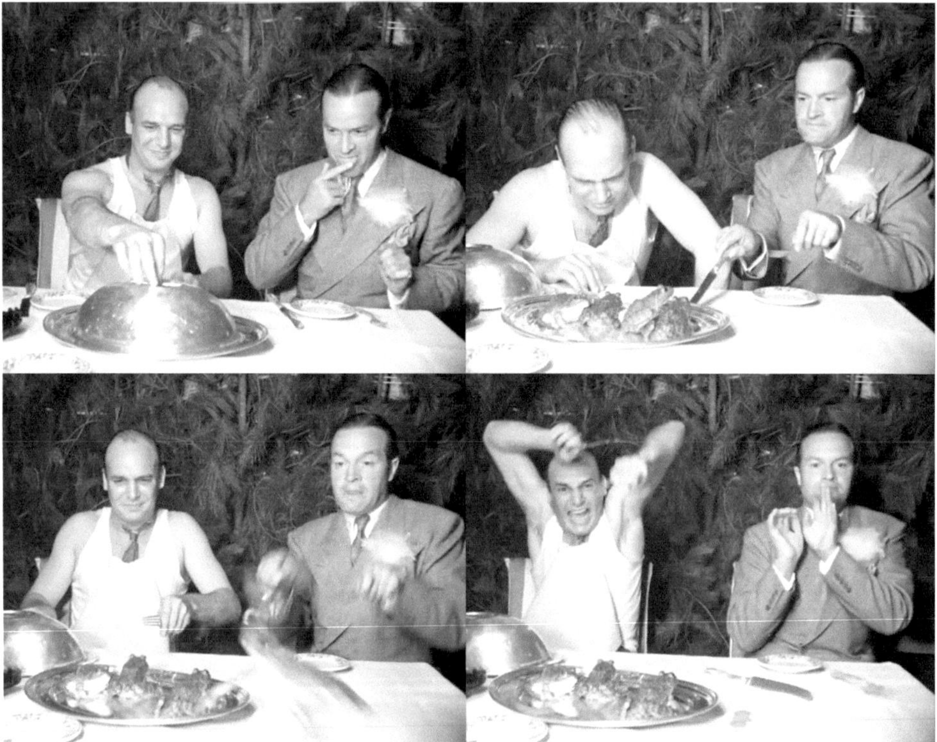

Figure 4.3 *Dizzy Dalí Dinner*, Paramount newsreel, 1941.

Dalí captioned a photograph of Antoni Gaudí's architecture 'fossilized waves from the sea' and describes Art Nouveau architects as operating per the 'convulsing–undulating formula'.[12] Invoking that sense of transformation, Dalí adopted numerous decorative motifs for the façade of his *Dream of Venus* pavilion that recalled hybrid sources: the plants of Art Nouveau, the water and tree nymphs of Antiquity and the undulating surfaces of Gaudí.[13]

Through live performers, watery waves and fossilized waves, Dalí's *Dream of Venus* featured various states of animacy, both real and imagined. Together, these different features reveal that animation is not confined to technological devices, nor is animacy confined to living beings; rather, effects of animacy can also appear in water, rocks and other elemental forms.

Film: the paranoiac–cinematic method

Lastly, for a full understanding of Dalí's interest in animation, we must (of course) examine Dalí's direct engagement with cinema both within and outside the medium of animation. Dalí worked on two completed films – *Un Chien andalou* (Andalusian Dog, Luis Buñuel, France, 1929) and *L'age d'or* (The Golden Age, France, 1930) – and wrote undeveloped screenplays of several others in the 1920s and 1930s.[14] Furthermore, he published several texts about cinema history. In Dalí's earliest writings on film, animation as a medium is absent – in part, because there were not yet the breakout, feature-length successes of the Walt Disney company that popularized the medium.

In his first published text on film in 1927, the closest reference to animation is in a section about the films of Man Ray and Fernand Léger, both of whom notably featured animated sequences using stop-motion animation in *Emak Bakia* (1926) and *Le Ballet Mécanique* (1924).[15] He does not call these animation; nonetheless, these films featured objects that seemingly moved of their own volition – a quality Dalí admired in other films. Dalí's later 'Short Critical History of Cinema' (1932) is peppered with references to the disturbances of everyday objects. He writes, 'the beginnings of the cinema having an experimental nature, up to and including [Georges] Méliès', and attributes that era's innovative nature to 'the contemplative and questioning exhibition of things and phenomena'.[16]

Closer to his own era, he celebrates the 'hysterical' films produced by Italians in the 1930s for maintaining that interest from the fantastical era of Méliès.[17] In his description of this body of films, Dalí writes in passive voice, often starting with the objects themselves: 'palm trees and magnolias were materially bitten, uprooted with the teeth by these women'.[18] He describes a shot showing an actor descending into a lake with almost complete detachment from the human agent. He writes that, after the character disappears, the camera lingers on the water 'until the usual expanding concentric circles subsided and the calm of the water was restored'.[19] Of course, a human actor caused the reactions of water in this film, but the motion Dalí focuses on is of water's responsive patterns of movement. Like his interest in waves in Gaudí's architecture, his *Dream of Venus* façade, or the wet tanks of that pavilion, water's fluid motions captivated Dalí cinematically as well.

Dalí's first writing that references the medium of illustrated animation is 'Surrealism in Hollywood' (1937), when he writes 'one always believes to have "dreamed" those dazzling "cataclysmic rainbows" which are the Silly Symphonies of Disney'.[20] The timing of this essay follows the inclusion of Disney films in the 'Fantastic Art, Dada, Surrealism' show which opened at MoMA in 1936 – a show that Dalí participated in.[21] Alfred Barr, the curator of the exhibit, believed – like many people at the time – that Walt Disney productions offered surrealist sensibilities for a mass public. Dalí's interest in Disney eventually turned into an opportunity to make his own Disney film, *Destino* in 1946. The project was never completed in his lifetime – although, in 2003, Dominique Monféry directed a version of the film based in part on the extant storyboards, in consultation with Dalí's original partner John Hench.

Looking at the original storyboards, we see Dalí's surrealist approach to animation. In one sequence of four images, Dalí transmutes the face of a clock into a bird and other objects, then into the face of a man. The multiplicity of forms that emerge out of that scene evokes the transformational possibilities inherent to his paranoiac–critical method. Dalí vividly described this mode of seeing in a text published in *Le Surréalisme au service de la révolution* (1931) in which he relays having erroneously spotted a face in a postcard of Africans in a village.[22] He explained that 'suddenly the face fades and I became aware of the illusion (?) The analysis of the paranoiac image in question allows me to rediscover, by a symbolic interpretation, all the ideas that had preceded the vision of the face'.[23] Once Dalí becomes aware of the two facets of the illusion, he can then analyse the different forms residing within the image: that is, the actual photographed subjects of the image as well as the imagined face.

Oscillating between differing interpretations of the same visual stimuli, viewers can imagine the figures literally morphing between the two – a person into an eye, a hut into a cheekbone. In an earlier, unpublished screenplay, *Cinq minutes à propos du surréalisme* (Five Minutes About Surrealism, c.1931–4), Dalí illustrates how an ambiguous image of a reclining woman can be transformed into a lion and a horse. In fact, this exact transformation is one he describes in his 1930 essay 'The Rotting Donkey', another essay that offers an overview of the paranoiac–critical method.[24] These motifs also appear in a painting of 1930, *Invisible Sleeping Woman, Horse, Lion*. But, fixed on a canvas, the image of the woman–lion–horse is all of these things all at once, requiring the viewer to decipher the various forms and only ever imagine the transformation from one to another. With animation, however, Dalí would be able to illustrate the optical transformations he hopes viewers will experience. Perhaps teaching his paranoiac–critical method is what he meant when he said in an interview that film 'is an effort intended to initiate the public into surrealism, better than painting or the written word'.[25]

Other avant-garde film-makers praised precisely this transformational possibility of animation, including Sergei Eisenstein who celebrated Disney's 'plasmatic' qualities.[26] This 'plasmaticicity' (or in more familiar terms, 'plasticity') refers to the possibility of figures to grow, shrink and otherwise change their shapes. In fact, Dalí uses a similar word for architecture, saying that Art Nouveau's essential characteristic is that it is 'extra-plastique',[27] suggesting that these various animated media – whether in stone or in drawings – were never far apart for Dalí.

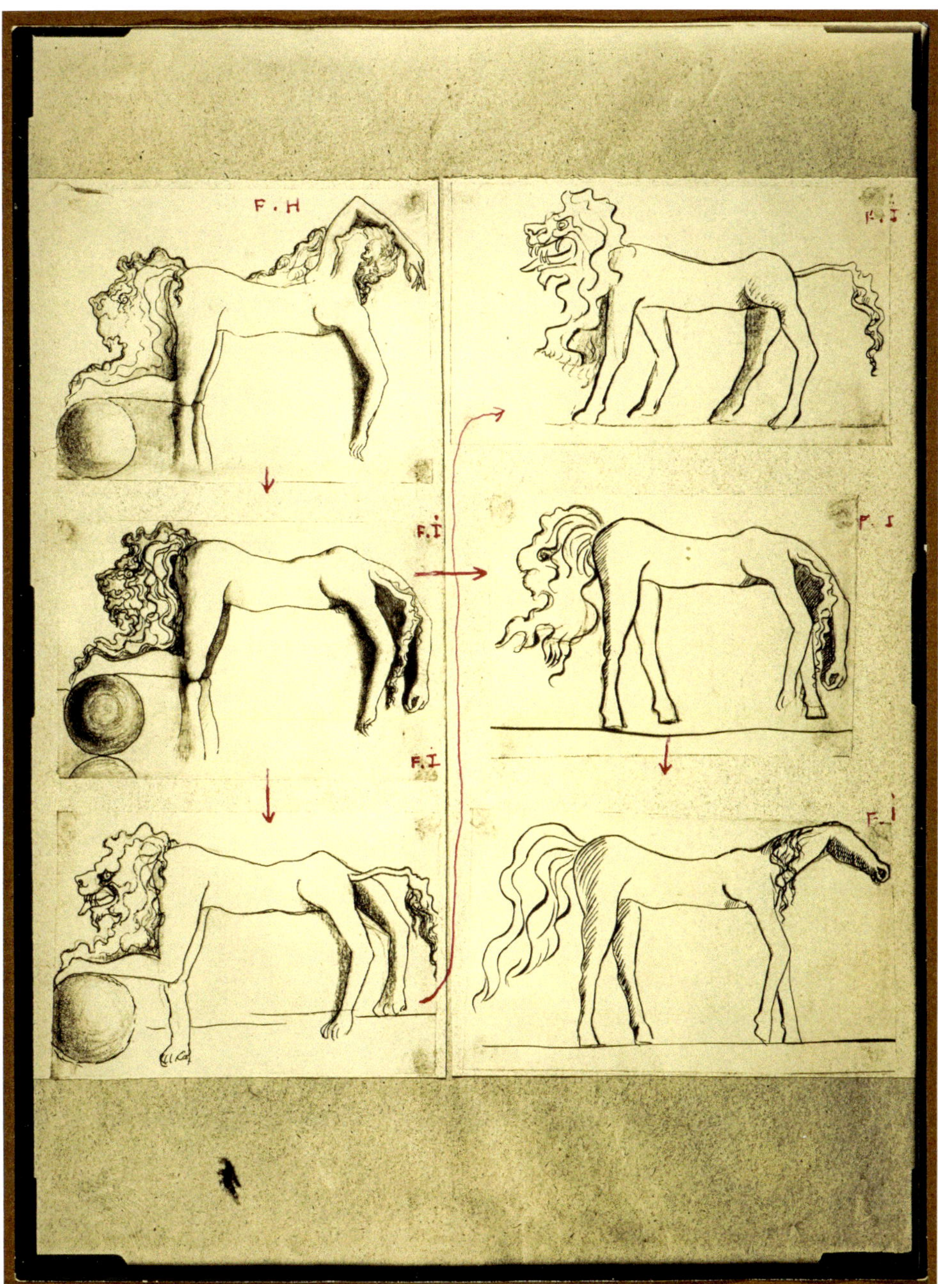

Figure 4.4 Salvador Dalí, Schematic drawing for *Invisible Sleeping Woman, Horse, Lion*, from Dalí's unpublished film script, *Cinq minutes à propos du surréalisme*, c.1931–4. National Galleries of Scotland. Bequeathed by Gabrielle Keiller 1995. © 2024 Salvador Dalí, Fundació Gala-Salvador Dalí, Artists Rights Society.

Animated film could have been Dalí's perfect medium. His sketches for animation reveal that he wanted to help viewers to see as he sees – both during the course of his films and, perhaps, even after the movie ends. But these possibilities ultimately remained undeveloped, as no animated films were completed in his lifetime. Instead, ideas of animacy and actual animation history hover around most of his artworks – evoking the inner spirit of things as well as the workings of his paranoid–critical mind that saw such shifting forms all around. Like an interest in the unconscious as the substrate of surrealist art, these projects reveal an interest in animacy as another underlying principle of Dalí's multimedia art. In the 1930s, surrealism escaped Dalí's paintings: emerging in constellations of objects, images, elements and animals that Dalí brought together – demonstrating not just that surrealism is alive, but that life itself can be surreal.

Notes

1 Dawn Ades, *Dalí's Optical Illusions* (New Haven, CT: Yale University Press, 2000), 12–13. His references appear in Salvador Dalí, *The Unspeakable Confession*s (London: W. H. Allen/Virgun Books, 1977), 27 and Salvador Dalí, *The Secret Life of Salvador Dalí* (London: Vision Press 1968), 41.

2 Ades, *Dali's Optical Illusions*, 12–13.

3 Meredith A. Bak, *Playful Visions: Optical Toys and the Emergence of Children's Media Culture* (Cambridge, MA: MIT Press, 2020), Barbara Maria Stafford, *Devices of Wonder: From the World in a Box to Images on a Screen* (Los Angeles, CA: Getty Research Institute, 2001).

4 Alla Gadassik, 'Tracing the Multiplane: Toward a Genealogy of Animation Apparatuses', *JCMS: Journal of Cinema and Media Studies*, 61, no. 1 (2021): 160–5.

5 The so-called multiplane camera was created multiple times around these years to make several animated films, including Lotte Reiniger's *The Adventures of Prince Achmed* (1927), a few 1930s films by Ub Iwerks, and then various Disney films including a Silly Symphony short film *The Old Mill* (1937) and their first feature-length film, *Snow White and the Seven Dwarves* (1937). Christiane Schönfeld, 'Lotte Reiniger and the Art of Animation', in *Practicing Modernity: Female Creativity in the Weimar Republic*, eds. Christiane Schönfeld and Carmel Finnan (Würzburg: Königshausen & Neumann, 2006), 169–85; J. P. Telotte, 'Ub Iwerks' (Multi) Plain Cinema', *Animation*, 1, no. 1 (July 1, 2006): 9–24.

6 Lewis Kachur, *Displaying the Marvelous: Marcel Duchamp, Salvador Dalí, and Surrealist Exhibition Installations* (London: MIT Press, 2003), 34.

7 Annette Michelson, 'Dr. Crase and Mr. Clair', *October*, 11 (1979): 31–53.

8 'Surrealist House' proposal by Julien Levy and I. [Ian] Woodner-Silverman, New York World's Fair 1939 and 1940 Incorporated, D.W.F. Inc. Manuscripts and Archives Division, New York Public Library, MssCol 2233, b. 540 f. 16.

9 Department of Feature Publicity press release, New York World's Fair 1939 and 1940 Incorporated, D.W.F. Inc. Manuscripts and Archives Division, New York Public Library, MssCol 2233, b. 540 f. 16.

10 Letter from George P. Smith, Jr. to William M. Gardner, New York World's Fair 1939 and 1940 Incorporated, D.W.F. Inc. Manuscripts and Archives Division, New York Public Library, MssCol 2233, b. 540 f. 15.

11 Margaret Cohen, 'Underwater Optics as Symbolic Form', *French Politics, Culture & Society*, 32, no. 3 (1 December 2014): 1–23, https://doi.org/10.3167/fpcs.2014.320301/

12 Salvador Dalí, 'De la beauté terrifiante et comestible, de l'architecture Modern Style', *Minotaure*, 3–4 (1933): 69–76. Author's translation.`

13 The architectural historian Spyros Papapetros has written that this aspect of the pavilion expresses what he calls 'Daphne's *anima vegetativa*' and writes that the nymph 'externalizes her presence in a series of *protrusions*'. Spyros Papapetros, *On the Animation of the Inorganic: Art, Architecture, and the Extension of Life* (Chicago, IL: University of Chicago Press, 2012), 284–5.

14 See Elliott H. King, *Dalí, Surrealism and Cinema* (Harpenden: Kamera Books, 2007).

15 Salvador Dalí, 'Art Film, Antiartistic Film', in *Dalí & Film*, ed. Matthew Gale (New York: Museum of Modern Art, 2007), 74.

16 Salvador Dalí, 'Short Critical History of Cinema', in *Dalí & Film*, ed. Matthew Gale (New York: Museum of Modern Art, 2007), 75.

17 Dalí, 'Short Critical History of Cinema', 75.

18 Dalí, 'Short Critical History of Cinema', 76.

19 Dalí, 'Short Critical History of Cinema', 76.

20 Salvador Dalí, 'Surrealism in Hollywood', in *Dalí & Film*, ed. Matthew Gale (New York: Museum of Modern Art, 2007), 154.

21 Jorgelina Orfila and Francisco Ortega Grimaldo, 'Fantasyland or Wackyland?: Animation and Surrealism in 1930s America', *Journal of Surrealism and the Americas*, 11, no. 1 (20 September, 2020): 1–19.

22 Salvador Dalí, 'Communication: Visage Paranoïaque', *Le Surréalisme au service de la révolution*, 3 (1931): 40.

23 Dalí, 'Communication: Visage Paranoïaque', 40. Author's translation.

24 Salvador Dalí, 'The Rotting Donkey', in *The Collected Writings of Salvador Dalí*, ed. and trans. Haim N. Finkelstein (Cambridge: Cambridge University Press, 1998), 224.

25 Quoted in Fèlix Fanés, 'Destino', in *Dalí & Film*, ed. Matthew Gale (New York: Museum of Modern Art, 2007), 189.

26 Sergei Eisenstein, *Eisenstein on Disney*, ed. Jay Leyda, trans. Alan Upchurch (Calcutta: Seagull Books, 1986).

27 Dalí, 'De la beauté terrifiante et comestible, de l'architecture Modern Style', 70.

Chapter 5

Max Ernst's Cartoon Modernism: Brentano, Disney and *Dream and Revolution*

David Hopkins

Max Ernst's work has become the stuff of connoisseurship. Numerous major exhibitions have elevated him to the status of modern Old Master.[1] Surrealism, and surrealist painting especially, has been assimilated into the standard modernist accounts of art history, however antimodernist its exponents considered themselves, and Ernst – especially the Ernst of the large forest and jungle paintings of the 1930s – has been fitted, rather too neatly I would suggest, into such narratives. How do we rescue him from a too-easy absorption into this story? One way is to consider the political stakes of his work and its scathing critique of aesthetic Modernism. With this in mind, the bulk of this essay focuses on the artist's work in America between 1942 and 1948, a subject that is rarely considered in depth. In this context, Ernst seized on animation – or more exactly the pictorial devices and idioms of animation associated with Disney – to intervene satirically in debates around aesthetic Modernism, producing highly disjunctive, antimodernist provocations.

Part of the reason the politics of Ernst's practice have been occluded is that the roots of his visual output in popular visual culture – particularly book illustration – are rarely given enough emphasis. This might seem questionable. There has been an enormous amount of source-hunting; Werner Spies, notably, uncovered multiple borrowings from *La Nature* and other populist science journals of the nineteenth century in Ernst's work.[2] However, the critical function of Ernst's integration of popular illustration into his collages in particular – which dovetails with his broad commitment to a collage aesthetic (and hence a questioning of autographic authorial intervention) – gets lost from sight. Most accounts of Ernst's collage-based works have recourse, reflex-like, to concepts of surrealist *dépaysement* informed by Breton's influential reading of Ernst's images in terms of the meeting of divergent realities.[3] Although perfectly accurate given Ernst's surrealist affinities, these readings tell us little about the *structural* and *dialectical* role of the demotic in Ernst's collages. If, as I will show, Ernst responded directly to Disney in the early 1940s, it is important to appreciate that popular or populist imagery had always played a disruptive internal role in his productions, offsetting and often destabilizing the erudite high-cultural allusions he otherwise made.

Ernst is an unusual artist in that art-historical precedents do not necessarily illuminate the stylistic foundations of his work. In the crucial years between 1919 and 1922, we can, it is true, talk about his absorption of expressionism and de Chirico into a distinctive proto-dada/surrealist style, but his surrealism, as I have argued elsewhere, owes as much to the sardonic grotesquerie of Wilhelm Busch's popular cartoon imagery, or the archaicizing imagery of Heinrich Hoffmann's children's picture books, as to contemporary 'high art' precedents.[4] In fact, if we want to get to the roots of Ernst's dialectical collage aesthetic, we should go back to the illustrational idioms that Busch and Hoffmann were themselves familiar with. Both, as Ernst fully appreciated, were involved with satirizing German fairy-tale traditions, and their dark, sometimes violent, reworkings of folk imagery had German Romantic roots. It is here that the internal mechanisms of Ernst's collage aesthetic were derived, and I shall begin this essay with a reconsideration of this formative cultural context.

*****

Among the names of his 'Favourite Poets and Painters', published in *View* magazine in 1942, Ernst included that of Achim von Arnim, a German Romantic writer whose work has long been understood to have had an impact on surrealism, particularly his *Contes Bizarres*, and notably *Isabella von Ägypten*, which Breton admired and wrote an introduction to in 1931.[5] However, the highly educated Ernst, whose first-hand knowledge of German literary culture was crucial for Breton, would have been well aware that Arnim's activities extended beyond this. Within German Romanticism, Arnim's name was closely associated with that of Clemens Brentano (1778–1842). Together they had produced *Des Knaben Wunderhorn* (1805–8), a hugely influential collection of German folk songs that fed the nationalistic mood of early Romanticism in the country. It was Brentano who exhorted the Brothers Grimm to begin collecting fairy tales, as well as writing several tales of his own.

If we looked to Brentano, rather than Arnim, as an exemplar for Ernst, it is significant that one of his fairy tales, *Gockel, Hinkel und Gackeleia* (first published in Frankfurt in 1838) – the story of a noble rooster, Alektryo, who after various misfortunes recovers the lost magic ring which properly belongs to him – contained a set of lithographic illustrations that are remarkably proto-surrealistic and make use of collage-like juxtapositions.[6] Produced partly by Brentano himself and partly, under his close direction, by Caspar Braun, they are unique within early German Romanticism. *Das Knaben Wunderhorn* had possessed few illustrations, but in this publication an attempt was made to evoke, in visual terms, the magic and enchantment of folk- and fairy-tale traditions. The book was reprinted, complete with illustrations, in facsimile form in 1912. Given that, many years later, Ernst would acknowledge his interest in Brentano, the proto-surrealist iconography of this publication, rooted in popular motifs of magic and transformation, may well have made a formative impression on him.[7]

A brief look through its pages is now required. In the first instance Brentano and Braun as illustrators are themselves indebted to two artists whom Ernst admired. One of these is Phillip Otto Runge, who will be returned to shortly; the other is Hieronymous Bosch, who provided the basis for a remarkable fantasy image in which Gackeleia, the daughter of Gockel and Hinkel, the main human protagonists of the tale, falls asleep and dreams of a mouse kingdom in which there are towers of cheese rind and houses made of hollow pumpkins.[8] Although these images would have appealed to Ernst, it is the frontispiece to the volume that most overtly foregrounds the aesthetic implications that all of the illustrations possess. Here, there is a fusion not only of high-art allusions to the Runge of the *Tageszeiten* (*Times of Day* sequence) and to Dürer but also to Germanic popular fairy tales and folk myths in terms of images such as the Easter bunny laying an egg, a child emerging from a broken eggshell, a stork carrying a swaddled baby in its beak and two dominant images of roosters, which draw attention both to the role of cockerels throughout the text and to the multiple linguistic puns, relating to eggs and hatching, that pepper the narrative.

This frontispiece thus produces a paradigmatic image of the weaving together of high-art quotations and popular folkoric imagery. That this melding of cultural frameworks was at one with an aesthetic of *collage* is suggested by the disjunctions of scale in the frontispiece, where the roosters completely dwarf the figures placed beneath them (although other images in the book contain even more dramatic jumps of scale). Indeed, as recent scholarship has emphasized, Brentano specifically talked about his visual method (a method duly followed by his artist-collaborator Braun) in terms of a collaging of diverse scraps of cultural matter. In the lengthy preface to his tale he outlined an aesthetic of 'remaindering' whereby human, doll and animal forms were assembled inspired by memories of his grandmother's 'moldering collection of clothing scraps, jewellery, dried flowers, church decorations and cut-out pictures'.[9]

Of course, it may not be so great a step from Brentano as bricoleur to Ernst as collagist. In Ernst we find comparable disjunctions of scale, and in his 1934 collage novel, *Une Semaine de Bonté*, he may have followed Brentano by making a rooster the recurrent leitmotif of an entire section titled 'Le rire du coq'. Furthermore, one conjectures whether the alchemically tinged motif of egg-hatching, which is such a dominant element of Brentano's *Gockel, Hinkel und Gackeleia*, has its counterpart in various aspects of the Ernstian universe: his mock-biographical account of being hatched from an egg, for instance, or his concentration on the egg motif in the *L'Intérieure de la Vue: L'oeuf* pictures of 1929.[10] Admittedly, the sources of Ernst's human–bird transformations – famously set in motion by the death of a favourite pet cockatoo when the artist was fifteen – have been shown in the art-historical literature to be heavily overdetermined, but it is interesting that, in two key works dealing with his alter ego of the late 1920s and early 1930s, Loplop, Ernst chooses to supply his alternative persona with the distinctive 'comb' of a rooster.[11]

Whether or not we can discern specific echoes of Brentano in Ernst, the overriding point is that the fairy-tale images of Brentano/Caspar Braun provided a cultural template for Ernst's collaging of high art and popular illustrational motifs. Furthermore, by invoking the likes of illustrators like Busch and Hoffmann, Ernst could reinforce the sense that his work arose out of a fund of enchantment lodged in his own cultural ancestry. When, in 1923, he transplanted to Paris from Cologne, he had a readymade tradition to draw on, alongside the modernist dislocations of dada, in order to satisfy surrealism's yearning for the marvellous (to say nothing of its revolutionary opposition to bourgeois taste).

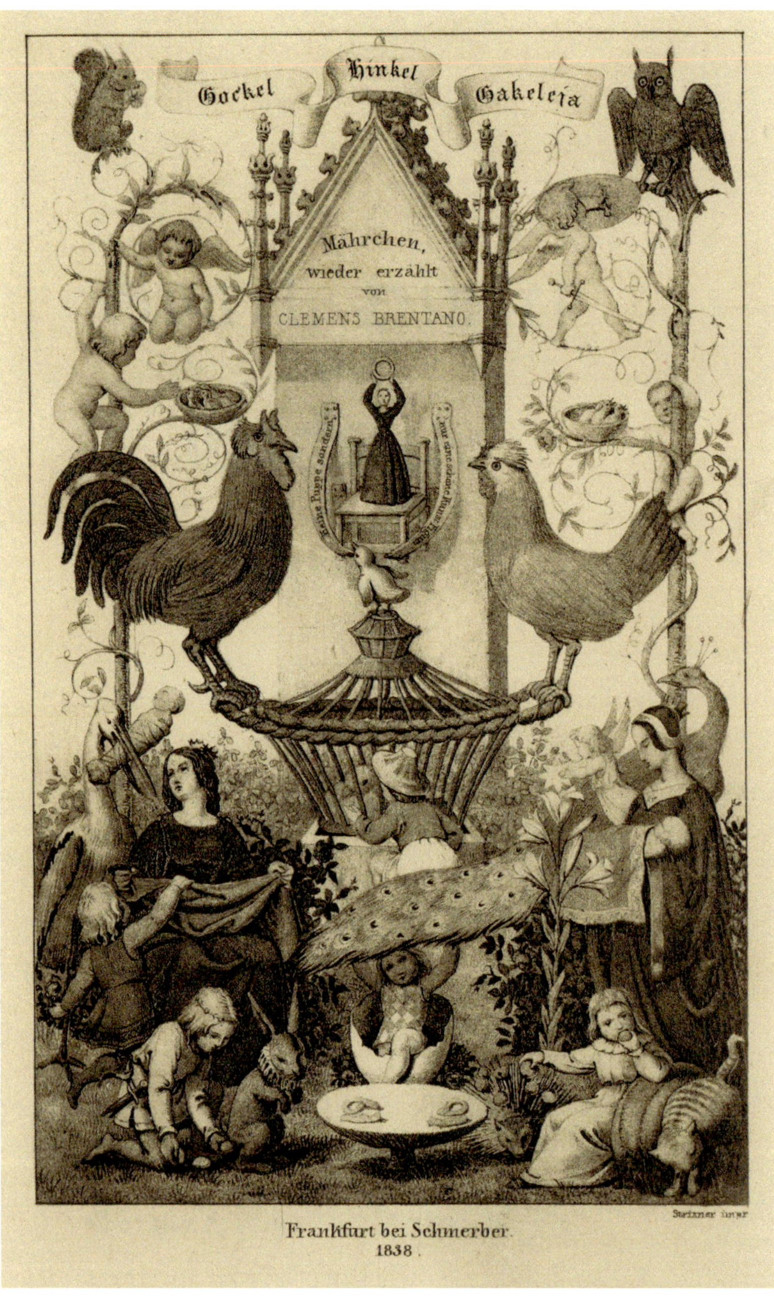

Figure 5.1 Frontispiece: Clemens Brentano, *Gockel, Hinkel und Gackeleia*. Facsimile of first edition (Frankfurt: Schmerber, 1838), Berlin: Morawe and Scheffelt, 1912. Private collection.

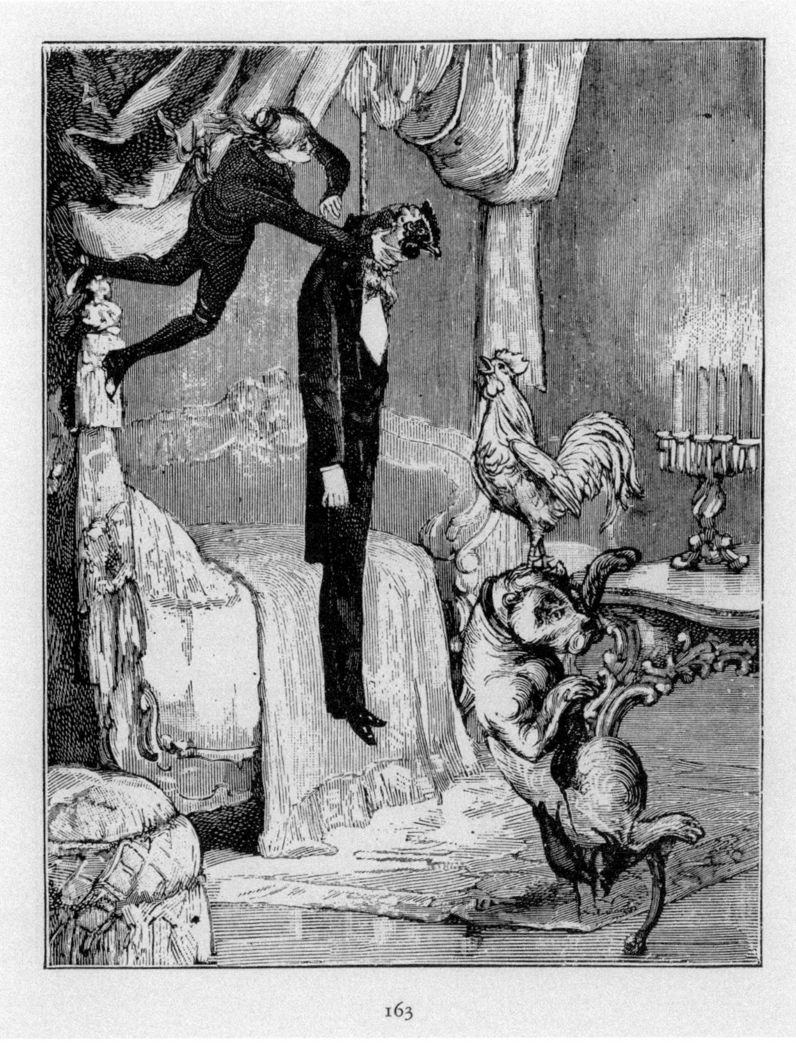

Figure 5.2 Max Ernst, From *Une Semaine de Bonté*: plate 15 of 'Le Rire du Coq' section (Paris: Éditions Jeanne Bucher, 1934). © ADAGP, Paris and DACS, London 2024.

The question I want to raise here is how this internal dialogue between 'high' and 'low' imagery manifested itself at a later stage in Ernst's career and how it took on the overtly political function I alluded to earlier. The polemical nature of Ernst's early production in the USA, after his exile from France during the Second World War, is hardly ever considered, but in that context issues of 'high' and 'low' took on a special urgency. Ernst threw off his visual models in European popular culture and turned to American ones. Brentano gave way to Walt Disney.

*****

Having arrived in New York as an émigré in 1941, largely via the support of Peggy Guggenheim, Ernst is often seen as directionless and unsettled in his five years in the city, only beginning to feel comfortable in the USA after meeting Dorothea Tanning and moving to Sedona, Arizona in 1946. There is no space here to discuss the entire New York and early Sedona period, but it was characterized by stylistic vacillation, as Ernst revisited his earlier output and reacted to a range of new stimuli. One mode from Ernst's past work might be set against another; as, for instance, in the compartmentalized *Vox Angelica* (1943) where automatist passages are juxtaposed with veristic ones as though thematizing cultural relativism or a sense of dislocation. As already suggested, Ernst turned to Disney in this new climate. He did this in a painting that has eluded the in-depth examination it deserves: *Dream and Revolution* of 1945–6.

The components of this painting can be briefly itemized. Leaving aside its Disney dimension for a moment, we have here a red-capped figure wearing what partly reads as a painter's apron and partly as armour, surrounded by the accoutrements of the painter's craft. A deliberately historicist dimension is incorporated into the image. The long red and yellow coloured poles in the foreground could be read as a painter's maul sticks, but they also allude to the lances that feature, almost as decorative elements, in Uccello's *Battle of San Romano* paintings of the mid-fifteenth century, especially the one in the collection of the Uffizi Gallery, Florence.[12] Such associations are upheld by the large

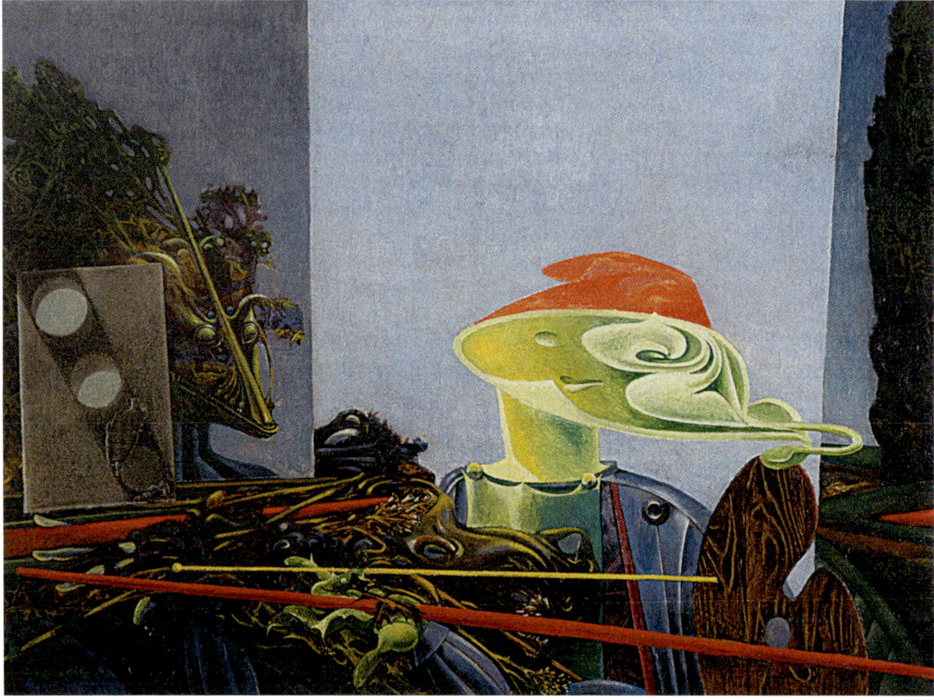

Figure 5.3 Max Ernst, *Dream and Revolution*, 1945–6. Oil on canvas, 108 × 149 cm. Private collection. © ADAGP, Paris and DACS, London 2024.

brown palette propped up next to the figure's left shoulder, which also reads as a shield. (Its prominent woodgraining incidentally alludes to Ernst's deployment of the technique of frottage, derived from wooden surfaces, as a chance-invoking medium in the mid-1920s.) All of this suggests that this may well be a tongue-in-cheek self-portrayal by Ernst as a kind of artist-warrior. Beyond this, there are also glimpses in the painting of the kind of monstrous animals that peopled the artist's recently completed entry to a competition related to Albert Lewin's Bel Ami film, *The Temptation of St Anthony*: one of these, a distant relative of the ghastly horse from Fuseli's *The Nightmare* of 1781, leans into the picture with unseeing eyes at the left, whilst various eyes and beaks are depicted in a compacted mass beneath the maul sticks/lances, as though belonging to demons held in check by this painter-warrior.

If many aspects of the picture invoke the tradition of painting, with its historical associations stretching back to the early Renaissance, the head of the central red-capped figure suggests something utterly different. Gunter Metken initially observed that this head looks strangely like the Disney cartoon character Donald Duck and Werner Spies later concurred with this, stating that the link is 'obvious'.[13] Donald's head, however, has been subjected to radical levels of transformation (or possibly disguise). Its green colouration suggests a plant, and the head further doubles as some kind of leaf form, with its Art Nouveau–like floriate curlicues serving to form the three-quarter view of Donald Duck's eye and beak. The hat confirms Donald's identity. Rather than being his familiar blue sailor's cap, however, it is transformed into what Spies identified as a Phrygian Cap.[14] Hence the reference to revolution in the title of the picture – which itself looks back to the title of a 1923 work by Ernst, *Pietà ou la Révolution la nuit* – and adds to the sense that Ernst is presenting himself, somewhat ironically, as a revolutionary warrior-artist.

What are we to make, then, of the presence of Donald Duck? Neither Spies nor Metken pursued this, but I think it likely that the famous duck is actually a humorous incarnation of Ernst's birdman alter ego, Loplop, which further supports the idea that this is a self-portrait. Beyond this, Ernst is clearly thinking deeply about Disney and the implications of animation. The duck's familiar features are stretched out horizontally in such a way that, to

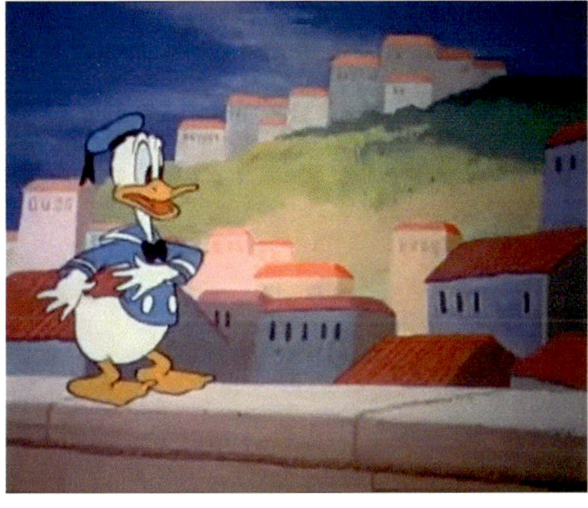

Figure 5.4 Walt Disney, dir., *The Three Caballeros* (Brazil section), Walt Disney Productions, 1944.

render them identifiable, one has to view them obliquely from the side. This is an example of anamorphosis, unusual for Ernst but familiar to surrealist discourse ever since it had been used in Bataille's *Documents* to illuminate Dalí's late 1920s paintings.[15] Its most famous historical usage had been in the work of Hans Holbein whose *Ambassadors* (National Gallery, London, 1533) was popular with the surrealists and especially important to an early surrealist associate, the psychoanalyst Jacques Lacan, who would later investigate the vanitas associations of the image, along with its phallic connotations.[16] Ernst would have appreciated that the device was a forerunner of the distortions of animation, which frequently involve recognizable forms being distended or yanked out of their familiar configurations. In terms of the avant-garde, the Russian film-maker Eisenstein had been an advocate of Disney's distortions, especially in the early Mickey Mouse films, feeling that a quasi-political principle of 'plasmaticness' could be adduced from them; a revolutionary impulse to defy stasis and the fixity of form.[17]

We cannot be certain Eisenstein's theorizations of Disney were known to Ernst, but he would certainly have seen the affinities between the looping caricatural rhythms of the style of animation drawing in early Disney films – Mickey Mouse especially – and surrealist procedures of automatism (as in his own *One Night of Love* of 1927, for example). As well as Donald Duck's fluorescent green face, the bright red and yellow colouration of the lances/maul sticks in this painting surely owe something to the vibrant effects of Disney's use of 'Technicolor', a process that had been used in films since 1916, but which Disney in particular had perfected, in animation films such as *Fantasia* (1940). The issue of colour will be returned to shortly, but Ernst's overlaying of animation techniques onto art-historical allusions suggests that, at some level, he was aware of the historicity embedded in Disney-style animation; the fact that it relied on 'high-art' precedents such as the perspectival researches of Uccello or Piero della Francesca, to say nothing of the scenographic tropes found in the work of early twentieth-century popular illustrators such as Arthur Rackham and Kay Nielsen.[18]

The fact that Uccello is brought up against Disney in terms of the signifying economy of *Dream and Revolution* alerts us to the coexistence, internal to the mechanics of the picture, of so-called 'high' and 'low' cultural idioms. This characteristic Ernstian dialectic, whose roots were earlier traced back to Brentano and German fairy-tale traditions, now seems to have a specific ideological target, but to appreciate this one first needs to sketch in a few contextual factors.

For one thing, the production of the picture coincided with a period when left-wing film critics were beginning to register the cultural importance of Disney, albeit in rather negative terms. In an essay in *Partisan Review* of Spring 1945, exactly contemporaneous with the production of Ernst's painting, Barbara Deming saw Disney's latest Donald Duck film, *The Three Caballeros* – a sequence of Latin American adventures – as constituting a nightmare vision of the contemporary world. 'Nothing holds its shape', she argued, clearly discombobulated by the proto-surrealist metamorphoses of the film. More than anything, though, she was disconcerted by the experimental mixing of stylistic registers indulged in by Disney's animators: 'techniques are mixed incongruously: conventional cartoon drawing, live action, calendar art, chic illustration'.[19] Ernst, with his leftist sympathies, is likely to have been aware of debates that raged in the pages of *Partisan Review*, and it is perfectly possible that *The Three Caballeros*, which had premièred in the USA in February 1945, provided his introduction, while in New York, to Donald Duck. The stylistic discontinuities of his *Dream and Revolution* might easily be seen as paralleling Deming's vision of the cartoon duck caught up amid incompatible visual registers and thereby allegorizing a fragmented world, emerging from world war.

An even more significant publication than the Deming essay, which appeared just months before Ernst began work on his picture, was Clement Greenberg's influential critical assessment of surrealist painting, which was published in two venues: first as a two-part article in *The Nation* in August 1944, and then in *Horizon* in January 1945.[20] Here, as the advocate of an artistic Modernism synonymous with formal innovation, Greenberg was positive about the abstracting tendencies of automatists such as Miró and Masson but scathing about what he considered the 'vulgarized' and 'literary' aspects of the work of other surrealists. Criticizing their revivalist and antiquarian tendencies, he asserted: 'For the sake of hallucinatory vividness the Surrealists have copied the effects of the calendar reproduction, postal card chromeotype and magazine illustration.'[21] Significantly, the populist forms denigrated by Greenberg here are similar to those that mixed indiscriminately in Disney's recent Donald Duck film according to Deming. In the light of this, and particularly in view of Greenberg's pinpointing of Ernst as one of the literary or 'illustrational' surrealists he was opposed to ('Ernst's volcanic landscapes look like exceptionally well manufactured seaside postcards', he fumed), *Dream and Revolution* may be seen as a riposte to him.[22] Disney animation epitomized precisely what the critic was against: the incursion of 'vulgarized' popular imagery into the precincts of culture; a theme which had been established in his seminal position statements, 'Avant-Garde and Kitsch' and 'Towards a Newer Laocoon', published in *Partisan Review* in 1939 and 1940, respectively.[23]

By placing Donald Duck at the very centre of his painting, Ernst effectively confronts Greenberg's newfound modernist orthodoxy with its ideological antithesis: the imagery of mass culture. At the same time, he challenges Greenberg's assumption that his modernist avant-gardism could lay claim to the left-wing political high ground. Ernst would have known that Greenberg's political sympathies, at this point in his career, were Trotskyist, which would have made him broadly acceptable from a surrealist point of view, but by placing a Phrygian Cap on the head of a Disney character, Ernst ironically supplies himself, and surrealism, with more assertive revolutionary credentials. The red cap had further surrealist left-wing antecedents, in that it had appeared as a Catalan peasant's 'barretina' in certain of Joan Miró's *Tête de paysan Catalan* paintings of 1925.[24] The image, therefore, re-asserted the libertarian 'revolutionary' spirit of surrealism at a time when Greenberg was downplaying the importance of the movement, and proposed a fusion of the dialectic of 'high' and 'low' cultural forms in defiance of Greenberg's élite Modernism.

All of this makes *Dream and Revolution* a highly pertinent intervention in art world politics. By the same token, aside from its broad allusions to liberatory principles – which, however generalized, were far from inconsequential when intellectuals in Europe and the USA were feeling the need to make crystal-clear distinctions between fascism and communism – it would be unwise, I think, to see it as directly responding to 'hard politics'.[25] Contrary to the view that sees him as largely apolitical, Ernst, at this point, was acutely sensitized to politics, but they were the newly relevant politics of 'high' and 'low' culture, and of the modernist cult of formal innovation versus the surrealist fascination with the phantasms of the popular imaginary.

To return to the earlier stages of this discussion, Donald Duck is mobilized by Ernst in much the same way as he borrowed the Brentano-derived model of fairy-tale illustration in the 1920s and 1930s: to produce an inner dialectic between the 'low' of folk imagery and the 'high' of artistic tradition. Donald Duck was, in effect, the American heir to Germanic mythical protypes. That Ernst harboured a certain fondness for the duck – one in a long line of bird avatars in his work that included the roosters from Brentano's tale mentioned earlier and frequently contributed to articulations of his Loplop alter ego – is underlined by the fact that another duck cropped up in a later painting of 1948, produced after Ernst had moved to Sedona: *Le canard du doute aux lèvres de vermouth* (*The duck of doubt with lips of vermouth*).[26] In this peculiar rebus-like fusion of word and image – almost unprecedented in Ernst's work – the cartoonish features of the central duck image are clearly not those of Donald. They may, however, be interpreted as belonging to a female cousin of the Disney character. Her gender is suggested by the schematized back view that is juxtaposed with the head. Ernst would concoct further bird heads out of cartoonish elements around the same time.[27] One such head appears in the left foreground of *Le régal des dieux*, also of 1948. It appears next to other mask-like heads, all of them schematized in similar fashion, whereas the large hands of the central personage are almost absurdly Disneyesque in style.

As noted earlier, colour has to be taken into account as a distinguishing feature of these works. In *Le régal des dieux* the range of highly saturated swatches of colour – vibrant reds, yellows, oranges and greens – above the head of the central character approximate, I would suggest, to those of contemporary Technicolor animation, and one could find similar effects in further works of the period such as *Design in Nature* (1947) and *Chemical Nuptials* (1948).[28] It would be mistaken, though, to think that animation is the privileged point of reference. A whole variety of discursive contexts jostle beside each other in these pictures. These include, for instance, mathematical and geometrical figures from models in the Parisian Institut Poincaré and D'Arcy Thompson's writings, allusions to Hopi and Zuni Indian regalia, and passages of decalcomania and frottage that refer back, autobiographically, to Ernst's classic surrealist practice.[29] Of particular significance are the backgrounds of certain images – *The Cocktail-drinker* of 1945 being a notable example – in which geometrical subdivisions of the canvas both play with ideas from Einsteinian physics, such as the curvature of space–time, and allude satirically to the contemporaneous abstraction of the likes of Mondrian, in full awareness that this was the kind of Modernism currently being touted by Greenberg.[30]

More than anything the mask assumes a major significance in Ernst's work at this time. Ernst's appropriative 'primitivism' had been evident earlier in his career, but it now assumed an overriding importance.[31] But, however much these works teem with allusions to Kachina dolls, Native American masks and totems and Ivory Coast carvings, they simultaneously offer up an array of impenetrable or unknowable personae. Perhaps the masks say something about Ernst's lack of assurance in this transitional period living in New York. One might, of course, think of Donald Duck's head in *Dream and Revolution*

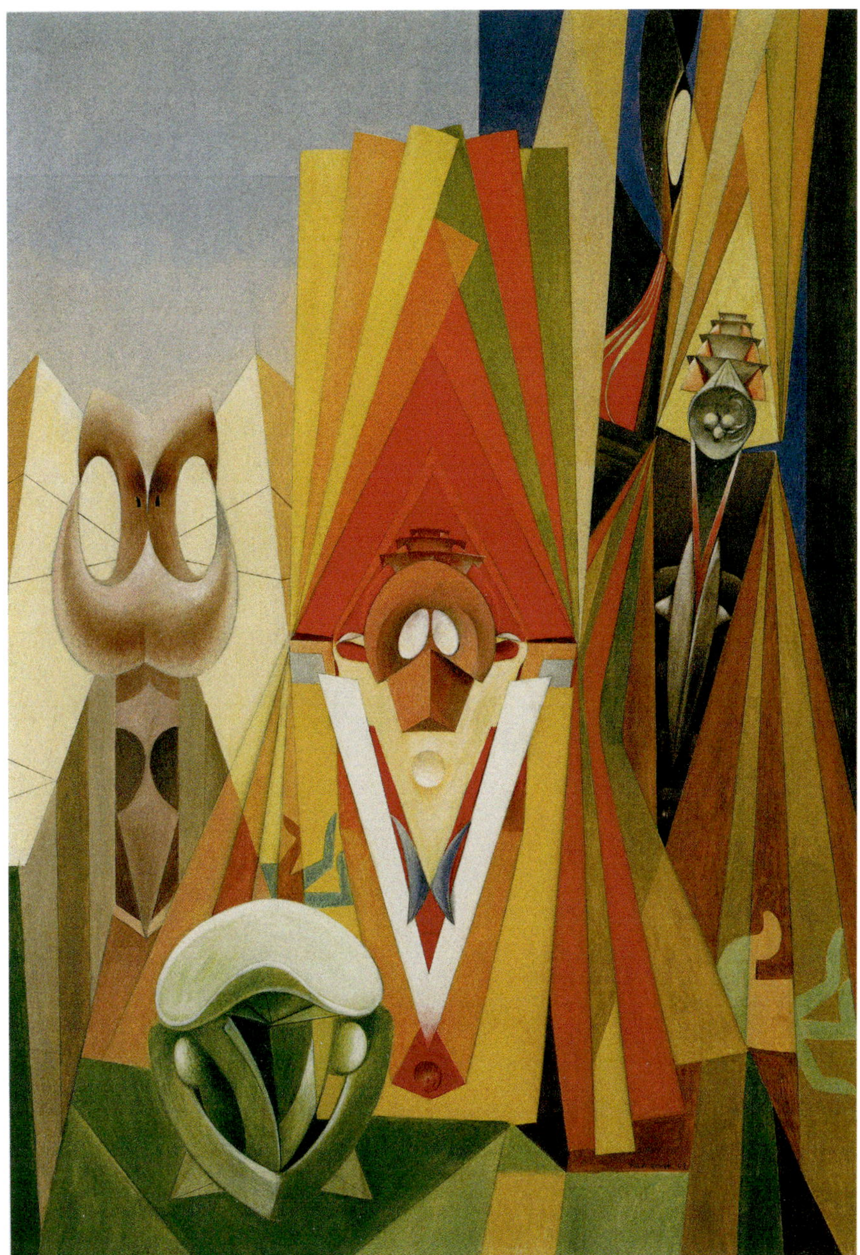

Figure 5.5 Max Ernst, *Le régal des dieux*, 1948. Oil canvas, 153 × 106 cm. Museum Moderner Kunst Stiftung Ludwig, Vienna. Reproduced in *Max Ernst: Dream and Revolution*, eds. Spies et al., ex cat: Moderna Museet, Stockholm and Louisiana Museum of Modern Art, 2008. © ADAGP, Paris and DACS, London 2024.

as a kind of mask, ironically standing in for the identifying features of the artist, but masks recur in painting after painting and, beyond hinting at Ernst's multiple identities, they metaphoricize a broader sense of the hermetic and the impervious or inaccessible. They are cartoon-like to varying degrees. In *Euclid*, *Gardenia* and *The Cocktail-drinker*, all of 1945, they appear whimsical in their conflations of decorative devices, geometry and bird-like features, but they can also be tragic, as in the ironically titled *Mask of Comedy* (1947).[32] Sometimes they are absurdly cartoonish, as in *Witch* of 1948.[33]

Set amid the proto-postmodern rubble of allusions in the paintings of the period, the masks underline the impenetrability of Ernst's practice, on both iconographic and aesthetic levels. The flat, hard nature of the surfaces of these paintings, with their smooth Technicolor finishes, finally suggest a certain order of cultural mimicry. In a memorable phrase in the early part of his *Aesthetic Theory*, which was later to be isolated for special emphasis by Peter Bürger, Adorno asserted that 'Art is modern through mimesis of the hardened and alienated.'[34] The phrase seems remarkably apt in relation to these works, which take on the quality of masks in their entirety, and contain within themselves a dialectical stand-off between the culture industry and an officially sanctioned aesthetic Modernism.

In the absence of any serious art-historical commentary on the significance of Ernst's work of this period, I would suggest that he was developing a disjunctive response to the climate of the times; a hybrid style for which I would propose the term: *cartoon modernism*. The neologism conveys the strange collision we have been discussing in Ernst's work between the cartoonish simplifications and colour of Disney animation and the high-cultural forms of modernist abstraction and 'primitivism'. This cartoon modernism, in which the high-minded tropes of modernist painting are rendered in a strategically 'vulgarized' manner, might be discerned in the output of other surrealists – the Dalí of the late 1930s springs to mind – but it is the Ernst of the 1940s who embodies it most fully, especially given his parodic play with abstraction. This phase in Ernst's career was relatively short. Once he had built a new home for himself with Dorothea Tanning and settled in Sedona, Arizona he would set in motion a new chapter in his art involving the mythic landscape themes he had explored in canvases of the late 1920s and 1930s. However, for those few years in New York and Sedona between 1942 and 1948 Ernst intervened symbolically in a tussle between Disney and Greenberg that had considerable critical, as well as political, urgency.

Notes

1 Werner Spies was instrumental in organizing many of these exhibitions. For my comments about this defining curatorial rationale see my 'Max Ernst: Retrospective' (review of the 2013 Albertina, Vienna exhibition), *Burlington Magazine* (June 2013): 430–1. Also see David Hopkins, 'Max Ernst', *Burlington Magazine* (February 2013): 196–9.

2 Werner Spies, *Max Ernst: Collages* (London: Thames & Hudson, 1991), 485–526.

3 André Breton, 'Max Ernst', in *Breton: The Lost Steps* [1921], trans. Mark Polizzotti (Lincoln, NB and London: University of Nebraska Press, 1996), 60–1.

4 See my *Dark Toys: Surrealism and the Culture of Childhood* (New Haven, CT and London: Yale University Press, 2021), 54–61. See also Abigail Susik, 'Surrealism and Jules Verne', in *Surrealism, Science Fiction and Comics*, ed. Gavin Parkinson (Liverpool: Liverpool University Press, 2015), 16–39.

5 Max Ernst, 'Favorite Poets and Painters of the Past', *View*, 2nd series, no. 1 (1942). André Breton, 'Centenaire Arnim – fragment de l'introduction a la réédition française des Contes Bizarres', *Le Surréalisme au service de la révolution*, 6 (May 1933): 5–9.

6 Clemens Brentano, *Gockel, Hinkel und Gackeleia* (Berlin: Morawe and Scheffelt, 1912).

7 Brentano's name does not figure in early texts by Ernst. Later, however, Ernst produced a homage to Brentano, along with Arnim and other key figures of German Romanticism, in the form of *For Kleist*, *Brentano*, *Arnim*, *Caspar David Friedrich: Seelandschaft mit Kapuziner* (Zurich: Edition Hans Bolliger, 1972).

8 The two illustrations appear opposite pages 214 and 112, respectively, of Brentano, *Gockel*.

9 Catriona MacLeod, 'Brentano's Remains: Visual and Verbal Bricolage in "Gockel, Hinkel and Gackeleia"(1838)', *Goethe Yearbook*, 23 (2016): 221.

10 For the mock-autobiographical reference see Max Ernst, 'Some Data on the Youth of M.E. (as told by himself)', in *Max Ernst: Beyond Painting* (New York: Wittenborn, Schultz, Inc., 1948), 26, 29. For the *L'Intérieure de la Vue: L'oeuf* sequence see Werner Spies, Günter Metken and Sigrid Metken, *Max Ernst Oeuvre-Katalog, 1929–1938* (Houston, TX and Cologne: Menil Foundation; DuMont Schauberg, 1979), 1564–5, 1574–9.

11 For Ernst's account of the cockatoo's death see Ernst, 'Some Data', 28. The Loplop works with rooster characteristics are *Loplop présente une fleur* (1930) and *Loplop présente Loplop* (1930). Spies et al., *Max Ernst Oeuvre-Katalog, 1929–1938*, 1794, 1710. For an overview of the role of Loplop in Ernst's oeuvre see Werner Spies, *Max Ernst: Loplop: The Artist's Other Self* (London: Thames & Hudson, 1983). Brentano, and German Romanticism in general, play no part in Spies' account.

12 Uccello was a favourite artist of the surrealists. See Georges Pudelko, 'Paolo Uccello Peintre Lunaire', *Minotaure*, 7 (June 1935): 33–41.

13 Werner Spies and Günter Metken, *Max Ernst: Retrospective* (Munich: Haus der Kunst, Munich, 1979), 324. Werner Spies, 'Dream and Revolution: On the Exhibition', in *Max Ernst: Dream and Revolution*, eds. Werner Spies, Iris Müller-Westermann and Kirsten Degel (Stockholm: Moderna Museet), 11.

14 Werner Spies: 'Dream and Revolution', 12.

15 Visual comparisons were made between anamorphosis and Dalí's imagery in *Documents*, no. 4 (September 1929.) Dawn Ades, 'Dalí's Optical Illusions', in *Dalí's Optical Illusions* (Hartfort, CT: Wadworth Atheneum Museum of Art, 2000), 21–23.

16 David Macey, *Lacan in Contexts* (London and New York: Verso, 1988), 46, 62.

17 For a full discussion of this see Esther Leslie, *Hollywood Flatlands: Animation, Critical Theory and the Avant-Garde* (London and New York: Verso, 2002), 231–7 and *passim* .

18 Rackham and other Edwardian illustrators also affected surrealism, especially Dalí. See my *Dark Toys*, 41–6 and *passim*.

19 Barbara Deming, 'The Artlessness of Walt Disney', *Partisan Review* (Spring 1945): 230.

20 Deming, 'The Artlessness', 228.

21 Clement Greenberg, 'Surrealist Painting', *The Nation* (12 and 19 August 1944); *Horizon* (January 1945), as reprinted in John O'Brian, ed., *Clement Greenberg: The Collected Essays, Vol. 1: Perceptions and Judgements 1939–1944* (Chicago, IL: University of Chicago Press, 1986), 229.

22 Greenberg, 'Surrealist Painting', 229.

23 Clement Greenberg, 'Avant-Garde and Kitsch', *Partisan Review* (Fall 1939); Clement Greenberg, 'Towards a Newer Laocoon', *Partisan Review* (July–August 1940).

24 See, for instance, *Tête de paysan Catalan* (Tate/Scottish National Gallery of Modern Art, Edinburgh).

25 Werner Spies wrongly asserted that *Dream and Revolution* responds to the hysteria of McCarthyism. Spies, 'Dream and Revolution', 12, n. 13.

26 Spies et al., *Max Ernst Oeuvre-Katalog, 1939–1953* (Houston, TX and Cologne: Menil Foundation; DuMont Schauberg, 1987), 2585.

27 See *Head of a Bird*: Spies et al., *Max Ernst Oeuvre-Katalog, 1939–1953*, 2590.

28 Spies et al., *Max Ernst Oeuvre-Katalog, 1939–1953*, 2562 and 2594.

29 Ludger Derenthal, 'In the American West: *Capricorne* and the Influences of Native American Cultures', in *Max Ernst: Dream and Revolution*, 177–8.

30 For Ernst and Mondrian, as well as Ernst's allusions to mathematics and physics at this time, see my *Marcel Duchamp and Max Ernst: The Bride Shared* (Oxford: Oxford University Press, Clarendon Studies in the History of Art, 1998), 182–3.

31 For Ernst's 'primitive' sources see Evan Maurer, 'Dada and Surrealism', in *'Primitivism' in 20th Century Art*, ed. William Rubin, vol. 2 (New York: Museum of Modern Art, 1984), 561–75 and *passim*.

32 Spies et al., *Max Ernst Oeuvre-Katalog, 1939–1953*, 2496–9, and 2556. Masks also play a key role in the sculptures of the period. There is too little space to discuss them here, but they generally have a lighter, more playful character than those in the paintings. Spies et al., *Max Ernst Oeuvre-Katalog, 1939–1953*, 2464–75.

33 Spies et al., *Max Ernst Oeuvre-Katalog, 1939–1953*, 2585.

34 Theodor Adorno, *Aesthetic Theory*, eds. Gretel Adorno and Rolf Tiedemann, trans. Robert Hullot-Kentor (London: Athlone Press, 1999), 21.

Chapter 6

'Woe to the sperm whale that fought against a louse!': On the Surrealist Reception of Tex Avery in the 1950s

Gavin Parkinson

In a widely read essay first published in 1992, Timothy R. White revisited a crucial juncture in the critical history of animation, 'in the sixties', he wrote, when 'critical opinion began to shift away from Disney towards Warner Bros. and, to a lesser extent, MGM (especially the cartoons of Tex Avery)'.[1] Stating received wisdom that '[t]his shift, which continued into the seventies, has been attributed to the general irreverence and "anti-establishment" attitudes of the sixties and early seventies, which seemed better suited to the non-Disney animation', White argued instead for the evaluation of European art cinema as the impetus for the critical shift.[2] For this, he took his cue from the film theorist and historian David Bordwell, who had earlier argued similarly for the new attention given European movies as the root cause for the reinterpretation of classic Hollywood cinema from the 1960s.[3] 'These critics', concluded White, 'justified their preference for the Warner Bros. cartoons on the grounds that they were "just like" the art cinema of [Luis] Buñuel, [Jean-Luc] Godard, and the like.'[4]

White was aware, no doubt, of the significant differences between the surrealist films of Buñuel originating in the 1920s and the New Wave ones of Godard that arrived in 1960 (and therefore made a neater fit with his historical paradigm than Buñuel's). However, it is unlikely that he would have stated them as vociferously as the surrealist Robert Benayoun, who was profoundly averse to the New Wave and would also have taken issue with the detail of White's historical argument about animation.[5] It was not merely a matter of taste or a different disposition towards film theory. Benayoun and his friends mainly at the French film magazine *Positif* had long agitated against New Wave cinema and the rival magazine *Cahiers du cinéma* where it originated and where it received enthusiastic support.[6] More to the point, Benayoun, the surrealists and the surrealist influence on the writing at *Positif* had been largely responsible for a favourable reception of Avery's cartoons produced by Warner Brothers (1936–42), Paramount (1942), MGM (1942–57) and Universal (1954–5). That commentary began as early as the late 1940s, long pre-empting White's critical shift. In fact, most of the components of that narrative, written in the French language, had been collected and published by Benayoun before White's article appeared in 1992. This chapter expands on the specifically surrealist viewpoints in that earlier interpretation, drawing out the surrealist traits of favoured cartoons and uncovering the pioneering role of surrealism in the critical history of animation.

The Swiftian Mad Hatter: Disney, Robert Benayoun and the 'anti-Disney'

The differences between Disney, Warner Brothers and MGM cartoons have long been identified by critics and were explored by Benayoun and other surrealists in the period after the Second World War. Yet in the earlier part of the twentieth century, Disney had occasionally been a point of reference for surrealists and commentators on the movement. The British artist Paul Nash, who worked primarily in a surrealist mode from 1936 and showed at the landmark International Exhibition of Surrealism in London that year, wrote in an essay on colour film around that time of his admiration for Disney's early cartoons ('one of the few geniuses of the cinema'), as White was the first to point out, calling them 'sensitive drawings charged with a rather pale bright colour, reminiscent of certain drawings by William Blake' and going on to give credit to *The Band Concert* (1935, USA), *Mickey's Polo Team* (1936, USA) and *Mickey's Garden* (1935, USA) as 'successful experiments in sound and colour pyrotechnics', peaking with the last of these: 'a kind of surrealist extravaganza, full of imagination, and heightened at every point by rich outrageous colour'.[7] Nash was quite right: Mickey's botched garden maintenance is caused and furthered through hallucination and inebriation courtesy of a toxic substance (super strength, reverse insecticide) in a cartoon that revels in the kind of Lilliputian theme, life or death struggle and oneiric pay-off recognizable in the cartoons to come of Avery and his contemporaries at Warner Brothers and MGM.

In the same year, four drawings of the 'wolf pacifier' contraption that serves as the main plot device in Disney's recent and, again, proto-Warner Brothers *Three Little Wolves* (1936, USA) were displayed at *Fantastic Art, Dada, Surrealism* at the Museum of Modern Art in New York in the category of 'comparative material' (subcategory 'commercial and journalistic art') where the point seems to be less to do with animation or even drawing than the surrealist object (which had reached the height of its theoretical and curatorial trajectory that year); also, the first Mickey Mouse film *Plane Crazy* (1928, USA) was mentioned in Disney's brief biography in the exhibition catalogue and the classic cartoon *The Skeleton Dance* (1929, USA) was listed among the 'fantastic or surrealist films' in the MoMA film library alongside those of others including George Méliès, Man Ray, and Buñuel and Salvador Dalí.[8]

In 1937, a starstruck Dalí would write to André Breton from Hollywood where he claimed to have 'made contact with the three American surrealists, Harpo Marx, Disney and Cecil B. DeMille'.[9] Similarly to Nash, he would also align 'those dazzling "cataclysmic rainbows" which are the Silly Symphonies of Disney' with the strand of surrealist research and analysis of dreams in an essay of the same year inspired by his visit to Hollywood and published in *Harper's Bazaar*, a few months before the première of Disney's first full-length feature, *Snow White and the Seven Dwarfs* (1937, USA), which would bring near-universal acclaim to Disney and his studio.[10] The success of that film helps explain the aside in the article on Piero di Cosimo in the surrealist-dominated *Minotaure* by the German art historian Georg Pudelko, who argued that after psychoanalysis it became 'possible to detect, from the surrealist point of view … the dark regions, the unconscious, the demonic that is crystallized very clearly in some artists',[11] focusing by way of demonstration on remarkable details reproduced full page from the wooded background to left and right of Piero's painting *The Immaculate Conception with Saints* of circa 1510 (cropped in *Minotaure* to omit both Virgin and saints), in which '[t]he metamorphosis of forms, the artist's hallucinations … reinforces their unreal character … just as, in a drawing by Walt Disney, we intuit with amazement the mad masquerade of nature'.[12]

For the next twenty-five years or so, Disney would be cited in glowing terms by critics, artists, writers and film-makers either in thrall to his artistry, or pretending to be so in order to feign at least some acquaintance with popular taste. Sergei Eisenstein's on–off writings on Disney from 1932 to 1943 are full of praise (even of *Bambi* with a few reservations), already comparing Disney's first 'plasmatic' (stretching or distorted) drawing of Mickey Mouse to comparable objects in the art of 'the surrealists: Dalí, for example' (the soft objects in his paintings) as early as 1932.[13] Dalí seems to have been equally genuine in his admiration of Disney, happily accepting the invitation extended to him in late 1945 by the Disney studio to work on the film *Destino*, which would stall in 1946.[14] The involvement of the vilified post- and even anti-surrealist Dalí at Disney may well have contributed to Benayoun's critique and his closely related, ardent advocacy of Avery as 'by nature, by vocation and by career the indisputable Anti-Disney', that were frequent and extensive from 1951.[15] But where did Benayoun's fervent attraction to Avery's cartoons begin, what paths did it follow up to this peak of interest in the mid-1960s, and what forms did it take in the larger surrealist group in France and elsewhere?

***

It is beyond doubt that European surrealists and the larger circle of émigrés who took refuge in the United States during the Second World War were exposed to Avery's cartoons as well as Disney's, preceding feature films on cinema programmes, but there is no record of commentary on this from the surrealists themselves or historians of the movement. Paul Hammond has argued that the flood of Hollywood films into Europe that had been held up by the conflict meant that in the immediate postwar period 'various factions within a renascent French film culture began to tackle the ideological and aesthetic problems of popular Hollywood film'.[16] The extension of that argument to animation is what brings the critical shift of the 1960s hypothesized by White into question, or at least reveals an incomplete reception history that has absented surrealism.

That history must be re-established around Benayoun, a fluent English speaker and Anglophile. Born in Morocco in 1926, he encountered comics following the arrival of US forces in that country in November 1942 at a time such materials were banned in France under the occupation. His subsequent discovery of surrealism in 1946 was a revelation and he visited the sixth International Exhibition of Surrealism, titled *Le Surréalisme en 1947*, held that year from 7 July to 30 September at the galerie Maeght in Paris. Of this and his subsequent closeness to the surrealists, he recalled later: 'I arrived in a group that was in an energetic renewal, where all the old debates were already being called upon to reevaluate themselves, a surrealism re-energised by America.'[17] Writing on animation in *Positif* in 1963, he wrote of the 'more than fifteen years that I have been an enthusiastic follower of animation', which places the beginnings of his fervent exploration of the medium at precisely the same moment around 1947–8 (he actually joined the Paris Group in 1950) when Avery's cartoons were first shown in Europe.[18] Benayoun himself identified an article of 1947 on Avery's *The Shooting of Dan McGoo* (1945, USA) in *Revue du cinéma* by future co-founder of *Cahiers du cinéma* Jacques Doniol-Valcroze as the first on the anti-Disney, which goes some way towards confirming the inference I have drawn from Hammond.[19] The launch of *L'Âge du cinéma* in March 1951, published and edited from March by surrealists Ado Kyrou and Benayoun, respectively, with frequent contributions from other surrealists, gave Avery his earliest visibility in a specifically surrealist context and apparently only his second bout of critical publicity in France. This came in the article in the first issue signed by one 'Abner Lepetit' – Benayoun, in fact, concealed beneath a pseudonym drawn from one of his favourite comic characters, Li'l Abner, star of Al Capp's astonishingly successful, eponymous tale of life in the Deep South (1934–77). So began a tradition of fictive characters and pseudonymity that would expand later in the decade in *Positif* then in the 1960s in its Bureau d'études texaveriennes.

Under the guise of Abner Lepetit, Benayoun was pitiless in his assessment of the decline of Disney, its 'laziness and vulgarity' over the preceding ten years, the time and great technical skill wasted on 'established formulas' that hit rock bottom in its current 'bland' and 'garish' fare.[20] His judgement is easily borne out by a viewing of the now largely forgotten, sugar-bloated musical trio he brings up: the pedestrian, multichapter, animation-set-to-music *Make Mine Music* (1946, USA; a characterless squib in spite of its opera-singing whale), the twee, fairy-tale–themed two-parter *Fun and Fancy Free* (1947, USA) and the religio-patriotic frontierist propaganda multi-story flick *Melody Time* (1948, USA), relentlessly optimistic escapist churn that seems to have numbed the evaluative capacities of postwar critics and audiences alike. By contrast, Benayoun lauded the 'cruel comedy' of Tom and Jerry cartoons, amazed and bemused by their extreme violence by comparison with the very Hollywood feature films diluted by censorship with which they were billed.[21]

The particular appeal of Avery's work lay partly in those characteristics of malice and bleak comedy, evident in *The Shooting of Dan McGoo* as indicated by Doniol-Valcroze, and also in three cartoons that appeared close together over a period of eleven months and would compose the core of the surrealist canon of Avery's oeuvre: the sadistic *Slap-Happy Lion* (1947, USA), the freakish *King-Size Canary* (1947, USA) and the sadistic and freakish *Half-Pint Pygmy* (1948, USA), masterpieces of the moral ambiguity that Disney had long deserted. But it was their use of scale that made them, according to Benayoun:

> the surreal tribute to a *mis en scène* that shakes off its servility. Juggling with dimensions, Avery makes us advance, by a rigourously logical progression, from the infinitely small

> to the infinitely large. Raising the absurd as a totem, as much through the subject matter as the development of the action, he breaks the laws of the three-dimensional world one after the other. Next to this Swiftian Mad Hatter, Disney truly cuts the figure of a pygmy.[22]

Benayoun's own tribute at this stage was hesitant and limited mainly to a discussion of this issue of scale, motivated partly by certain much quoted lines from the revered precursor of surrealism, the Comte de Lautréamont (Isidore Ducasse): '[b]ut woe to the sperm-whale that fought against a louse! … An elephant can be stroked. But not a louse.'[23] Yet it was the beginning of a consistent contrast with Disney in which Avery always came off best, and a debate on the surrealist traits of Avery and the merits of his art, which coincided with Benayoun's first attempt to contact him.[24]

In 1951, *L'Âge du cinéma* placed Disney in the 'Don't See' column of its list of film-makers in the special August–November surrealist issue,[25] while the 'magician of Burbank' is rechristened the 'Henry Ford of animation' and, Michael Richardson reminds us, 'advised that "having swallowed his umbrella," he ought to digest it'.[26] A more specifically ideological aspect of the surrealist grievance lay there, in the industrial nature of Disney's operation, and as the critique evolved, Benayoun's own verdict would lie partly in a contrast between Disney's inflated corporatism and expansionism on the one hand and Avery's smaller-scale, almost fringe activity on the other, carried out in the company of fellow directors Chuck Jones and Bob Clampett on the Warner Brothers lot in Culver City, in fact, not Hollywood, in the run-down bungalow known as 'Termite Terrace'.[27]

But the surrealists also took aim at the distinct type of humour manufactured by Disney, contrasted with Avery's from the standpoint of theory. This strategy can be found in an early guise in the brief text of 1953 by the writer and future actor François Valorbe that appeared in the first number of *Médium: Communication surréaliste* (four issues, 1953–5). In place of a psychic economy in which emotion is turned rationally to engineer humorous excess (entertainment), Valorbe advocated a 'poetic shortcut' that relied 'on the rational structures of the mind to disarticulate its mechanism by means of the absurd' (criticism).[28] Violence mixed with suddenness was the key to this 'mad humour' in which logic undermined logic (Valorbe used boxing as an analogy for its spontaneity and unanticipated impact).[29] In language, its sovereign was Alfred Jarry and its chief contemporary practitioner was Eugène Ionesco; in the realm of the image, wrote Valorbe, 'it is absent from Chaplin's comedy and abundant in that of the Marx Brothers, almost zero in the animation of Disney, everywhere in that of Tex Avery'.[30]

As a contributor to *Médium*, Benayoun obviously knew Valorbe's text and even mentioned Ionesco when he weighed in again the following year in *Positif*. Still recovering from the 'painful farce' of Disney's *Peter Pan* (1953, USA), he speculated that Avery's treatment of scale in *King-Size Canary*, *Half-Pint Pygmy* and others was a symptom of anxiety in a United States obsessed by material security, aligning it not only with US science fiction of the 1930s in that regard but Breton's myth of the 'Great Invisibles', which had just preceded these cartoons in 1942.[31] In dialectical opposition to this cosmic strand of his work, argued Benayoun, was the frankly down-to-earth, sexual one in *Red Hot Riding*

Hood (1943, USA) and *Swing Shift Cinderella* (1945, USA), among a series of Warner Brothers and MGM cartoons made since 1937 that were thought by the surrealists to reinvest long-expurgated fairy tales with their original, explicit and often menacing themes of temptation, cruelty and conflict, obviously meant by Avery as antidotes to Disney's pure-as-Snow White.[32] Further coverage of Avery's oeuvre would take place in the pages of *Positif* in the 1950s by writers such as Maurice Ranchal, Louis Seguin and Paul-Louis Thirard, long before the creation of the Bureau d'études texaveriennes at the journal encouraged deeper and more systematic study by a larger group of writers in the 1960s.

The mortal enemy of sentimentality: André Breton and *King-Size Canary*

Significant traction for these speculations had been gained from the surrealist programme of comedy musicals and cartoons that took place in June 1951 in Paris at the Studio Parnasse on rue Jules-Chaplain, presumably associated with the launch of *L'Âge du cinéma*, where surrealists present viewed movies such as *Ziegfeld Follies* (1945) and cartoons by Avery.[33] This was the moment that Benayoun was able to identify more concretely their surrealist traits because two icons of surrealism were present and turned out to be enthusiastic: 'André Breton and Benjamin Péret', he reported, 'expressed publicly their liking for *King-Size Canary* and *Half-Pint Pygmy*.'[34]

In *King-Size Canary*, a typically famished alley cat seeking food spies a large fridge through the window of a suburban house. Neutralizing the guard dog Atom (not Spike, for once) with sleeping pills, he enters to find the fridge empty, beautifully rendered with precision, an economy of detail and ripe untinted colours by Ray Abrams, Robert Bentley and Walter Clinton; it also serves to introduce the shifts of scale that dominate the action of the cartoon and introduce a theme that appealed to the surrealists. Disappointed by the tiny, emaciated bird he discovers, the cat spots a bottle of garden 'Jumbo Gro' and one (very literal) 'BRAIN STORM' later pours it down the canary's throat. It grows to large enough proportions to threaten the cat, like Alice in the 'eat me' episode in *Alice's Adventures in Wonderland* (1865), which might well have been Heck Allen's inspiration for the story in *King-Size Canary* and, a few years later, for René Magritte's room-sized apple of *The Listening Room* (1952). What follows is a novel take on the dog-chases-cat, cat-chases-bird-or-mouse staple, as all the characters in turn swig from the bottle of 'Jumbo Gro', as though it were an animated comedy sequel to that other masterpiece of gigantism *King Kong* (1933), long admired by surrealists since the days of *Minotaure*.

Finally, the overgrown cat and enormous mouse, who had indeed saved the cat's life (from the dog) as predicted, fight to the death, pitching across the western United States to recognizable landmarks in the desert like Monument Valley and the Grand Canyon. Breaking the fourth wall for the last time, they sup the last of the 'Jumbo Gro' and bid the audience farewell, at which point the frame widens to show the two colossal combatants astride the Earth. Analogy with Kong at the summit of the Empire

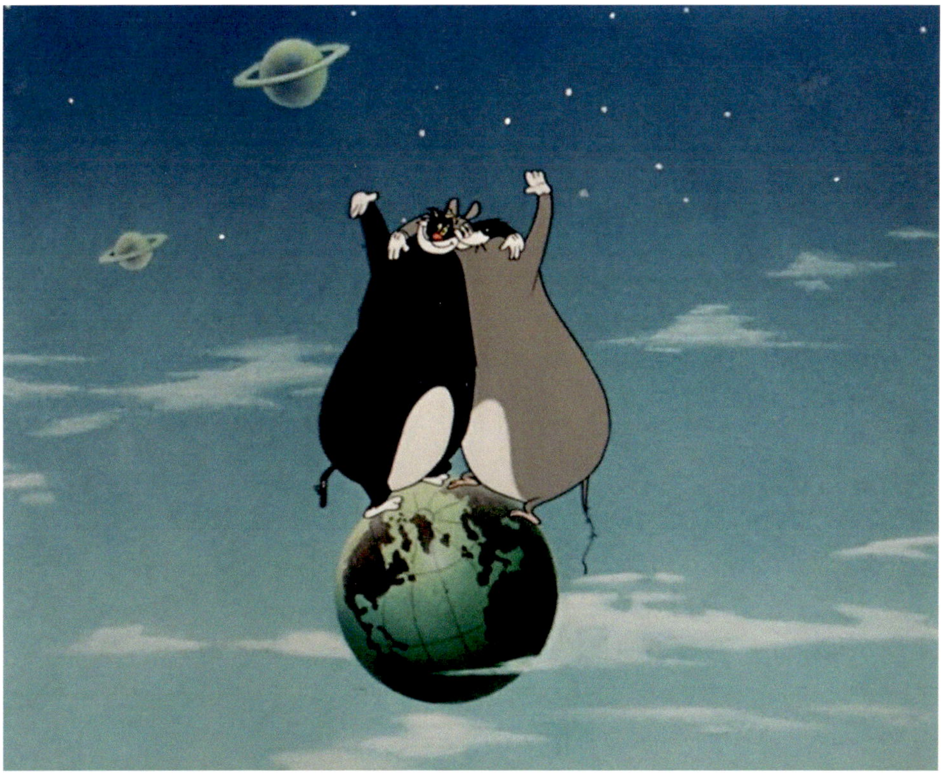

Figure 6.1 Tex Avery, dir., *King-Size Canary*, Metro-Goldwyn-Mayer, 1947.

State Building at the climax of *King Kong* is available, yet Kong remains throughout a recognizably proportioned ape, whereas the hideously enlarged protagonists of *King-Sized Canary* never merely grow, but grow fat or fattened, in tune with the hunger–food theme of the cartoon, serving also to introduce properties of the grotesque through their flaccidly distorted bodies.

Even as the culmination of a tale that monstrously surpasses the laws of nature in the service of humour, it is a strikingly excessive dream image created around the time the first photograph of Earth from space was taken, but well before it was known. Nevertheless, comparatively gargantuan fantasy imagery had been around in popular culture since at least the early years of the twentieth century, notably in Winsor McCay's *Little Nemo in Slumberland* (1905–11, 1924–7) venerated by later surrealists in Chicago, where growth and disproportion of figures and objects were commonplace and sometimes characters lay across, stood astride or looked from a distance at the globe of the Earth as, for instance, in the strips of Sunday 27 December 1908, Sunday 14 March 1909 and Sunday 21 August 1910.

Dating from the moment of Benayoun's initiatory beguilement by animation, *King-Size Canary* 'entranced' Breton, he recalled, but he made surprisingly little of the (surrealist) roots of Breton's fascination, linking it only briefly to Breton's rarely mentioned statement on Muller and Bower's *It's a Bird* (1930, USA), placed at the front of *Minotaure* 10 in 1937.[35] All the same, Benayoun's intuition was good and we can deepen it into a fuller surrealist reading of Avery by further comparison with ex-chauffeur Charley Chucklehead's adventure with the African metal-eating bird. This is facilitated by the knowledge that not only is the period of Breton's reference to *It's a Bird* that of Avery's stint at Warner Brothers but that there are some points of comparison available, such as the roundabout journey via Greenland and Europe taken by Charley to the Belgian Congo to catch the bird, recorded frantically on a map like the one in Warner Brothers cartoons such as *The Isle of Pingo Pongo* (1938, USA). The second half of *It's a Bird* contained the still remarkable combination of animation and live action and has thematic similarities with the kidnap–freak plot of *King Kong* and anticipates Avery's baby goat that will eat anything in the excellent *Billy Boy* (1954, USA), unsurprisingly lauded in the pages of *Positif* in 1956 by Seguin (Billy Boy devours the engine of a car along with part of the cartoon he is appearing in, the entire railway track to California ('2360 miles'), and, in another example of Averian universal disorder, the Moon).[36]

The two stills from *It's a Bird* reproduced in *Minotaure* that accompany Breton's brief statement on the film show the bird consuming a trombone and could easily be associated with Breton's suspicion of music.[37] However, the main concern is with a particular kind of humour that Breton had recently begun to term 'black'. Benayoun's speculation, therefore, about Breton's admiration of *King-Size Canary* for its echo of *It's a Bird* can be rooted in the black humour displayed in both animations.[38] In the *Anthology of Black Humour* (1940/1945) – delayed publication until 1945 due to wartime censorship, so possibly formative to Benayoun's early understanding of surrealism, just as its republication in a revised edition in 1950 might have shaped the surrealists' reception of cartoons in that decade – Breton went on to characterize black humour by drawing partly (with some reservations) on Sigmund Freud's discussion of the subject. We have long since become familiar on a much broader scale in our culture with a humour representative of an economy of feeling that leavens violence, suffering, sorrow and danger with laughter. Nevertheless, in exploring Breton and the surrealists' enthusiasm for the fanatical mayhem of Avery's cartoons, usually careening riotously across the adjoining terrains of sex and violence – see, for instance, the classic *Red Hot Riding Hood* and the sadistic *Slap-Happy Lion* mentioned earlier, the incredibly cruel *Bad Luck Blackie* (1949, USA) and even more so, plotless and gratuitous, *The Cat That Hated People* (1948, USA), and the brutally funny, trickster-themed duo *Rock-a-bye Bear* (1952, USA) and *Legend of Rockabye Point* (1955, USA), all much-loved by surrealists – it is useful here and in my next section to situate and expand Benayoun's own tentative interpretation of Breton's enthusiasm for *King-Size Canary*. That approach is further justified not only by Avery specialist Joe Adamson's objective discernment of black humour as 'increasingly in evidence' from the wartime manic–reflexive, bird-outsmarted-by-worm caper *The Early Bird Dood It!* (1942, USA) with atypical conclusion,[39] one of Avery's first cartoons for MGM and nearly contemporary with Breton's writing on the subject, but also because it is stated bluntly in the *Anthology* that black humour is 'the mortal enemy of sentimentality', underlining the rejection of Disney.[40]

Everything is permitted: Benjamin Péret and *Half-Pint Pygmy*

In a second account of the event at Studio Parnasse, Péret is said by Benayoun to have 'adored' as much as Breton 'the proliferating universes of Tex Avery, that poet of the irresistible attraction of opposites, with his cyclopean canaries, shrinking fleas and madly dashing half-sized pygmies'.[41] A closer exploration of the surrealist qualities of Avery's animation is possible through analogy with the tumultuous poetry of Péret, who had long been considered the surrealist's surrealist since his earliest work in 1923 using automatic writing. One early instance, the '"impossible" film scenario' titled 'Bonny Wants a Car' (1923), has even been called 'closely related to the animated cartoon … an extraordinary fairy tale of extreme and hilarious violence'.[42]

Péret's writing has a particularly privileged place in the *Anthology* where Breton wrote as follows of its lawless world of bizarre objects and events, generated through a juxtaposition of nouns, verbs and adjectives that constantly destabilizes readerly expectation, further placed at the mercy of conjunctions and prepositions located aberrantly, which are, nevertheless, in themselves perfectly familiar:

> censorship no longer obtains, and one takes it as a given that 'everything is permitted.' Never had words and what they designate, finally freed from domestication, shown such glee. It is not only that natural objects succeed in dragging even manufactured objects into the hullabaloo; each side vies with the other for availability. We have finished once and for all with old-fashionedness, with dust. Frantic joy has returned … Everything is set free, everything is poetically saved by the reactivation of a generalized principle of mutation and metamorphosis.[43]

Péret's poetry and prose bear a close relationship with the tradition of 'nonsense' esteemed by Benayoun, who was mentored by Péret in his early days in the surrealist group and was a devoted admirer.[44] In 1969, a decade after Péret's death, Benayoun contributed the introduction to the republication of Péret's volume *Le Grand jeu* or *The Big Game* (1928), where he averred that there are in his poems 'those mad pursuits, those flamboyant collisions, those unexpected falls that we find in the short films of Mack Sennett and the cartoons of Tex Avery'.[45]

The master metaphor in Péret's poetry is freedom, the mind consummately unshackled from routine constraints, overwritten on every runaway image, while the talking sheep, humming sheers and ship in distress in *The Big Game* conjure situations that await their animator, resembling the warring sheep and domesticated cattle caught up in the 'grazing land battles' in one of Avery's greatest cartoons *Drag-a-long Droopy* (1954, USA). The same could be said for the car full of water in Péret's 'Etiquette', the 'donkey of straw' and 'jockey/cherry limp and rubbery' of 'Daily Double', the mouth opening 'to vomit the landscape' of 'The Enemy Beats Him', the 'blonde woman' who 'split a rock/with a celestial razor' in 'Domestic Bliss' and the 'calf/which would come one night to devour my ears' in 'The Dead and Their Children', among so many other fantastic images described elsewhere in *The Big Game*.[46]

Péret's reported adoration of Avery's *King-Size Canary* and *Half-Pint Pygmy* was partly determined by a kindred attraction to abrupt and matter-of-fact juxtaposition as well as by a pleasure taken in the mutation of scale, but also by a particular poetic attitude towards the natural world that warrants closer investigation. In *Half-Pint Pygmy*, the bears George and Junior (based on the characters of George Milton and Lennie Small as they were portrayed in Lewis Milestone's 1939 film version of John Steinbeck's *Of Mice and Men*) go to Africa seeking a $10,000 reward for the capture of the world's smallest pygmy. Their arrival at a pygmy village in the jungle by descending a purple elephant's trunk shaped like a staircase cues the fantastic attitude to the natural world and the overriding chase structure and theme of the cartoon, as well as its racism; indeed, given its ethnic stereotyping, it is surprising that *Half-Pint Pygmy* has not been added to the three cartoons by Avery – *Uncle Tom's Bungalow* (1937), *The Isle of Pingo Pongo* and *All This and Rabbit Stew* (1941) – among the 'censored eleven' withheld from television broadcast in the United States from 1968 due to their depiction of race, unremarked by the surrealists or anyone else in the 1950s.

The larger part of the plot of *Half-Pint Pygmy* ends there and the rest of the cartoon is given over to remarkably quick-fire gags and ingenious, immoderate violence, even by Avery's standards. In pursuit of their prey, Junior is deformed by a snake hanging from a tree; the duo chase the pygmy over a lake using the legs of flamingos as stilts; all three leap into one kangaroo's pouch only to emerge out of the pouch of another; the pygmy inflates himself using a balloon to masquerade as a giant (in a theme comparable to

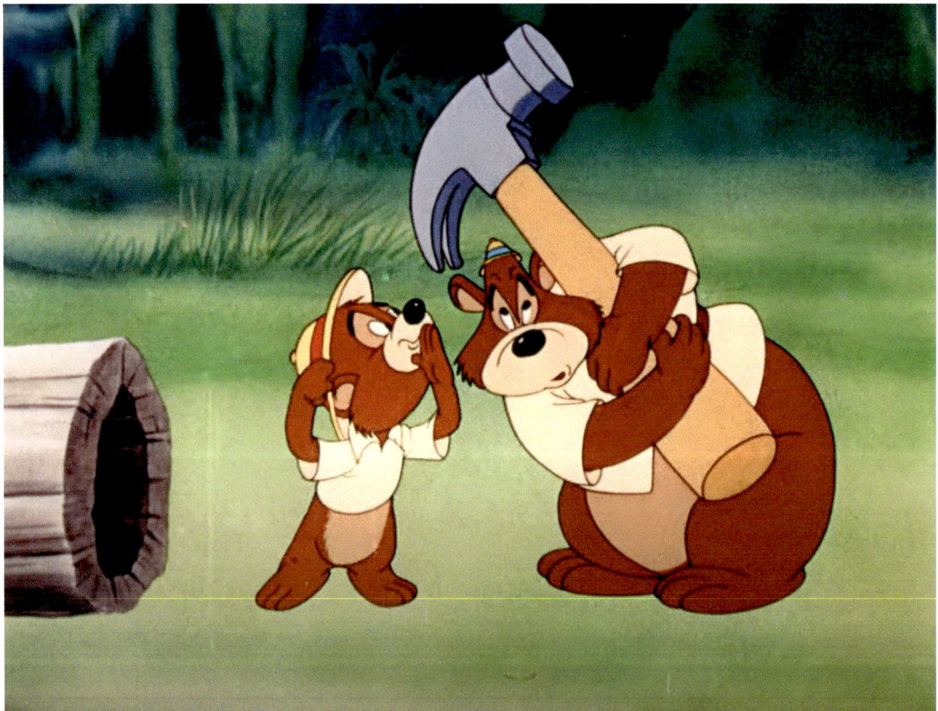

Figure 6.2 Tex Avery, dir., *Half-Pint Pygmy*, Metro-Goldwyn-Mayer, 1948.

that of *King-Size Canary* of the previous year); they race up the neck of one giraffe to slide uninterrupted down the neck of another (the wider view reveals the single-necked, two-bodied, no-headed creature). The skirmish speeds up in the final minute through a sequence of ten gags to accentuate Avery's quick-fire virtuosity, as though we have been transplanted from the jungle to the circus.

The cartoon, and especially its abrasive conclusion, are dosed with a grim humour that jar today, but they do little to reduce the overall clout of *Half-Pint Pygmy*, owed not to a plot but to the wild inventiveness of its natural history lesson combined with the casualness of its staging through extraordinary compression, relying heavily on precisely those strategies of juxtaposition and metamorphosis by which we might recognize surrealism. Its vigour and agility invoke more specifically the poetry of Péret, whose most self-conscious application of his own poetic vision to a mutation and metamorphosis of the natural world can be found in *Histoire naturelle* (1958), which appeared in the course of the reception of Avery by surrealists.[47]

Like Péret's 'Turkish baths, which come from kneading damp earth with yoghurt', his air 'used for mending inner tubes, and if salt is added, it makes beds', his 'dusty-water, which is useful in carpentry' and 'stinking-fire ... obtained by soaking bishops in cod-liver oil' in *Histoire naturelle*,[48] Avery's zebra that sheds its stripes like iron hoops and his leopard that surrenders its spots like coins in *Half-Pint Pygmy*, but also, in his early satirical documentaries and travelogues, the cigarette-smoking camels at the beginning of *A Day at the Zoo* (1939, USA), the human basketball of *Believe it or Else* (1939, USA), the expectorating geyser and 'rolling plains of Texas' swelling like ocean waves in *Detouring America* (1939, USA), the natural (dental) bridge in Bryce Canyon, Utah and stripping lizard in *Cross Country Detours* (1940, USA), the thigh-slapping horse in *Wacky Wildlife* (1940, USA), the cow caught suspended in a spider's web and picketing silk worms of *The Bug Parade* (1941, USA), and the kangaroo in *Slap-Happy Lion* that dives into its own pouch and disappears (one of the 'Lichtenbergian shortcuts' named by Benayoun after the sometimes absurdist aphorisms of Georg Christoph Lichtenberg, treated by Breton in the *Anthology*, such as 'a knife without a blade, which is missing the handle'),[49] all show, in J. H. Matthews' words on Péret, that 'poetic natural history may be governed by imaginative laws of myth-making that ignore scientific law'.[50]

Péret was a small press poet with a very limited audience, not a worker in the entertainment industry, of course, and he had even made his feelings known in the first issue of *L'Âge du cinéma* about a film business 'governed by sordid market forces' in perhaps his best-known statement about cinema, so there are distinct differences from Avery in his intentions, tone and use of language.[51] These can be viewed especially in his enraged, often-explicit condemnation of religion and militarism, his scatological language that goes far beyond the limits self-assigned to Avery's commercial cartoons, and the non-pictorial nature of some of his imagery that contrasts with the hyper-literalism of Avery's, most obvious in the latter in those self-consciously corny in-jokes that literalize metaphor, prized by Doniol-Valcroze and *Positif* writers in the 1950s such as Ranchal, particularly accessible through the cartoon medium.[52] Nevertheless, Benayoun was right to twin them again in a related discussion of the 'surrealist' nature of Woody Allen's imagery, 'characteristic of certain poetic techniques used by the surrealists'.[53] As a film-maker and short story writer, Allen's work forms an unexpected yet convincing bridge between the cartoons of Avery and poetry of Péret and leads back to an ancestry that had been earlier traced by Breton, as both Forneret's letterbox and Lichtenberg's gallows are present in the *Anthology*.[54] Their nonchalance with the macabre is equalled by the widow of Péret's dead 'gas man' whose 'ears will be unpaid bills/unpaid because you're dead' in 'Spilled Blood' and in 'Never Wait' the 'execution of Louis XVI/and the head of the executed bounces on that of his wife/who faints';[55] alternatively, by the twin gallows of Avery's *The Shooting of Dan McGoo*, signed 'DOUBLE HEADER TODAY 2 O'CLOCK' next to a smaller gallows marked, incredibly, 'KIDS 15 CENTS', examples of the 'unique humour' and 'audacity' of Avery identified by Doniol-Valcroze in his early review of that cartoon; also by the opening tracking shot of a corridor of 'Alka-Fizz Prison' (motto: 'No Noose is Good Noose') in *Northwest Hounded Police* (1946, USA) where a sign 'COME IN – HAVE A SEAT' indicates a room containing an electric chair.[56]

It is a poetic humour that has little to do with the New Wave but might be associated with movies of the Marx Brothers, often compared with and sometimes even seen as the inspiration for Avery's cartoons, occasionally by the master himself. Another means of discerning such humour in the movies before Avery and in parallel with surrealism is, of course, through the films of Buñuel, as suggested by White. Péret's poetry was held in the highest regard by Buñuel because, he stated, it 'seems to flow freely, untrammelled by any cultural effort, from a hidden source of inspiration, spontaneously recreating a wholly new and different world. In 1929, Dalí and I used to read from *The Big Game* and weep with laughter'.[57] Much later, he made a self-conscious tribute to the surrealist poet through the darkly humorous non-plot of his penultimate film *The Phantom of Liberty* (1974), in which we are led apparently randomly through bizarre encounters and events by means of the disjointure of dream logic: a postman arrives by bicycle in a bedroom and delivers a letter to a couple in bed; dinner guests sit on toilets around a table reading magazines and excuse themselves to eat privately; a missing child is entirely present throughout the investigation into her disappearance; a 'killer poet' shoots citizens from a high-rise building, is captured, condemned to death, celebrates and goes free. The consensus within the surrealist group, according to Benayoun, that 'there are only two film-makers who are authentically and completely surrealist: Buñuel and Tex Avery'[58] was, then, the outcome of a poetic disposition and substance-over-style in both that Benayoun regarded as quite contradictory to the technical preoccupation and formalism that were common to both Disney and the 'quotation films' of New Wave where 'the mere process of direction has taken the place of an act of creation'.[59]

Epilogue, or the absolute enemy of the Oedipus Complex: the Bureau d'études texaveriennes

Benayoun visited Disneyland and carried out the first interview with Avery and one with Jones on his trip across the United States in 1963, which confirmed in his eyes Disney's corporatism and Avery's 'primitivism' (in the sense of the painter Henri Rousseau).[60] The development of Averian studies in and close to surrealism had led to the opening of a Bureau d'études texaveriennes that year at *Positif*.[61] As well as the authors mentioned in this chapter, it included the surrealist Ado Kyrou, who had written of Avery as the 'veritable poet of the explosive cartoon', giving special treatment to *King-Size Canary* and confirming the larger surrealist–Averian canon of *Half-Pint Pygmy*, *Slap-Happy Lion* and *Red Hot Riding Hood*, while adding the unruly adventures of Screwy Squirrel in *Screwball Squirrel* (1944, USA), *Happy-Go-Nutty* (1944, USA) and others.[62] Benayoun's contributions were extensive and included his summary of his own activities and the writings in or close to *Positif* up to then in his essay 'Le dossier Tex Avery' plus annex, in an issue of the journal given over to animation.[63]

Petr Král extended Averian studies into the 1970s in an important essay in *Positif* that saw Avery 'pushing the absurd to the point of delirium, nonsense to the point of the surrealist "marvelous" and the gag to the point of a nightmare'.[64] Král included one of Avery's drawings for *King-Size Canary*, an inevitable focus for discussion, which also commented on the 'surrealist' features of several others such as the 'Magrittean rain' (piano, steamroller, aeroplane, bus, battleship) that menaces the dog at the conclusion of *Bad Luck Blackie*, demonstrating that as in Péret's poetry, '*everything*, in a cartoon, is possible' on Avery's watch.[65]

Avery received honourable mention from at least 1971 in the list of US forerunners to Chicago surrealism. Then, in the same year as Král's text, the final nightmare image of his 'magisterial' *King-Size Canary* prompted an analogy with the 'infamous "power blocs" careen[ing] over the globe' in a major statement by the Chicago surrealists.[66] It was followed a few years later by extensive discussion of Avery by Franklin Rosemont in a volume by US surrealists given over to popular culture, which is largely a scroll through many of the cartoons referred to in this chapter while giving unusual emphasis to Screwy Squirrel, 'Avery's exterminating angel', and arguing that black humour transports us 'to the very heart of the Averian dialectic' in the animation of 'this absolute enemy of the Oedipus Complex'.[67] Rosemont's text was accompanied by a section of brief quotations by previous surrealist commentators on Avery, several of whom had been referred to back in 1976 in Rosemont's critical review of Adamson's *Tex Avery: King of the Cartoons* (1975), which insisted on the surrealist qualities of Avery's work in the face of Adamson's tentativeness, partly by sketching in highlights of its surrealist reception since 1951.[68] These writings that emerged within the group in Chicago stand as both summary and continuation of a passionate enquiry within surrealism across thirty years, yet to be either fully documented or grasped in its theoretical implications within studies of surrealism or animation.

Notes

I thank Krzysztof Fijalkowski, Kristoffer Noheden and Michael Richardson for help and advice with this chapter.

1 Timothy R. White, 'From Disney to Warner Bros.: The Critical Shift' [1992], in *Reading the Rabbit: Explorations in Warner Bros. Animation*, ed. Kevin S. Sandler (New Brunswick, NJ and London: Rutgers University Press, 1998), 38–48, 38.

2 White in Sandler (ed.), *Reading the Rabbit*, 38–9.

3 White in Sandler (ed.), *Reading the Rabbit*, 39. See David Bordwell, *Narration in the Fiction Film* (Madison: University of Wisconsin Press, 1985), 232.

4 White in Sandler, *Reading the Rabbit*, 39.

5 See Robert Benayoun, *Le mystère Tex Avery: biographie* (Paris: Éditions du Seuil, 1988). This volume either refers to or includes material going back as far as 1947, but is not mentioned by White, who does allude briefly to Benayoun (as a 'critic', not a surrealist) who, he states, 'discussed animation as an art form, not a medium; Disney is not mentioned, but Avery, [Chuck] Jones, and [Friz] Freleng were'; White in Sandler, *Reading the Rabbit*, 44. His source is Robert Benayoun, 'The Phoenix and the Road-Runner' [1963], *Film Quarterly*, 17, no. 3 (Spring 1964): 17–25, 24, 25. Disney is discussed in Benayoun's earliest writing on cartoons; Robert Benayoun, *Le Dessin animé après Walt Disney* (Paris: Jean-Jacques Pauvert, 1961), 8–13; and in Benayoun, *Le mystère*, 10–12, 14, 54, 59–69, 100, 104–05, 109–10.

6 Paul Hammond (ed. and trans.), *The Shadow & Its Shadow: Surrealist Writings on the Cinema* [1978] (San Francisco, CA: City Lights, 2000), 36.

7 Paul Nash, 'The Colour Film', in *Footnotes to the Film*, ed. Charles Davy (London: Lovat Dickson Ltd, 1937), 116–34, 128, 129, 131–2.

8 Alfred H. Barr (ed.), *Fantastic Art, Dada, Surrealism* (New York: Museum of Modern Art, 1936), 233, 242.

9 Quoted in Fèlix Fanés, 'Film as Metaphor', trans. Alayne Pullen, in *Dalí & Film*, ed. Matthew Gale (London: Tate Publishing, 2007), 32–51, 43.

10 Salvador Dalí, 'Surrealism in Hollywood' [1937], trans. George Davis, *Dalí & Film*, 154–6, 154.

11 Georges Pudelko, 'Picro di Cosimo, peintre bizarre', *Minotaure*, 11 (1938): 19–26, 19 (all translations are by the author unless otherwise stated).

12 Pudelko, 'Piero di Cosimo', 24.

13 Sergei Eisenstein, *Eisenstein on Disney*, ed. Jay Leyda, trans. Alan Upchurch (London: Methuen, 1988), 70.

14 Fèlix Fanés, '*Destino*', trans. Alayne Pullen, *Dalí & Film*, 186–95, 189.

15 Benayoun, *Le mystère*, 59.

16 Hammond, *The Shadow & Its Shadow*, 34.

17 Robert Benayoun, *Le Rire des surréalistes* (Paris: La Bougie du Sapeur, 1988), 18.

18 Benayoun, 'The Phoenix', 19; see Robert Benayoun, 'Le Phénix de l'Animation', *Positif*, 54/55 ('L'Animation en 1963', July–August 1963): 1–14, 4; Benayoun, *Le Rire*, 21.

19 Benayoun, *Le mystère*, 119. See Jacques Doniol-Valcroze, 'Un savoureux *western* dessiné', *Revue du cinéma*, 5 (February 1947): 71–2, 72. This was preceded by an earlier, rare appreciation of Warner Brothers cartoons in the United States by a film critic and painter: 'Tex Avery is a visual surrealist proving nothing is permanent … while Jones's speciality, comic character, is unusual for the chopping up motion and the surrealist imposition', Manny Farber, 'Saccharine Symphony' [1942] and 'Short and Happy' [1943], *Farber on Film: The Complete Film Writings of Manny Farber*, ed. Robert Polito (New York: The Library of America, 2009), 16–18, 17 and 103–06, 105.

20 Abner Lepetit, 'Bilan du dessin animé', *L'Âge du cinéma*, 1 (March 1951): 18–19, 18.

21 Lepetit, 'Bilan', 19.

22 Lepetit, 'Bilan', 19.

23 Comte de Lautréamont, *Maldoror and Poems* [1869 and 1870], trans. Paul Knight (Harmondsworth: Penguin, 1988), 88–9.

24 Benayoun, *Le mystère*, 14.

25 Reprinted in Hammond, *The Shadow & Its Shadow*, 46–7.

26 Quoted in Michael Richardson, '"Open the Locksmiths": On the Collaboration between Surrealism and *Positif*', in *Surrealism and Film after 1945: Absolutely Modern Mysteries*, eds. Kristoffer Noheden and Abigail Susik (Manchester: Manchester University Press, 2021), 147–64, 149.

27 See Adamson, *Tex Avery*, 160.

28 François Valorbe, 'L'humour critique', *Médium: Communication surréaliste*, 1 (November 1953): 8.

29 Valorbe, 'L'humour', 8.

30 Valorbe, 'L'humour', 8.

31 Robert Benayoun, 'Bilan du nouveau dessin animé', *Positif*, 12 (November–December 1954): 17–23, 17, 20.

32 Benayoun, 'Bilan', 21.

33 Benayoun, *Le mystère*, 97; Benayoun, *Le Rire*, 94.

34 Benayoun, *Le mystère*, 97.

35 Benayoun, *Le mystère*, 97.

36 Seguin, 'Le Phénix', *Positif*, 18 (November 1956): 38–40.

37 Harold Muller, '*It's a Bird*', *Minotaure*, 10 (Winter 1937): 2. The film was known to Benayoun's generation only through these two images: Benayoun, *Le Rire*, 94. André Breton, *Anthology of Black Humour* [1940/45], trans. Mark Polizzotti (San Francisco, CA: City Lights, 1997), xvii–xviii.

38 A chapter devoted by Benayoun to black humour includes Avery's giant canary, 'dont nous raffolions tous', among the nonsensical bestiaries of Charles Cros, Guillaume Apollinaire and Lewis Carroll (all present in Breton's *Anthology*): Benayoun, *Le Rire*, 62–3.

39 Joe Adamson, *Tex Avery: King of the Cartoons* [1975] (New York: Da Capo, 1985), 59.

40 Breton, *Anthology*, xix.

41 Benayoun, *Le Rire*, 94–5.

42 Dawn Ades, 'Why Film?' *Dalí & Film*, 14–31, 26.

43 Breton, *Anthology*, 301–02.

44 Benayoun, *Le Rire*, 94. Quotations from Péret's poetry serve as epigraphs at the beginning of *Le mystère Tex Avery* and for its brief chapter concerned with Avery's reception among surrealists, the former – 'The mystery eats our steak' – derived from a volume that Benayoun thought was titled ideally for Avery's typical subject matter: Benjamin Péret, *The Leg of a Lamb its Life and Works* [1957], trans. Marc Lowenthal (Cambridge, MA: Wakefield Press, 2011), 134; Benayoun, *Le mystère*, 7, 96, 98.

45 Robert Benayoun, 'A plus d'un titre', Benjamin Péret, *Le Grand Jeu* [1928] (Paris: Gallimard, 1969), 7–17, 11 (tellingly, Benayoun refers in the next sentence to 'Bonny Wants a Car').

46 Benjamin Péret, *The Big Game* [1928], trans. Marilyn Kallet (Boston, MA: Black Widow Press, 2011), 161, 171, 193, 215, 217.

47 See J. H. Matthews, *Benjamin Péret* (Boston, MA: Twayne Publishers, 1975), 1975, 52.

48 Benjamin Péret, *Death to the Pigs: Selected Writings*, ed. and trans. Rachel Stella (London: Atlas Press, 1988), 133, 135, 137, 138.

49 Benayoun, *Le mystère*, 75; Breton, *Anthology*, 32.

50 J. H. Matthews, *Benjamin Péret* (Boston, MA: Twayne Publishers), 43.

51 Benjamin Péret, ‘Against Commercial Cinema’ [1951], Hammond, *The Shadow & Its Shadow*, 59–60, 59.

52 Doniol-Valcroze, ‘Un savoureux’, 72. For the pictorialization of metaphor afforded by ‘la grand liberté du dessin animé automatique’, see Marcel Ranchal, ‘En la fête de Saint Tex et de quelque autres’, *Positif*, 21 (February 1957): 46–8, 47.

53 Robert Benayoun, *Woody Allen: Beyond Words* [1985], trans. Alexander Walker (London: Pavilion, 1987), 23–4.

54 Breton, *Anthology*, 37, 96.

55 Péret, *The Big Game*, 227, 253.

56 Doniol-Valcroze, ‘Un savoureux’, 72.

57 Luis Buñuel, *My Last Breath* [1982], trans. Abigail Israel (London: Flamingo, 1987), 110.

58 Benayoun, *Le Rire*, 96.

59 Benayoun in Graham with Vincendeau (eds), 70.

60 Benayoun, *Le mystère*, 64, 67. See Robert Benayoun, ‘Un entretien avec l’insaisissable’ and ‘Disneyland mis à nu’, *Positif*, 57 (‘Hollywood!’) (December 1963): 11–16 and 25–32; Robert Benayoun,‘Le mimiracle (Cinq jours avec Chuck Jones)’, *Positif*, 54/55 (‘L’Animation en 1963’) (July–August 1963): 41–51. That year, the Surrealist Georges Goldfayn introduced an article on Ernest Pintoff by matter-of-factly calling Disney a routine litigator and ‘une marquee de jouets’, Georges Goldfayn, ‘Le Jeune Homme et la Fleur’, *Positif*, 54/55 (‘L’Animation en 1963’) (July–August 1963): 59–62.

61 Benayoun, *Le mystère*, 32–44.

62 Kyrou, *Le Surréalisme au cinéma* (Paris: Arcanes, 1953), 103.

63 Robert Benayoun, ‘Le dossier Tex Avery’, *Positif*, 54/55 (‘L’Animation en 1963’) (July–August 1963): 63–7.

64 Petr Král, ‘Tex Avery ou le délire lucide’, *Positif*, 160 (June 1974): 40–3, 41.

65 Král, ‘Tex Avery’, 41, 43.

66 The Surrealist Group, ‘Lighthouse of the Future’ [1974], Franklin Rosemont, Penelope Rosemont and Paul Garon (eds), *The Forecast is Hot: Tracts & Other Collective Declarations of the Surrealist Movement in the United States, 1966–1976* (Chicago, IL: Black Swan Press, 1997), 200–6, 202.

67 Franklin Rosemont, ‘Homage to Tex Avery’, in *Surrealism & its Popular Accomplices*, ed. Franklin Rosemont (San Francisco, CA: City Lights Books, 1980), 53–5, 53, 55.

68 Franklin Rosemont, ‘Tex Avery’ (book review), *Arsenal: Surrealist Subversion*, 3 (Spring 1976): 70–1.

PART TWO

Animacy Transforming the World: Postwar Transnational Surrealism and Animation

Introduction to Part Two

Abigail Susik

The second part of *Surrealism and Animation* explores how it was only after the Second World War that a thriving surrealist discourse on animation developed thanks to surrealist film critics Ado Kyrou and Robert Benayoun. Certainly, surrealist or surrealist-adjacent film-makers continued to use special effects and animation sequences in their live-action films made during wartime and in the postwar period. For instance, American film-maker Maya Deren employed slow or reverse motion in *Meshes of the Afternoon* (1943; co-directed with Alexandr Hackenschmied) and *At Land* (1944), whereas *Eaten Horizons* (1950) by Jørgen Roos and Wilhelm Freddie featured limited stop motion. *L'invention du monde* (1952) by Jean-Louis Bédouin and Michel Zimbacca included some cut-out animation.[1] Surrealist-adjacent critics wrote about the dynamism and animated quality of cinematic techniques used by several film-makers like Deren, such as Parker Tyler, whose 1954 essay, 'The Film Sense and the Painting Sense', Ann Reynolds discusses in this part. But, as Kristoffer Noheden shows ahead, it took the vision of Czech artist and film-maker Jan Švankmajer to manifest a surrealist animation practice as such starting in the 1960s (Švankmajer became a member of the Prague surrealist group in 1970).

Partly as a result of Švankmajer's arrival onto the international scene, the 1960s witnessed the first efflorescence of surrealist animation accompanied by a surrealist critical reception of those films. Likewise, the animations of American film-maker Lawrence Jordan, discussed in this part by Jorgelina Orfila and Francisco Ortega in comparison with the work of Harry Smith, also contributed to the dissemination of surrealist techniques via collage and cut-out animations, which became prevalent in the 1960s–1970s international counterculture in the work of film-makers such as Terry Gilliam.[2] Other animators with surrealist affinities worked in greater isolation. As explained here by Cheri Donaldson, Czech film-maker Dušan Tomáš Marek produced a series of 16-mm animations in Australia between 1952 and 1963.

By the late 1930s, if not before, Hollywood animation began to incorporate popularized and satirical tropes about surrealism into cartoons such as Robert (Bob) Clampett's 'surrealistic' cartoon *Porky in Wackyland* (1938), part of the Warner Brothers *Looney Tunes* series. The commercialization of a mass market pseudo-surrealism in American animated shorts was amplified in the 1940s. This was partly as a result of surrealism's growing fame in the United States following the temporary relocation to North America of many European surrealists fleeing the war, and also because of the outsized influence of the showman Dalí, who was expelled from the Paris Surrealist Group in 1939 because of his capitalist-bourgeois and fascist-sympathetic activities and pronouncements, among other concerns.[3] In 1949 Warner Brothers released *Dough for the Do-Do* by director Friz Freleng, a Technicolor remake of *Porky in Wackyland* for the *Merrie Melodies* series that made direct allusions to Dalí's painting *The Persistence of Memory* (1931), a work of art which in itself may have been influenced by the time-based art of cinema.[4]

To be sure, Dalí's extensive involvement with American mass media starting in the 1930s is no doubt one of the factors – besides the war itself – that contributed to the lag in writings by anti-capitalist surrealists on animation during the 1940s. Dalí's collaboration with Walt Disney Studios and Disney animator John Hench between 1945 and 1946 on the unfinished animated short *Destino* (completed posthumously and released by Disney Studios in 2003) may have been part of the reason that the surrealist special double issue of the journal *L'Âge du cinéma* (nos. 4–5, September 1951) included a 'watch/don't watch' list of surrealist advice on film from the Paris Group and the journal's editorial board, which comprised surrealist cinephiles Benayoun, Kyrou, Georges Goldfayn and Gérard Legrand. Under the 'watch' column, Méliès and Cohl are named first, for example, while Disney is prominently placed as the second name on the 'don't watch' list.[5]

This was a state of affairs that quickly began to shift during the early 1950s in publications such as Kyrou's *Le Surréalisme au cinéma*, with its notable section on animation, 'Les Êtres dessinés'. Meanwhile, *L'Âge du cinéma* ran to just six total issues between 1951 and 1952, but, given the journal's surrealist affiliation, it had a pivotal impact on the surrealist discourse on animation. It featured essays devoted to animation in all but one of its numbers, and helped launch the surrealist obsession with American animator Tex Avery, discussed by Gavin Parkinson in the previous part. *L'Âge du cinéma* 1 featured Abner Lepetit's (a pseudonym for Benayoun) overview of contemporary animation and Kyrou's discussion of Méliès in relation to illustrations by Grandville and Gustave Doré. Issue 3 published Lepetit's essay on French animator Jean Image (whose feature-length animated fantasy *Johnny the Giant Killer* was released in 1950) alongside an essay by Simone Dubreuilh discussing the work of Scottish-Canadian animator Norman McLaren, who was much-loved by the surrealists.[6] The surrealist double issue (4–5) included an essay by Goldfayn lauding Méliès and alluding to Breton's 1921 essay on Ernst and special effects, discussed in the first pages of this volume. The final issue of *L'Âge du cinéma*, number 6, boasted the most coverage of animation and related subjects, including, among other texts on the subject, an essay about McLaren by surrealist actor, director and long-time film critic Jacques B. Brunius, as well as an essay by the Russian-born French film-maker Alexandre Alexeïeff, who with his wife Claire Parker, an American animator, invented the painstaking pinscreen animation technique during the first half of the 1930s.[7]

With the arrival of *L'Âge du cinéma*, the surrealist discourse on animation became an indispensable and prominent strain in the movement's broader cinematic imaginary, an elective imaginary positing that what was of concern was not so much whether such and such a film could be considered surrealist or was made by a surrealist, but rather that quintessentially surrealist energies could be identified at will (largely by surrealists themselves) in certain movies. Such a model is replicated in Kyrou's chapter 'Drawn Beings', in *Le Surréalisme au cinéma* (1953), published a year after *L'Âge du cinéma*

VOYEZ	NE VOYEZ PAS
Méliès	Lumière
Cohl	Disney
Feuillade	Delluc
Mack Sennett	Capra
Chaplin	
Stroheim	Gance
Langdon	
Christiensen	Dreyer
Wiene	Dupont
Murnau	Griffith
Paul Leni	Leni Riefenstahl
Koulechov	Nicolas Ekk
Poudovkine	Dovjenko
Eisenstein	Dziga Vertov
Richter	Deslaw
Fritz Lang	Lubitsch
Pabst (mort en 1932)	Steinhoff
Renoir	
Cavalcanti	Grierson
Dickinson	Carol Reed
Man Ray	Kirsanoff
Bunuel	
Vigo	L'Herbier
Tod Browning	Duvivier
De Santis	Rouquier
Van Dyke	Wyler
Storck	Machaty
Clouzot	Cocteau
Sternberg	
Lewin	Pagnol
Cooper-Shoedsack	Bresson
Sjoberg	Sjostrom
King Vidor	David Lean
Pierre Prévert	P. Sturges
James Whale	Feyder
John Huston	René Clément
Visconti	Genina
Lewis	Leenhardt
Hamer	Rossellini

Figure II.1 'Voyez/Ne voyez pas', *L'Âge du cinéma* (nos. 4–5, September 1951): 2. Author's collection.

concluded and Kyrou resigned from his managing editorial position for the journal. Méliès is lionized throughout Kyrou's book, and, in the initial pages he compares the imaginative colour schemes in Disney's animated feature *Dumbo* (1941) to costume elements in Hans Richter's avant-garde omnibus film, *Dreams that Money Can Buy* (1947; which includes sequences of stop-motion animated mannequins in Fernand Léger's chapter, 'The Girl with the Prefabricated Heart'). Following these preliminaries, Kyrou's chapter on animation surveys far and wide for its chosen material. Kyrou identifies what he calls 'surrealist aptitudes' in animation despite the perils of excessive 'cuteness' and 'anthropomorphism', censorship (he mentions Popeye and Betty Boop), the 'facile' and 'bourgeois' failures of Disney, and vain attempts to render an animated form of cinéma verité.[8] He clarifies that these surrealist aptitudes of animation will facilitate the 'penetration' of life by 'latent content', the unconscious drives that surrealism thought could eventually bring about a collective revolution in human ways of life.[9] Kyrou examines an enormous number of international animators, films and animated characters in this effort: he likens Cohl's films to surrealist paintings; he praises the autonomy of Koko the Clown by Fleischer Studios; and he namechecks Pat Sullivan's Felix the Cat. The list continues, including Woody Woodpecker, Bugs Bunny, Tom and Jerry; Avery, Jiří Trnka, McLaren, Pal, Ptouchko, Starevich, Goldschmidt, Painlevé, Reiniger, Alexeïeff & Parker and many others. Building on the foundation of a surrealist animation discourse in *L'Âge du cinéma*, Kyrou's book explodes the parameters of this line of inquiry, pointing the way toward a potential future field of surrealist animation studies.

One of the most interesting features of Kyrou's chapter on animation in *Le Surréalisme au cinéma* is his comparison of cartoon gags by Tex Avery to the effects of the surrealist exquisite corpse, the collaborative drawing game named in 1925 by poet and screenwriter Jacques Prévert, who was involved with the Paris Surrealist Group between 1924 and 1929 and retained close connections to it throughout his life.[10] For Kyrou, Avery's gags in films such as *King-Size Canary* (1947) create extreme disorientation in the viewer, akin to the visual shock afforded by the results of a *cadavre exquis* drawn by various players, thus awakening a 'deep anxiety' and forcing us to 'reconsider all our beliefs'.[11] That the cinephile and future animation screenwriter Prévert named the exquisite corpse game is significant, for it suggests that he might have been associating this surrealist practice with the anthropomorphic metamorphoses made possible by cinematic animation or montage effects in 1925. Without explicitly linking Prévert to the invention of the *cadavre exquis*, Kyrou mentions Prévert's earliest collaborations as a screenwriter for animated films, singling out the marvellous qualities of the cartoon short *Le Petit soldat* [1948], the story of a wounded toy soldier who returns from war to find his beloved ballerina, which Prévert wrote with French animator Paul Grimault.[12] Kyrou might have taken cues from the former dadaist Georges Ribemont-Dessaignes, who in a 1946 article acclaims the unfolding poetic potential of the developing medium of animation, excoriates Dalí for 'the liquidation of an entire surrealist marketplace' in Hollywood and hails the animation of Paul Grimault (with scenarios by Prévert) as 'pure surrealism on screen'.[13]

In 1957, the year that Breton's book *L'Art magique* gave passing consideration to Méliès' invocation of magic in cinema, Kyrou would go on to publish the tome *Amour-érotisme et cinéma*, which included a chapter on animated films that argued for an expansion of the cartoon beyond a children's genre.[14] The notion of animation for adults was rooted not in the violent or abject tendencies of some cartoons, but in what Kyrou considered to be the inherent erotic pleasure of characters such as Betty Boop, a subject that Michael Richardson discussed in Part One.[15] In *Amour-érotisme et cinéma*, Kyrou also celebrates a second collaboration between Prévert and Grimault, another love story commenced circa 1946: the feature-length animated film *La Bergère et le Ramoneur*, which remained unfinished and was released against Grimault's wishes in 1953 (Grimault completed the film in 1980, when it was released as *Le Roi et l'oiseau*).[16] It is also interesting to note that Kyrou's discussion includes what might be the earliest surrrealist reference to Japanese anime, a topic explored in this part by Catherine L. Hansen via the work of Kōbō, Shūzō, Kuri, Yamamoto, Miyazaki and others. Kyrou mentions Noburō Ōfuji's explicit short, *Kujira* [The Whale] (1952), which deploys the silhouette animation pioneered by Lotte Reiniger in the mid-1920s to tell the story of a mermaid sexually tormented by a group of sailors.[17]

For all of Kyrou's influential writing on animation from a surrealist point of view, it was Robert Benayoun who ultimately wrote the most about this subject. In 1954, he penned his first article for the influential cinema journal *Positif* on contemporary animation, focusing on a generous range of topics related to the Hollywood cartoon industry in the wake of the widespread use of the multiplane camera.[18] Walerian Borowczyk and Jan Lenica were two of Benayoun's favourite animators, as I detail in my chapter ahead, which also discusses 1960s animation by René Laloux and Roland Topor, such as the feature-length animated film that is featured on the cover of this volume, *Fantastic Planet* (1973). Benayoun even experimented with stop-motion animated sequences in his directorial debut, the live-action feature *Paris n'existe pas* (1969).

In his first book, *L'Anthologie du non-sens* (1957), devoted mostly to humour in international literature and poetry since the medieval era, Benayoun included a chapter titled 'Absurdity of the Image' in which he compares animators such as Avery and McLaren, and cartoon characters such as Bugs Bunny and Woody Woodpecker, to slapstick directors Mack Sennett and others.[19] A few years later, certain animators had already solidified in Benayoun's criticism as the key names for surrealist concerns. In February 1960 he curated a screening at Studio Parnasse in Paris in conjunction with the 1959–60 *Exposition InteRnatiOnale du Surréalisme* (EROS) at the Galerie Daniel Cordier, which included animated shorts by Tex Avery, Walerian Borowczyk and Norman McLaren alongside live-action films by Buñuel and others.[20] This was around the time that a larger community of international artists began to realize the experimental and avant-garde potential of cut-out animation as an updated version of dada and surrealist collage techniques, in particular the series of three collage novels based on nineteenth-century illustrations that Max Ernst published between 1929 and 1934. The Paris-based American artist Norman Rubington, who published a series of collage novels with Olympia Press starting in 1959 under the nom de plume Akbar Del Piombo, was one of the earliest to engage in this tradition, even though his remarkable cut-out animations *The Birth of Venus* (1958), *Oh Frabjous Day* (1959) and *Fuzz Against Junk* (c.1962) unfortunately remain obscure and difficult to access. Not even Benayoun, for all his vast knowledge about animation in this period, appears to have known about Rubington's

Pendant la première guerre mondiale, une chanteuse, Helen Kane, connaissait quelques triomphes passagers. Elle était petite, potelée, assez agréable à regarder et sa voix enfantine contrastait étrangement avec l'aspect très féminin et adulte de toute sa personne et les paroles impudiques de ses chansons. Comme Fields remplaçant le juron interdit « God damn » par un autre de son invention, « Godfrey Daniel », Helen Kane créa un refrain abstrait mais beaucoup plus érotique que tous les mots concrets :

Boop a dopp a dopp
Bopp boop a dopp
Boop boop a dopp girl
Betty Boop !

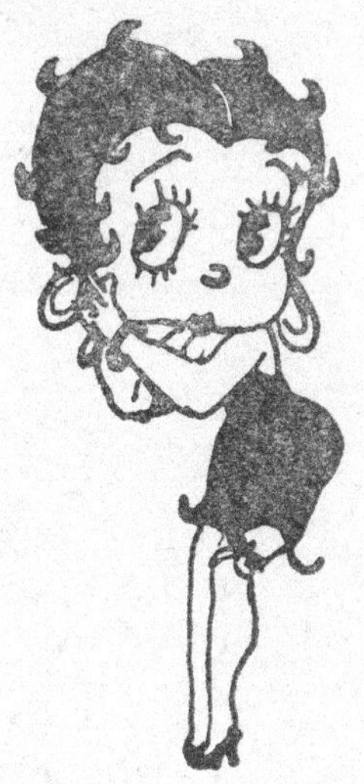

Betty Boop fut le nom de la créature dessinée par Fleischer et pour laquelle Helen Kane, mitigée de Clara Bow, servit de modèle. Son cri de ralliement : « Poo-poo-pi-doo ! » est le plus impudent appel à l'amour que je connaisse. Mais décrivons Betty, pour le cas où certains lecteurs ne la connaîtraient pas : visage rond, poupin, cheveux noirs, peignés en accro-

272

Figure II.2 Ado Kyrou, *Amour-érotisme et cinéma* (Paris: Le Terrain Vague, 1957), 272. Author's collection.

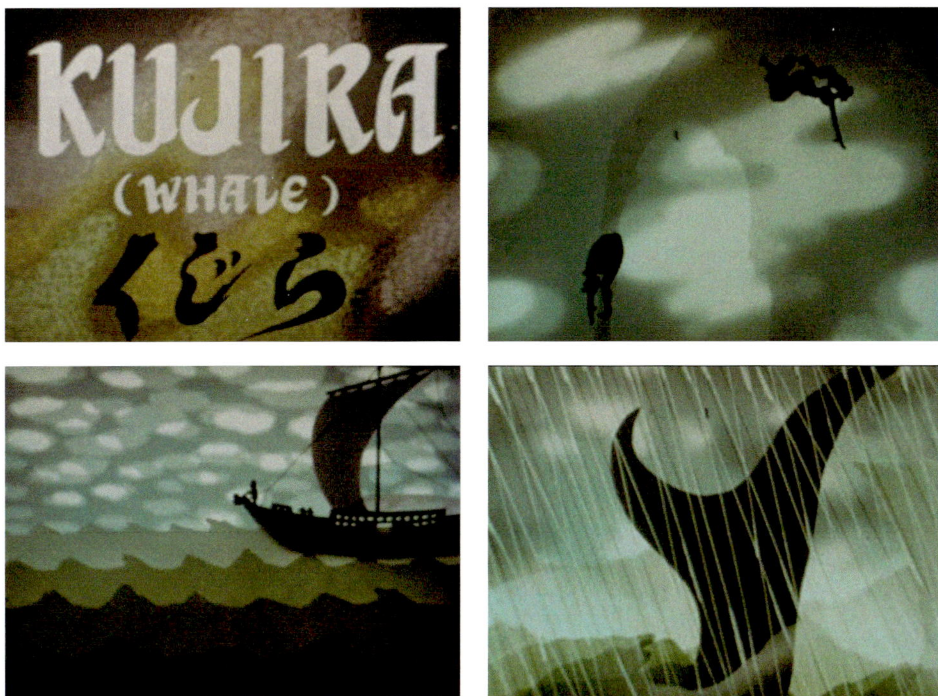

Figure II.3 a–d Noburō Ōfuji, dir., *Kujira* [The Whale], 1952.

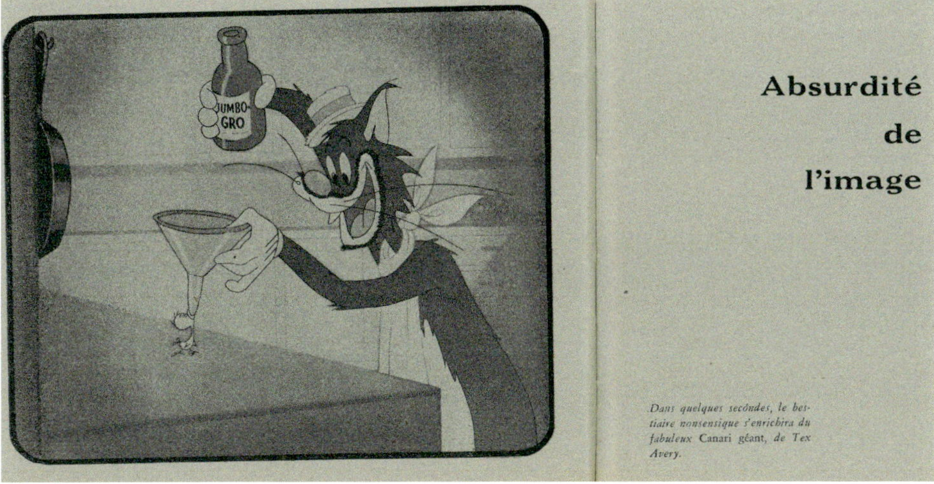

Figure II.4 Robert Benayoun, *L'Anthologie du non-sens* (Paris: Jean-Jacques Pauvert, 1957), 'Absurdité de l'image', 358–9. Author's collection.

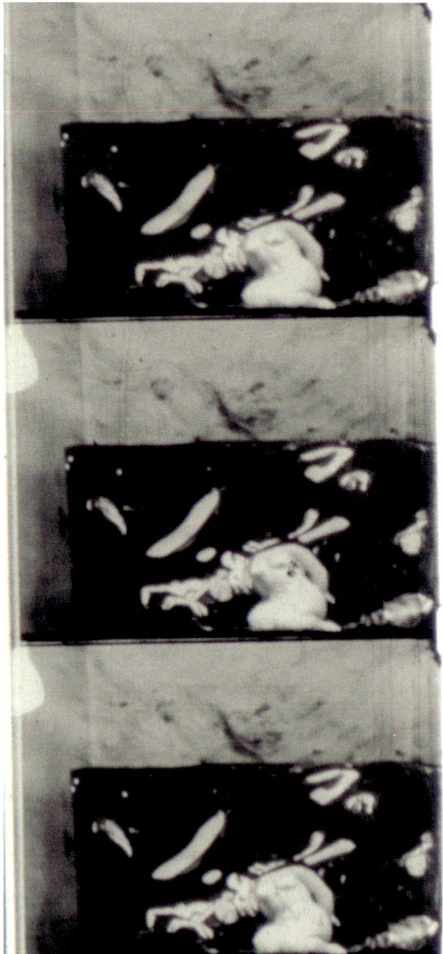

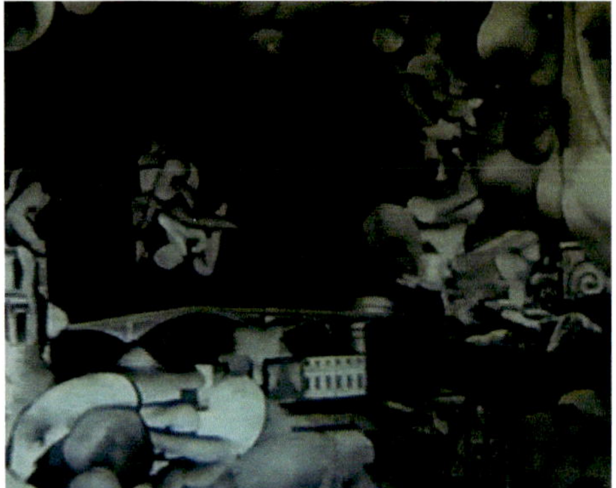

Figure II.5 a/b Norman Rubington, dir., *The Birth of Venus*, 1958. Scans from original film reel. Courtesy of the Norman Rubington Estate.

films, although in the 1980s Benayoun did express his admiration for animator Terry Gilliam's Rubington-like contributions to the British sketch comedy television series *Monty Python's Flying Circus* (1969–74).[21]

In 1961, the year that Jean Desvilles released his collage and cut-out animation short *Une Semaine de Bonté*, based on the Max Ernst collage novel of the same name from 1934, Benayoun published his most important statement on animation – and also the most extensive commentary on animation to ever emerge from the Surrealist movement – the book *Le Dessin animé après Walt Disney*.[22] Taking the format of an international anthology of recent animation with a more limited historical view, Benayoun analysed American and European animated features and shorts accompanied by brief nods to Asian animation in China and Japan. He discusses an enormous number of animators, animated characters and animated films from around the world, while giving less attention

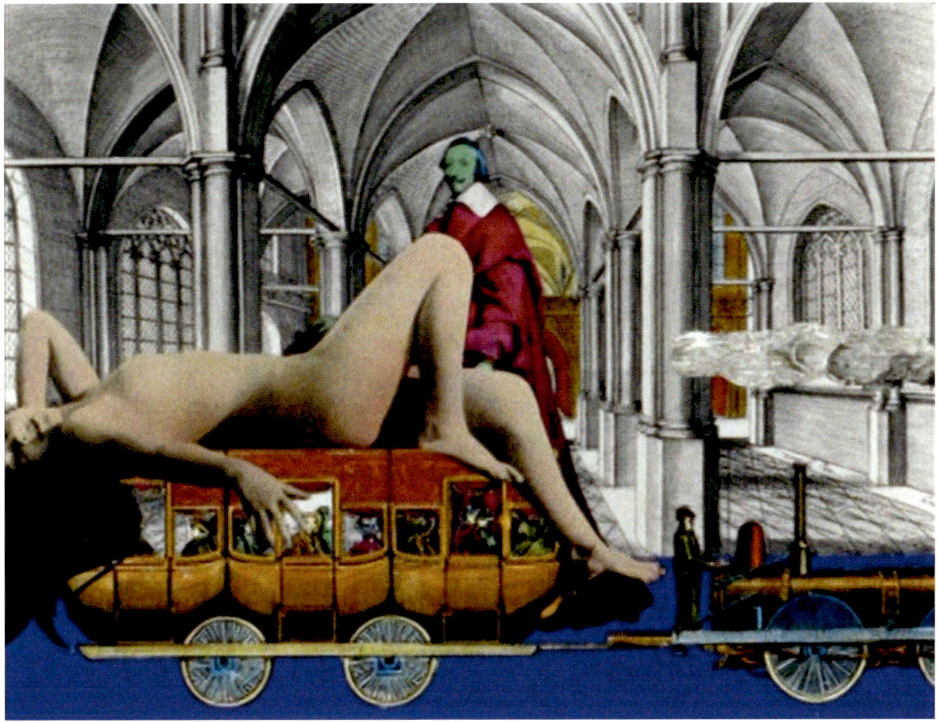

Figure II.6 Terry Gilliam, Opening animation sequence from Monty Python's Flying Circus, *Whither Canada?*, October 1969.

to different animation techniques and technologies such as pixilation, the stop-motion animation of live actors. Hailing the contemporary cartoon as a poetic form of art that permits a unique continuity between thought and realization for the animator, Benayoun claimed that in the 1960s, animators must be fully versed in the history of the avant-garde if they are to seize the opportunity for independent rather than Taylorist animation production.[23]

Although surrealism is not Benayoun's primary concern in the book, he did highlight films that bear a close connection to surrealism, such as Jean Jabely's *Ballade chromo* (1957), which featured words and collages from Prévert. Jiří Trnka, Stephen Bosustow (UPA), Chuck Jones, Disney, McLaren, Avery, Alexeïeff and Grimault are the focus of Benayoun's analysis, as are the intertwined sadism and eroticism of popular cartoons. Yet, Benayoun also revels in an inclusive discourse that considers the work of American animators such as Mary Ellen Bute and John Hubley (Benayoun does not mention Faith Hubley) alongside that of John Halas and Joy Batchelor (England), Wan Laiming (China), Lev Atamanov (Soviet Russia) and many others. Declaring the innate affinity of animation and the avant-garde, Benayoun's book arrests the eye with striking visual comparisons between cartoons and surrealist artworks, such as the juxtaposition of a surrealist painting by Yves Tanguy with a still from Norman McLaren's *A Phantasy* (1952). According to Benayoun, surrealism and animation were made for one another.

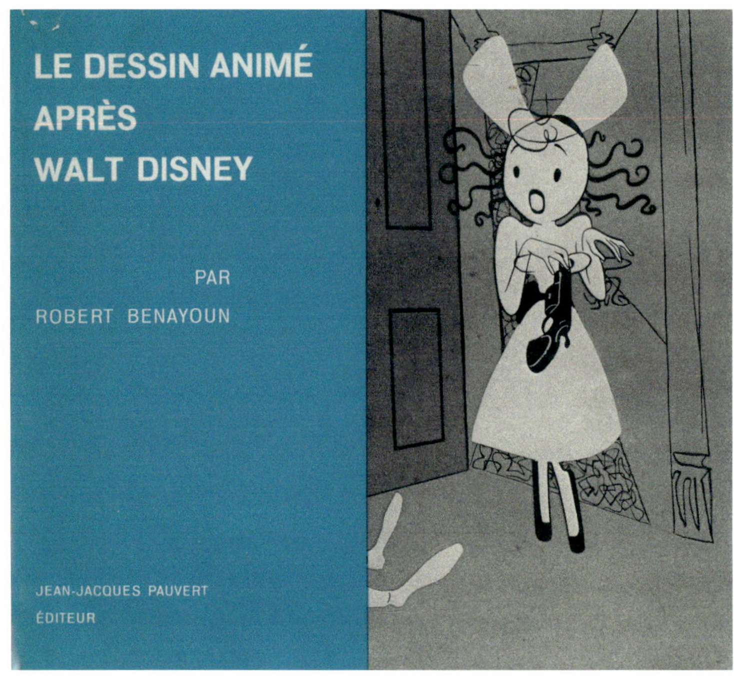

Front cover

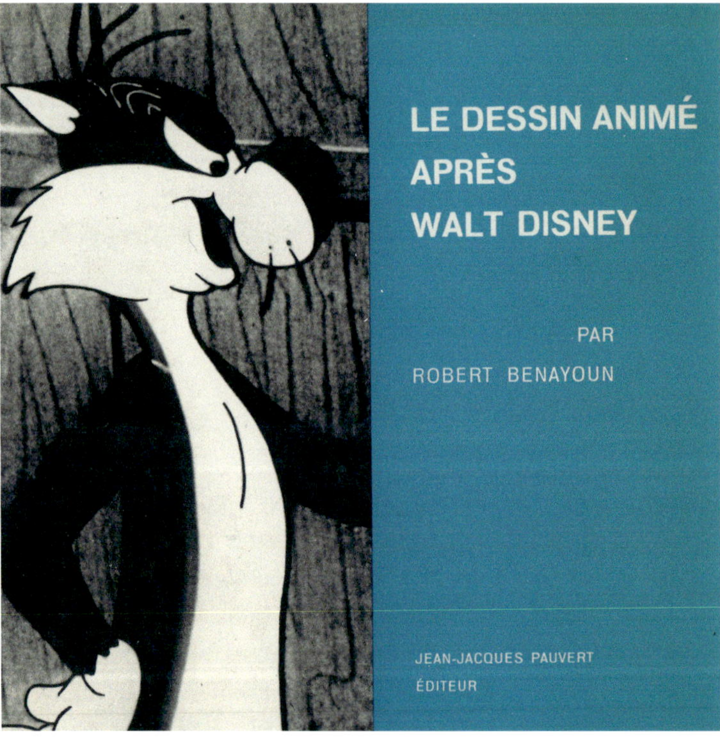

Back cover

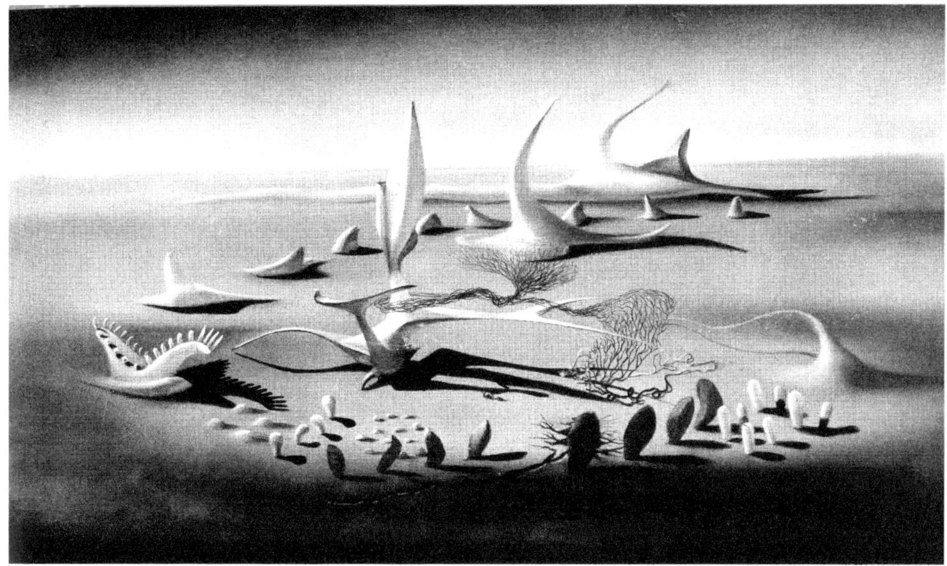

A Phantasy, de Norman Mac Laren (1952)

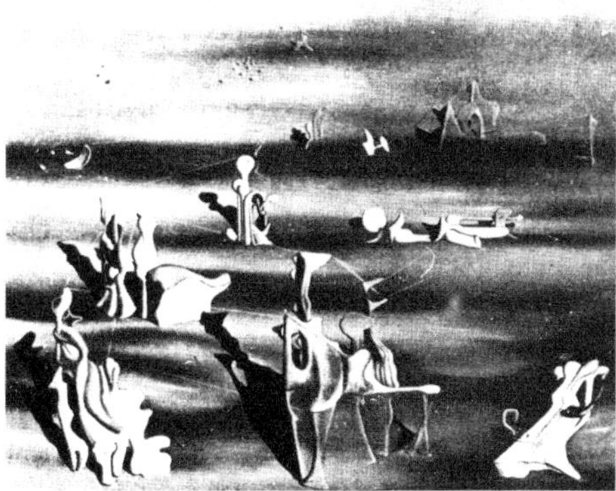

Yves Tanguy : Le temps entretenu (1939)

Figure II.8 Robert Benayoun, *Le Dessin animé après Walt Disney* (Paris: Jean-Jacques Pauvert, 1961), 65. Author's collection.

Figure II.7 a/b Robert Benayoun, *Le Dessin animé après Walt Disney* (Paris: Jean-Jacques Pauvert, 1961), front and back covers. Author's collection.

Notes

1 Kristoffer Noheden, *Surrealism, Cinema, and the Search for a New Myth* (Cham: Palgrave Macmillan, 2017), 163.

2 On Jordan, see R. Bruce Elder, *Dada, Surrealism, and the Cinematic Effect* (Waterloo: Wilfrid Laurier University Press, 2013), 433–8, 488–506.

3 Ulrich Lehmann, 'Assimilation: Objects; Commodities; Fashion', in *A Companion to Dada and Surrealism* (Boston, MA: Wiley-Blackwell, 2015), 432–4. See also Van Norris, '"Interior Logic": The Appropriation and Incorporation of Popular Surrealism into Classical American Animation',

in *The Unsilvered Screen: Surrealism on Film*, eds. Graeme Harper and Rob Stone (London and New York: Wallflower Press, 2007), 75–7.

4 Jorgelina Orfila and Francisco Ortega Grimaldo, 'Fantasyland or Wackyland?: Animation and Surrealism in 1930s America', *Journal of Surrealism and the Americas* 11, no. 1 (20 September 2020): 15.

5 'Voyez/ne voyez pas', *L'Âge du cinéma*, no. 4–5 (August–November, 1951): 2. In 1957, Disney visited Dalí in Spain and discussed a collaboration on an animated version of *Don Quixote*, a project that was never realized. An animated sequence from Dante's *Inferno* was also considered. *Impressions de la haute Mongolie (Hommage à Raymond Roussel)* (1976), a documentary by Salvador Dalí and José Montes-Baquer, includes animated sequences. *Dalí & Film*, ed. Matthew Gale (New York: Museum of Modern Art, 2007), 26, 194. Elliott H. King, *Dalí, Surrealism and Cinema* (Harpenden: Kamera, 2007), 7, 88, 91.

6 Richard Walter, '*L'Âge du cinéma*, entre nostalgie assumée et lendemains rêveurs', *La Revue des revues*, 1, 65 (2021): 66–85.

7 Jacques B. Brunius, 'Stéréoscopique et en couleurs', *L'Âge du cinéma*, 6 (1952): 25. Brunius briefly invokes Mickey Mouse in his book on avant-garde film. Jacques B. Brunius, *En marge du cinéma français* (Paris: Arcanes, 1954), 183.

8 Ado Kyrou, *Le Surréalisme au cinéma* (Paris: Arcanes, 1953), 109. Note that the 1963 edition of Kyrou's book by Le Terrain Vague added text to the 'Drawn Beings' chapter on the following subjects, listed in order of appearance throughout the book: the surrealist poetry of phantasmagorias and magic lanterns; Karel Zeman; William Hurtz; John Hubley; Saul Bass; Władysław Nehrebecki; Richard William; and the collage films of Stan VanDerBeek, Jan Lenica, Walerian Borowczyk, Carmen D'Avino and others. The 1963 edition also discussed McLaren's animated films in relation to 'animated sound' (34–5). Ado Kyrou, *Le Surréalisme au cinéma*, 2nd edn (Paris: Terrain Vague, 1963).

9 Kyrou, *Le Surréalisme au cinéma*, 112.

10 Kyrou, *Le Surréalisme au cinéma*, 110.

11 Kyrou, *Le Surréalisme au cinéma*, 110.

12 Kyrou, *Le Surréalisme au cinéma*, 110. Prévert wrote two other scenarios for animated shorts with Grimault: *Le Diamant* (1970) and *Le Chien mélomane* (1973). See also Michael Richardson, *Surrealism and Cinema* (New York: Berg, 2006), 45–60.

13 Georges Ribemont-Dessaignes, 'Printemps, surréalisme, et cinéma', *L'Écran français*, 45 (8 May 1946): 7.

14 André Breton with Gérard Legrand, *L'Art magique* [1957] (Paris: Adam Biro, 1991), 248.

15 Ado Kyrou, *Amour-érotisme et cinéma* (Paris: Le Terrain Vague, 1957), 271–2.

16 Kyrou, *Amour-érotisme et cinéma*, 274.

17 Kyrou, *Amour-érotisme et cinéma*, 274.

18 Robert Benayoun, 'Bilan du nouveau dessin animé', *Positif*, 12 (Nov–Dec 1954): 17.

19 Robert Benayoun, *L'Anthologie du non-sens* (Paris: Jean-Jacques Pauvert, 1957), 359–67.

20 Alain Joubert, *Le Cinéma des surréalistes* (Paris: Maurice Nadeau, 2018), 77, 202. Robert Benayoun, *Le mystère Tex Avery: biographie* (Paris: Éditions du Seuil, 1988), 59. Robert Benayoun, *Le Rire des surréalistes* (Paris: La Bougie du Sapeur, 1988), 94, 96.

21 Robert Benayoun, *Les dingues du nonsense, de Lewis Carroll à Woody Allen* (Paris: Seuil, 1984), 267–73.

22 Robert Benayoun, *Le Dessin animé après Walt Disney* (Paris: Jean-Jacques Pauvert, 1961).

23 Benayoun, *Le Dessin animé*, 6–7. On Desvilles' *Une Semaine de Bonté* (1961), see Arnaud Maillet, 'From Max Ernst's Collage to Jean Desvilles' Cut-out Animation: Transposing *Une semaine de bonté* to Film', in *Surrealism and Film after 1945*, 92–107.

Chapter 7

Parker Tyler's 'Film as the Problem of Space Control'

Ann Reynolds

In 1954, the critic and poet Parker Tyler published an essay in *Art Digest* entitled 'The Film Sense and the Painting Sense', one of several essays he wrote about film's capacity to transform one's experience of works of art – and confound the alleged distinctions among media – and, ultimately, its potential to fundamentally alter one's relation to the world.[1] Ostensibly, the essay addresses the affinities between film and painting, but Tyler's true subject is, in fact, what initially appears to be just an expedient device for linking the two: animation.

Tyler begins the essay by stating that the movie camera, beyond its more mundane ability to faithfully record real life in motion, can animate lifeless objects and two-dimensional still images: 'A rudimentary plastic design such as Mickey Mouse or a highly complex one such as Bosch's *Garden of Delight* are "stills", inanimate subjects, which the movie camera – as we have seen – can approach as raw material, just as though they were life itself.'[2] When Tyler turns to a discussion of several sequences from Richard Lyford's documentary *The Titan: Story of Michelangelo* (1951; henceforth *The Titan*) that feature two of the artist's sculptural works, *Bacchus* and the recumbent Medici Chapel figures, his argument markedly deepens into a description of the actively interpretative capacities of such cinematic animations.[3] The camera's ability here to choose not only what spectators see and in what order but *how* they see it – what Tyler calls *controlled spectatorship* – manifests in two primary qualities of the images it produces: their black-and-white tonalities and their rectangular shape.[4] These qualities, which presumably limit the camera's capacity to faithfully – and passively – record the physical world in front of it, can, alternatively, enhance the camera's ability to actively generate a new world of sensation to take its place. Dramatic images of inanimate figures rendered as if in motion elicit embodied emotion within the viewer: 'Signally, too, with the *Bacchus*, the movie camera "narrated" a way-of-looking that was a way-of-feeling the rectangularly isolated views achieving a special plastic effect that would not have been thus precise without the camera's use.'[5]

The *Bacchus* sequence in *The Titan* opens with a still image of a sketch by Michelangelo of a Bacchus figure – itself suggestive of the shared roots of sculpture, painting, and

---

This essay is drawn, in part, from my forthcoming book *Imagining an Altogether: Cinema, Surrealism, and New York 1940–1970*.

animation in drawing – that soon fades to an establishing shot of Michelangelo's *Bacchus* standing amidst other figurative sculpture in Florence's Bargello Museum. This shot is succeeded by a much tighter framing shot of the *Bacchus*' upper torso that effectively releases the sculpture from its physical surroundings; the sculpture's now isolated, dramatically lit, white marble surfaces provide a striking contrast to an ambiguous deep black background. Then the camera begins to move to the left and then to the right, generating a series of quick, wide, curving shots, from the figure's head and left shoulder around to its extended right arm and hand, which grasps a kylix, and then back to its head; at moments the camera allows the *Bacchus*' head to almost drop out of the frame completely. Although some of these shots are quite rapid and sweeping, they all manage to maintain a tight focus on the *Bacchus*. As a result, the figure's only spatial frame of reference becomes the limit terms established by the moving camera's lens and the resulting image's quadrangular frame. Cumulatively, the attenuated absence of a defined background, the relative rapidity of the camera's movements, and the tight focus of its lens that reduces the sculpture to a sequence of fragments, underscored at moments when the figure comes perilously close to disappearing from view, create the illusion that the *Bacchus*, not the camera, is moving, turning away from or coming to meet it in a series of somewhat loopy, lurching or swaying gestures. The cumulative effect is of giddy drunkenness, a state totally appropriate to the sculpture's subject, and one that also translates into an equivalent spectatorial experience of both seeing and, perhaps, feeling as if in a state of disequilibrium.[6]

It is important to note that the *Bacchus*' 'movements' are in no way life-like. They are clearly the result of the film-maker's efforts to bring the sculpture 'to life' on the camera's own terms and in terms of its two-dimensional counterpart, painting, a 'conception of film not as a representation of a three-dimensional world in terms that (like those of sculpture and bas-relief) remind us literally of the third dimension, but rather in terms that remind us literally of the two dimensions of painting'.[7] Michelangelo's *Bacchus* moves and is moving because of the film-maker's abilities to temporarily animate it through the two-dimensional terms of the camera's image field. The effect is one of attempted escapes from and returns to these medium-specific terms, transforming one's sense of both, and producing emotional content and a particular 'way-of-feeling' in the process.

Tyler relished images produced by the high-speed still camera and the movie camera because they revealed or animated what he elsewhere calls unexpected 'sculptures in time', which, in turn, narrated analogous feelings and interpretations, without regard for the presumed realities of their ostensible subjects.[8] Still life, such as Michelangelo's *Bacchus*, when animated by the camera's moving frame, operates in terms of the basic rules of animation proper and not those of the so-called real world:

> A distinctive aspect of the animated cartoons is the absence of motion in the background in contrast with the cavorting figure in front. We sense the background simply as a drawing. It is likewise with the blank ground of drawing-paper or canvas on which the designs of artists, through the film, acquire the magic attribute of 'organic growth'. Yet this blank 'background' is not a void but a physical plane surface limited by edges; in this sense, the sides of the paper are equivalent to the

> sides of a film frame as projected. In the old days when animation was becoming popular, a clown used to be born illusorily from an ink bottle in lines of ink, and the humor of it was his dependence on his creator for things to use, a world to live in, and sometimes even ground to stand on. This was a comic version of the myth of divine creation and like all myths its elements reverberate in time and space … the world is shown as *man*-created, and this is what, in our urban civilization, the visible world often is.[9]

Tyler's seemingly eclectic constellation of references to animated shorts by Walt Disney and Max Fleischer's *Out of the Inkwell* series, and to documentaries on artists – called art films at the time – were probably prompted by his viewing experiences at the Museum of Modern Art's Sunday Night Film Shows, which juxtaposed art films, animated cartoons and surrealist films within a single evening's viewing.[10] However, Tyler provides his own unifying logic and set of potential outcomes for their '*man*-created worlds': they can dictate life's terms for viewers who offer no resistance, but, as something made, they also have the potential to be remade according to individual or collective needs and desires. Tyler claims that certain 'imaginative workers in the experimental-film field', such as Jean Cocteau, have offered insights into this situation. Cocteau's 1930 film *The Blood of a Poet* includes numerous instances of simple cinematic animation. For example, the main character's inadvertent superimposition of a 'living' animated mouth from his charcoal drawing of a face onto his own hand as he tries to erase the mouth and, eventually, his transfer of this mouth onto an armless plaster copy of a classical female figure, which then transforms into a living woman. The film's entire *mise en scène* is also a manifestation of Cocteau's imagination, each element dictated by his exploitation of the material conditions and limitations of film itself, its own artifice as an equally enclosing quadrangular two-dimensional world. But, for Tyler, the even larger stakes involve how Cocteau generates this world through a 'basic odyssey: that of the human creator'. This odyssey takes the main character through a sequence of 'man-made' interior spaces: plunging through a mirror onto a narrow corridor of closed sequential 'interiors like small stage-sets, visible to him only through a keyhole', a return through this mirror to his studio, then to a larger interior courtyard, which becomes a small theatre, complete with audience, which eventually opens up into a spatially ambiguous black void delimited solely by the filmic image's rectangular frame, through which the statue/woman moves.

Tyler describes this final space as 'cosmic', where 'the hero's destiny, and implicitly that of all artists, is finally transmuted into glory by the artistic instinct'.[11] Tyler's conception of Cocteau's filmic space as a potentially cosmic space derives, in part, from his long-held desire for movies 'to focus attention on the dream world *as a place*; that is, as a three-dimensional theatre like the physical world held in common by everyone but individualized like artistic vision itself and holding another mental dimension, that of the fabulous and impossible'.[12] In his writings, he frequently characterizes *The Blood of a Poet* as 'the crux of the avant-garde viewpoint' because it achieves this.[13]

In Maya Deren's 1945 *A Study in Choreography for Camera*, Tyler's second example of a cinematic odyssey, the artist hero has now internalized a 'man-made' world that

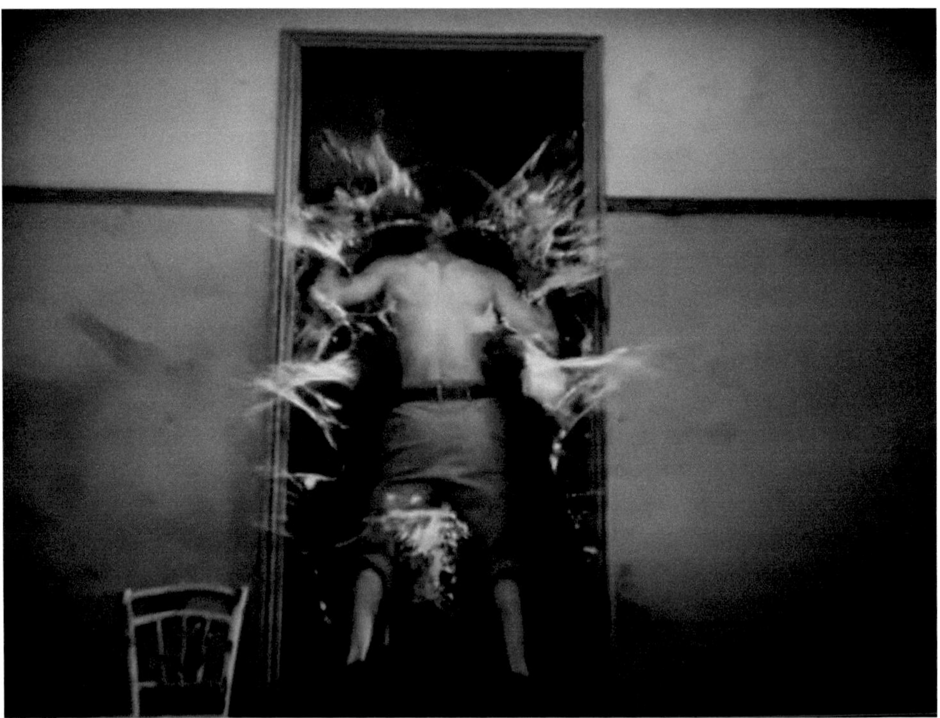

Figure 7.1 Jean Cocteau, dir., *The Blood of a Poet*, 1933. Tyler's caption: 'Cocteau created a basic Odyssey: that of the human creator'. 'The Film Sense and the Painting Sense', *Art Digest*, 29, no. 10 (15 February 1954): 12.

contrasts with the background filmic 'reality' through which he moves. As Tyler describes it, when this artist, the dancer Talley Beatty:

> begins his movement in a wood, continues it without the least interruption as the scene shifts to a private interior, then to a hall in a museum, then to another interior and back to the wood, reaching his climax with a triumphant sense of dance-flow, we have an active, self-contained figure seen before a background whose seemingly arbitrary and sudden mutations are independent of his movements and of which he seems quite unaware.[14]

Tyler attributes what he describes as Beatty's confidence in his individual 'integrity in a changeable environment' to the artist's creation of his own internal space, based on his own rhythm in time, which he consistently follows. 'The "ground" he assumes', states Tyler, 'is the basic, limited ground which every artist uses.'[15] Yet in his efforts to find equilibrium within this ground, Beatty also functions like an animated character, actively generating, and operating within, his own imagined world, in contrast to – or even in defiance of – his background. Tyler offers the analogy of the short-sighted cartoon character Mr Magoo, who is blissfully unaware of the constant dangers in the world he physically moves through, as he confidently imagines another that conforms to his own

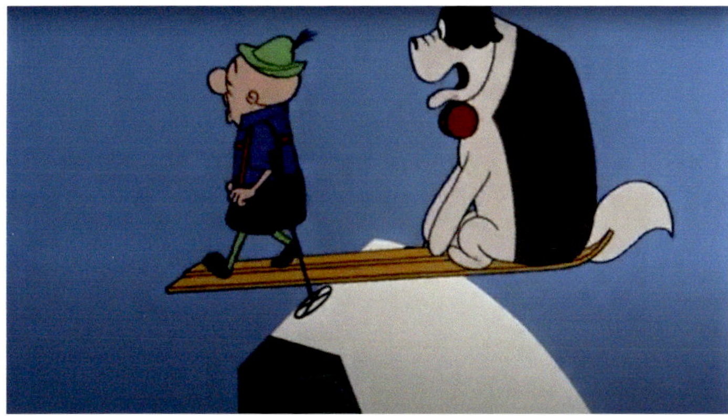

Figure 7.2 Pete Burness, dir., *Magoo Goes Skiing*, 1954. Published as an example of 'Adventure of the individual in space' in Tyler's 'The Film Sense and the Painting Sense', *Perspectives USA*, 11 (Spring 1955): n.p.

internal sense of the world, and which the background or 'outside' world miraculously accommodates, usually at the very last minute.

In a longer version of 'The Film Sense and the Painting Sense', published about one year later, Tyler had an opportunity to add discussions of films by many more contemporary US experimental film-makers, such as Sidney Peterson, Curtis Harrington, James Broughton, Kenneth Anger, Willard Maas, Stan Brakhage and Gregory Markopoulos. Although he added this material towards the end of the essay, just before the penultimate paragraph, and made relatively few changes to the original text, his additions shift the primary focus of his argument from the relationship between film and painting to one between film and space. Retrospectively, Tyler directly acknowledged this shift by adding in pencil at the top of the first page of an offprint of the 1955 version: 'new title: "Film as the Problem of Space Control"'.[16] The most obvious marker within the text itself is Tyler's selection of a new progenitor who was neither a relative contemporary nor a film-maker:

> I should say that the recently prominent experimental school in the United States is notably 'Proustian' as well as expressionist and surrealist, inasmuch as the quasi-autobiographic hero or heroine is usually the psychic as well as the optical center of the screen. As Proust seems to gather space about his private person and modulate it with the music of his heartbeat and his very optic nerve, so in principle does the American experimentalist compose space – with the screen rectangle as his visible limit – about a sort of cosmic adventurer who is the self.[17]

Through this analogy, an individual internalization of space, which Tyler evocatively calls an 'atmosphere of subjectivity', not only drives the world-making, it proceeds from a way of feeling that produces a way of seeing mental, and eventually textual or visual, images, and not from *a priori* images that dictate both things, as in the *Bacchus* footage.[18] One could say that this way of feeling as a way of seeing has been shaped by the camera and by the types of imagery it can produce, but now it has been internalized and belongs to the makers and viewers of images who shape their own personal mental images, what they see *and* seek to capture on film, and ultimately their attitude towards life itself. Tyler states:

> The film strip rotating swiftly through the camera projects a limited perspective no matter how often its viewpoint may be changed: this perspective is equivalent to each man's mental image of the world and of those numerous, more or less fanciful, perspectives which inevitably are everyone's subjective possession – the way you or I or someone else 'sees life' at some given moment. It is when someone's internal assurance of existence tends to vanish, to represent 'spacelessness', that the appetite for life and the future also vanishes.[19]

So for Tyler, when Cocteau's hero plunges into the mirror/pool, or Beatty confidently and consistently assumes and sustains the rhythmic momentum of his own internalized, choreographed space, or Mr Magoo blithely steps toward the end of a pair of skis precariously balanced on a narrow cliff and secured only by the counterweight of his St Bernard, they signal an 'absolute faith in the future', despite a contrary or even perilous 'reality' that might surround them.[20] This spatial attitude provides a stark contrast to what Tyler calls the plot-driven, 'frantic drive of Hollywood cameras to "eat up" space on their recurrent "trips to the moon"', which 'directly reflects the general commercial viewpoint toward space as a jungle, a *chaos*, whether void or occupied. Art, on the contrary, is produced by the controlling principles of a *cosmos*, which underlies all casual aspects of confusion and variety and represents destiny as opposed to chance, form as opposed to formlessness'.[21]

Two Disney films, *Three Caballeros* (1945) and *The Clown of the Jungle* (1947), attracted the attention of several of Tyler's contemporaries as they also grappled with describing problems of space control in films made during and soon after the Second World War. The animated short *The Clown of the Jungle* stars Donald Duck as a photographer hoping to capture images of the ever-elusive exotic tropical birds in an unspecified Latin American rainforest. Throughout, his efforts are thwarted by the 'clown' of the jungle, the fantastical Aracuan bird. The film opens with a slow pan of a colourful if muted landscape accompanied by a generic bucolic soundtrack. A large white heron-like bird flies across this background landscape at a more rapid, looping pace than the camera pan till it lands on a branch, and the camera then follows its gaze to a group of hummingbirds who sing in barbershop quartet-like harmony, using a flower as a microphone. The film's narrator describes this scene as charming, but as the camera resumes its pan, he expresses even greater interest in 'a treat that awaits us behind every twig and vine': the Aracuan. Although the Aracuan initially appears in the frame reclining on a branch, smoking a cigar and playing with a yo-yo, as the pan threatens to pass beyond him, he leaps up and begins to dart across the branch, seemingly chasing the camera's movements. But once the camera ceases to move, he takes control, moving rapidly around its fixed rectangular edges in ways that both underscore and defy its logic by disappearing and then popping his head in and out of the frame's four edges in rapid succession while constantly repeating a simple, pseudo-Latin-inflected tune.

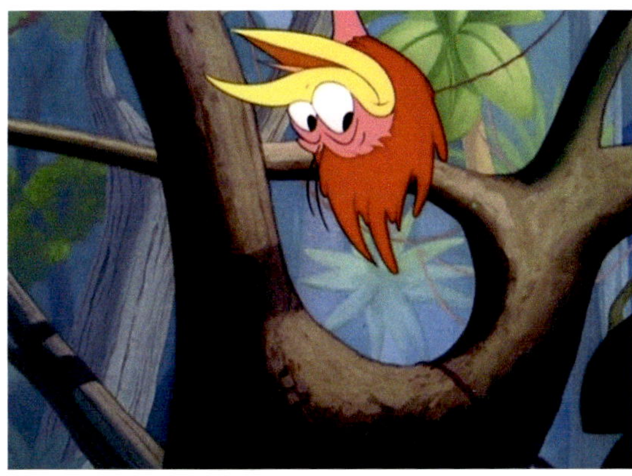

Figure 7.3 Walt Disney, dir., *The Clown of the Jungle*, 1947.

Eventually, the Aracuan disrupts Donald's concentration and destroys his equipment, but most of all, through his constant movement and the movements he generates in Donald's ostensible subjects and his self-serving alterations of the space's ostensible terms, he renders the jungle and its inhabitants 'inauthentic' to the eyes of an outsider and impossible to photograph. For example, he rapidly crosses Donald's camera's line of vision while the latter is attempting to photograph the only still bird that he has encountered – one that is asleep – and then he inserts himself into a group of hummingbirds that Donald is attempting to photograph, transforming them into a troupe of 'Russian' dancers who follow his choreographic lead. As the conflict between the two birds escalates – after all, Donald is also a bird – the Aracuan draws a door onto a rockface to escape into an unseen space, which Donald unsuccessfully tries to access, and then emerges from a previously non-existent trapdoor in the jungle floor. In the end, a defeated Donald internalizes the Aracuan's movements, song and relation to the film's spatial terms, becoming the only other figure to break the fourth wall by popping in and out of the frame, walking along the black iris, and shrinking with it at the film's conclusion. In doing so, such apparent signs of plot-driven conflict between characters are revealed to be signifiers of different relationships to the space of animation. Not just a jungle chaos, but potentially a cosmos – a coherent if dissociated world born of the artist creator and the clown of the inkwell.

The film critic Barbara Deming identifies the Aracuan as the sole character in *The Three Caballeros* who dictates the terms of his own world by 'dissociating himself from the world the film has been creating, giving it the wink'.[22] But in this feature-length film his actions are dwarfed by a dizzying array of animation techniques, including footage of actual actors and landscapes shared with animated characters and backdrops that generate a much more complex and relentless visual chaos and spatial discontinuity, and which sometimes abandon the film's ostensible hero, Donald Duck, to a black void, seemingly situated nowhere at all. As a result, Deming concludes, 'What we can learn of Latin America from *The Three Caballeros* is less than little. But what we can learn of where *we* live is a great deal. For it is through *this* world that, quite unknown to Mr. Disney, Donald makes his voyage.'[23] According to Deming, 'The bulk of films today display – though in less enthusiastic fashion – this formlessness.'[24] Quests ultimately emptied of meaning, 'too psychopathically chaotic … as much an ordeal to view as a real nightmare is to undergo'.[25] Deming claims that '*The Three Caballeros* is not Disney's private monster, his personal nightmare. It is a nightmare of these times.'[26] In another review, she notes that Donald Duck's pursuits always fail, as the coherent 'worlds unto themselves' these pursuits require are only 'a hallucination', like those constituted in contemporary advertisements.[27] Here Deming uses Tyler's term 'hallucination' for the superficial, passive waking dreams Hollywood offers; they are not the dream worlds that Tyler advocates or that artists he champions actively create.[28]

In 'Hollywood's Terror Films', Siegfried Kracauer describes Disney's *Three Caballeros* as 'show[ing] us a universe torn to pieces as though it had been hit by a cluster of atomic bombs. That shattered universe is symptomatic of the way we feel about the world now around us, as Barbara Demining has suggested'.[29] In his first review published in English after arriving in New York in 1941, Kracauer had already distinguished between Disney's classic short cartoons, which 'sought to build a world which had as little to do with ours as Mickey with a living mouse; his creatures strolled through a cartoonist's space in a time which, like the space itself, spread or shrank to his liking', and what he perceives in *Dumbo* and more recent feature-length films to be a reinforcement of a more conventional reality and a too-ready submission to current social conventions, which could be better photographed than drawn.[30]

Tyler never wrote about *Three Caballeros* or *The Clown of the Jungle*, but his assessments of animation and Hollywood's attitude toward space were fully in line with those of his contemporaries. Each critic acknowledges the tension between figures and the spaces they are made to occupy and identifies heroes who inhabit their own internalized sense of reality regardless of the inconstancy or impositions of their surroundings – a divergence that may manifest as conflict for the viewer, but to which the hero is wilfully oblivious. Deming and Kracauer view this conflict in terms of Cold War paranoia or atomic devastation, Hollywood's distorted or chaotic spaces becoming projections of psychic trauma, whereas Tyler avoids discussing the broader terms of the 'backgrounds' from which his heroes are disencumbered. Most strikingly, he makes no reference to *The Titan*'s complicated history as a re-edited version of a 1940 film written, directed and primarily shot by Curt Oertel, entitled *Michelangelo – Das Leben eines Titanen*, one in a series of so-called 'patriotic' films Oertel made in Germany during the late 1930s.[31] Oertel does represent Michelangelo as an artist hero, often through dramatic animations of individual works, but as Oertel's chosen genre was documentary, and his frame of reference was Nazi Germany, Michelangelo and his art are meant to glorify the fascist state. The aims of Robert Flaherty and the others involved in reshaping the film in the late 1940s were also hagiographic, even though their intended audiences and message were shaped by Cold War humanism.[32]

In both versions of 'The Film Sense and the Painting Sense', Tyler frames his consideration of *The Titan* in relation to other 'art', animated and surrealist films, and in terms of shared manifestations of alternate visual worlds. His analysis is underscored in the 1954 version by his pairing of five stills from *The Titan* with five stills from Deren's *A Study in Choreography for Camera*, both out of their original sequence, removing the former even further from its initial context.

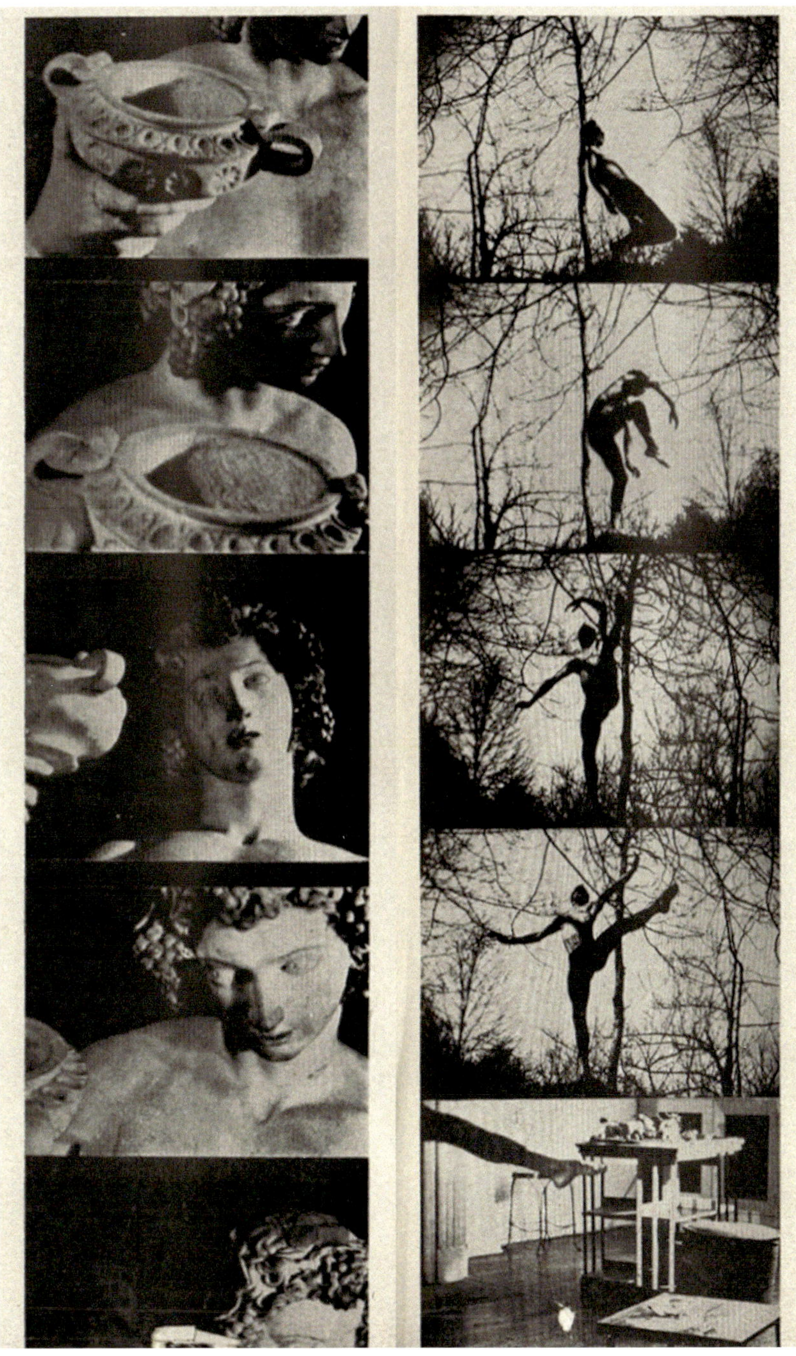

Figure 7.4 Richard Lyford, dir., *The Titan: Story of Michelangelo*, 1950, and Maya Deren, dir., *Study in Choreography for Camera*, 1945, as published in Tyler, 'The Film Sense and the Painting Sense', *Art Digest*, 29, no. 10 (15 February 1954): 10–11.

Tyler's way of looking situates the artifice of the original documentary and, most centrally, the shaping eye of the camera frame at the fore, aligning them with a surrealist approach to life, one that rewrites reality on its – and animation's – own terms.

Notes

1 By 1954, Tyler had been an active participant in New York cultural and intellectual circles for over fifteen years. He collaborated with Charles Henri Ford on the surrealist-identified magazine *View* (1940–1947), he published several volumes of poetry, two equally well-received books on Hollywood film, *The Hollywood Hallucination* (1944) and *Magic and Myth of the Movies* (1947), and one on Charlie Chaplin (1947); and he wrote articles and regular film and art reviews for a wide variety of journals such as *American Quarterly*, *ArtNews*, *Art Digest*, *Kenyon Review*, *Magazine of Art*, *The Nation*, *The Sewanee Review*, *Sight and Sound*, *Theatre Arts* and *View*.

2 Parker Tyler, 'The Film Sense and the Painting Sense', *Art Digest*, 29, no. 10 (15 February 1954): 10. Tyler is not the first to make this argument. It is a recurrent theme, especially in the early writing on film. Tyler was probably aware of some of this writing, although only through translation, but he rarely cites other film critics or theorists.

3 *The Titan: Story of Michelangelo*, directed by Richard Lyford, and produced by Ralph Alswang, Robert Flaherty and Robert Snyder, was screened at the Museum of Modern Art, New York (MoMA) in 1949, had a wider release in 1950 and won the Academy award for best documentary feature in 1951.

4 Tyler, 'Film Sense', 12. Italics in original. Tyler almost always subscribes agency to the camera and not to cinematographers or directors, as he is intent on describing the relationships established between actors and viewers via the camera's disembodied eye and its material terms. He also never mentions sound in this essay, as he is focused on making visual analogies between painting and film: 'The latter [the rectangular screen] was always an element of the movies' artistic function and was apt to operate best in the pre-talkie era since in the talkies the film often tends merely to photograph actors speaking, and to follow them about as though they were on a theatre stage … thereby destroying all opportunities for true cinematic composition in the "still" sense.' Tyler, 'Film Sense', 12. Tyler's avoidance of colour, both through his preponderant choice of black-and-white films as examples and his lack of reference to colour in the colour films he does discuss, is not equivalent as just over 50 per cent of films produced in the United States were made in colour by 1954, the year Tyler's article was published, whereas sound film, in contrast, was well established and practically ubiquitous by the mid-1950s. See Pam Cook ed. *The Cinema Book* (London: British Film Institute Publishing, 1985), 29.

5 Tyler, 'Film Sense', 12. Tyler is not the first to make the argument that the camera, as an active agent, can produce an emotional response in the spectator. See, for example, Maya Deren, 'Magic is New', *Mademoiselle* (22 January 1946): 180–1, 260–5.

6 This drunken effect is not solely the invention of the camera. Michelangelo's *Bacchus* has often been referred to as 'the drunken Bacchus' because of the figure's attributes, its somewhat precarious contrapposto stance, slack musculature and glazed facial expression. The narration accompanying this sequence describes the drunken Bacchic rites that Michelangelo's sculpture is meant to suggest and informs a viewer's sense of the significance of the figure's movements as generated by the camera.

7 Tyler, 'Film Sense', 12.

8 Parker Tyler, 'The Ivory Tower of Judo', *View*, 3, no. 1 (April 1943): 34.

9 Tyler, 'Film Sense', 27. Italics in original.

10 This series included three documentary films about art: *Michelangelo – Das Leben eines Titanen* (1940), directed by Curt Oertel and the source for *The Titan* (see endnote 31); *Italian Monuments and the War* (1948), which addresses the American Committee for the Restoration of Art Objects in Italy's reconstruction of frescoes damaged by the War; and *In Paradiso Terrestre* (1946), a film about cinematic techniques for analysing works of art; two surrealist films: Luis Buñuel and Salvador Dalí's *Un Chien andalou* (1929) and Germaine Dulac's *La Coquille et Le Clergyman* (1928); and *Hare-Raising Hare* (1945), an animated Bugs Bunny film. Press release, Sunday Night Film Shows, Museum of Modern Art, 30 January to 22 May 1949. https://www.moma.org/momaorg/shared/pdfs/docs/press_archives/1289/releases/MOMA_1949_0003_1949-01-07_490107-3.pdf/ MoMA also demonstrated its commitment to animation as a modern art form in other roughly contemporary exhibitions, such as 'UPA: Form in the Animated Cartoon', 1955. This exhibition's press release includes the supporting claim 'The first movies were drawings.' https://www.moma.org/documents/moma_press-release_325991.pdf?_ga=2.77825879.234392392.1683902115-806680238.1683902114/

11 Tyler, 'Film Sense', 27.

12 Tyler, 'Finding Freudism Photogenic', *Magic and Myth of the Movies* (New York: Henry Holt and Company, 1947), 116.

13 Tyler, 'The "Hollywood Hallucination" Rampant: An Introduction', in *The Three Faces of the Film*, revised edn (South Brunswick and New York: A.S. Barnes and Co., 1967), 14. In 'Dream Structure: The Basis of Experimental Film', Tyler claims that experimental films, such as *The Blood of a Poet*, are dedicated to mending the dream/reality split by viewing dreams 'as a means *through which the protagonists are able to recognize their ultimate desires*'. Italics in original. Tyler, *Three Faces*, 65. Tyler describes Cocteau's film in terms of surrealism throughout his writings, but most notably in 'The Movies as a Fine Art', *Partisan Review*, 24, no. 3 (Summer 1957): 422–7.

14 Tyler, 'Film Sense', 27. Hannah Durkin argues that Deren highlights Beatty's individual artistic skills as a dancer and equal collaborator on the film through the tension he creates between his independent movements in relation to the camera's movements. She attributes this deliberate independence to Deren's respect for Beatty as an artist and her desire to heighten his visibility as a Black artist. Although I am not so convinced by Durkin's characterization of Deren's representation of Beatty – Deren seems to use Beatty more than she collaborates with him – Durkin's careful reading of the film, and particularly the moments when Beatty's awareness of where he is in space and in relation to the camera become clear, such as when his reflection and gaze are captured in a full-length mirror, points to how Tyler's reading of the film is agenda-driven, as he fails to mention such moments that would compromise his argument about Beatty's discrete, internalized sense of an alternate world. Hannah Durkin, 'Cinematic "Pas de Deux": The Dialogue between Maya Deren's Experimental Filmmaking and Talley Beatty's Black Ballet Dancer in *A Study in Choreography for Camera* (1945)', *Journal of American Studies*, 47, no. 2 (May 2013): 385–403.

15 Tyler, 'Film Sense', 27.

16 Parker Tyler Papers, Harry Ransom Center, Box 58.1. All further references to these papers are cited as Tyler Papers, HRC. Tyler's proposal for a new title eventually led to a 1971 book project entitled 'Film as the Conquest of Time and Space'; his retitled 'The Film Sense and The Painting Sense' essay constituted one chapter in this book. Tyler Papers, HRC, Box 16.2.

17 Tyler, 'The Film Sense and the Painting Sense', *Perspectives USA*, 11 (Spring 1955): 103.

18 Tyler, 'Film Sense', 1955, 103.

19 Tyler, 'Film Sense', 1955, 101–2.

20 Tyler, 'Film Sense', 1955, 101.

21 Tyler, 'Film Sense', 1955, 104. Italics in original.

22 Barbara Deming, 'The Artlessness of Walt Disney', *Partisan Review*, 12, no. 2 (Spring 1945): 228.

23 Deming, 'Artlessness of Disney', 226. Italics in original. The Spanish-language version of the film, *Saludos Amigos*, was released in 1942. For a discussion of this film's role in US Cold War cultural politics, see Antonio Pedro Tota, *The Seduction of Brazil: The Americanization of Brazil during World War II* (São Paulo: Conpanhia das Letras, 2000). Translated by Lorena B. Ellis (Austin: University of Texas Press, 2009). For a foundational text on Disney and Imperialism, see Ariel Dorfman and Armand Matterlart, *How to Read Donald Duck: Imperialist Ideology in the Disney Comic* [1971], trans. David Kunzle (New York: International General, 1975).

24 Deming, 'Artlessness of Disney', 228.

25 Deming, 'Artlessness of Disney', 230.

26 Deming, 'Artlessness of Disney', 226. Deming opens the essay with the question posed by Wolcott Gibbs when reviewing *The Three Caballeros* for *The New Yorker* – 'What Hath Walt Wrought' – to illustrate the collective sense of Disney as having gone awry and how changes in his work are symptomatic of much larger, psychosocial conditions. See Gibbs, 'What Hath Walt Wrought?', *The New Yorker* (10 February 1945); reprinted in Gibbs, *Backward Ran Sentences: The Best of Wolcott Gibbs from The New Yorker*, ed. Thomas Vinciguerra (New York, Berlin, London and Sydney: Bloomsbury, 2011), 598–9.

27 Barbara Deming, 'The Close-Up of Love', *Partisan Review*, 12, no. 3 (Summer 1945): 396.

28 Tyler, *The Hollywood Hallucination*, as quoted in Deming, 'The Close-Up of Love', 393. Her essay is, in part, of review of *The Hollywood Hallucination*.

29 Siegfried Kracauer, 'Hollywood's Terror Films: Do They Reflect an American State of Mind?' *Commentary*, 2, no. 2 (August 1946): 135. For an excellent analysis of Kracauer's argument, see Edward Dimendberg, 'Down These Seen Streets A Man Must Go: Siegfried Kracauer, "Hollywood's Terror Films", and the Spatiality of Film Noir', *New German Critique*, 89 (Spring-Summer 2003): 113–43.

30 Siegfried Kracauer, 'Dumbo', *The Nation*, 19 (18 November 1941): 463. Robert Feild, in his 1942 book on Disney, acknowledges this increasingly compromised balancing act between animation and reality: 'truth to nature is the goal though no photographic verisimilitude is required'. Such verisimilitude is transcended for 'a more powerful impression in a shorter time'. Robert Feild, *The Art of Walt Disney* (New York: The Macmillan Company, 1942), 242. Gibbs, on the other hand, when describing the humorous compressions of Donald Duck into a conventional Aztec design in *The Three Caballaros*, claims that this 'is the sort of thing Mr. Disney should be doing instead of pretending he is either Salvador Dali or the operator of a magic lantern'. Gibbs, 'What Hath Walt Wrought?', 599.

31 Oertel presented the first version of this film to an audience of art historians on 16 October 1938, at the Scala Cinema in Zurich. Due to positive reaction then and a bit later at the Venice Biennale, Oertel went on to produce a feature-length version in collaboration with Berlin Tobis; it premièred in Berlin on 15 March 1940. *Michelangelo: The Life of a Titan*, Wikipedia page, accessed 4 November 2019. The film was 'recovered' by Robert Snyder while he was serving in the Office of War Information during the Second World War. Tyler could have seen both films at MoMA, and, because of his friendship with Norman Borisoff, who wrote the script for the 1950 version, he would have known the film's history.

32 Arvind Rajagopal, 'Communicationism: Cold War Humanism', *Critical Inquiry*, 46 (Winter 2020): 353–80.

Chapter 8

Harry Smith and Lawrence Jordan in San Francisco, 1946–64

Jorgelina Orfila and Francisco Ortega

The animations that Harry Smith and Lawrence (Larry) Jordan produced in San Francisco between 1946 and 1964 bookend the lifespan of a community of multidisciplinary creators working at a time when surrealism was in the air.[1] San Francisco poets Philip Lamantia and Robert Duncan met André Breton in New York City in the early 1940s, and Lamantia contributed his work to the surrealist magazine *VVV*. Bay Area artist Richard Diebenkorn noted the prevalence of surrealist automatism and assemblage on the West Coast after the Second World War, linking the practice of assemblage to surrealist collages and *object trouvés*.[2] Art critic Peter Plagens considered assemblage art 'the product of a Bay Area bric-a-brac sensibility whose natural home was the city of San Francisco'.[3]

Smith's early direct animation style and Jordan's collage animations reflect this sensibility. In general, a surrealist attitude encouraged these artists to attempt the reconciliation of life and art, one whose influence extended 'beyond the rarefied circles of art'.[4] In hindsight, Smith and Jordan – like most of the San Francisco scene artists – acknowledged surrealism's ubiquitous influence in the community in interviews from later decades. This essay focuses on the performative character of the animations that Smith and Jordan created in San Francisco in the context of the dissemination of surrealist cultural strategies in postwar America. The spectatorial conditions for which Smith and Jordan intended their films differed from the paradigmatic theatrical screening of films before an absorbed audience. Their films were conceived as integral parts of performative events incorporated into music recitals or shown in public places where the film-maker, as projectionist, had the ability to improvisationally and creatively adapt the speed, duration and order of sequences.

Born in Portland, Oregon in 1923, Harry Smith – a musicologist, experimental film-maker, anthropologist, painter, linguist and occultist – spent his childhood in the Pacific Northwest. He lived primarily in Anacortes, Washington, where he recorded rituals and collected artefacts from the Lummi and Salish tribes of the Pacific Northwest. After studying anthropology at the University of Washington in the early 1940s he moved to Berkeley, where he intended to pursue his studies. Swayed by San Francisco's cultural life and jazz scene, he moved into the city in 1947. Jordan Belson, a painter turned abstract animator, was Smith's close acquaintance at this time. Both Smith and Belson collaborated with Frank Stauffacher and Richard Foster in the programming for *Art in*

Cinema, a San Francisco film society that from 1946 to 1954 organized programmes of independent and experimental film at the San Francisco Museum of Art (later, the San Francisco Museum of Modern Art).

Lawrence Jordan arrived in San Francisco when he was twenty years old. He was not able to meet Smith but got acquainted with and was heavily influenced by the poets of the San Francisco Renaissance movement, particularly Robert Duncan and his partner Jess Collins, known as Jess. Jordan was in close contact with Wallace Berman, Bruce Conner and other assemblage artists who used collage to express their disdain for rampant consumerism. Jordan's manifold activities reflect these artists' blurring of strict definitions in art practice. While mastering the use of the film camera. he also wrote poetry, painted and performed in plays written by his friends.[5] Stan Brakhage and Jordan met surrealist artist Joseph Cornell while working together in New York City in the mid-1950s. In 1965, Jordan would assist Cornell in the creation of his boxes and films.

Both Smith and Jordan were self-taught animators who used unsophisticated, unpretentious, low-tech, low-cost techniques (direct animation and stop-motion/collage/cut-out animation). Still, they needed cheap, accessible cameras and film. The affluent, post-Second World War American economy and the technological advances boosted by the consumer demand of industrial commodities provided what they needed: small-gauge (16-mm) portable film cameras and affordable film material. Nevertheless, the key to the success of this cinema was the wide availability of 16-mm projectors, which in the immediate postwar period were marketed and perceived as a means of communal engagement.

Film scholar Haidee Wasson has demonstrated that the user-driven, accessible, highly adaptable 16-mm projector promoted improvised and inventive modes of presentation that encouraged social interaction.[6] These projectors became dynamic media machines that allowed the user to stop, reverse or repeat parts of the film. Projectionists could influence the reception of the film and the intentions of the film-maker by controlling the speed, brightness and size of the image. The apparatus, Wasson concludes, 'invited a controlled, creative kind of techno-cultural performance'.[7] Small-gauge film technology buttressed the creation of animations conceived to be part of unique and ephemeral events that reflected the alternative lifestyles and hybrid art production of the San Francisco artists. These performances were the result of impromptu modes of working as they were conceived for 'the moment' and the reactions they would produce *in situ*.[8]

The exhibitory and spectatorial conditions afforded by small-gauge technology resembled those of early cinema. Screening could happen in ad-hoc locations where ambient noise and the public's exclamations, comments and general activity became part of the experience. These environments made evident the materiality of both the equipment (the crackling and whirring sounds of the projector) and the film (scratches, dust and hair on the celluloid; the breaks of edited splices, and even the smell of the film as it passed through the projector). Portable and widely distributed, the malleability of these 16-mm machines encouraged and allowed the San Francisco film-makers to transform the projection into a performance. Thanks to them, animation was not a passive media but could be conceived of as part of performative film events. Animation scholar William

Moritz relates that using a 'multi-speed projector, Smith could modulate the images to fit the jazz improvisations'.[9]

Smith identified neither as a film-maker nor animator, but rather as a painter – he called his films 'cinematic excreta'.[10] Artistically, Belson characterized the work Smith was doing at this time as 'being highly influenced by Surrealism and Dadaism'.[11] The two friends created drawings in the tradition of the surrealist exquisite corpse. At the same time, Belson and Smith's fascination with abstract film went hand in hand with their passion for jazz. They became bebop fanatics and strove to incorporate it into their art. In Smith's 1948 *Five Instruments with Optical Solo*, the animation was one of the instruments of a jazz band jam session. Bebop – a fast-tempo, highly improvisatory form of jazz, unsuitable for dance – uniquely befitted Smith's artistic practice. As Smith was exploring the incorporation of jazz in his art, he began creating what he called 'brain drawings', which were purportedly done without the interference of the mind. The technique is closely related to surrealist automatism. In 1965, Smith avowed that he removed his consciousness as much as possible from his work and allowed the material to dictate the animation.[12] In the extant hand-painted animations squares, rectangles and circles slide in and out of frame. The visual impression is nevertheless dominated by what is known as his batik technique, which involved: masking areas of the film; using the mouth as an atomizer to spray colour on it; gumming little forms on its surface; dyeing and soaking the celluloid in different substances; and drawing or scratching on its surface.[13]

Smith's and Jordan's early artistic careers frame the golden years of the artist community that thrived in the Fillmore district, the area where most San Francisco scene poets and artists would eventually live and work in the 1950s. Smith settled there in 1947, living in an apartment above Jimbo's Bop City, a waffle house that became an after-hours jazz club where local musicians and some of the best contemporary jazz players held jam sessions. Arriving in San Francisco in 1954, Jordan befriended Belson but did not meet

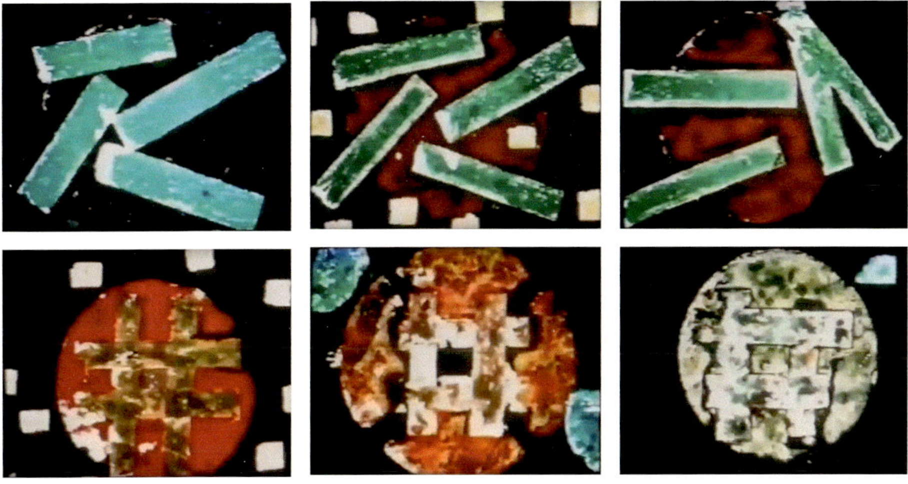

Figure 8.1 Harry Smith, dir., *Early Abstractions*, 1939–56.

Smith.[14] His mentors were Duncan and Jess. At the time of Jordan's arrival, the couple resided in a house/studio at the edge of the Fillmore district. In 1961, Jess loaned Jordan copies of Max Ernst's collage novels *La Femme 100 têtes* (1929) and *Une Semaine de Bonté* (1934). Having no funds to purchase the books for himself, Jordan photographed each page with a Rolleiflex camera and in the process discerned their potential to be transformed into 'moving images'. This inspired him to animate collages made from Victorian engravings – 'things that have been thrown away, definitely not valued' – that he purchased at local bookstores.[15] These stop-motion films included *The Centennial Exposition* (1961–4) and *Patricia Gives Birth to a Dream by the Doorway* (1961–4), which he would eventually combine into *Duo Concertantes.*

Jordan's stop-motion animation technique involved what for Ernst had been a stylistic choice: rephotographing the original collages, a step that helped to conceal the sutures between the collaged elements. These are the foundations of the surrealist technique that followed automatism in the early 1930s; the juxtaposition of disparate objects set on an outlandish background challenged observers' conditioned perception of reality and revealed the objects' latent potential for signification. Jordan linked the use of discarded Victorian engravings with ideas about redemption: 'there's a kind of working with ephemerality and mortality and there's a kind of making sense of eternal values out of very fragile, perishable goods'.[16] He explained that '[t]he basic act in my work is freeing the objects from the chains of convention and connotation. The whole thing is symbolic of the Surrealist philosophy … I believe strongly in the process of free association in combining image'.[17] His interest was in the images' effects on the public, who had to actively engage with works whose illogical appearance prompted the unconscious to attempt to make sense of them.[18] Nevertheless, the film-maker noted that '[t]o call the image surreal is fully inadequate, because the term should not be applied to art but to life … Surrealism is a way of life, the works that fall out of that way of life are accidental'.[19]

The painstaking character of the stop-motion technique allowed Jordan the freedom to, as he said, follow the material or 'find it half-way'.[20] He also explained that '[m]eticulousness is an act of freedom and through seeing and living in timelessness. It is an act of concentration and intense living'.[21] One of Jordan's main concerns was to create an alternative cinema structured around non-commercial systems for the distribution of art films, freed from both the art institutions and the film industry. In *Duo Concertantes* there are several allusions to the cinematic apparatus. Film historian P. Adams Sitney noticed early on the presence of a film-within-the-film in *Patricia Gives Birth to a Dream by the Doorway*.[22] The animated action is framed by the motionless figure of a woman, who, reclined in a doorway, looks towards the background. Close to the end of the film, a movie screen replaces one of the objects seen on the horizon. By representing the screening of an animation within the animation, the film-maker reminds the audience of the cinematic apparatus that sustains their experience of the film. In *The Centennial Exposition*, Jordan represented the projectionist in action when he introduced a man operating a mechanic contraption emitting flickering lights that controls the rotation of the moon.

Smith's and Jordan's animations and the San Francisco artists' multimedia performances can be construed as both a reaction against the film industry and as precursors of the

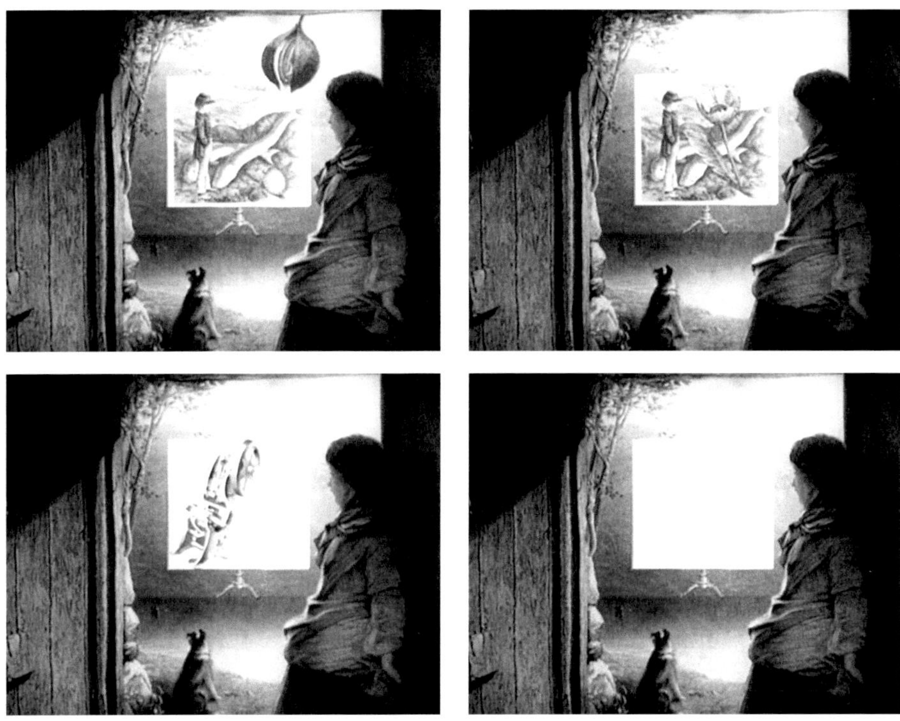

Figure 8.2 Larry Jordan, dir., *Patricia Gives Birth to a Dream by the Doorway*, 1964.

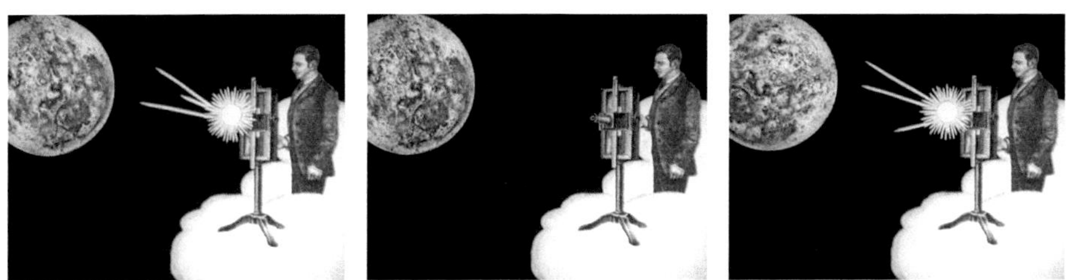

Figure 8.3 Larry Jordan, dir., *The Centennial Exposition*, 1964.

expanded cinema of the 1960s. The availability of 16-mm film and equipment also promoted the creation of artists' cooperatives independent from the circuit of commercial cinema for the distribution and exhibition of art films.

Notes

1 Sandra Leonard Starr, *Lost and Found in California: Four Decades of Assemblage Art* (Santa Monica, CA: James Corcoran Gallery, Shoshana Wayne Gallery, and Pense Gallery, 1988), 15, 17.

2 Starr, *Lost and Found in California*, 61.

3 Quoted in Gillian Whiteley, *Junk: Art and the Politics of Trash* (London: I.B. Tauris: 2011), 57.

4 Starr, *Lost and Found in California*, 16.

5 Michael Duncan and Kristin McKenna (eds), *Semina Culture: Wallace Berman and His Circle* (Los Angeles, CA: D.A.P./Santa Monica Museum of Art, 2015), 188–91.

6 Haidee Wasson, *Everyday Movies: Portable Film Projectors and the Transformation of American Culture* (Berkeley: University of California Press, 2020), 145.

7 Wasson, *Everyday Movies*, 173.

8 Richard Cándida Smith, *The Modern Moves West: California Artists and Democratic Culture in the Twentieth Century* (Philadelphia: University of Pennsylvania Press, 2009), 103.

9 William Moritz, 'Hy Hirsh and The Fifties: Jazz and Abstraction in Beat Era Film', *Kinetica*, 3 (2001): 3–8.

10 Harry Smith as cited in P. Adams Sitney, *Visionary Film: The American Avant-Garde, 1943–2000* (New York: Oxford University Press, 1979; revised 2nd edn 2002), 232.

11 Foye, 'Delineators', 90–6 at 92; Jordan Belson, '[Interview with] Jordan Belson' by Paula Igliori in *American Magus Harry Smith: A Modern Alchemist*, ed. Paola Igliori (New York: Inanout Press, 1996), 19–29. Also see John F. Szwed, Cosmic *Scholar: The Life and Times of Harry Smith* (New York: Farrar, Straus and Giroux, 2023).

12 Interview with Harry Smith in *Think of the Self Speaking: Harry Smith – Selected Interviews*, ed. Rani Singh (Seattle, WA: Elbow/Cityful Press, 1999), 58.

13 Belson commented that Smith used to call this technique 'batik' in the interview published in Igliori (ed.) *American Magus*, 23. Also see *Harry Smith: The Avant-Garde in the American Vernacular*, eds. Andrew Perchuk and Rani Singh (Los Angeles: Getty Research Institute, 2010), 115–27.

14 G. T. Collins, 'Larry Jordan's Underworld', *Animation Journal* (Fall 1997): 54–67.

15 Paul Karlstrom, 'Oral History Interview with Larry Jordan, 1995 Dec. 19–1996 July 30'. Smithsonian Online Virtual Archives https://www.aaa.si.edu/collections/interviews/oral-history-interview-larry-jordan-12216 (accessed April 2014).

16 Karlstrom, 'Oral History'.

17 Karlstrom, 'Oral History'.

18 Karlstrom, 'Oral History'.

19 Karlstrom, 'Oral History'.

20 Karlstrom, 'Oral History'.

21 Quoted in Robert Roussett and Cecile Starr, eds. *Experimental Animation: Origins of a New Art* (New York: Da Capo Press, 1988), 158.

22 Sitney, *Visionary Film*, 313.

Chapter 9

'Magical Dreams': The Surrealist Animations of Dušan Tomáš Marek in Czechoslovakia and Australia

Cheri Donaldson

When the history of Surrealism is written from an international standpoint, the work of many Czech artists will be included.

FRANTIŠEK ŠMEJKAL, 1990[1]

The timing and location of Dušan Tomáš Marek's birth was significant in his development as a surrealist. Born in Bohemia in 1926, he was a child during the cultural renaissance initiated by the 'President Liberator' Tomáš Garrigue Masaryk, following the First World War. The arts benefited from Masaryk's progressive agenda with its goal to internationalize Czechoslovakia. During the 1920s and 1930s, Prague became a centre for international exchange, a veritable nexus for creative and intellectual activity. Devětsil became the ideological heart of the Czech avant-garde in 1920 when the creative arts united under the auspices of poet Vitězslav Nezval and theorist Karel Teige. The film branch, the Klub za nový (club for new film) was established in 1927.[2] The Czech surrealist group formed in 1934 and Prague became the second largest hub of surrealism after Paris.[3]

At the first exhibition of his paintings in the late 1930s, when he was just thirteen years old, Marek declared himself a surrealist. Marek attended the UMPRUM (School of Art, Architecture and Design) in Prague during the late 1940s. Immersed in the zeitgeist of surrealism, Prague became a major influence on Marek's art, as it later did for Jan Švankmajer.[4] Another major influence for Marek was Teige, the 'architect' of Poetism and Constructivism who was considered 'one of the few whose stature in surrealism is comparable to André Breton'.[5] Teige was at the core of a 'friendly circle of young, independent artists', which appears to have included Marek, the painter Mikuláš Medek, and his wife, the photographer Emila Medková.[6]

Three-dimensional puppet animation emerged in the 1940s in Czechoslovakia and film production flourished there in 1946 when the Film and Television School of the Academy of Performing Arts (FAMU) opened.[7] An avid filmgoer, Marek would have seen puppet film animations by Jiří Trnka and Karel Zeman before leaving Czechoslovakia for

Australia in 1948. Giannalberti Bendazzi claims that 'great Czechoslovakian animation … was rooted in Prague'.[8] Having seen Marek's first animations, Australian experimental film-maker Arthur Cantrill states, 'the animation and design in these films is advanced – certainly not like the work of a beginner'.[9] It is probable that Marek was exposed to the work of Trnka and Zeman and was active in animation in some way before he left Czechoslovakia.

Unlike Marek, who largely worked alone in Australia and was financially unsupported, Trnka's studio, which was set up in 1936 and closed during the war, had the advantage of receiving subsidies from the government from 1948. Whereas Marek was a painter receiving money from the inconsistent sale of his works, Trnka had secure, paid work as an illustrator. Many of Trnka's animations were inspired by works of popular and classical literature, a technique used by Marek in his *8 Nursery Rhymes* (1960). Trnka's approach also diverged from Marek's in that Trnka, who had a trained team of animators working for him, was mainly involved in developing scripts and making puppets. In contrast, Marek largely worked alone on the production of his animations, except for the involvement of his wife Helena, who made costumes for the puppets. Marek wrote the scripts for his animations, although this was not the case with *The Magic Trumpet* (1962), which was written by Tim Burstall. Another distinct difference between the work of the two puppet-makers was that Trnka's puppets were expressionless, whereas Marek built facial expressions into his puppets and also used colour in sets and costumes to express emotion. One strong connection between them, however, is that both artists considered music integral to their films. Marek also saw musical composition as a time-based means of connecting the film with an audience. He explains:

> I think it is very important in film to use a musical way of composing, a musical structure – for then the difficulty that the film is not easily understood should slowly vanish, because the film will become like a musical composition, a form with which we are already familiar.[10]

Although these two film-makers divided their time between other art forms – painting in Marek's case and illustration in Trnka's – Zeman is best known for his feature film combining live action and animation. Zeman was a strong influence on Švankmajer, whereas Marek used combined live action and animation in only one of his films, *Cobweb on a Parachute* (1966–7).

Švankmajer joined the Prague surrealist group in 1970 and continued the Czech tradition in his film-making.[11] Michael Richardson suggests that Švankmajer is 'the only major film-maker whose work fully belongs to surrealism' in that he 'conceived and realised' most of his films in 'the heart of the Czechoslovak Surrealist Group'.[12] This body of work included Švankmajer's 'theatrical skills of masks and puppets', combined with animation techniques using clay models, cut-outs and inanimate objects.[13] Švankmajer's oeuvre forms a historical link with Marek, Trnka and Zeman, although the connection to Marek's work was distanced due to his emigration to Australia in the late 1940s.

Marek's animations in the Antipodes

At the outset of the communist era in Czechoslovakia (1948–89), Teige gathered together a group of new adherents and surrealists from the remaining avant-garde groups.[14] Cantrill suggests that Marek would undoubtedly have joined these artists had he remained in Czechoslovakia.[15] After the Soviet-backed communist putsch in February 1948, Marek escaped to freedom in Allied-occupied Germany and sailed to Australia. From that time Marek was considered 'dead' to the regime. When he arrived in Sydney on 29 October 1948, he stepped into a notoriously conservative world, resulting in what he called 'a particularly vexed atmosphere for surrealist art practice'.[16] Until his death, Marek claimed that his surrealist style remained misunderstood in Australia.

Disillusioned by the negative reception of his surrealist painting,[17] between 1952 and 1963 he produced a series of 16-mm animations. Curator Danni Zuvela suggests that:

> With the many hallmarks of Czech animation in these films – grotesque puppets and Claymation maquettes navigating neurotic interior journeys, undercut with a mordant wit – the artist's arrival in Australia in 1948 predates the great age of animation in Czechoslovakia which produced international luminaries such as Jan Švankmajer and Jiří Trnka.[18]

Arthur Cantrill remarks that when Marek embarked on his film-making in Australia his early animations became 'arguably the first Australian avant-garde films'.[19] As Marek's film had its genesis in the same Czech tradition, his film-making in the Antipodes is an invaluable link in the history of Czech film-making ruptured by the mass emigration from Europe following the Second World War.

Light of the Darkness (1952) is Marek's earliest example of surrealist animation. Plasticine figures interact in a sequence of strange events in a dimension where time does not exist. A streetscape suggests Marek's European 'world' of apartments, but Australian cues punctuate the non-linear narrative. These include Victorian terrace houses, a milk bar displaying an iconic Australian Peter's ice cream sign bearing a nonsensical message; a strange goanna-like creature; a dust-up at a police station; a randy male and bikini-clad female on a sunny beach; and decapitating and re-capitating boxing kangaroos. The *mise en scène* is indicative of the hybridized style emerging from Marek's memories of Europe and his still-unfolding experience of Australia. In the final scene, the man floats upwards, disintegrates and disappears. A wizard's face appears, intercut with flashing single frames of Marek's contorted visage.

Fisherman's Holiday (1952) uses articulated figures and is shot on black-and-white reversal film, its monochrome palette suggesting mysterious forces operating in a medieval village. A man fishes from an arched bridge; a statue of a nude woman stands nearby; a passing cyclist is caught on the fisherman's line and his head is then used as bait; a friend arrives with a bottle of wine and the head of the cyclist re-attaches. The film concludes with the three inebriated men toppling the statue.

Nightmare (1956) demonstrates the surrealist potential of stop-motion puppetry using wooden puppets carved by Marek in the Czech tradition.[20] A ceiling fan suggests the heat

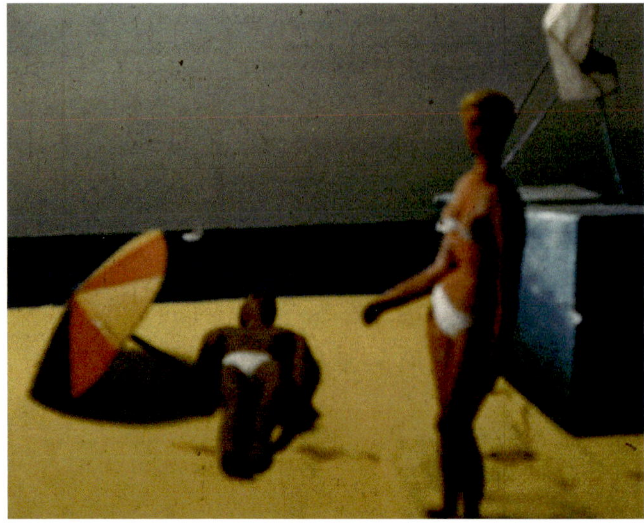

Figure 9.1 Dušan Marek, dir., *Light of the Darkness*, 1952. National Film and Sound Archive of Australia.

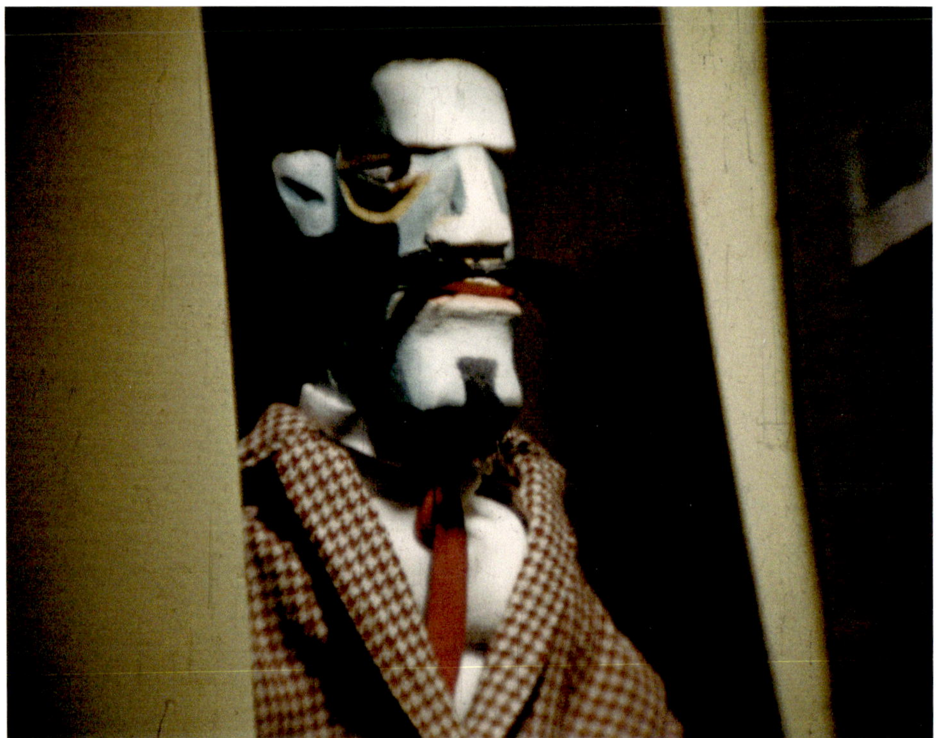

Figure 9.2 Dušan Marek, dir., *Nightmare* (or *The Magician*), 1956. National Film and Sound Archive of Australia.

and humidity of Rabaul, where the film was produced. A green-faced visitor arrives at a small-town hotel and drinks a bottle of sulphuric acid; the waitress' hair stands on end; the manager collapses; a drunken patron passes out, scattering the broken discs from a record player; and the visitor leaves, then returns to knock on the door. The film concludes with a view through the keyhole as seen by the unwelcome visitor. Cantrill suggests that the 'dark playfulness and feeling for the psychology of the characters' is a tendency Marek shares with Trnka.[21]

Marek discovered a burgeoning centre of experimental film-making in Adelaide when he returned to Australia in 1959. During the 1960s he was prolific, producing a series of around fifteen short films including *One Dotty Adventure* (1960–1; precursor to *Adam and Eve*); *Three Wise Men of Gotham* (1959–60); *Eight Nursery Rhymes* (1959–60); *The Magic Trumpet* (1962); and his most celebrated film, *Adam and Eve* (1962). Cantrill remarks:

> Marek's design and animation techniques were formidable by this time – his sense of timing and characterization is brilliant ... He was obviously a leading Australian animator although not working in the mainstream.[22]

In *The Magic Trumpet*, Marek uses a technique whereby the boy's eyes expand, contract and vibrate at moments of emotion using rapid two-framed animation of textured

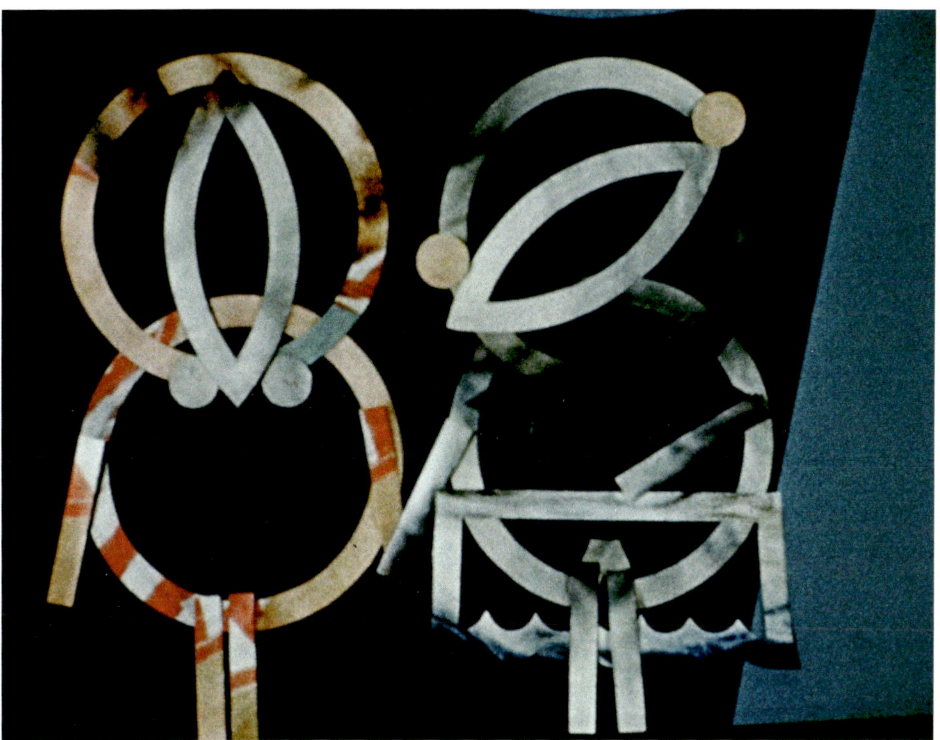

Figure 9.3 Dušan Marek, dir., *Adam and Eve*, 1962. National Film and Sound Archive of Australia.

and coloured discs. This strategy for expressing emotion was also used in *Adam and Eve*, Marek's allegory on humanity 'from creation to the bomb', which uses cut-out figures, dots, circles and lines. The figures have interchangeable decorative elements whose rapid animation generates a vibrating energy field that mixes optically to achieve whiteness.[23] The film was awarded the inaugural Australian Film Industry's Grand Prix in 1963, and gained awards in Venice, Vancouver and Chicago. According to Cantrill, the unusual method of mixing four sound sources in the sound composition accompanying the animation was improvised with Ian Davidson's technical assistance. It prefigured the 'sampling' method now used in sound composition and suited Marek's predilection for experimentation.[24]

These animations are infused with the traditions of Czech dark humour, poetism, puppetry, film-making and surrealism. *Windmills*, produced in 1963, was Marek's last animated film. It is structured to reflect the non-linear, syncretistic sensibility of childhood, using children's paintings. Marek thought of his work in film and painting as being like a child playing with a new object, discovering its properties freshly without the influence of others.[25] He was fascinated with the concept of time, and the time-based medium of film-making facilitated his deeper understanding of it. Cantrill notes that Marek's use of non-linear narrative showed events in an 'unnatural' order that he believed led the viewer to an 'inner space' where perceiving replaced the motivation for understanding.[26]

Conclusion

Between 1966 and 1975, Marek also produced three feature films. *Cobweb on a Parachute* is a seventy-minute depiction of the conflict between Marek's conscious and subconscious mind. It was produced in Sydney in 1966–7, set against the coastal landscape. It features a short animated sequence and is interspersed with Marek's poetry. Marek and his alter ego (who wears a de Chirico-like mask) are the only characters in the film apart from a fleeting view of a nude woman. Marek's voice is mixed with bird calls and other sounds of nature, and shots of strange objects found in the Australian bush – an empty chrysalis case, smoke curling up from a seed pod – are intercut into the film. His treatment of found objects is similar to Medková's. Fellow film-maker Davidson comments that:

> [In the film] Dusan shows his remarkable ability to make magic out of everyday life, and to capture and sustain a rare atmosphere of something just beyond reach being made obtainable.[27]

Marek felt strongly about the importance of retaining one's inner freedom by remaining completely unaffected by outside influences. In an interview with Cantrill, Marek emphasizes the need to:

> … retain his inside freedom, and not be molded by the outside, because the outside has not much to do with the inner truth and inner crystallization, and I think one should allow the outside to be modelled with.[28]

In his search for freedom from the ravages of a world at war, Marek chose to live as far away as one could go, to the surrealist 'down under' of the southern hemisphere. When he fled Czechoslovakia, he took with him a deeply spiritual connection with nature; the legacy of Czech surrealism with its strong currents of poetism; the Czech tradition of puppetry and film-making; and the lasting influence of the city of Prague with its dynamic avant-garde.

Marek described his animations as 'magical dreams'.[29] In film, Marek found the ideal medium through which he could create his magical dreamscapes and combine his early experience of Czech surrealism into a unique response to his life in the vast, surreal landscapes of Australia and Papua New Guinea. A hybrid style unique to Marek formed through the amalgam of memory, adventures of discovery, and journeys into the inner self, which were then reintegrated into his consciousness through film.

Marek died in Adelaide in March 1993 on the eve of the major exhibition held in the Australian National Gallery, *Revolution by Night*, in which his paintings were hung alongside those of Dalí, Ernst, Magritte and others. Not until 2021 were excerpts from Marek's home movies, documentaries, advertising films, animations, and feature films first screened as part of the Art Gallery of South Australia's exhibition *Dušan and Voitre Marek: Surrealists at Sea*.[30]

Notes

1 František Šmejkal, 'After Devětsil: Surrealism in Czechoslovakia', in *Devětsil: Czech Avant-Garde Art, Architecture and Design of the 1920s and 30s*, ed. Rotislav Švacha (Oxford: Museum of Modern Art, London: Design Museum, 1990), 93.

2 Peter Hames, 'The Film Experiment', in *The Cinema of Jan Švankmajer: Dark Alchemy*, ed. Peter Hames (London: Wallflower Press, 2008),11.

3 Jana Claverie and Alena Kubova, *Prague* (Paris: Vilo Publishing, 2002), 73.

4 Michael O'Pray, 'Jan Švankmajer: A Mannerist Surrealist', in *The Cinema of Jan Švankmajer: Dark Alchemy*, ed. Peter Hames (London: Wallflower Press, 2008), 55.

5 Franklin Rosemont, *André Breton and the First Principles of Surrealism: A Companion Volume to What is Surrealism?: Selected Writings of André Breton* (London: Pluto Press, 1978), 52.

6 Lenka Bydžovska, 'Against the Current: The Story of the Surrealist Group of Czechoslovakia', *Papers of Surrealism*, 1 (Winter 2003): 9.

7 Cheri Donaldson, 'Prague the Magic Capital', in *Dušan and Voitre Marek: Surrealists at Sea*, ed. Elle Freak (Adelaide: AGSA, 2021), 29.

8 Giannalberti Bendazzi, *Cartoons: One Hundred Years of Cinema Animation* (London: John Libbey, 1994), 164.

9 Arthur Cantrill, 'A Surrealist Film Practice – the Animated Films of Dušan Marek', *ASIFA Magazine: the International Animation Journal*, 21, no. 2 (Winter 2008): 46.

10 Marek quoted in Arthur Cantrill, 'The Knife of Light: Surrealism and Violence to the Eye', in *Cantrills Filmnotes* 93–100 (Dec. 1999–Jan. 2000): 51.

11 O'Pray, 'Jan Švankmajer', 40; Cantrill, *A Surrealist Film Practice*, 41.

12 Michael Richardson, *Surrealism and Cinema* (Oxford: Berg, 2006), 11.

13 Brian Sibley, *Creating 3-D Animations* (New York: Abrams, 1998), 27.

14 Krzysztof Fijalkowski, 'Dada and Surrealism in Central and Eastern Europe', in *A Companion to Dada and Surrealism*, ed. David Hopkins (New York: Wiley-Blackwell, 2016), 171.

15 Cantrill, *A Surrealist Film Practice*, 41.

16 Danni Zuvela, '"A Haze of Visions": Dream Work in Early Australian Avant-Garde Cinema', *emajartjournal*, 6 (2011–12): 4.

17 Cheri Donaldson, *In Pursuit of the Marvellous: Exploring the Role of Memory in the Surrealism of Czech Émigré Dušan Marek 1926–1993* (PhD diss., University of South Australia, 2018), 186–7.

18 Zuvela, '*A Haze*', 7.

19 Cantrill, *A Surrealist Film Practice*, 41.

20 The puppets are operated in real-time by manipulating wire armatures. In wide shots, the freestanding figures are animated single frame.

21 Cantrill, 'Light of the Darkness: Dušan Marek's Films and Animations', in *Dušan and Voitre Marek*: *Surrealists at Sea*, ed. Elle Freak (Adelaide: AGSA, 2021), 119.

22 Cantrill, *A Surrealist Film Practice*, 45.

23 Cantrill, *Light of the Darkness*, 120.

24 Cantrill, *Light of the Darkness*, 122.

25 Arthur Cantrill, 'Dušan Marek, 1926–1993', in *Cantrills Filmnotes*, 69, 70 (March 1993): 9.

26 Cantrill, *Light of the Darkness*, 117.

27 Ian Davidson, 'Remembered', *Agenda*, 30/31: 21.

28 Arthur Cantrill, 'Dušan Marek: And the Word Was Made Flesh', in *Cantrills Filmnotes*, 6 (Oct. 1971): 5.

29 Arthur Cantrill email to author, 7 March 2012.

30 *Dušan and Voitre Marek: Surrealists at Sea*.

Chapter 10

Animating Death and Deadening Life in 1964: *Angels' Games* by Walerian Borowczyk and *Les Temps morts* by René Laloux and Roland Topor

Abigail Susik

Most animators are unconsciously … Surrealists.
ROBERT BENAYOUN, 'THE CABINET OF JAN ŠVANKMAJER', 1984[1]

*This sublime and distressing surrealist poem (*Les Jeux des anges*), sumptuous in its plastic richness, today crowns a body of work which has no equivalent.*
MARCEL MARTIN, *LES LETTRES FRANÇAISES*[2]

Introduction

In January 1965 the opening night of the exhibition *Camera Obscura* at the Le Ranelagh cinema in Paris featured a special programme of film shorts called *Two Hours with Walerian Borowczyk*. The literary and film community turned out in force to the exhibition *vernissage* and screening of films by the émigré visual artist and film director. Borowczyk had moved to France from the communist Polish People's Republic in 1958 to follow up on a favour he couldn't refuse from French film-maker Chris Marker: a job offer to become a maverick auteur-*animateur* at Les Cinéastes Associés, a leading animation company near Paris where other international animators such as Alexandre Alexeïeff and Claire Parker also worked.[3] Thanks to his reputation as an award-winning animator, the exhibition and screening organized by Les Cinéastes Associés at Théâtre Le Ranelagh was a triumph.[4] Artworks, objects, drawings and storyboards by Borowczyk were on display. Film directors Agnès Varda and François Truffaut were among those in the audience, along with writers Alain Robbe-Grillet and Lotte Eisner.[5] French surrealist André Breton was also

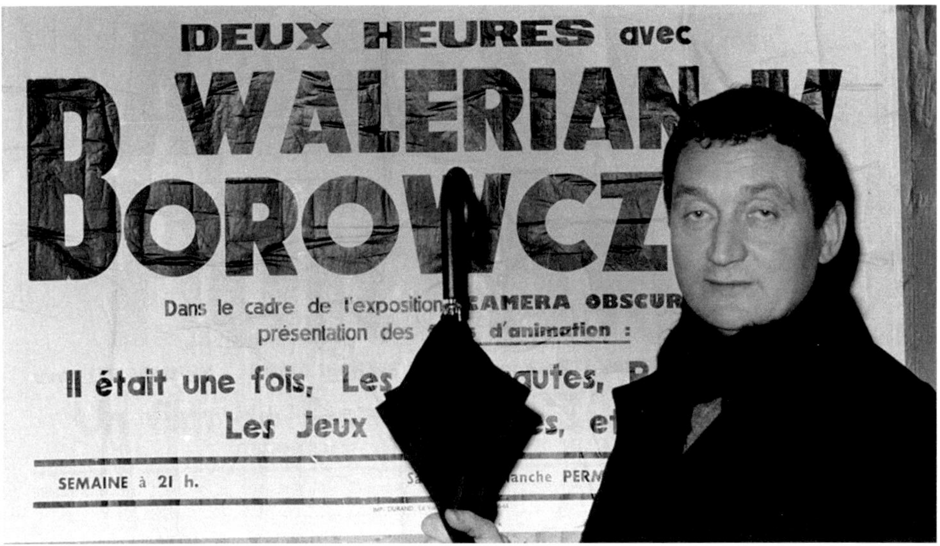

Figure 10.1 Władysław Sławny, Walerian Borowczyk at the *vernissage* for *Two Hours with Walerian Borowczyk*, Le Ranelagh cinema, Paris, Tuesday, 26 January 1965. Photograph.

watching alongside his surrealist comrade Robert Benayoun, a French-Moroccan film critic who had written the feature essay in the programme. After the screening, Breton praised the Polish film-maker for his 'dazzling imagination' (l'imagination fulgurante) – words that would thereafter remain significant for Borowczyk.[6]

It is in the context of Borowczyk's Bretonian 'dazzling imagination' and his reception of and by surrealism that I want to examine the Polish auteur's striking animated short *Les Jeux des anges* (*Angels' Games*; 1964, 35 mm, approx. 11 min.) in relation to the rest of Borowczyk's animated filmography and in comparison with an animated short by René Laloux and Roland Topor from the same year titled *Les Temps morts*. *Les Jeux des anges* was one of the thirteen short films Breton and others viewed at the Ranelagh, but it played an important role in the Camera Obscura Exhibition because original gouaches used for the film composed the major part of the display.[7] The printed invitation for the screening mailed out to one thousand guests also featured a drawing from *Les Jeux des anges*.[8]

A minimalist exercise in sombre watercolour animation, *Angels' Games* is a stylized and deeply disturbing meditation on a mechanized death camp. Borowczyk described it as a film in the style of a documentary about an imaginary country, a nation of angels who seek to destroy all life forms and see violence as a form of play.[9] Although the film is allegorical in its lack of visual and narrative specificity, explicit reference to the Holocaust and Nazi concentration camps in Poland is made in the music credit at the beginning of the film, which was not featured in the original release print but only added later.

For Benayoun, in his essay written for the *Camera Obscura* programme, 'Les crocs du machiniste' (The Dolly Grip's Fangs), it was this diffused evocation of the horrors of the Holocaust combined with the film's detached observation of an elaborate killing apparatus that resulted in the film's achievement of a spectacular–traumatic surrealist aesthetic.[10] Such a surrealist ambiance conjures the affect of historical trauma without

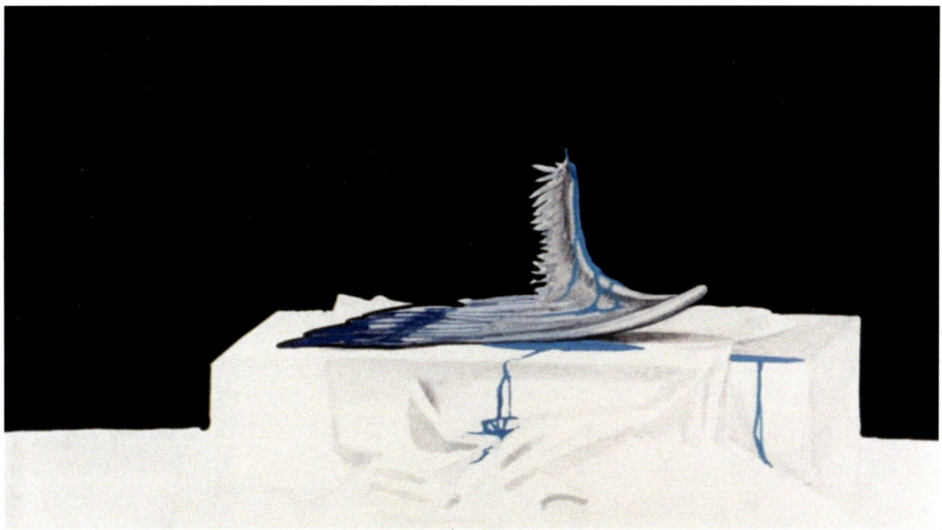

Figure 10.2 Walerian Borowczyk, dir., *Les Jeux des anges*, Les Cinéastes Associés, 1964. 35 mm.

engaging in the retrospectivism of memorials to historical events. In the case of *Angels' Games*, it is the dynamism of Borowczyk's rhythmic, abstract watercolour animation that achieves an immediacy of heightened sensory and emotional impact while avoiding any narrative objective.

Although starting in the late 1960s with *Goto, l'île d'amour* (1968) Borowczyk became best known for the erotic (and later pornographic) character of his live-action cinema, it was his animation practice beginning in the late 1950s that caught the attention of the surrealists and likewise piqued his own interest in the movement. Through an analysis of the French and American surrealist reception of Borowczyk's animation between the late 1950s and the 1970s, with a focus on texts by Benayoun that discuss *Angels' Games*, I assess the nature of surrealist resonances in this film and in Borowczyk's animated work at large. Even though Borowczyk was not a member of any surrealist group, he repeatedly framed his cinematography and animation in relation to the movement in published statements and interviews.

Angels' Games was aligned with surrealism for Borowczyk and for surrealists like Benayoun not only because of its symbolic and expressive approach to the anti-fascist critique of industrialized genocide in the Holocaust via a disorienting ilk of visual abstraction. *Angels' Games* also synergizes with surrealism because of its technical and symbolic exploration of the medium of animation as a mode of both enlivening the inanimate and deadening life, what animation theorist Alan Cholodenko has termed 'lifedeath' in animation.[11] As a form of hybrid lifedeath and movement–stillness, animation had the capacity to become a cinematic correlate to the longstanding surrealist obsession with the mechanical automaton. This collective surrealist fascination emerged precisely because the automaton's semblance of life was poised in balance with its parallel corpse-like motionlessness. In *Angels' Games*, Borowczyk accentuates this tension between movement and stillness by minimizing straight animation in favour of using the rostrum camera to complete elaborate pans across the watercolours that were painted in advance and only later served as the visual basis for the film.

To extend this point, my essay compares Borowczyk's *Angels' Games* with another important animated short made in Paris during the same year that deals allegorically with the subject of violent death and systematic murder through the staccato movements of stop-motion – *Les Temps morts* (*Killing Time*, 1964) by René Laloux and surrealist associate Roland Topor. Animation, via mid-1960s films like *Angels' Games* and *Killing Time*, provided an ideal medium and critical sociopolitical vehicle for the symbolic envisioning of a troubling and phantasmagoric dialectic: the simultaneous vivification of things and zombification or demise of living beings in a militarized–industrialized sphere.

Borowczyk on surrealism and surrealism on Borowczyk

It is not coincidental that the event at the Ranelagh theatre at the beginning of 1965 brought surrealism even more forcefully to the fore in considerations of Borowczyk's filmography to date. This repertoire consisted of thirteen shorts made in Poland starting in 1957 and later in France using an impressive variety of methods of animation. Five of these films were collaborations with fellow countryman Jan Lenica.

Anikó Imre has discussed Borowczyk's 'Buñuelian surreal sensibility' as being related in part to the 'surrealist investigation of the potential life of graphic forms and inanimate objects', as seen in the celebrated short film *Dom* (*House*, 1958), a Borowczyk–Lenica collaboration that salutes French film pioneer Georges Méliès and combines live action with stop-motion, cut-out animation, stills and pixilation.[12] Featuring sequences such as a wig furiously drinking a bottle of milk, *Dom* was seen in an explicitly surrealist light by American critic and surrealist associate Parker Tyler. In a 1959 review in *Film Quarterly*, Tyler cited surrealism multiple times as a primary influence for *Dom* and compared the film broadly to artworks by surrealists such as Max Ernst, Salvador Dalí and Man Ray. Man Ray, it happened, served as one of the judges at the 1958 World Expo Experimental Film Festival (Expo' 58) in Brussels, where *Dom* won the immensely prestigious grand prix.[13]

Tyler's assessment of Borowczyk as a surrealist affiliate proved durable. Following the 1967 debut of his feature-length animated film *Le Théâtre de monsieur et madame Kabal*, Borowczyk won the Max Ernst Prize for his contributions to the art of animation, underscoring the reception of his work as surrealist in tenor.[14] In addition, Tyler's 1959 review of *Dom* inaugurated a tradition of comparing Borowczyk's filmography to surrealism in film criticism. In Benayoun's ground-breaking 1961 book *Le Dessin animé après Walt Disney*, *Dom* is praised for its marvellous Lautréamontian qualities, a sentiment echoed in the expanded second edition of surrealist critic Ado Kyrou's *Le Surréalisme au cinéma* (1963).[15]

Benayoun remained an avid supporter of Borowczyk's animation and published a series of essays about the auteur starting in the mid-1960s.[16] It is therefore not surprising that several scholars consider Borowczyk's filmography, especially his early, animated films, central to the surrealist movement.[17] For instance, Michael Richardson has called

Borowczyk 'the Polish director whose sensibility is closest to surrealism'.[18] Moreover, beyond any question of overarching surrealist tendencies, Borowczyk was close with surrealists such as writer André Pieyre de Mandiargues, whose fiction was adapted in Borowczyk's live-action features such as *Immoral Tales* (1974).[19] The first episode of *Immoral Tales* was based on Mandiargues' short story about an act of fellatio on the beach, 'The Tide', which was commissioned by André Breton for the *Boîte alerte* box of facsimiles printed for the 1959 Exposition inteRnatiOnale du Surréalisme (EROS) Exhibition in Paris.[20] Borowczyk actively engaged surrealist material in his films.[21]

Contemporary critics have also connected this surrealist tendency to Borowczyk's interest in the ontology of objects, especially outmoded ones.[22] Yet, it is important to remember that Borowczyk had his own things to say about surrealism and that such commentary sheds light on why surrealists such as Breton and Benayoun viewed the Polish director's animation as close to the movement. Following the 1965 *Camera Obscura* screening, for example, Borowczyk was invited to submit a statement about his work in the context of surrealism as part of a survey of contemporary film-makers in a special double issue of *Études cinématographiques* published in spring 1965. Appearing alongside testimonies by peer directors in Polish cinema Roman Polanski and Andrzej Wajda (Borowczyk's classmate from art school in Kraków) and other international cinematographers such as Stan Brakhage, Georges Franju and Nelly Kaplan, Borowczyk's short essay evinces a profound consideration of the cinematic applications of surrealism and the reasons why cinema by non-surrealists was embraced by the international movement.

'Surrealism is a program of absolute non-conformity, in life and in poetry, that speaks equally to the cinema. I'm all for it', Borowczyk began.[23] Deploying language that resonated with the title of the Paris surrealist group's upcoming exhibition *L'Écart absolu* (at the Galerie de l'Œil in Paris in December 1965), Borowczyk's oxymoronic description of surrealism as a 'program of absolute non-conformity' reflects the subtlety of his knowledge about contemporary preoccupations of the movement. He continued, contemplating the mythical possibility of an automatist film medium with flawless immediacy, 'There is no real surrealist film except in the form of an imagined scenario, a speculative film. A truly surrealist film would require that the film-maker be freed from the camera, the celluloid, and the projection device, so that the film could be communicated directly from an emitting brain to a receiving brain.'[24]

For Borowczyk, the fantasy of immediacy embedded in surrealism's psychic automatism rendered the film medium too cumbersome for any approximation of perfect transmission – film was limited in its automatism precisely because of its proliferation of technological supports. Even though Borowczyk stated that his film refrained from deploying automatist techniques, an orientation he would reiterate throughout his career, he was firm in his understanding of surrealism as something greater than a cultural groupuscule located in a certain place and time.[25] His film could perform as an automatist instrument when needed, he asserted, and his cinema could be surrealist at will:

> I don't work in a state of psychic automatism. But that doesn't mean that I am incapable of rendering myself a 'modest recording instrument'. Surrealist traditions of

> past centuries considered today, as well as any involuntary surrealism, demonstrate that it is the beholder who is the source of surrealism. There are more discoverers than creators of surrealism. This same subjective approach has made it possible to inventory a rather impressive number of surrealist films. Rarely have these films been distinguished by their merits. If we consider cinema in itself as a surrealist manifestation, any cinematographic projection can be surrealist.[26]

Surrealism was, in his mind, essentially transhistorical and elective, and therefore one could infer that his filmography could be, in turn, situated within the surrealist tradition. Although the film medium was not practical as an instrument of surrealism, according to Borowczyk, the whole of cinema itself, as an art of equally agentic makers and beholders, was for him a 'surrealist manifestation'. He suggested that if one were to piece together all the extracts of sequences from different films that surrealists love, then one might have something like the ultimate surrealist film.[27]

Four years later, Borowczyk returned to some of these ideas in a 1969 interview for *Cahiers du cinéma*. There he asserted that he saw no difference between animated and live-action film. Rather, all film was animation, and all actors were puppets manipulated by the director.[28] Once again, he spoke of his unconscious and involuntary surrealism.[29]

If Borowczyk was able to relate his cinematography to surrealism because he viewed cinema itself as inherently surrealist, Benayoun was more specific in his assessment. In 'Les crocs du machiniste', Benayoun appraised the medium of animation and what he considered to be Borowczyk's mastery of it in light of the surrealist fascination with the ability of the magician or optical illusionist to animate the inanimate.[30] Importantly, Benayoun opened his essay with a quote about the innate vital force of matter and the human drive to shape it from a short story by Bruno Schulz, a Holocaust victim: the three-part 'Treatise on Tailors' Dummies' from the 1934 volume of short stories *The Street of Crocodiles*. Evoking the heresiarch in Schulz's story, Benayoun stated that 'Boro', whom he calls a 'camelopard of graphic art', is literally an animator or life-giver to things miniscule and massive who, like a demiurge, can deploy the medium of animation, a 'micro-active branch of the seventh art', to enliven objects.[31] Thus animation, for Benayoun, has the capacity to approximate the demented atmosphere of *Les Chants de Maldoror* (1868–9) by the Comte de Lautréamont or the disorientation of an eighteenth-century Gothic novel in the space of just a few minutes.[32]

Benayoun singled out *Angels' Games* as the Giorgio de Chirico-esque animated film that best demonstrates how Borowczyk is alternately an 'inventor and saboteur', someone who destroys even as he creates.[33] 'We witness, in a sinister warehouse, the simultaneous fine-tuning and dismantling of who knows what primordial automata … We don't know if the destruction (Cruel? Irresponsible?) shares in creation, or if the two activities aren't in some mistakenly linked hell of perpetual death and rebirth', Benayoun wrote of *Angels' Games*.[34] The 'shock' of the film results from this meeting of 'Frankenstein' with 'Auschwitz', he asserted – a scenario in which the dead are brought back to life and the living are murdered en masse, ultimately resulting in a 'metaphysical parade' and the annihilation of the difference between life and death.[35]

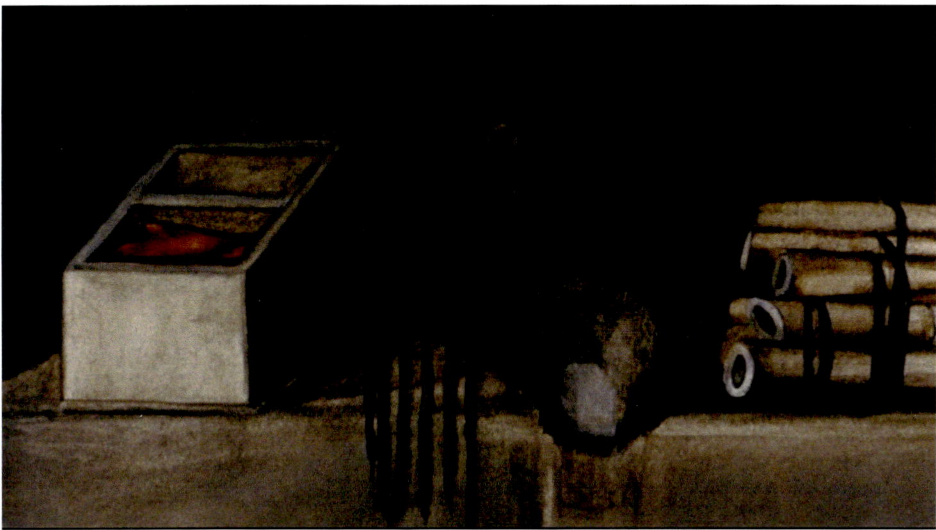

Figure 10.3 Walerian Borowczyk, dir., *Les Jeux des anges*, Les Cinéastes Associés, 1964. 35 mm.

Seven years later, in an essay in *Dossiers du cinéma* from 1971, Benayoun was still writing about the tortured and torturing automatons of *Angels' Games*, declaring that Borowczyk 'became the absolute master of a type of terror opera' with this 1964 short.[36] Although Borowczyk had moved away from animation starting in 1968 with his first live-action feature, *Goto, l'île d'amour*, Benayoun lingered on the director's uncanny powers as an animator, comparing his work to that of the contemporary Canadian animator Norman McLaren: 'Borowczyk is a modest demiurge, a perpetual inventor of himself and his accessories. He is, like McLaren, a Robinson who creates his world entirely from almost nothing … A patient, stubborn animator … His interest in surrealism can be deduced from the works themselves and does not seem to have constituted an a priori element.'[37] For Benayoun, Borowczyk's animated films did not need to be approved as surrealist. The director's demiurgic ability to give and take life via the eminently flexible medium of animation automatically allied him with the surrealist aim to re-enchant life while critiquing industrial capitalism's ceaseless exploitation of living beings.

Painted animation: *Angels' Games*

As an émigré auteur in Paris, Borowczyk completed the short film *Angels' Games* in 1964, writing, directing and animating his entirely hand-drawn scenography with a small crew of collaborators.[38] The idea for the film emerged from a cycle of paintings by Borowczyk that were prepared in the late 1950s for an exhibition, works that were influenced by what Daniel Bird has called the 'quasi-surrealism' of certain Kraków-based painters who were his friends at the time.[39] Borowczyk's employer in Paris, Jacques Forgeot of the Cinéastes Associés, suggested a film based on the paintings. The Polish director assented, describing *Angels' Games* as a 'documentary filmed in an imaginary land' using a 'new means of expression': '"hand-made" film'.[40] 'The events to be depicted in this film will be created gradually while the pictures are being painted', Borowczyk added.[41]

The sombre, figurative gouaches for *Angels' Games* were a far cry from the crude line drawings he had employed for his Ubuesque animated short *The Concert* (1962), the film that debuted his mutually sadistic characters, the husband-and-wife maelstrom Mr and Mrs Kabal. The Kabals starred five years later in his only animated feature, *Le Théâtre de monsieur et madame Kabal*, a work that Benayoun classified as 'anti-Disney'.[42] *Angels' Games* was also totally distinct from a snappy cut-out and purposefully crude film still animation hybrid short like *Les Astronautes* (1959), supposedly co-directed with Chris Marker, who lent his name to the film although he was not extensively involved in its production.[43]

In fact, *Angels' Games* is one of the few handmade animated films in Borowczyk's oeuvre, and its distinctive quality was recognized in awards from the main jury and the critics jury at the Tour Film Festival in 1964.[44] Having studied painting at the Academy of Fine Arts in Kraków, Borowczyk was highly experienced in the film's medium of watercolour as well as the print medium of lithography, which he practised as a poster designer in Poland.[45] The painting techniques deployed in *Angels' Games* resulted in a stark and seamless ilk of animation: gouaches in hues of black, umber, olive, ecru, plum and dark grey are brought to life through pans, zooms, vertical tilts and reframing, whereas cut-out animation and accelerated montages create more jarring effects. Jeremy Robinson clarified that in *Angels' Games* Borowczyk reused the same hand-painted scenes multiple times in the film, flipping them in reverse or turning them upside down, piecing shots together with dissolves and straight cuts, and recycling the footage in what Robinson

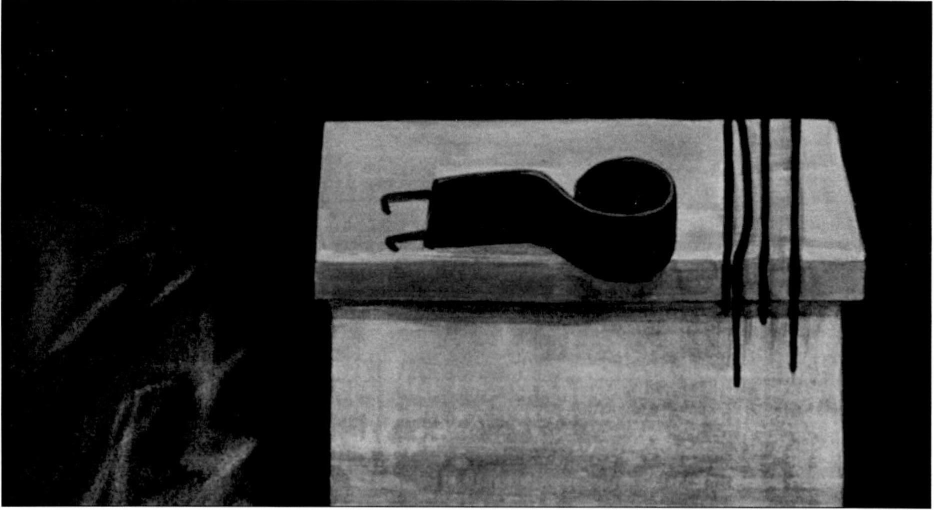

Figure 10.4 Walerian Borowczyk, dir., *Les Jeux des anges*, Les Cinéastes Associés, 1964. 35 mm.

termed his 'bleak humour' short.[46] The cinematography has a disorienting and frantic quality, what Benayoun called in a 1969 comparison of *Angels' Games* with *Goto, l'île d'amour*, 'a cyclopean world of cellars and corridors … designed with the true genius of a mad architect or a Babylonian librarian'.[47]

A similar animation of painted scenes via pans and montage constitutes his 1957 collaboration with Jan Lenica, the eight-minute homage to kitsch, *Rewarded Feelings*, based on the folk-art paintings of Polish artist Jan Płaskociński. However, the unique graphic character of *Angels' Games*, which is reminiscent of works by artists such as Toyen, Yves Tanguy, René Magritte, Konrad Klapheck and Francis Bacon – not to mention the slaughterhouse (*abbatoir*) photographs of Eli Lotar from the late 1920s – nevertheless remains entirely distinct in Borowczyk's oeuvre. If his 1963 animated shorts *Renaissance* and *Grandmother's Encyclopedia in 13 Volumes* are probably his most surrealist animated films, reminiscent as they are of Max Ernst's collages or the contemporary cinematography of Czech surrealist director Jan Švankmajer, *Angels' Games* connects with surrealism on an obvious level through the movement's painterly legacies.[48] Whereas *Renaissance*, for example, depicts the reconstruction of a room of family possessions after the explosion of a bomb via the meticulous reverse stop-motion animation of everyday objects, the Kafkaesque penal colony of *Angels' Games* unfolds a scenario of brutally rationalized dismemberment, leading from capture, confinement, torture and execution to the mass industrial processing of bodies.

Angels' Games begins with an accelerated montage of pans that resembles one continuous high-speed pan. The striking soundtrack by French electronic music composer Bernard Parmegiani, who later worked with Borowczyk on the soundtrack of the horror live-action feature *Docteur Jekyll et les femmes* (1981), blends in the most subtle fashion with the scenario and graphics. Indeed, the full significance of the scenario of *Angels' Games* is arguably not comprehendible without Parmegiani's ponderous audio-scape. The credit sequence for *Angels' Games* states, 'The music from this film is based on an original chant from Polish concentration camps.' Accordingly, the music accentuates the mood of the allegorical visuals, which suggest only the most basic narrative elements, such as a prison setting, guillotine, and acts of pitiless violence in a war between angels.

The film's allusions to the Holocaust are strong enough to provoke scholars such as Michael Richardson to observe that the film 'recalls Borowczyk's memories of the Nazi occupation and the collapse of civil society it involved'.[49] Following concepts of the Holocaust-inflected 'concentrationary universe' depicted in Borowczyk's filmography as described by Raymond Durgnat in a 1976 essay, Jonathan Owen has explored the thematic of traumatic penitentiary spaces that evoke Kafkaesque repressive regimes as well as 'Nazi or Stalinist political tyranny' in the Polish film-maker's works, including *Angels' Games*.[50] Rather than confronting the Second World War and the Holocaust directly, Owen argued in a related essay, Borowczyk and other Polish émigré film-makers like Polanski engaged in 'concentration camp allegory' or dreamlike allegories of 'twentieth-century atrocity' in films such as Borowczyk's *Angels' Games* and *Goto, Island of Love*, which depicts an outlandish dictatorship.[51]

If allegory is one of the modalities deployed in *Angels' Games*, there is nevertheless a significant personal resonance to the film, because Borowczyk was a direct witness to Nazi Holocaust crimes in Poland. In his 2007 autobiography, he described doing forced labour as a teenager in the village of Luboń – including working in a potato processing plant – during the Nazi occupation of Poland between 1939 and 1945.[52] Iwona Kurz and Kuba Mikurda have inferred that, because of his father's work as a railway inspector, Borowczyk probably heard about the transport of prisoners to concentration camps such as the Fort VII camp in Poznań.[53] In January 1945, when the nearby concentration camp in a former brick factory, Żabikowo, was liberated, Borowczyk witnessed the charred remains of prisoners the Germans mass executed and burned in an attempt to hide evidence from the incoming Soviet Red Army. Roughly 150 Polish prisoners deemed unfit for deportation by the Nazis were shoved into barns that were then set alight. In his early twenties at the time, Borowczyk made a drawing of this experience called *The Evidence of German Crime*, which was reproduced in the local newspaper, becoming his first published work.[54]

Borowczyk refused to connect *Angels' Games* to his witnessing of the horrors of the concentration camps.[55] Yet, abstract though the rendering of scenes from *Angels' Games* are, the sense of place is ominously concrete. One wonders, for example, whether the graffiti on the wall of one of the cells in *Angels' Games*, reading 'D-A-N-T-E' and 'U-K-R-A-N-Y', visible only when the footage is viewed on a Moviola editing machine, was something that Borowczyk witnessed as he explored the abandoned Nazi prison in Żabikowo.[56] Nevertheless, the overarching sensibility in *Angels' Games* is one of terrifying placelessness, claustrophobia and confinement. Over the course of a few cycles of disorienting and minutely gradual changes in darkness and light, we perceive that we are confined in a grey box that resembles a prison cell. As the camera alternates between vertical tilts and zooms in this breathless space, it becomes clear that many of these chambers abut one another. The cells are not unlike the frames of the celluloid itself as it moves through the camera and the projector. The movement of the celluloid that creates the illusion of animation is the 'train' that has delivered the viewer, in near total darkness and at high speeds, to the faceless death camp of the film.

At about four and a half minutes into *Angels' Games*, Parmegiani's soundtrack switches into a striding organ sonata based on the aforementioned chant sung by prisoners in Nazi concentration camps in Poland. A dismembered angel's wing falls onto a platform and begins to bleed Prussian blue fluid. Agitated camera pans and tilts proceed, and a panorama of amputated angel bodies unfurls, with heaps of detached wings and headless, armless torsos like so many mannequins filling dim corners. As these rattling forms attempt to morph and reconstitute themselves in flashes of light, the body of a pale, immobile and hairless female entity is uncovered via a steady downward wipe shot. Perhaps an android or some other revivified monster, she has eyes frozen open, and her arms are truncated and locked behind her where they disappear into the wall. The striptease downward wipe shot reveals more and more of the leaden female android, who begins to come to life thanks to a strange fluid. Dark hair appears on her head, and she blinks once. She seems to be the final product sought by this angel slaughterhouse and processing plant.

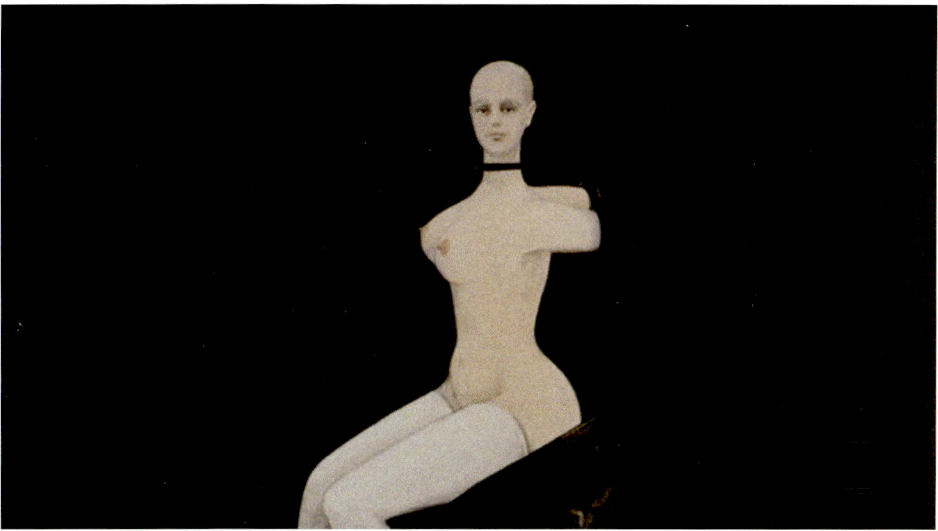

Figure 10.5 Walerian Borowczyk, dir., *Les Jeux des anges*, Les Cinéastes Associés, 1964. 35 mm.

Animating death in 1964: *Killing Time* by René Laloux and Roland Topor

Like Borowczyk's *Angels' Games*, a film from the same year called *Les Temps morts* by René Laloux and surrealist associate Roland Topor combines various animation techniques with a surrealist aesthetic to make a misanthropic statement about the inhuman atrocities perpetrated by humans. Completed two years after the conclusion of the Algerian War and during a year of heightened activity in the ongoing Vietnam War, *Angels' Games* and *Killing Time* draw upon the aesthetic corpus of surrealism in their deployment of nightmare imagery alongside graphic brutality.

However, in other regards the two films could not be more different in terms of format and storytelling. Whereas *Angels' Games* is a wordless hand-drawn scenario, *Killing Time* features a prominent narration that connects the film's experimental combination of stop-motion animation, filmed stills and stock footage and photographs.[57] *Killing Time* was directed by Laloux and co-written by Laloux and artist–author Roland Topor, a child of Jewish refugees from Poland, who also created the drawings that populate the film. The French science fiction and fantasy writer Jacques Sternberg wrote the text for the film's voiceover. It was the first of three animated film collaborations in which Laloux served as the director for scenarios co-written with Topor using Topor's drawings. The sardonic tall tale *The Snails* followed a year later in 1965, while the legendary feature-length cut-out science fiction animation *La Planète sauvage* (*Fantastic Planet*) made animation history in 1973.[58] All three included memorable scores by jazz pianist and composer Alain Goraguer and dystopian scenarios that showed the human race on the brink of extinction. In *Fantastic Planet*, for example, Laloux and Topor speculated on the resilience of human

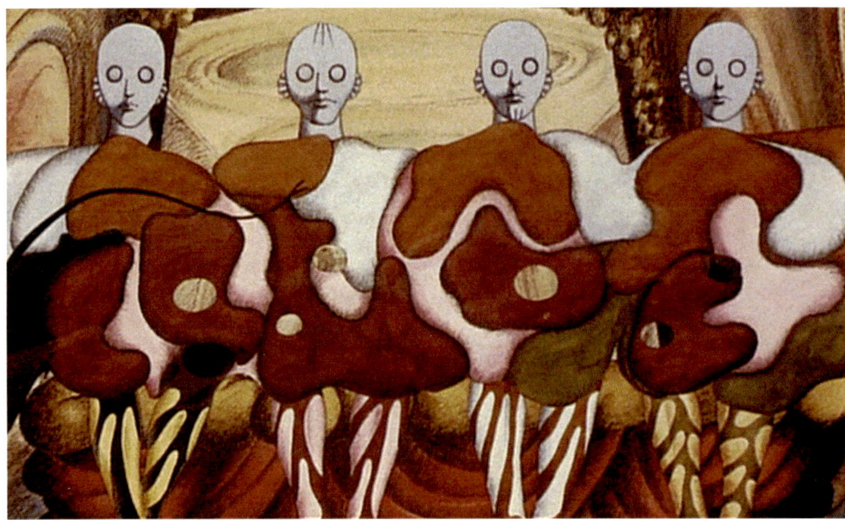

Figure 10.6 René Laloux, dir., *Planète sauvage*, 1973.

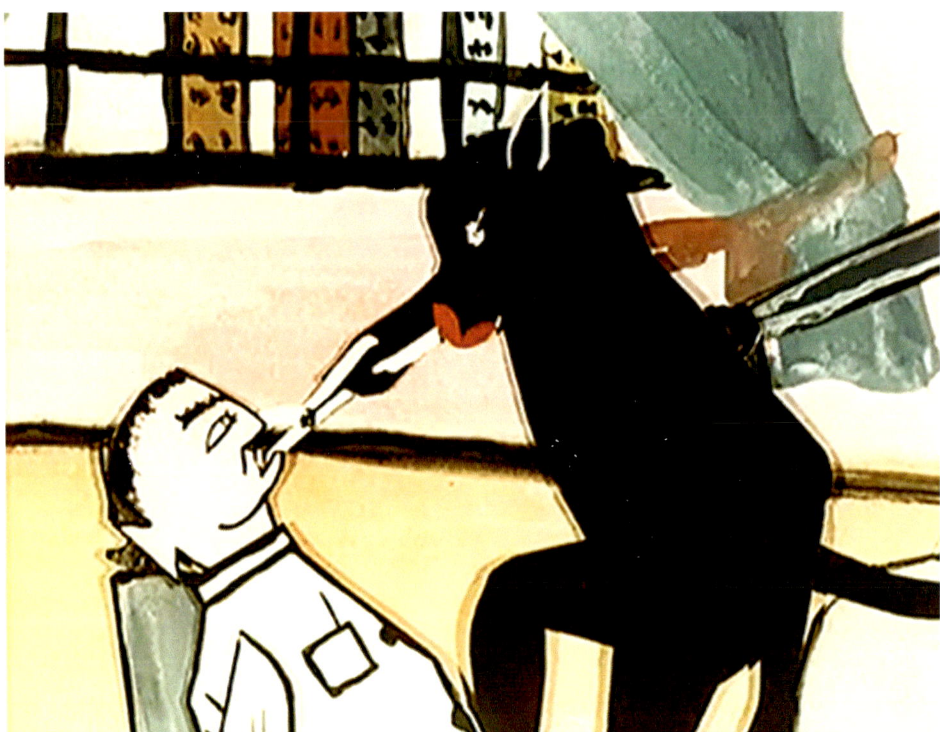

Figure 10.7 René Laloux, dir., *Les Dents du singe*, 1960.

autonomy under conditions of enslavement by an alien race of blue giants (the Draags). On the distant planet Ygam, the Draags have harnessed telepathy for their pleasure, but they fail to see the barbarism in their treatment of the humans (Oms), who retaliate against their oppression.

Laloux and Topor met in France in 1960 when Laloux's third short film, the cut-out animation *Les Dents du singe* (*Monkey's Teeth*; 1960), won an award, and Topor was involved in a screening of the film.[59] Laloux was almost a decade older than Topor, but given their mutual background in fine arts and Laloux's attraction to a macabre black humour aesthetic, as exemplified by Laloux's *Monkey's Teeth*, the two had quite a bit in common. Like his two previous films, *Tic Tac* (1957) and *Les Achalunés* (1958), *Monkey's Teeth* was made with the help of doctors and patients at La Borde Clinic in the Loire Valley, a facility founded by Lacanian psychotherapist Jean Oury in 1953. With the help of Oury and a young Félix Guattari, who appears briefly in the film, Laloux worked with the patients to create the colourful Art Brut-style cut-outs and the scenario. *Monkey's Teeth* features an evil dentist who brutally steals all the teeth from his poor, unconscious patients and sells them to the rich – until a frightful monkey magician reaps vengeance against the dentist by pulling out all his teeth and giving them to the victims.

In contrast with *Monkey's Teeth*, in which the creators were situated in the social reality of the clinic even while they created a fantastic horror tale, *Killing Time* juxtaposes appropriated documentary film footage and photographs with Topor's convulsed black ink drawings, some of which are stop-motion animated. Although the footage, photographs and drawings in *Killing Time* contain scenes of death and mutilation of humans and animals, the tone is closer to a melancholic poem than any horror genre. Nevertheless, Laloux's interest in themes of greed, crime and retribution in *Monkey's Teeth* carries over through the tone of Topor's drawings, which evoke a range of precursors, including Bosch, Goya, J. J. Grandville, and Max Klinger.

Killing Time commences with a science fiction perspective: flying through a galaxy, a planet comes into focus. The narrator (Roland Dubillard) explains that we are examining the beings of this nameless planet, who from a very young age practice the act of murder. The narrator states, 'Somewhere, in a sparsely populated galaxy, there is a world like any other. The creatures of this world have four limbs. The two lower limbs enable them to move forward and backward, and the two upper limbs allow them to kill.' The voice

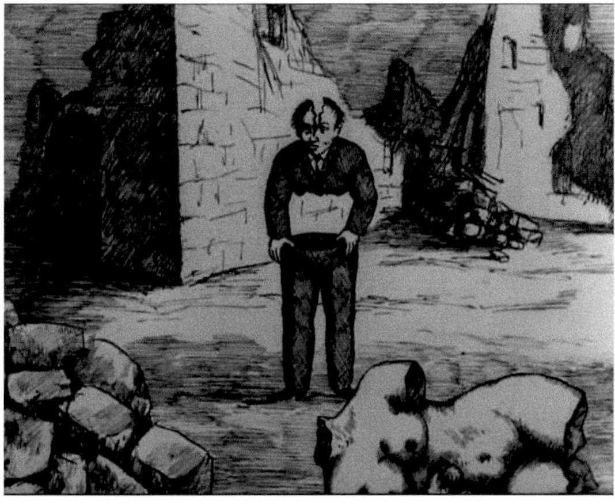

Figure 10.8 René Laloux, dir., with Félix Guattari (including drawings by Roland Topor), *Les Temps morts*, 1964.

continues, 'Man. Principal resource: death. He lives on it; he also perishes from it.'[60] Stock footage borrowed from French animator Paul Grimault's studio reveals a montage of children in Japan engaged in a play-fighting shoot-out. Play turns into practice when the footage shifts into scenes of heavy artillery firing, soldiers running across battlefields and fighter planes exploding into flames. Goraguer's mournful score, pierced with sonorous flutes, accentuates the heaviness of the atmosphere, as the camera shifts to a series of zooms, pans and tilts at varying speeds across Topor's drawings. These scenes depict, for instance, a dismembered, hanged man, a pile of naked bodies and ruined buildings in a barren landscape – along with impossible vignettes such as a dismembered and partially decapitated man walking his still-living dog in front of the roof of a house that floats in the air. Jerky cut-out animation sequences bring one corner of a ghastly funeral procession to life, while the rest of the drawing remains inanimate.

Les Temps morts, literally 'dead times', suggests in French the notion of a pause, such as 'down time' or 'time out', but it could also be translated as 'dead beats'. In a screening of short films, you might have 'temps mort' between each film. In Laloux's short, such 'dead time' refers to the intimacy of human life with the state of death. The narrator explains that humans get bored between near-constant bouts of war and that, ironically, they must suffer the continuation and reproduction of life so as to proceed with their beloved game of death. Even time is murdered by humans who loiter in their addiction to violence, because time is spent killing and dying rather than living.

Given this view of humanity, the significance of the multimedia construction of the film becomes more evident, as do the connections with the surrealist animation of death in Borowczyk's *Angels' Games* from the same year. The montage of appropriated footage and photographs interspersed with Topor's drawings, which have been animated via stop-motion or filmed stills, creates an uneasy and forced continuity between cinema and two-dimensional fine art. Animated drawings – which become the vivification of still life, *nature morte* (literally dead nature) – are the corollary to the moving stillness that is celluloid-based cinema, sequences of photographs sped up to create the illusion of movement. Killing time is equated with the essence of filmic animation and therefore the fabric that bridges and binds together found footage, photographs and Topor's drawings.

Conclusion

The scenario of *Killing Time* devised by Laloux and Topor, which cuts in and out of documentary footage, found illustrations, and Topor's drawings, ultimately emerges as a misanthropic satire and a stark critique of war. The stream of life, which cinema's durational aspect attempts to approximate, is embedded in death's rigor mortis and obscurity: this is the immobility of the still images and the eerie jerkiness of the stop-motion animation. Sternberg's dour text describes the globe as enthralled in a vicious circle of murder and death.

In comparison, Borowczyk's *Angels' Games* depicts the anonymous cruelty of the death camp or slaughterhouse without drawing any obvious moral conclusions about the human race and its activities. Although the film's title indicates that we are witnessing games engaged in by angels, it is also clear from the scenario that these angels are the victims of their own games. Like supernatural children, they orchestrate the torture and simultaneously become entangled in its trap, as in a game of hide-and-seek wherein the seeker ultimately becomes the concealed fugitive.[61] Just as surrealists assemble a Frankensteinian *cadavre exquis* through the collective action of folding and passing a drawing, Borowczyk's angels dismember and reassemble their toys in the act of play. The director's animation becomes the realm of adult games, in which trauma and Thanatos coexist with pleasure and Eros.[62] As Roy Armes wrote of *Angels' Games*, 'With this film one can say that the drawn cartoon is vindicated as a totally adult form of expression of the fears and anxieties of our age.'[63]

Notes

1. Quoted in Jonathan L. Owen, 'Motion without Escape: The Bleak Surrealism of Czech and Polish Animation', in *A Story of Sin: Surrealism in Polish Cinema*, eds. Kamila Wielebska and Kuba Mikurda (Kraków: Korporacja Halart, 2010), 49–50.
2. Quoted and translated, *sans date*, in Walerian Borowczyk, *Boro: Walerian Borowczyk L'imagination fulgurante, André Breton* (Annecy: Centre International du Cinéma d'Animation, 1997), 69.
3. Kuba Mikurda, 'Boro: Escape Artist', in *Boro*, *L'île d'amour*, eds. Kamila Kuc, Kuba Mikurda and Michał Oleszczyk (Oxford: Berghahn, 2015), 19–20; and Aga Skrodzka, 'Leaving the Art-house: Commerce and Commodity in Borowczyk's Controversial Cinema', *Studies in Eastern European Cinema*, 9, no. 2 (2018): 118.
4. Daniel Bird, 'Devil's Games: Surrealism in Polish Émigré Cinema', in Wielebska and Mikurda, *Story of Sin*, 77.
5. Mikurda, 'Boro: Escape Artist', 20.
6. Walerian Borowczyk, *Co Myślę Patrząc na Rozebraną Polkę* (Warsaw: Rytm, 2007), 51.
7. Pascal Vimenet, ed., *Walerian Borowczyk* (Montreuil: Editions de l'oeil Annecy, 2009), 170; and Walerian Borowczyk, 'Walerian Borowczyk Collection', BOROWCZYK112-B18, Cinémathèque française / Bibliothèque du film de la Cinémathèque française.
8. Borowczyk, 'Walerian Borowczyk Collection'.
9. Typescript scenario dated 21 April 1967, Borowczyk, 'Walerian Borowczyk Collection'.
10. Borowczyk, 'Walerian Borowczyk Collection'; Owen, 'Motion without Escape', 44–5.
11. Karen Beckman, 'Animating Film Theory: An Introduction', in *Animating Film Theory*, ed. Karen Beckman (Durham, NC: Duke University Press, 2014), 1–22; and Alan Cholodenko, 'Speculations on the Animatic Automaton', in *Illusion of Life 2: More Essays on Animation*, ed. Alan Cholodenko (Sydney: Power Publications, 2007), 486–528.
12. Anikó Imre, *A Companion to Eastern European Cinemas* (Hoboken, NJ: John Wiley & Sons, 2012), 277, 279; and Marcin Giżycki, 'Avant-garde and the Thaw: Experimentation in Polish Cinema of the 1950s and 1960s', in *The Struggle for Form: Perspectives on Polish Avant-garde Film, 1916–1989*, eds. Kamila Kuc and Michael O'Pray (London: Wallflower Press, 2014), 87–8. Lenica attended a surrealist gathering in this era. Owen, 'Motion without Escape', 51–2.

13 Parker Tyler, '*Dom*: A Film by Walerian Borowczyk and Jan Lenica; *Loving*: A Film by Stan Brakhage; *L'Opéra Mouffe*: A Film by Agnès Varda', *Film Quarterly*, 12, no. 3 (Spring 1959): 50–3.

14 Ronald Bergan, 'Obituary: Walerian Borowczyk: Surrealist Whose Films Blurred the Lines between Erotic Art and Exploitation', *The Guardian*, 23 February 2006, 37. On Borowczyk's collage *Hommage à Max* [Ernst], see Bird, 'Devil's Games', 77.

15 Robert Benayoun, *Le Dessin animé après Walt Disney* (Paris: J. J. Pauvert, 1961), 40, 134–5, 139, 165; Ado Kyrou, *Le Surréalisme au cinéma* (Paris: Le Terrain Vague, 1963), 203. Robert Benayoun, 'Walerian Borowczyk', *Dossiers du cinéma*, 1 (1971): 29.

16 Robert Benayoun, 'Les crocs du machiniste', *Cinéma*, 65, no. 98 (July–August 1965): 44–51; Benayoun, 'Annecy, sept, oui', *Positif*, 87 (September 1967): 27, 30–1; Benayoun, 'Les Volets de fer de Boro-Boro', *Positif*, 105 (May 1969): 60–3; Benayoun, 'Walerian Borowczyk', 29–32; Benayoun, 'L'Ingénieur des extases: (Contes immoraux)', *Positif*, 162 (October 1974): 62; and Benayoun, 'Interieur de pupille: aqua micans', in *Borowczyk: Cinéaste onirique*, eds. Walerian Borowczyk et al. (Paris: Editions Walter/Albatros, 1981), 11–16.

17 Krzysztof Fijalkowski, 'Dada and Surrealism in Central and Eastern Europe', in *A Companion to Dada and Surrealism*, ed. David Hopkins (Hoboken, NJ: Wiley-Blackwell, 2016), 165, 173; Kacper Nowacki, 'Eroticism and Surrealism in the Cinema of Walerian Borowczyk', in *Rethinking the Erotic: Eroticism in Literature, Film, Art and Society*, eds. Katarzyna Popak-Bernat and Sara D'Arcy (Leiden: Brill, 2019), 55–7; Jonathan Owen, 'Avant-garde Exploits: The Cultural Highs and Lows of Polish Émigré Cinema', in Kuc and O'Pray, *Struggle for Form*, 93–114; Jonathan Owen, 'An Island Near the Left Bank: Walerian Borowczyk as a French Left Bank Filmmaker', in *Polish Cinema in a Transnational Context*, eds. Ewa Mazierska and Michael Goddard (Rochester, NY: University of Rochester Press, 2014), 219–20; Robert Short, *The Age of Gold*: *Dalí, Buñuel, Artaud: Surrealist Cinema*, 2nd edn (Los Angeles, CA: Solar Books, 2008), 185; David Thompson, 'Pleasures of the Flesh: Walerian Borowczyk', in *Exile Cinema: Filmmakers at Work Beyond Hollywood*, ed. Michael Atkinson (Albany: State University of New York Press, 2008), 165; and Amos Vogel, *Film as a Subversive Art* (London: Weidenfeld & Nicolson, 1974), 145.

18 Michael Richardson, 'Walerian Borowczyk and the Touch of Desire', in *Surrealism and Cinema*, ed. Michael Richardson (New York: Berg, 2006), 107.

19 Bird, 'Devil's Games', 77–80.

20 Jonathan Owen, 'The Beach, the Bubble, and the Boudoir: The Meeting Spaces of Walerian Borowczyk and André Pieyre de Mandiargues', in Kuc, Mikurda and Oleszczyk, *Boro, L'île d'amour*, 149; and 'Walerian Borowczyk', in Michael Richardson et al., *The International Encyclopedia of Surrealism* (London: Bloomsbury, 219), 2:80. Madiargues singled out *Docteur Jekyll et les femmes* (1981) as surrealist. Walerian Borowczyk et al., *Borowczyk: Cinéaste Onirique* (Paris: Editions Walter/Albatros, 1981), 8.

21 On Borowczyk's film adaptation of a Valentine Penrose novel, see Iwona Kurz, 'Cruel Imagination: Borowczyk's Post-traumatic Surrealism', in Kuc, Mikurda and Oleszczyk, *Boro, L'île d'amour*, 71.

22 Richardson, 'Walerian Borowczyk', 108. Daniel Bird, 'The Ghost of Goto: Walerian Borowczyk Remembered', *Vertigo*, 3, no. 1 (Spring 2006): 57–9.

23 'Walerian Borowczyk on Surrealism', trans. Jim Knox, UbuWeb (accessed 12 June 2012), http://www.ubu.com/film/borowczyk.html; and Walerian Borowczyk, 'Témoignages: W. Borowczyk', in 'Surréalisme et cinéma', ed. Yves Kovacs, special issue, *Études cinématographiques* 40–2 (April–May–June 1965): 155.

24 Borowczyk, 'Témoignages', 155. Translations are by the author unless otherwise noted.

25 Owen, 'Avant-garde Exploits', 113.

26 Borowczyk, 'Témoignages', 156.

27 Borowczyk, 156.

28 Walerian Borowczyk et al., 'Entretien avec Walerian Borowczyk: par Michel Delahaye, Sylvie Pierre, et Jacques Rivette', *Cahiers du cinéma*, 209 (February 1969): 31, 33.

29 Borowczyk et al., 37.

30 Borowczyk, *Boro*, 12. Benayoun's essay for the *Camera Obscura* programme was republished in *Cinéma*, 65 (July–August 1965): 44–51. All citations below are from the *Cinéma* reprint.

31 Benayoun, 'Les crocs', 45, 46.

32 Benayoun, 45.

33 Benayoun, 46.

34 Benayoun, 50.

35 Benayoun, 50–1.

36 Benayoun, 'Walerian Borowczyk', 30.

37 Benayoun, 29.

38 Vimenet, *Walerian Borowczyk*, 170.

39 Daniel Bird, 'Walerian Borowczyk', in *Boro: Walerian Borowczyk* (Paris: Centre Pompidou, 2017), 29–30.

40 Bird, 29–30.

41 Quoted in Bird, 'Walerian Borowczyk', 30; Vimenet, *Walerian Borowczyk*, 44, 46, 47, 52, 53; and Borowczyk, *Boro*, *passim*.

42 Benayoun, 'Walerian Borowczyk', 30.

43 Owen, 'Island near the Left Bank', 215; Bird, 'Walerian Borowczyk', 13–14. Anatole Dauman, producer of *Les Astronautes*, collected surrealist artworks and introduced Borowczyk to Mandiargues. Bird, 'Devil's Games', 77.

44 Kurz, 'Cruel Imagination', 65.

45 David Thompson, 'Pleasures of the Flesh', 164. Jonathan Owen has argued for the surrealist tendencies in the Polish poster scene of Borowczyk's era. 'Motion without Escape', 50.

46 Jeremy Mark Robinson, *Walerian Borowczyk, Cinema of Erotic Dreams* (London: Crescent Moon, 2012), 144.

47 Benayoun, 'Les Volets', 62.

48 Alison Frank, 'The Artistry of Walerian Borowczyk', *CineAction*, 94 (Summer 2014): 59.

49 Richardson, 'Walerian Borowczyk', 109.

50 Owen, 'Island near the Left Bank', 218; and Raymond Durgnat, 'Borowczyk and the Cartoon Renaissance', *Film Comment* (January–February 1976): 42.

51 Owen, 'Avant-garde Exploits', 101–2.

52 Borowczyk, *Co Myślę*, 29, 60–1; and Vimenet, *Walerian Borowczyk*, 90.

53 Kurz, 'Cruel Imagination', 65, 67; and Mikurda, 'Boro: Escape Artist', 13–14. Conversation with Filip Bajon, quoted in Mikurda, 'Boro: Escape Artist', 14.

54 Borowczyk, *Co Myślę*, 29, 60–1.

55 Borowczyk, 60.

56 Durgnat, 'Borowczyk', 41.

57 Owen, 'Avant-garde Exploits', 103–4.

58 Fabrice Blin, *Les Mondes fantastiques de René Laloux* (Chaumont: Pythagore, 2004), *passim*; and René Laloux, *Ces dessins qui bougent: 1892–1992, cent ans de cinéma d'animation* (Paris: Dreamland, 1996).

59 Laurence Engel et al., *Le Monde selon Topor* (Paris: Les Cahiers dessinés, 2017), 78–9; Frantz Vaillant, *Roland Topor, ou, le rire étranglé: biographie* (Paris: Buchet-Chastel, 2007); and Alexandre Devaux et al., *Topor: dessinateur de presse* (Paris: Les Cahiers dessinés, 2014).

60 Author's translations.

61 Durgnat, 'Borowczyk', 42; and Kurz, 'Cruel Imagination', 68–70.

62 Vimenet, *Walerian Borowczyk*, 44–7.

63 Roy Armes, *The Ambiguous Image: Narrative Style in Modern European Cinema* (Bloomington: Indiana University Press, 1976), 169.

Chapter 11

Everyday Dreamlife: Surrealism and Animation in Japan

Catherine L. Hansen

A stop-motion introduction

The ‘AkeruE’ children’s museum in Odaiba, Tokyo, with a range of interactive STEAM exhibits meant to foster a spirit of ‘creative action’, features a stop-motion animation studio room, complete with boxes of toys arrestingly grouped by colour, a large theatre screen, and private green-screen booths. It takes about ten minutes of repetitive shooting and object-shifting to create a jerky, minute-long, stop-motion film. What is startling is how quickly the imagination – lulled into a trance state by the increasingly automatic movements of the hands incrementally adjusting figurines and taking snapshots – drifts into pure surrealism. An intrepid pair of hourglass-lovers rescue each other from an onslaught of fried eggs; an enormous slab of bacon pursues a tiny bear, who escapes by becoming a bird. The surreal state of grace attained in such marginal, fleeting moments tends to slip through the social and institutional cracks of meaning-making. But the fact that both surrealism and animation are things that just about anyone can ‘do’, filling an endless supply of surreal and of animated things, creates both problems and opportunities for practitioners and scholars.

One commonplace of the study of surrealism is that it will not hold still under investigation. Surrealism is a set of methods or obsessions, a conceptual–imaginative palette, a set of historical facts and their aftermaths, a way of articulating politics to art, a thing one does with others, or a strong tendency to import new objects into consensus reality. ‘Japanese animation’, in much the same way, strikes a highly coloured figure in the collective mind – but refracts and fragments up close.

What is more, in the project of considering surrealism, Japan, and animation all together, ‘Japanese surrealism’ is also a slippery fish. Yuko Ishii and Michael Richardson comment that ‘surrealism as it became manifest in Japan contains so many diffuse, not to say contradictory, elements that it is incredibly difficult to pin down’. Each of its many collective and individual instances proves to be either ‘highly original, or … [not] surrealism at all’.[1] But one reason for this is, as Richardson suggests, ‘surrealism had a more widespread impact [in Japan] than anywhere else, even France’, dissolving so thoroughly into the air that it became both imperceptible and inescapable.[2] This condition may owe to a prevailing impatience, among surrealist practitioners in Japan, with forms

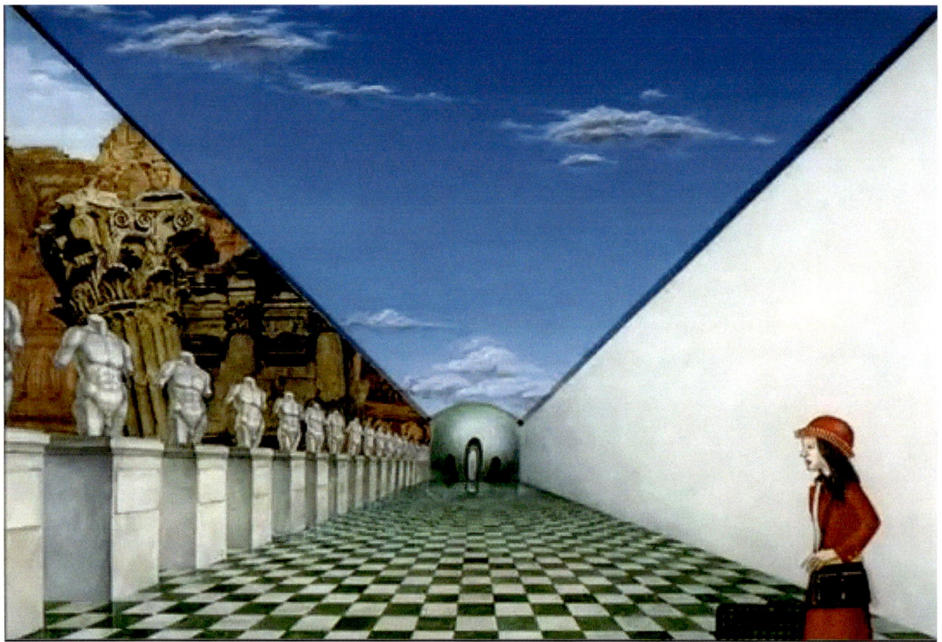

Figure 11.1 Kawamoto Kihachirō, dir., *Tabi*, 1973.

of art and action that do not draw from or spill out into everyday life and practice. This insistence on the everyday – its abundance, its strangeness – is well documented in Japanese art and avant-garde discourse low and high, including both surrealism and animation. The 'everyday surreal', as encountered throughout this essay, is the lived experience of the body, with its fluid boundaries and uncanny margins; of everyday objects, with their inexhaustible details and dreamlike self-evidence; and of the mind that domesticates what it encounters and makes it feel routine and 'real'. To be surreal is to spell out the lived realities of the most impossible premises, including those of the world accepted as real.

Kawamoto Kihachirō's journey

One of many promising points of entry into what is involved in discussing surrealism and animation in Japan is the career of Kawamoto Kihachirō (1925–2010), a stop-motion puppet animator who also made a small number of cut-paper works with painted backdrops, including *Tabi* (Journey; 1973; 12 minutes; Japan). The film was inspired in part by Kawamoto's trip to Prague in the 1960s to study under the Czech stop-motion animator Jiří Trnka, whose work was increasingly screened and admired in Tokyo at the time. Kawamoto's memories of his complete disorientation in the new city, and his rage over the suffering caused by the August 1968 Soviet invasion of Czechoslovakia, come together in a tale of a woman leaving Japan and returning transformed, set to lines by the Song dynasty poet Su Shi. Her plane descends onto empty city streets that visually cite landscapes from Giorgio de Chirico, Paul Delvaux and Remedios Varo. In her red cloche and matching fitted suit, haunted by rows of headless male marble sculptures, she crosses subterranean spaces composed of heaped-up strata, resembling one of Piranesi's *grotteschi* – the unconscious as a cross-section of an architectural dig. It becomes clear across the collage-scapes that follow – with Dalínian sliced-up crucifixions and other non-sequiturs scattered between crepuscular skies and checkerboard floors, in a surrealist junkyard mashup – that 'surrealism' has been made into the site of a nightmare-encounter with Europe, where sinister things lurk amid classical, columned splendour: cadaverous ghouls, faceless de Chirico soldiers, Soviet tanks.

In the sixties and seventies – according to Miryam Sas, an authority on surrealism's crosscurrents in Japan – artists 'often took Surrealist thought for granted, incorporating it freely into their ideas and purposes'.[3] Although postwar groups and individuals could often trace their inspiration (or drew their membership) from prewar surrealist projects, the result was less often a programme of collective action and more often a vocabulary and toolkit for 'understanding the role of art in society [or] … delving into the dark areas of the soul or unconscious'.[4] Kawamoto, who in 1989 took the presidency of the Japanese Animation Association, was among those who used this readily available vocabulary.

Kawamoto made another cut-paper animation the following year. Titled *Shijin no Shōgai* (A Poet's Life; 1974; 19 minutes; Japan), its source was an eponymous short story by Abe Kōbō, written when the latter was a part of the surrealist/Marxist group Yoru no Kai, 'The Night Society' – founded in 1947 by Hanada Kiyoteru and Tarō Okamoto (who, a decade earlier, had been part of Georges Bataille's Acéphale group and had shown his work in the 1938 International Surrealist Exhibition). *Shijin no Shōgai* is a brown-and-grey socialist realist story that has strayed into a dreamworld – vibrating with fury at the owner class and truly disturbing in its imagery. An apocalyptic cold has descended on a small city, freezing rich and poor alike. The 'dreams, souls, and desires' have 'evaporated' from the poor who can't afford sweaters, have cut off the sun, and are now falling as relentless snow.

The film's broader context is significant. The period immediately after the Second World War marked the second time that the Japanese animation profession had to rebuild itself almost entirely (the first was after the 1923 Great Kantō earthquake), amid growing pressure and censorship under the Occupation and its aftermath, along with disheartening competition from Disney. Animation historian Jonathan Clements writes: 'the scramble for subsistence and fierce competition over jobs in a shrunken film industry meant animation was side-lined for a decade. By the beginning of the 1960s, [the animator] Yamamoto Eiichi … estimated the size of the Japanese animation "industry" at roughly 500 people' (incidentally, this was also the number of self-reported 'surrealists' working in Tokyo in the mid-1930s, a figure that startled André Breton).[5] In the forties, amid union-related conflict, purges and schisms, the enthusiastically Red-hating Watanabe Tetsuzō took command of the Tōhō film studio and fired a large number of 'communist sympathizers', including almost fifty animators. Events intensified with a union occupation of Tōhō headquarters, followed by surreal scenes on barricades, in which special effects materiel like rain and wind machines were creatively weaponized; Watanabe, backed by US occupation

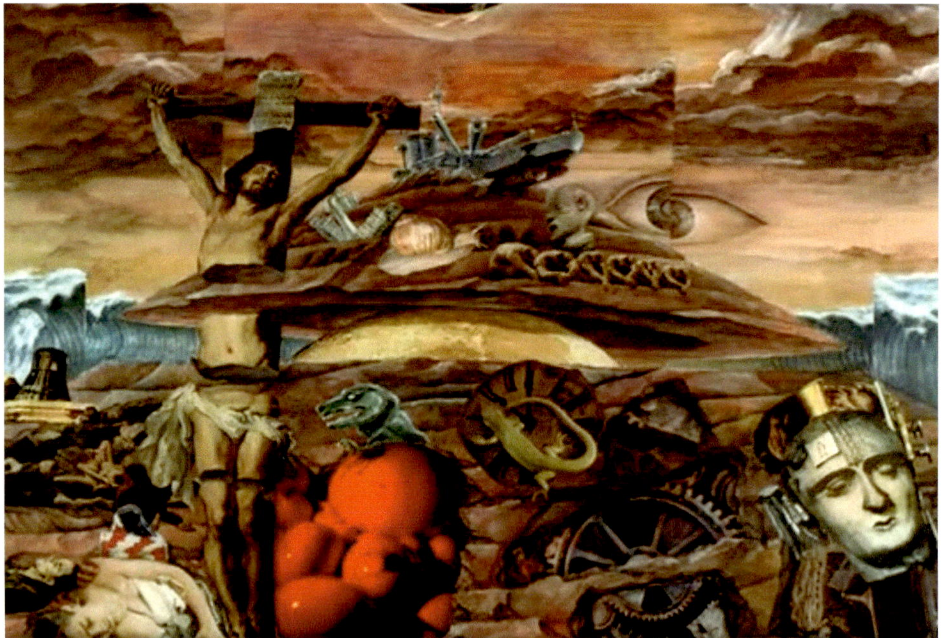

Figure 11.2 Kawamoto Kihachirō, dir., *Tabi*, 1973.

authorities, fought back with armed units and literal tanks.[6] Kawamoto was among those who became jobless during these events, and partially based *Shijin no Shōgai* on them.

A third significant moment in Kawamoto's career opens another window onto the converging worlds of the literary–artistic avant-garde and of animation. Beginning in the late fifties, the animation profession managed to hitch itself to a generous patron: advertising. Kawamoto, working with the great cut-paper animator Ōfuji Noburō, created puppet-based commercials for Asahi Beer and other companies, and finally created his own animation studio, Shiba Production. Clements evokes a vast, 'uncommemorated' world of Japanese animation for TV commercials, where candy and pharmaceutical companies became 'patrons of the arts'. This was the case for the early, avant-garde efforts of the 'Group of Three' (Sannin no Kai), comprising the work of Kuri Yōji, Yanagihara Ryōhei and Manabe Hiroshi. It was their 'day jobs in advertising',[7] Clements points out, that supported preparations for their first public screening at the Sōgetsu Art Centre on 26 November 1960, with a one-hour programme of 8-mm black-and-white films and a manifesto calling for new kinds of experimentation to arrive hand in hand with new modes of consciousness. These activities soon evolved into a series of Sōgetsu 'animation festivals', to which Kawamoto's studio also contributed.

These three episodes serve to colour and 'animate' the questions that undergird this investigation. Were any Japanese animators linked to the Surrealist movement and its central or peripheral figures? Yes, but at varying degrees of separation. In what ways did animators participate in and/or gain momentum from Surrealism as a distributed international movement? Many, but it can take some telling to show how. Did any individuals associated with surrealist groups in Japan or elsewhere act as mediators with the practice and profession of animation and/or its adjacent arts? Yes, but it's often complicated. In what ways have animators in Japan 'received' surrealism, and what have they made of it, by way of citation, inspiration, caricature or critique? The answer potentially reaches any and all examples of animated art in Japan, from mid-century art-house experiments to the participatory, intermedial worlds of the contemporary consumption of anime, where the secular 'surreal', using the plastic resources of animation, draws from the same wells frequented by the Surrealist movement (dreams, the unconscious, automatism, unexplored plasticities of form). The 'limitless world' of animation (in Kuri Yōji's words) is perhaps equalled only by what the First Manifesto of Surrealism called the limitless 'real functioning of thought'.[8]

Prewar: new plasticities

In 1925, just as the earliest translations of European surrealist writing and the earliest exhibitions of surrealist art were showing up in Japan, the so-called Peace Preservation Law instated a pre-Orwellian and quite literal 'thought police' that oversaw ideological transgressions and threats to the 'national body'. Barriers to avant-garde experimentation in all domains grew increasingly steep, as militarism tightened its grip and artists were called to demonstrate their nationalist credentials. Even in these circumstances, amateur, experimental and radically inclined animators made films. The abstract animated works of pre-Second World War small-gauge film-makers like Ogino Shigeji (1899–1991) are the tip of the iceberg of a largely overlooked world of 'significant experimentation in cinematic technique by amateur filmmakers', including animators.[9] The Proletarian Film League (Prokino, 1929–34) also somehow managed to put out animated works of agitprop on dangerous topics like Japanese imperialism, as well as to screen films by amateur groups.[10] In the very small animation scene at the time, it is likely that experimental and political zones overlapped.

At a time when celluloid (used in cel animation) was difficult to obtain, animators in the late twenties through the thirties used a broad range of techniques – including cut paper, collage and sequences of still images set to music or sound – that resembled the practices of the self-identified surrealist photographers and visual artists who were their contemporaries. These surrealists experimented not only with photocollage, photomontage and narratively sequenced photographs, but with hybrid techniques like the 'photo-dessin' and the 'photo-gram', the latter inspired by Man Ray.[11] Man Ray's 1926 film *Emak Bakia*, which he called a 'cinépoème', is also the source of the 'cinepoem' (シネ・ポエム) genre-designation that will show up in independent and art-house animations (e.g. Manabe Hiroshi's 'Cinepoem Work No. 1' shown at the Sōgetsu in 1961).

In the spring of 1941, two prominent and influential surrealists – the painter Fukuzawa Ichiro and the artist, essayist and poet Takiguchi Shūzō, who played a role in Japanese surrealism rivalling that of Breton in Paris – were arrested under the Peace Preservation Law. The authorities had tended to take surrealism seriously, as a 'cultural mission' of international communism, and Takiguchi was interrogated for months. In the thirties, practicing surrealists had already been forced to be evasive in their visual and verbal language. Jelena Stojković shows how the word 'avant-garde' (*zen'ei*) came to stand in for 'surrealism' when the latter could not openly be admitted, and how Takiguchi then urged further evasive measures, replacing 'avant-garde' with 'plastic' (*zōkei* – referring to the shaping of form, used to denote 'plastic arts'). Founded in 1934, the 'New Plasticity Art Association' – including Takiguchi in its membership – was 'the most established and immediately recognizable surrealist outpost in the country' before the war.[12] For the surrealist photographers and collagist–montagists of the Association (and other surrealist-leaning groups of the thirties) 'plasticity' was a term that stood for the braiding of art with life: 'in the avant-garde discourse of that time [it] connoted the relevance of everyday experience to revolutionary politics and social change'.[13] This crypto-surrealist 'formativity' was perhaps not far, as well, from the 'plasmatic' quality that Sergei Eisenstein found in the metamorphic animated lines of Disney, but also in Salvador Dalí's painting: 'the plasmaticness of existence, from which everything can arise'.[14]

The impact of Dalí's art as well as his writing in surrealist Japan was immense, partly due to the efforts of Takiguchi himself as a translator and interpreter of Dalí – on the level not only of visual citation (e.g. distorted, displaced, hyper-detailed objects set against vast horizons) but of method and concept. This included Dalí's 'paranoia critique': surrealist artists and photographers used pareidolia and creative misprision to seek surreality in the 'deep folds of the everyday' (in Takiguchi's words).[15] It speaks to how deeply this concept took root in Tokyo's visual art worlds that in 1965, Kaji Yūsuke – an advertising copywriter and designer – reached easily for the vocabulary of 'paranoia critique' to describe an animated film by Uno Akira (stylized as 'Uno Aquirax') shown at one of the Sōgetsu Animation festivals, where a woman's lower limbs pan down into flower stems, among other transformations.[16] Dalí's writings on the mysteries and formal possibilities of material things also informed the creation of photomontages teeming with strange and ordinary objects, resembling stills from an imponderable stop-motion drama. Such projects were part and parcel of the plasticians' declared commitment to material and everyday life, understood also as a commitment to its undoing and remaking – modest, intimate and up close.

Similar practices continued with Jikken Kōbō (the 'Experimental Workshop'), a group founded, named and mentored after the war by Takiguchi, as the experiments, magazines and theoretical writings of the prewar constellation of Japanese surrealism were taken up by a new generation.

Postwar: Jikken Kōbō animates the world

Around the time that Jikken Kōbō – a loose affiliation of like-minded friends and amateurs, designers, musicians, writers, and visual and proto-multimedia artists – was founded in 1951, film and animated works from abroad were becoming increasingly available for general viewing, carried on an Occupation-mediated flood of new information about the art world and its movements. Chronologically and geographically mixed up, this all came as a jolt to a cultural system already humming with new commercialism. The young photographer Ōtsuji Kiyoji, however, was in Tokyo's second-hand bookshops, discovering surrealist Japan in old issues of *Photo Times*, where essays by Takiguchi accompanied 'plastic' experiments. Ōtsuji soon joined Jikken Kōbō, and later as part of the 'Graphic Group' (1953–6) created an abstract animation that he and his collaborators called *Kine Calligraph* (1955). This experimental film was inspired by Norman McLaren's 'direct animation' techniques of scratching or inscribing the film stock or the optical soundtrack or applying colour directly to 16mm film.[17] In Japanese, the term 'cine-calligraphy' (rather than 'kine-calligraphy') is strongly associated with McLaren and in particular with his 1955 animated film *Blinkety Blank*, which in Japan is known as 'Improvised Line and Colour Poem'. 'Cine-calligraphy' animations (along with 'cinepoems') later featured at Sōgetsu Festival screenings.

Jikken Kōbō created 'presentations', mixed-media performances, and 'functional spaces'[18] instead of exhibitions, linking the visual to the aural in wildly original fashion. The group also collaborated in early 1954 to create a series of photographic images for 'Asahi Picture News', which was a popular segment of the widely read illustrated magazine *Asahi Graph* edited by Izawa Tadasu. In consultation with Takiguchi and with Kitadai Shōzō of Jikken Kōbō, Izawa solicited fifty-five photographs of dramatic scenes and arrangements of everyday objects and materials. The photographs were done by Ōtsuji – the convert to surrealism – and the arrangements done by Jikken Kōbō members and a succession of new contacts. These included Hamada Hamao, who had founded a prewar surrealist group and who later joined the 'Graphic Group'; and Teshigahara Sōfū, whose son Hiroshi (the director of the 1964 film *Woman in the Dunes* and a Yoru no Kai member) also became the director of the Sōgetsu Centre. Kitadai arranged the first photo scene, made of 'millet husks, soy beans, red azuki, aluminium wire, piano wire, Kent paper, sawdust'.[19]

As Obinata Kin'ichi explains, 'the artists consistently manipulated common, ordinary materials found in the everyday environment to fabricate a new artistic world'.[20] In some cases these 'worlds' were sequences of different angles of the same object-scene, intimations of a hidden story. The pursuit of such a 'hidden animation in the object world' is how William Marotti characterizes a prevailing trend of the Japanese art world around this time, especially as it plays out in the Yomiuri Indépendant (or 'Yomiuri Anpan') exhibition series, initiated by a Takiguchi collaborator (Kaido Hideo). The mainstream in these exhibitions was to explore the 'uncanny potentials and eerie physicality of the discards of the everyday world', 'a hidden life of objects and debris emerging from new patterns of daily life'.[21]

Jikken Kōbō also 'animated' objects, and a wide variety of them – including figural mobiles created by Kitadai and others. One of Kitadai's mobiles appeared at the 1953 Abstract Art and Surrealism Exhibition at the National Museum of Modern Art, Tokyo – a response to the 1936 Fantastic Art, Dadaism, Surrealism Exhibition in New York[22] – and later in the 1960s he made multi-strobe images of objects in motion, for example falling sheets of paper, calling them 'visions of the unknown'.[23] In the early fifties, Yamaguchi Katsuhiro of Jikken Kōbō created a series of 'vitrines', with abstract shapes and other constructions set up behind rippled glass which animated the interior as the viewer moved. The vitrines, mobiles, and object-dioramas were all used in the Matsumoto Toshio-directed PR film *Ginrin* (Silver Ring; 1955; 12 minutes; Japan) where the Kōbō combined all its powers to give shape to the world of dreams, specifically a young boy's trippy dream about bicycles. There is even a simple animated sequence with diamond-shaped schematics of bicycle frames.[24]

Far more difficult to view in its original form is the series of 'surrealistic audio-visual stories' that Jikken Kōbō created with a then-brand-new technology by Tokyo Tsūshin Kōgyō (now Sony), called the Autoslide, a projector combined with a tape recorder that allowed slides to shift based on cues marked on the audio track.[25] Kōbō members produced their own slides, either by painting abstract compositions or creating object dioramas and figural or abstract constructions, sequentially photographed. One member wrote that watching the auto-slideshow felt like 'taking a stroll … the viewer is allowed to play as he wishes with his own images inside each still image. *At the same time, we are likely to notice that the compensatory operation of our senses fuses the fragmentary pictures into a single image*' (emphasis added).[26] This 'compensatory operation' is what visually fuses sequential images in any optical device, from phenakistiscopes to film projectors. One cannot help but imagine Kōbō members wanting to create an animated film and meeting too many obstacles along the way – as Takiguchi writes, the Autoslide project was conceived as plans for a film fell through.[27] Autoslide titles included 'Lespugue' (referring to the 26,000 year-old 'Venus de Lespugue' figurine), with abstract slides painted in primary colours of pastel and gouache by Komai Tetsurō; and 'An Unknown World', with composite-photo and sculptural compositions by Kitadai Shōzō that resemble stills from an animated science fiction cinepoem.

On the occasion of the fifth presentation programme of the Workshop in September 1953 at Daiichi Seimei Hall in Tokyo, where the Autoslide series was shown, Takiguchi wondered: 'What effects, what expressive values might result from the combination of still images with music?'[28] Of course, the combination of still images with music and narration is another way of describing 'limited animation' of the type famously practised by Tezuka Osamu, the creator of *Astro Boy*: the technique of approximating the expensive, labour-intensive effects of realistic 'full animation' with the creative use of still images, aided by music and the 'compensatory' senses.

The careers of individual members of the Kōbō continued, often internationally, even as they drifted away from collective action; notably, several former members were strongly involved in the activities of the Sōgetsu Art Centre, an avant-garde mecca from 1959 to 1971, alongside Takiguchi and many figures from avant-garde, visual arts and commercial worlds.

The historian and art critic Hamaguchi Ryūichi called the Sōgetsu the 'surreal salon', referring to its curious mix of opulence and emptiness – the 'gold fusuma and vermillion doors, the pillars, beams, and balustrades of polished oak'[29] – but where, as Uno Aquirax commented, you could easily mistake a fire hydrant for an *objet*.[30] It is tempting to claim that the Sōgetsu Art Centre was the fine instrument by which surrealist sensibilities – including a certain lack of inhibition with regard to formal possibilities – were instilled deep into the heart of animation as it is practised in Japan, from mass entertainment to experimental art.

The Sōgetsu Art Centre: threshold of the limitless world

The series of animation shows held at the Sōgetsu Art Centre between 1960 and 1966 were in part the result of director Teshigahara Hiroshi's interests in underground cinema, experimental theatre and dance, and performance art, as well as in 'transgenre collaboration' at the heart of a broader artworld 'rebellion against solemn modernist certitudes at the intersection of visual expression and the everyday'.[31] But they were also an outgrowth of a new 'Experimental Workshop' – the 'Kuri Jikken Kōbō', a modest animation studio in Kōjimachi maintained by Kuri Yōji of the Sannin no Kai, where Kuri encouraged newcomers – many of whom went on to brilliant careers – to make their first animations and show them at the Sōgetsu. They included Furukawa Taku, a Kuri protégé and later a Japan Animation Society president: Furukawa's 1968 animation 'Ushi Atama' (Bull Head) with its fluttering grim reaper–Minotaur, displays 'Kuri Jikken Manga Kōbō' in English letters at the beginning and fascinatingly, at the end, 'World Ordinarists Society'. (At Sōgetsu, Furukawa recalls, one would suddenly encounter Takiguchi with his 'radiant smile' in the lobby, alongside the artist and film-maker Terayama Shūji.)[32] The graphic artist Yokoo Tadanori was one of the first group of 'outsiders' invited to screen their work with the Sannin no Kai in 1964, along with Uno Aquirax and Makoto Wada (creator of an audience favourite, the very funny animation short 'Murder!') – all three learned the ropes at the Kuri Kōbō. The psychedelic pop artist and ex-Neo dada member Keiichi Tanaami made his first animation, 'Marionettes in Masks', at the Kuri Kōbō.

The Sannin no Kai came together before the advent of 'anime' as a distinctly Japanese phenomenon, which happened in the 'early to mid-1970s as the strands of limited animation, context-integrated merchandise, and active fandom began to coalesce' around animated works, later accelerated by the advent of videotape and niche audiences.[33] Despite a growing TV animation market, 'art animation' was not yet a thing: it was arguably the Sannin no Kai, working with the Sōgetsu Centre, that made it one. Kuri recalls that the group got started just as the manga and magazine era was becoming the TV era. The collaborators sensed, however, that the animated imagination could achieve more than the expensive, Disneyfied kids' entertainment (called 'manga eiga' or, already, 'TV anime') released by big studios like Tōei.[34]

Kuri Yōji, Manabe Hiroshi and Yanagihara Ryōhei, who had met amid the cultural and political upheaval surrounding the 'Anpo Protests' against the postwar US–Japan 'mutual cooperation and security treaty', presented their work to Sōgetsu as an animation spin-off of a modern jazz 'group of three' already associated with the Centre.[35] The first and second Sōgetsu animation festivals, in 1960 and 1961, screened only the group's work. The third event, in Spring 1963, included one foreign work ('Paper Paradise' by Carlos Marchiori). In September 1964 the event became an 'animation festival' proper, and brought in Uno, Yokoo and Wada. By 1965 and 1966, the festival was international, and included Japanese studios like Tezuka's Mushi Pro (short for 'Production') and Kawamoto's Shiba Pro. By the following year, however, Sōgetsu programming pivoted to experimental film, although it still showed animation and hosted an 'Invitation to Animation' event in 1967 that featured Disney, Grimault and Czech animators.

At Sōgetsu, where the old-guard avant-garde met the new, graphic designers and illustrators rubbed shoulders with both traditional artists and professional animators. The Sannin no Kai, characteristically in this sense, were initially artworld-outsiders with avant-garde instincts. Manabe writes that 'all three of us worked with manga, design, and painting, in other words on non-moving screens, but we wanted to make them move, and thought they could only fully be expressed if they moved'. The group's goal was thus to 'explore new kinds of movement'.[36] Many other festival contributors, also new to moving images, made extensive use of 'limited animation'. Wada, the creator of 'Murder!', wryly dismissed his own work as a bunch of 'no-account slides'.[37] The film writer Mori Takuya felt he was watching a festival of 'film-like illustration',[38] which he later called 'still animation' and 'unanimated animation'[39] – not far from Jikken Kōbō's Autoslide. Miryam Sas, looking at the Sōgetsu scene as a 'centre of a lively series of debates and writings on what, precisely, animation should be',[40] guesses toward links between this milieu and the 'sensibilities' of later anime – for example, between the festival and design work of Uno Aquirax and the visual style of Eiichi Yamamoto/Mushi Pro's 1973 feature-length *Belladonna of Sadness*. What also stands out in *Belladonna*, however, is how it achieves animation effects by panning over illustrations – especially illustrations that metamorphose by this means, like Uno's 'paranoiac-critical' panning above.

Uno, like others at the festivals, cultivated an inventive understanding of animation. In his festival film *Omae to watashi* (You and me; 1965; 10 min; Japan), for example, 'I drew illustrations on a human body, and photographed the way the picture moved with the movement of the flesh': a man sniffing a flower notably becomes a man with a pistol at his temple.[41] Commenting on Uno's self-described technique of regarding ordinary objects on the 'canvas of his mind' and waiting like a 'medium/spiritualist' to fix their transformations on the page, Sas sees 'a twenty-first century refraction of the fascination with that liminal space between intrapsychic and material structures'.[42] In a late interview, Uno confirms that he sketches figures not from models but 'in a state of automatism' – a state powered by a gap between the drawing hand and the unknown thing finding itself being drawn.[43]

Matsumoto Toshio wrote in 1966 that avant-garde films allow us to encounter what he calls 'things' (*mono*) – hitherto unrecognized objects inhabiting a still nascent world of experience.[44] The goal of the Sannin no Kai was to allow animation as a form to venture forth towards this world of immanent yet concealed potential, populated by objects that withdraw from existing modes of perception. The group writes in its 1960 manifesto, 'In Search of New Images': 'How often do we see someone who boldly sets out to do something completely new succeed in making only superficial changes because they are unable to break free of established thought patterns and methods? … New processes and technologies must go hand in hand with new modes of consciousness. Therein lies the path to the creation of truly new images. This is what we … want to achieve through animation.'[45] In addition to the vaunted 'cross-media collaboration' taking place at Sōgetsu, they want 'to transcend our own personal boundaries' and 'explor[e] different processes and modes of consciousness'. Although they want animation to 'evolve and

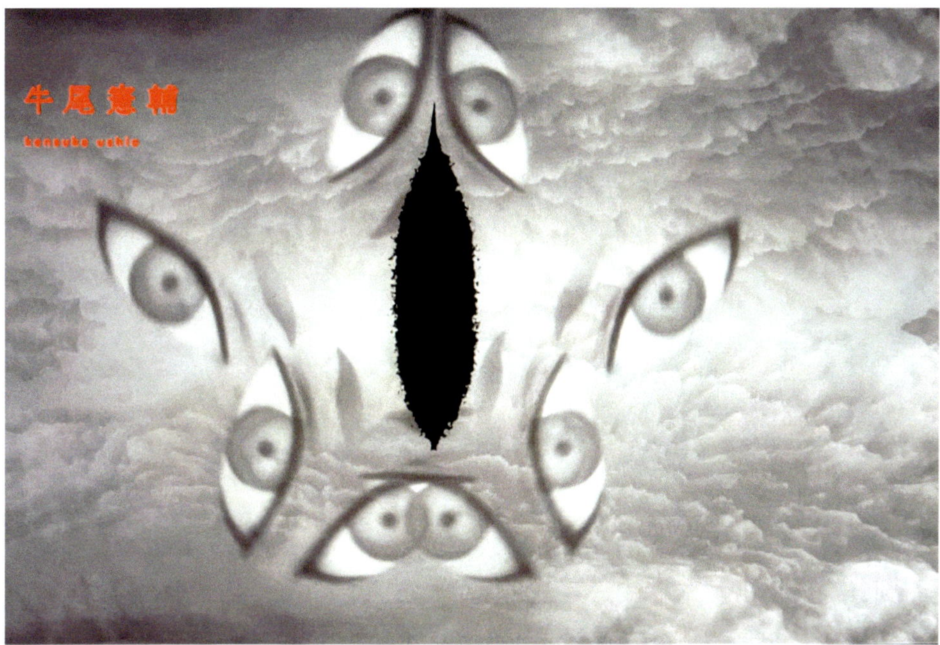

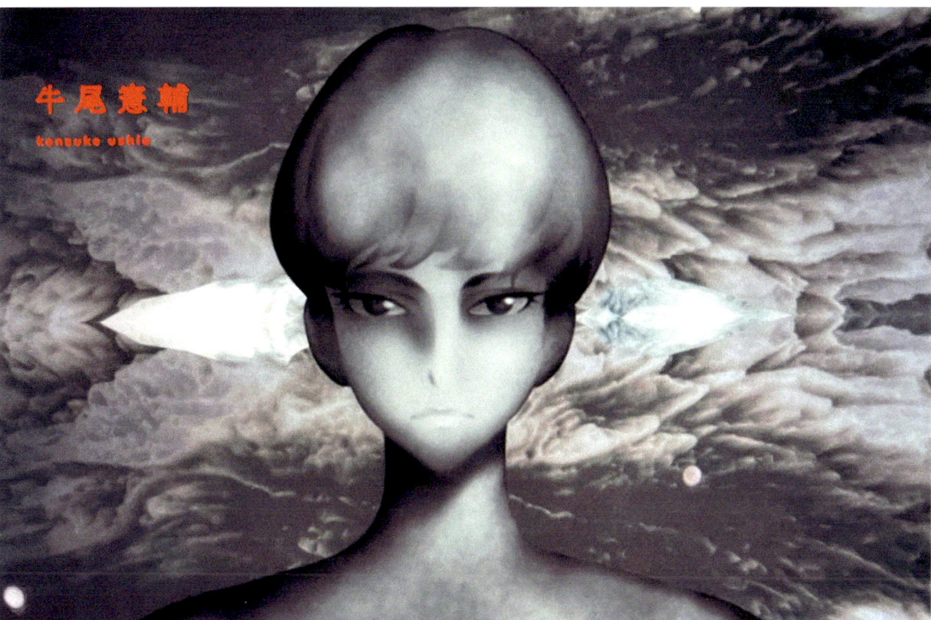

Figure 11.3 a/b Stills from Yuasa Masaaki, dir., *Devilman Crybaby*, 2018. The opening credits use the Rorschach-like 'decalcomania'-textures frequently seen in dreamlike or 'surreal' environments. Decalcomania is a technique used by surrealists such as Max Ernst and Óscar Domínguez.

stay truly contemporary' like other experimental arts, the goal of this evolution is the freeing of consciousness.

Others around Sōgetsu felt similarly. The science fiction writer Komatsu Sakyō, for example, claims that 'animation may hold a very important key to a future world in which we will need to process and attend to thousands of times more information than we do today'. Animation represents an entirely new domain of communication, for which we do not yet have a grammar. He urges Yokoo, Uno and others not to become mere artists, but instead to 'explore all possibilities'.[46]

In March 1959, the arch-surrealist Abe Kōbō published a short text in a 'Sōgetsu Liberal Arts Club' pamphlet called 'Keep your dreams in good repair'. It speaks to what was in the air at Sōgetsu on the eve of its rendezvous with animation. Night-dreams and day-dreams, Abe writes, have one thing in common: they envisage things that are not real as if they were. This power of 'anticipation' guides us through the 'forest of everyday life', but can also 'operate freely, unbound by direct reality (e.g., in the world of surrealism), and investigating them will help us discover realities of which we are not yet aware'. In this way, to be 'rich in dreams' is like having a ship with excellent radar – it doesn't make much difference crossing a river, but on the open sea it does, especially in a storm. That storm, Abe concludes, is the work of creation.[47]

A tendency to navigate by dream – and an appreciation for the limitless potential of animation that is an inheritance of not only the Sōgetsu era but the Japanese surrealist tradition it channelled – are visible in the work of those contemporary animators who have most deeply breathed the surreal air. Yuasa Masaaki, for example, names Salvador Dalí as a core inspiration, but also visually cites whole compressed histories of animation experiment in films like *Mind Game* (2004), whose death-defying protagonist witnesses God cycling through dozens of shapes in seconds, but also through vector and pixel graphics, stop-motion, cut-paper, early CGI, crayon drawings and live action, like an avatar of the 'storm' of creation. Yuasa's commitment, however, to the 'real functioning' of animation is also grounded in a close attention to the details and daily sensations of bodies, objects and relationships – to, as he puts it, the 'nameless flowers and grasses blooming on the road'.[48]

Coda: the persistence of cicadas

The twelve-episode anime series *Puella Magi Madoka Magica*, like many other anime series, centres on young women in high school – but it is a harrowing deconstruction of the tropes and assumptions of the 'magical girl' (*mahō shōjo*) genre of anime. The animation design collective Gekidan Inu Curry – influenced by Jiří Trnka and Jan Švankmajer – created the hallucinatory alternate dimensions inhabited by 'witches', the primary antagonists of the series. Each witch dimension is different, but they tend to feature a version of 'surrealism' that has become visually encoded in contemporary anime: floating checkerboard floors, heaped-up details and iterations, metamorphic faces, empty architectural vistas, decalcomania-textures and invasions of collage-like butterfly wings. (The butterflies also feature in Satoshi Kon's 2006 animated film *Paprika*,

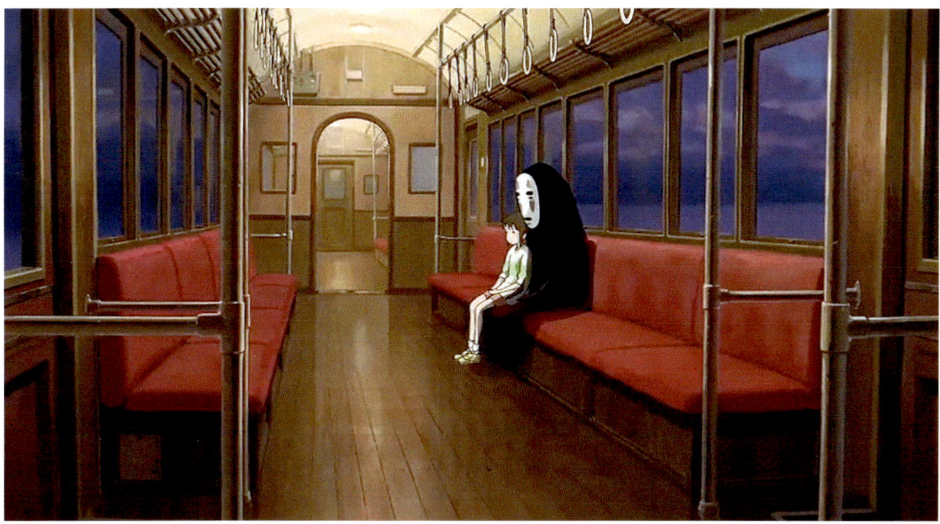

Figure 11.4 Miyazaki Hayao, dir., *Spirited Away*, 2001. Studio Ghibli films and other fantasy anime frequently use train scenes as icons of the 'everyday'.

a tale of a hubristic attempt to create a living, collective dream – like a nightmare version of a surrealist manifesto. Butterflies and moths are also frequent Dalí motifs.) In the copious, queasy carnivalerie of *Madoka*'s witch dimensions, surrealism, like for Kawamoto Kihachirō in *Tabi*, is the vocabulary of nightmare and despair.

But consider the 2011 Kyoto Animation comedy series *Nichijō* (Ordinary Life), another tale of young women in high school, where the surreal is the native grammar of all that happens in the most intimate corners of the everyday. In the reception of contemporary animation, from studio series to YouTube jetsam, 'Surr' (シュール, sometimes 'Surr-ism' or シュール系) is a genre-designation that most often refers to absurdist gags and late-night nonsense humour, but which also finds itself attached to *Nichijō*. The show, however, reaches for something more. Viewers have commented on the way *Nichijō* doubles down on its slice-of-dreamlife skits, extrapolating their lunatic premises to the point that they come to seem reasonable and inevitable. But it also zeroes in on the overlooked and insignificant crannies of human individual and interpersonal experience, heightening their inherent emotional and physical drama, and marshalling oneiric and metamorphic animation sequences in their service. Viewing these moments is like zooming in on the head of a pin to find frantic angels dancing. Each episode also keeps fixating on a particular city or suburb scene, where nothing of significance to the plot occurs: for example, a row of balconies in a *danchi* (a public housing apartment complex). The *danchi* tableau is shown in the morning, midday, late afternoon, evening and night – mostly silent, and as motionless as a limited animation 'slide', except for the changing light. Hanging laundry appears, then disappears. Balcony doors (single-pane, with aluminium siding) stand open or closed. What is the meaning of these scenes?

Certain indices of everyday experience seem to show up in no matter what the narrative or genre of contemporary anime: overhead power lines, cicadas in summer (seemingly the drone of 'reality' itself), the waning day flashing orange on windows, a half-empty train car filled with melancholy golden-hour light, sun dappling through leaves, narrow residential streets with cinderblock walls, steaming bowls of food, mothers washing dishes at a stainless steel sink/countertop. These details can both anchor a narrative in everyday reality and mark the distance of characters' inner or outer struggles from its comforting ordinariness. These moments – the droning cicadas, the silent balconies – map the dialectics of the surreal in contemporary Japanese popular anime, which has inherited much from the surrealist and animated experiments and manifestos of the past: everyday life, in its deepest 'folds', is surreal, whereas the surreal, at its extreme, resolves into the everyday. What they impart is both that *this* is not all there is (it is only a rippled surface), and that this *is* all there is – but it is limitless, and it is enough.

Notes

1. Yuko Ishii and Michael Richardson, 'Japan', in *The International Encyclopedia of Surrealism*, ed. Michael Richardson, vol. 1, *Movements* (London: Bloomsbury, 2019), 83.
2. Michael Richardson, 'Charting an Amorphous Past: Surrealism in Japan'. Review of Majella Munro, *Communicating Vessels: The Surrealist Movement in Japan, 1923–70*, in *Art History*, 37, no. 5 (November 2014).
3. Miryam Sas, *Faultlines: Cultural Memory and Japanese Surrealism* (Stanford, CA: Stanford University Press, 1999), 158–9.
4. Sas, *Faultlines*, 159.
5. Jonathan Clements, *Anime: A History* (Basingstoke: Palgrave Macmillan, 2013), 91. The Breton detail appears in Věra Linhartová, *Dada et surréalisme au Japon* (Paris: Publications Orientalistes de France, 1987), 4.
6. See for example Clements, *Anime*, 80–1. 'Surreal' is how Clements characterizes these events.
7. Clements, *Anime*, 87.
8. Kuri Yōji, 'The Limitless World of Animation', quoted in Jason Douglass, 'In Search of a "New Wind"', in *Animation Studies* (May 2019).
9. See Aaron Gerow, 'The Past of Japanese Science Fiction and Fantasy Movies', citing Nada Hisashi and others, in *Beyond Godzilla: Alternative Futures and Fantasies in Japanese Cinema*, ed. Mark Schilling (Japan Society, March–April 2017), 35.
10. The group Dōeisha, for example, screened an animated shadow play at Prokino's 31 May, 1930 'First Proletarian Film Evening'. See also Clements, *Anime*, 43–4, 48–50.
11. See Jelena Stojković, *The Impossible Avant-Garde: Surrealism and Photography in 1930s Japan* (Abingdon: Routledge, 2020). The 'photo-dessin' was an invention by the artist Ei-Kyu (also 'Ei-Q') (1911–60), which sought to 'realize reality beyond the conscious conclusions of thinking' (28).
12. Stojković, *The Impossible Avant-Garde*, 48.
13. Stojković, *The Impossible Avant-Garde*, 37.
14. In Jay Leyda (ed.), *Eisenstein on Disney* (Calcutta: Seagull Books, 1986), 46 and 70.
15. Takiguchi Shūzō, 'Photography and Surrealism' (February 1938), quoted in Stojković, *The Impossible Avant-Garde*, 67.

16 Kaji Yūsuke, 'Great Expectations for Films by Designers: Aesthetics of Animation', in *Kagayake 60-nendai* (輝け60年代：草月アートセンターの全記録 / Shine On, Sixties: A Complete Record of the Sōgetsu Art Centre) (SAC Records Publication Committee, 2002), 339.

17 See for example Machiko Kusahara, 'Proto-Media Art: Revisiting Japanese Postwar Avant-garde Art', in *A Companion to Digital Art*, ed. Christiane Paul (Chichester: Wiley-Blackwell, 2016).

18 Takiguchi Shūzō, 'Music Performance and the Plastic Arts', first published October 1952. In Fukuzumi Haruo, ed., *Jikken Kōbō and Shūzō Takiguchi: The 11th Exhibition Homage to Shūzō Takiguchi* (Tokyo: Satani Gallery, 1991), 15–17.

19 Obinata Kin'ichi, 'From Images/To Images: Exploring the Early Achievements of the Experimental Workshop', in *Jikken Kōbō*: *Opening Up Postwar Art*, ed. Harumi Nishizawa (Tokyo: Yomiuri Shimbun/Bijutsukan Renraku Kyōgikai, 2013), 324.

20 Obinata, 'From Images', 324.

21 William Marotti, *Money, Trains, and Guillotines: Art and Revolution in 1960s Japan* (Durham, NC: Duke University Press, 2013), 153, 161, 165.

22 Fumihiko Sumitomo, 'Heading towards the Unimaginable – Postwar Art and Technology', in *Possible Futures: Japanese Postwar Art and Technology* (Tokyo: NTT Shuppan, 2005), 16.

23 As in the 1967 work 'Vision of the Unknown: Fleeting Trace/Single Sheet', 1967, reproduced in Taro Okamoto Museum of Art, *Shozo Kitadai and Experimental Workshop* (2003).

24 Matsumoto called this film a 'cinema poem'. Miryam Sas, *Feeling Media: Potentiality and the Afterlife of Art* (Durham, NC: Duke University Press, 2022), 33.

25 These Autoslide works are discussed by Kusahara (the quoted phrase is hers) and by Sas (*Feeling Media*, 84).

26 Obinata, 'From Images', 325. Unsigned text from the 1953 pamphlet for the Autoslide 'presentation'.

27 Takiguchi Shūzō, 'Words for Some Friends', in Fukuzumi, ed, *Jikken Kōbō,* 19.

28 Takiguchi, 'Words', 19.

29 Hamaguchi Ryūichi, 'Surreal Salon', in *Kagayake*, 243.

30 Uno Akira, 'When Illustrators Were Active in Many Fields', in *Kagayake*, 141.

31 Thomas R. H. Havens, *Radicals and Realists in the Japanese Nonverbal Arts: The Avant-Garde Rejection of Modernism* (Honolulu: University of Hawaii Press, 2006), 107. See also Kusahara ('Proto-Media Art') and Sas (*Feeling Media*, 2022).

32 Furukawa Taku, 'My Sōgetsu Era', in *Kagayake*, 146.

33 Clements, *Anime*, 147.

34 Kuri Yōji, 'We Wanted to Animate Grownup Manga', in *Kagayake*, 138.

35 Kuri, 'We Wanted', 138.

36 Manabe Hiroshi, 'Next Time, an Omnibus: On the Group of Three', in *Kagayake*, 332.

37 Wada/Yokoo/Uno, 'Exhibiting at the Animation Festival', in *Kagayake*, 335.

38 Mori Takuya, 'Seeing the Sōgetsu Animation Festival', in *Kagayake*, 336.

39 Mori Takuya, 'Cartoons and Graphic Animation: The Aesthetics of Animation', in *Kagayake*, 338.

40 Sas, *Feeling Media*, 75.

41 Uno Akira, 'When Illustrators Were Active in Many Fields', in *Kagayake*, 140.

42 Sas, *Feeling Media*, 90.

43 Tara Sinn, 'Mollusks, Horses, and Nudes: Aquirax Uno in the Sixties', in *The Comics Journal* (31 March, 2011), www.tcj.com (accessed January 2023).

44 Toshio Matsumoto, 'On the Nature of the Avant-Garde', in *Kagayake*, 357.

45 Translation by Jason Douglass, 'In Search of a "New Wind"'. Manifesto reproduced in *Kagayake* (43) with significant omissions.

46 Komatsu Sakyō, 'Developing a New Dimension of Communication', in *Kagayake*, 341.

47 Abe Kōbō, 'Keep Your Dreams in Good Repair', in *Kagayake*, 243.

48 Chris Robison, 'Masaaki Yuasa Speaks in Many Colors', *Animation World Network* (5 December, 2017) (awn.com, accessed 3 January 2023).

Chapter 12

The Secret Life of the World: Jan Švankmajer's Documentary Animation

Kristoffer Noheden

Jan Švankmajer's latest film *Kunstkamera* (2022) is a documentary about the film-maker's *Wunderkammer*, which he has installed over the course of several years in his house in Horní Staňkov.[1] Lacking a voiceover, as well as any other kind of narration, the film documents Švankmajer's comprehensive collection with a camera that alternately roams the house and dwells on sets of objects and images, or zooms in on and pans across individual works and things. The camera registers alchemical alembics, African sculptures, surrealist artworks, taxidermied animals and many other curiosities, all arranged according to the associative logic of the *Wunderkammer*. In the absence of any on-camera human presence, this modern-day cabinet of curiosities appears remarkably ghostly. Across large parts of his vast oeuvre, Švankmajer excels in instilling a sense of life in things ranging from natural history specimens, animal body parts and puppets, to household objects, food and mud. But in *Kunstkamera*, we are shown these objects in their dormant state, prior to being animated by the film-maker.

Kunstkamera is something of a culmination of many of Švankmajer's central obsessions across nearly sixty years of film-making. 'If my films were perfect, I would like the viewer to think they had just watched a documentary', Švankmajer comments.[2] But in most of his earlier films, he combines these pursuits of documentary concretion with animation wielded as a tool for restoring life to objects. As he sees it, 'Animation is magic and the animator is a shaman. Apparently, our ancestors were able to bring inanimate natural objects to life through the magical power of their minds. We need technology to make this possible.'[3] Švankmajer often animates things that have been killed by civilization, whether literally, such as animals reduced to items for consumption, or ideologically, such as objects reduced to their utilitarian function or matter stripped of anything resembling life or a soul.

These two statements, about his films as simultaneously documentary-like and restorations of a magic sensibility, suggest that Švankmajer's poetics of film is predicated, on the one hand, on the observation of reality and, on the other, its transformation. In several of his films, the camera brings forth the innate marvels of reality, and it does so by imbuing the world with a sense of life all but eradicated from the inanimate world in, and

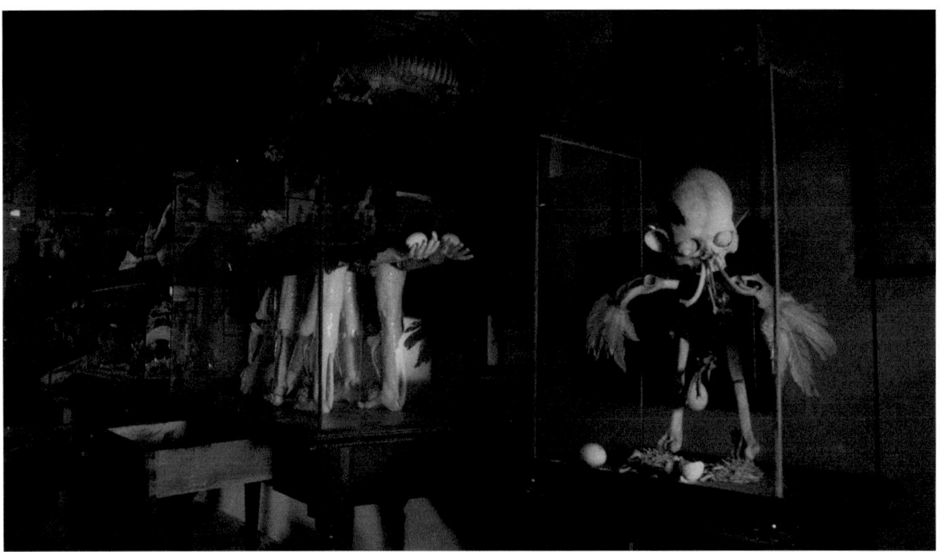

Figure 12.1 Jan Švankmajer, dir., *Kunstkamera*, 2022.

by, Western modernity.[4] The camera is an instrument of revelation and of transformation; animation is a tool of animist revitalization. Combined, they allow Švankmajer to depict the secret life of the world, beyond what André Breton once called the prevalent belief in 'the paucity of reality'.[5] Against the view of reality as inherently poor, Švankmajer's films show the world to be in the throes of unpredictable forces.

In this chapter, I explore Švankmajer's aspirations towards documentary veracity in his films. His appeal to the documentary, I argue, needs to be seen as part of a broader surrealist striving to discover and document the poetry immanent in reality. Švankmajer uses animation as a means to assert that the world has a secret life beyond that posited by Western modernity. His many allusions to animism, alchemy, and magic indicate that he is at one and the same time invested in discovering the hidden or repressed strata of reality and using reality as raw material for a transmutation in the furnace of the imagination. In other words, his works emerge out of a dialectics between the documentary and the fantastic, the objective and the subjective. Such a dialectic is central for surrealist practice overall, and, as we will see, it has been notably theorized in Czech surrealism.

Jan Švankmajer, surrealism and animation

Born in 1934 in Prague, Švankmajer studied fine art and puppetry in the 1950s. During his studies, he discovered art and writings by an earlier generation of Czech surrealists, including Karel Teige, Vítězslav Nezval, Toyen and Jindřich Štyrský; soon thereafter, he also came across reproductions of Paul Klee's and Salvador Dalí's art.[6] Because surrealism was considered illicit by the authoritarian regime, specimens of radical art only survived in private collections and in the odd book found in second-hand bookstores. By the late 1950s, Švankmajer made Klee-inspired drawings, and as his graduation project he put on a performance of the eighteenth-century play *King Stag*, which featured marionettes alongside live actors. In the same year, he worked with puppetry and animation on Emil Radok's film *Johanes Doktor Faust* (1958). Soon, Švankmajer also started making objects, often constructed from worn-down found things placed in vitrines or bottles.[7]

Švankmajer carried over these different artistic practices into his films. In 1964, he directed his first short, *Poslední trik pana Schwarcewalldea a pana Edgara* (The Last Trick), in which he combined marionette theatre and live actors wearing elaborate pâpier maché masks. The following year, he explored the potential of animation in two short films, *J. S. Bach: Fantasia G-Moll* (J. S. Bach: Fantasy in G Minor, 1965) and *Spiel mit Steinen* (A Game with Stones, 1965). In both of these shorts, the camera lingers on ordinary objects, from dilapidated walls to stones, only to liberate them from their everyday functions, in part through animation. In *J. S. Bach*, the stark black-and-white photography emphasizes cracks and fissures in walls, doors, and locks, and Švankmajer accelerates the decay as he uses animation to make the rifts widen and new cavities emerge. Time-lapse animation combines with animated collage imagery of coarse and corroded surfaces. *A Game with Stones* conducts a complex ritual in which stop-motion animated stones emerge out of a water tap and land in a bucket, only to arrange themselves in intricate patterns. In particular *J. S. Bach* demonstrates a palpable influence from the documentary photography of the Czech surrealist Emila Medková.[8] Placing her camera in unassuming Prague settings, Medková would extract from them a raw poetry oozing out of the dirty streets and run-down buildings, so that the very brute materiality and seeming desolation were transmuted into unlikely vehicles of a new kind of surrealist marvellous. In *J. S. Bach*, the camera pans, tilts, and zooms in on the worn-down surfaces; animation makes rifts and widening cavities appear in the walls or ghostly black shapes overtake them. Like Medková, Švankmajer seeks out the irrational streaks beneath the surface of everyday environments, and so provokes the emergence of poetry.

The second half of the 1960s was a prolific time for Švankmajer, during which he tried out a variety of different film-making techniques. In *Historia Naturae, Suita* (1967), he stop-motion animates a variety of natural history specimens, so turning the film into a riotous version of a *Wunderkammer*, in which the animal remains rebel against the human arrangements imposed on them. Although Švankmajer had been influenced by surrealism for a decade at that point, he considers his live-action short *Zahrada* (The Garden, 1968) to be his first truly surrealist film. Shot in black and white, and with costume design by his wife Eva Švankmajerová, with its depiction of a human fence surrounding the house of a dignitary, the film is also close in spirit to the theatre of the absurd. A similar sense of the absurdity of life under a totalitarian regime is brought out through a striking use of stop-motion animation in *Byt* (The Flat, 1968), in which a young man finds himself trapped in a small apartment. The furniture, food, and even the walls play constant tricks on him, by virtue of Švankmajer's combined use of animation and invention of surrealist objects, such as a spoon perforated with holes, so that soup passes right through it. A similar bewildering unpredictability of otherwise inert things come to life is the central theme of

Tichý týden v dome (A Quiet Week in the House, 1969), in which a spy watches a tongue, screws and other objects moving of their own volition.

Some of Švankmajer's films were made under the auspices of the Jiří Trnka Studio, and critics have found it tempting to situate Švankmajer's films in a Czech 'school' of animation, including such influential forerunners as Karel Zeman and Trnka himself. Švankmajer, however, has deliberately distanced himself from the tradition of Czech animation, in part because he has never limited himself to using animation. In fact, he does not consider himself an animator so much as a poet. As he states, 'There's only one poetry, and whichever tools or methods you use, poetics is all one.'[9] Švankmajer also considers his own use of animation to be distinctly different from that of his Czech forerunners, because they 'worked with representational illusion and I myself was attracted to brute reality'.[10] As we will see, under the sway of central ideas in Czechoslovak surrealism, Švankmajer would focus increasingly on the poetic potential inherent in this 'brute reality', which he opposes to the smooth flow of cinematic illusionism. Similarly, in his films, animation is often used to emphasize that imagination is not confined to any neatly constructed fantasy world, but may erupt from the fissures in worn-and-torn quotidian surroundings.

That approach was fortified when Švankmajer and Švankmajerová joined the surrealist group of Prague in 1970. Forced underground by the repressive Czechoslovak regime, the group was centred on poet and theoretician Vratislav Effenberger. He argued that changing historical, political and cultural conditions meant that Czech and Slovak surrealism could not pursue the wonders of the marvellous, but instead ought to locate poetry in the raw and brute material reality of postwar Czechoslovakia.[11] Probing the world's cracks and fissures, literal as well as figurative, would make an irrational poetry surge forth. Švankmajer's films already shared in these convictions and methods, in part as a consequence of his admiration for Medková's stark photography. In the more than fifty years since Švankmajer and Švankmajerová joined the surrealist group in Prague, his films have frequently related to their games, inquiries and other activities, and they have been critically discussed by the group.[12] Up until her untimely death in 2005, Švankmajerová contributed scenography and costume design to many of his films. Švankmajer kept making short films up until *Jídlo* (Food) in 1992, after which he has focused entirely on feature-length projects, a practice he started with *Něco z Alenky* (Alice) in 1987. Whether short or feature-length, the majority of his films share with the early examples discussed here a preoccupation with objects both natural and human-made, the materiality of the quotidian world, a combination of animation and live action, and an acidic black humour often directed against human pretentions to mastery of the world. Much as *The Flat* and *The Garden* implicitly critiqued the absurd conditions of life under a totalitarian regime, so the much later feature film *Šileni* (Lunacy, 2005) examines the tension between freedom and repression, prompted by the new forms of absurdity in a society undergoing swift changes as it transitioned into a so-called free market economy following the Velvet Revolution in 1989.

In Švankmajer's films, a self-professed perpetual childishness merges with a more cynical and corrosive approach to the dire state of the world.[13] Referring to his Lewis Carroll adaptation *Alice*, he states that, 'The animation of objects upholds the truth of our childhood', by giving his films 'the reality of a dream'.[14] But that dreamlike reality is inflected with pessimism, because Švankmajer, like Effenberger, believes that 'Atlantic civilization' cannot be saved.[15] All we can do is hope for a renewal once it collapses.

Surrealism and documentary

Švankmajer's wish for viewers to believe his films to be close to documentaries speaks to his pursuit of rendering credible the intrusion of the imagination into material reality. Among his prime means for doing so is to set them in everyday environments, with a pronounced emphasis on their materiality. The prominent role played in them by foodstuffs, cutlery and pieces of furniture relate the films to common, everyday experiences. The documentary quality Švankmajer aspires to emerges from his attempts to eradicate the presumed borders between waking and dreaming life, between external reality and internal mind, between objectivity and subjectivity. External reality turns unpredictable, and dreams and imaginary events take on the quality of the real. Moreover, with his propensity for locating poetry and play alike in unadorned quotidian objects, Švankmajer makes the fantastic and the marvellous emanate even from those things in his films that initially may appear to be firmly on the side of what we tend to take for reality. However, this is not a matter of seamless illusionism.

Švankmajer uses animation as well as the particular properties of the film camera in order to bring out the latent properties of settings and props. At the same time, he uses jarring cuts and jerky stop-motion to emphasize that the diegetic world he constructs is created like a collage, with noticeable splices connecting disparate things. In an interview, he states: 'What interests me about an object or a cinematic setting is not its artistic eloquence, but what it's made of, what affects it and in what circumstances, how it is altered by time, etc. This explains why I have used the close-up which precisely searches out every "scratch on the illusion".'[16] This attitude reflects Švankmajer's persistent sabotage of cinematic illusion as well as his fascination with objects as carriers of life, imprinted with the memories of the situations they have been in and the emotions they have been exposed to. Reality, as depicted in his films, is at one and the same time fissured and populated with things charged with their own histories. Švankmajer thus questions the smooth unity of the fictional world espoused by aesthetic realism, only to assert a deeper unity in which humans and objects come together through the workings of the imagination. Like the dolls in *Žvahlav aneb šatičky slaměného Huberta* (Jabberwocky, 1971), another adaptation of Carroll, which are first boiled upon a stove and then ironed flat, a cut used to replace the three-dimensional figures with drawings, many objects in Švankmajer's films are exposed to brute handling. They break down. They are disassembled. They crack open, like the white rabbit in *Alice* who leaks sawdust through a tear in his fur. The scratches on the illusion reveal the secret life of the world.

Since the inception of the movement, surrealists have trained their attention on locating oneiric undercurrents in the surrounding world as much as in the human mind. Such finds have frequently been documented in surrealist art and writings. In *City Gorged with Dreams*, his landmark study of surrealism and documentary photography in and of interwar Paris, Ian Walker proposes that surrealism even 'aspires to the condition of documentary'.[17] The abundance of dream transcripts, found objects, automatic writing conceived as revealing 'the true functioning of thought', records of chance encounters and photography of urban and natural sceneries alike, speaks to surrealism's attempts at 'objective documentation' of the fact that, as Breton asserts, the surreal is immanent in the real.[18] Early surrealists used film and photography, in particular, Walker says, 'to anchor the surreal in the real', by appealing to the widespread 'belief in the actuality of the image'.[19] Throughout the interwar period, the journal *La Révolution surréaliste*, Breton's autobiographical essays *Nadja* (1928) and *Mad Love* (1937), the magazine *Minotaure* and many other surrealist publications incorporated documentary photography, often as a way of heightening the veracity of the accompanying textual renditions of chance encounters and other unlikely events.

Walker's astute comment that 'we might think of the activity of Surrealist artists not so much as creation but observation' may, however, need to be nuanced.[20] Surrealism tends to evade any binary between observation and creation, revelation and transformation, much as it seeks a resolution of the otherwise conflicting states of waking and dreaming life, reality and imagination, and objectivity and subjectivity. In spite of the camera's purported objectivity, surrealist photographs may acquire their marvellous qualities from the sort of trained, subjective vigilance that allows a chance moment to be detected and captured. When textual descriptions of anomalous events are paired with documentary photography, as in *Nadja* and *Mad Love*, the photographs are infused with subjectivity. The marvellous is both found and created.

Objective poetry, subjective reality

Švankmajer's location of a raw poetry in the cracked and worn surfaces of walls, furniture and objects is an extension of this current of documentary attentiveness in surrealism. His use of animation to give life to and transform objects merges observation with creation and transmutation. In the former instances, the camera brings forth the latent poetry of the surroundings; in the latter, the found objects are made to speak their secrets through the magic of animation. Švankmajer's approach to this dialectic of observation and creation is indebted to an extensive lineage of thought and practice in Czechoslovak surrealism, which I can only sketch briefly here.[21]

In Czechoslovak surrealism, the appearance of the surrounding world as observed by surrealists acquired a particular significance. In a 1951 enquiry, Vratislav Effenberger proposed the concept of 'objective poetry' to describe how the result of surrealist activity 'could become an organic living whole that, uniquely, could encompass reality, a dialectic of the exterior and inner world – and still not cease to be poetry in the sense that human desire demand'.[22] Objectification is not about stripping away subjectivity, but 'has the task of bringing the author's and viewer's inner world to a common denominator'.[23] As Krzysztof Fijalkowski points out, Effenberger coined the concept of objective poetry in extension of Breton's notions of objective chance and objective humour.[24] Objective poetry is also linked to the Czechoslovak surrealist group's elaboration of what Dalí called concrete irrationality. In the interwar period, Dalí suspected surrealist automatism of being imprecise and arbitrary, and claimed that his paranoia-critical method concretized the sounding of irrationality.[25] Similarly, in the postwar period the Czechoslovak surrealists employed concrete irrationality to redirect attention from what they thought of as lofty surrealist ideals, as exemplified by Breton's call for 'love, liberty, and poetry' in *Arcanum 17*, to the crumbling materiality of the present.[26] Like Dalí before them, they emphasized the grounding of surrealist poetry in material reality.

Already in his earliest films, such as *J. S. Bach*, Švankmajer anticipates Effenberger's notion that reality under the Stalinist regime 'was replete with so much objective humour that one merely had to push it before the camera or onto the stage, and the rational shell shattered and set free a flame of purifying satire'.[27] Fijalkowski shows that the idea that a corrosive poetry was just waiting to be discovered in the streets was mined with stunning results by photographers including Medková, Alois Nožička and Vilém Reichmann.[28] Their stark photographs of deserted urban environments and found objects demonstrate something crucial about surrealist photography at this time and place: 'the less staged and interfered with it is, the greater its revelatory powers to peel back the skin of the real'.[29] At the same time, the photographers able to locate such places are inevitably trained in a specifically surrealist perception; imagination is there in perspective and framing, if nothing else.

In a similar vein, for all his use of unassuming settings, Švankmajer's films are staged and his incorporation in them of surrealist objects and employment of animation are obvious interferences with the reality in which they are set. It is nevertheless significant that his films are the result of a surrealist practice that has been shaped by what Fijalkowski describes as attempts to peel back the skin of the real through documentary photography. Additionally, from a surrealist perspective the marked intrusion of the imagination in Švankmajer's films does not necessarily lessen their ability to conjure up something vital about reality. Effenberger writes that, 'Imagination does not mean turning away from reality, but its antithesis: reaching through to the dynamic core of reality.'[30] Imagination need not be a retreat into interior recesses, but can be what allows for a deeper reality to appear on the screen or in a photograph. As effected by the film camera and animation, concrete irrationality at one and the same time documents and explodes reality. It uses subjective means – imagination, disorientation and other extrarational states – in order to tear the veil from the everyday world and uncover a multiplicity of meanings.

Although Švankmajer's pronounced wish for his films to be viewed as documentaries appears to apply to his filmography as a whole, some of his films engage directly with documentary modes. *Kostnice* (The Ossuary, 1970) is a documentary about the famous bone chapel in the Czech town of Sedlec. In the film, Švankmajer combines straight documentation of objects made from human bones with swift and disorienting cuts. A recurring close-up of a snail crawling slowly through the eye socket of a human skull takes on the appearance of a slimy vanitas image, a reminder of the messy, fleshy corporeality that has long since been stripped from the bones. The original soundtrack comprises a recording of a jaded tour guide who lectures to visiting school children, but the sound is dissociated from the images and we never see either the guide or the children. In *The Ossuary*, Švankmajer does not use animation, but simply films the interior and exterior of the bone church, and then edits together the footage with sometimes jarring cuts. There is no explicit agenda or argument in the film, and its resulting macabre ambiguity resonates with Effenberger's belief that the official rational shell of Czechoslovak society was easily cracked, and that an irrational poetry may surge forth once the surface was pierced. The authorities caught a whiff of the film's implicit sarcasm, and Švankmajer was forced to replace the soundtrack with music.[31]

Perhaps it makes sense to think of Švankmajer's ruptures of cinematic illusion as a further facet of his documentary leanings. Unlike the alienation effects often employed by Marxist film-makers in the wake of the various new waves in cinema, Švankmajer's breaks with illusion are not intended to be vehicles of disenchantment.[32] Instead, they display the dialectics between the subjective and the objective, the found and the created, in order to reveal their intermingling.

In Švankmajer's mockumentary *Otrantský zámek* (The Castle of Otranto, 1979), an amateur historian claims to have discovered that the Italian castle in Horace Walpole's eponymous Gothic novel was in fact located in Czechia.[33] The film alternates between a simulated black-and-white television interview with the idiosyncratic scholar and cut-out animation of colourized xylographic illustrations showing key scenes from Walpole's novel. The historian presents flimsy evidence for his thesis – including an oversize rivet, which he claims proves that the giant armour featured in the novel came crashing into

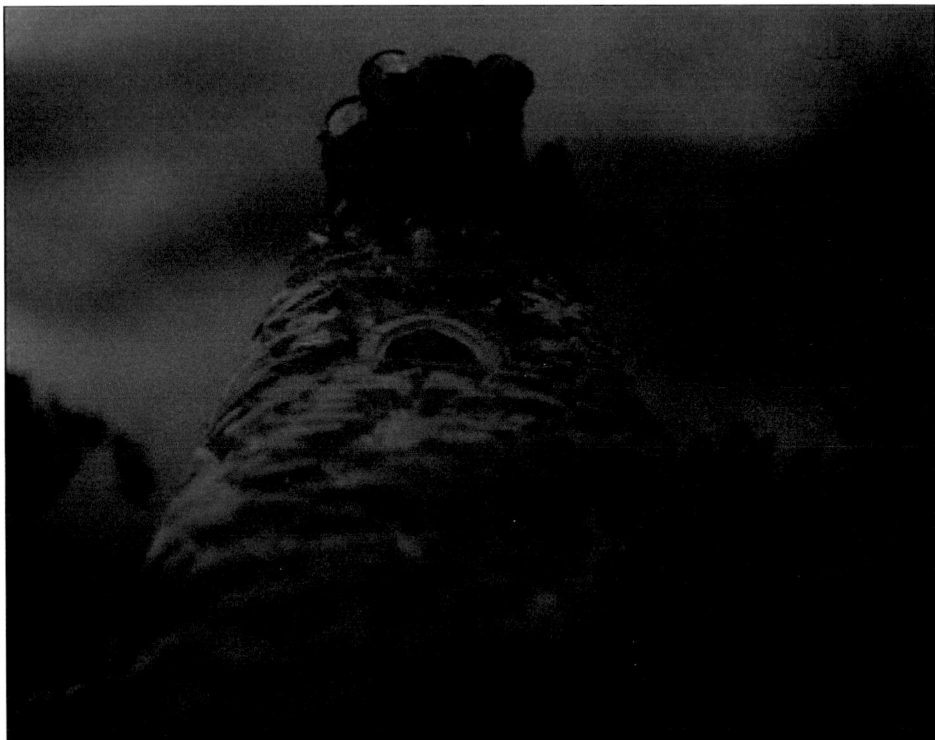

Figure 12.2 Jan Švankmajer, dir., *Otrantský zámek*, 1979.

the Czech castle – which rests on the premise that the events depicted by Walpole were actual rather than fictional. But while the television reporter dismantles the evidence with impeccable logic, the imagination has the last word. The reporter is interrupted mid-sentence when an enormous glove emerges out of the tower by which the interview is conducted. Stones come crashing down, marking the victory of the jubilant pleasure principle over the dreary reality principle. A cut, however, shows the scholar with his hand sticking out of a miniature model of the tower. The illusion is ruptured by this brief behind-the-scenes shot, but the expanded reality is nevertheless intact. The layering of interview, cut-out animation and behind-the-scenes footage amount to a mockumentary that nevertheless intends to say something true about reality. The imagination is not purged, but allowed to permeate all the layers of the film.

Some forty years later, in his last feature film *Hmyz* (Insects, 2018), Švankmajer incorporates documentary footage of the making of the film in the film itself. Several scenes featuring special effects, such as a character looking in the mirror and seeing the face of a two-dimensional animated insect looking back at him, are followed by sequences showing how the effects work. Part of the documentary footage also consists of some of the actors talking about their dreams. The actors' dream lives become part of the film, which in itself is largely about the slippages between and cross-fertilization of reality and imagination. Again, these breaks with illusion, whether created with special effects or by actors playing a role, seem to be intended to demonstrate the interpenetration of imagination and reality, rather than the deflation of either.

Ontological voyeurism and the magic of animation

Animation plays a crucial part in the fusing of reality and imagination in Švankmajer's films. As mentioned, he has professed his belief that animation is a form of animism, wielded by the animator-magician using technology for shamanistic purposes. Originally a derogatory concept coined by early anthropologists, animism was also significant for Sigmund Freud, who thought of it as a defining characteristic of a 'primitive' worldview of mysterious forces. Remnants of animism could still be found, Freud believed, among children and in the unconscious, springing to the surface in various mental disorders, in belief in magic and in art.[34] Bolstered by his interest in so-called 'primitive' art as well as his self-professed perpetual childishness, Švankmajer is one of many surrealists who has infused animism with a positive value.

In his 'Decalogue' with ten rules for film-making, Švankmajer thinks of animism and documentary as interrelated:

> Use animation as a magical operation. Animation isn't about making inanimate objects move, it is about bringing them to life. Before you bring an object to life, try to understand it first. Not its utilitarian function, but its inner life. Objects, especially the old ones, were witnesses to certain happenings, people's actions, their fortunes, which

> somehow marked them [...] If you want to disclose some of these hidden aspects of objects through your camera, you need to listen [...] Bringing objects to life through animation has to be a natural process. Life has to come from within them, and not from your whim. Never violate objects! Don't tell through them your stories, tell theirs.[35]

Animation, here, is not understood as a method of imposing life on objects, but as a shamanistic tool for activating their inner life. Instead of merely moving things around, Švankmajer believes that he reanimates them. Examples of such uses of animation-as-reanimation abound in his films. From the stones forming patterns in *A Game with Stones*, to the everyday objects running rampant in *The Flat*, to the taunting movements of the white rabbit and his hybrid animal cohorts in *Alice*, Švankmajer uses stop-motion animation to reanimate mineral objects, animal beings and human-made artefacts. Although these objects appear to contradict what is realistically possible, Švankmajer's statement suggests that he intends to show their latent reality. In doing so, he asserts an animistic ontology that counteracts the persistent modern Western idea that nature and objects are composed of inert matter, lacking anything like depth, an interior dimension, or agency. They have their own stories that can be retold by an attentive listener.

A longstanding critic of anthropocentrism, Švankmajer relishes in the way objects brought to life confound the neat and oppressive order imposed by modern humans on the entirety of the non-human world.[36] That is evident in particular in the stop-motion animated natural history specimens revolting against taxonomy in *Historia Naturae, Suita*, and the animal muscles, eyes, brains and skulls that are engaged in playful, animated activities in segments interspersed throughout *Lunacy*. Trying to understand the inner life of objects and listening to them is tantamount to channelling the secret life of the world through the magic act of animation. Magic, then, is not so much a manipulation of the world for one's own benefit, but a means of liberating inanimate objects from the stranglehold placed upon them by civilization.

Švankmajer sometimes draws attention to the act of looking at the secret life of the world. Depictions of voyeurism occur in surrealist films including Luis Buñuel's *Belle de Jour* (1967) and Nelly Kaplan's *Néa* (1975); in both films, peeping women discover hidden sexual undercurrents that enrich their worlds. In Švankmajer's films, illicit looking can just as well be focused on objects. In *The Flat*, the protagonist's attempts at peeping through a hole in the wall is punished when a boxing glove pops out and punches him in the face. Such slapstick antics give way to a more solemn look at the mysterious life of the material world in *A Quiet Week in the House*. A spy camouflaged with branches is first seen looking through a pair of binoculars at a house, before removing a rolled-up piece of paper from one of his nostrils. A close-up reveals the note to be a drawing of a floor plan. Once inside the house, he sets out on a strictly regimented spying scheme. Each day, he drills a hole in a door and peeks through it. His disciplined looking reveals objects behaving in unexpected ways, mainly through the use of stop-motion animation. As pieces of candy unwrap themselves, the colourful packaging turns out to contain screws, which parade across the desk and attach themselves to the keys of a typewriter. A tongue moves by its own volition and pushes its way through a meat grinder, which produces tightly rolled-up newspaper pages. So the week continues. The exteriors and the corridor in the house are shot with an often jerky handheld camera and in a sickly sepia. The scenes unfolding behind the closed doors, in contrast, are shot in colour, and although the camera is steadier, the objects are animated with a technique that makes them shudder. Psychoanalytical film theory has problematized scopophilia, or the desire to look.[37] In contrast, surrealist art and cinema tends to avoid pathologizing obsessive looking, instead mining it for its poetic potential of discovery through an indulgence in desire. In *A Quiet Week in the House*, the protagonist's looking is tantamount to what I would like to describe as an *ontological voyeurism*. Viewed from a vantage point removed from utilitarian engagement or use, the world displays qualities otherwise inaccessible. Such sequences imply that for surrealism, voyeuristic looking can surpass its associations with a negative objectification. It is not hidden erotic life that is discovered here; rather, it is the world itself that reveals its secret life.

The revelation of this secret life is, again, a consequence of relating to reality itself as shot through with subjectivity. The spy in *A Quiet Week in the House* seems to be on a mission to root out such instances of subjectivity, as he ends his stay in the house by blowing up the building. But the animist inflections of the spy's acts of ontological voyeurism are also readily apparent in Švankmajer's adaptation of Edgar Allan Poe's short story 'The Fall of the House of Usher' (1839/1845). In *Zánik domu Usherů* (The Fall of the House of Usher, 1980), Švankmajer jettisons human actors entirely in favour of letting objects, trees, mud and a dilapidated mansion act out the high-strung emotions of Poe's

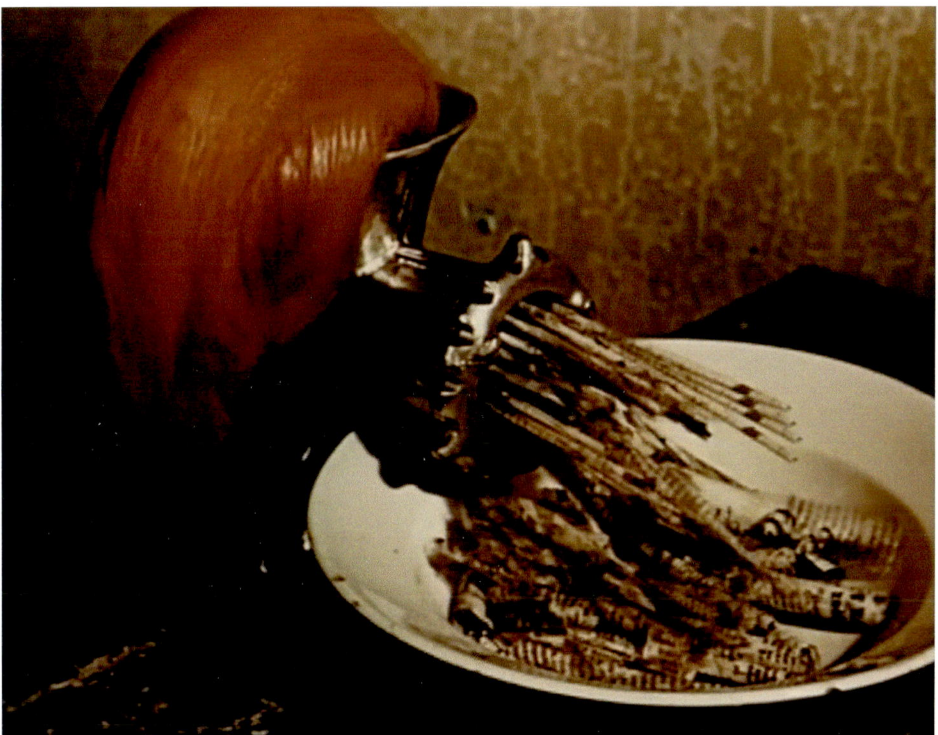

Figure 12.3 Jan Švankmajer, dir., *Tichý týden v dome*, 1969.

tragic tale. Stop-motion animated, a coffin and chairs display unruly behaviour inside the house. Their erratic movements impart a sense of life to the cracks and fissures in the walls, even as they are filmed without special effects, the camera panning across them. Outside the crumbling mansion, Švankmajer animates clay to make it appear as though the dirt on the ground takes on a vivid kind of life. Employing a technique he calls 'tactile gesture', which he developed making sculptures, Švankmajer seeks to make a direct imprint of emotions on clay.[38] A sequence featuring stop-motion of lumps of clay tortured by the animator is intended to illustrate Roderick Usher's descent into insanity.[39] As the clay throbs and takes on the shape of swirls and mounds, now and then torn apart by the visible imprint of fingers, Švankmajer believes that he eradicates the distinction between subject and object.[40] His gestural animation generates emotions that arise through the interaction between matter and mind mediated by the body of the animator. The ascription of tense emotional states to the non-human world is directly grounded in Poe's tale. Consider Poe's mention of Usher's belief in 'the sentience of all vegetable things. But, in his disordered fancy, the idea had assumed a more daring character, and trespassed, under certain conditions, upon the kingdom of inorganization'.[41] Usher does not merely conjure ancient ideas of the vegetable soul, but extends the presence of mind all the way to rocks, furniture and buildings.[42] Švankmajer seems to adhere to this animist and panpsychist view of the world, as he states that he shares 'Usher's opinions on inanimate nature'.[43]

In the ancient world, the soul was often defined as that which made things move, whether human, animal, plant or iron drawn to a lodestone.[44] Through animation, Švankmajer believes, 'a meaningful relationship arises between people and things, based on a dialogue, never on consumption. Objects are thus separated from their utilitarian function and return with their primordial, magical meanings'.[45] Entering into a dialogue with objects is tantamount to seeing them as ensouled, because the soul, in this sense, is both the cause of movement and an interior dimension. Švankmajer's attentive listening to objects detects the presence of souls; making visible the life and agency of objects is a very different proposition from treating them as mere things intended for human use and abuse. In *The Fall of the House of Usher*, each crack in the wall, each puddle of mud and each chair are shown to have an inner life, through which they enter into dialogue with the doomed story narrated in the voiceover.

Švankmajer's late documentary film *Kunstkamera* does not merely record his extensive collection on the model of the *Wunderkammer*. The film also documents his belief in the continuity of the imagination across different registers of reality. In an interview, he states,

> I make no distinction between imagination such as the kind we find [in] Hieronymus Bosch, or the imagination that we find in art brut, in surrealism and in the 'creations' of nature or in so-called primitive art, for example from Africa or Oceania. The differences are merely in the ways these treasures of the imagination are made visible.[46]

Like the writhing mud in *The Fall of the House of Usher*, the rocks, fetishes and alchemical engravings in *Kunstkamera* display the presence of subjectivity throughout the material world. Švankmajer's films show a world in which exterior and interior together constitute reality. As the director puts it in his 'Decalogue', 'The deeper you enter into the fantastic story the more realistic you need to be in the detail.'[47] His films reveal new facets of reality through a reanimating animation practice conducted in realistic settings in which the fantastic appears.

Acknowledgements

Research for this chapter was funded by the Swedish Research Council, 2021-01660.

Notes

1 *Kunstkamera* exists in a festival cut and a director's cut. In this chapter, I refer to the shorter festival cut.

2 Quoted in Ian Walker, *City Gorged with Dreams: Surrealism and Documentary Photography in Interwar Paris* (Manchester: Manchester University Press, 2002), 23.

3 In Carolina López Caballero, 'Jan Švankmajer: A Magical Outlook on Life and the World', in *Metamorfosis: Visiones fantásticas de Starevich, Švankmajer y los hermanos Quay*, eds. Carolina López Caballero and Andrés Hispano (Barcelona: Centre de Cultura Contemporània de Barcelona, 2014), 188.

4 See, e.g., Freya Mathews, *For Love of Matter: A Contemporary Panpsychism* (Albany, NY: SUNY Press, 2003).

5 André Breton, 'Introduction to the Discourse on the Paucity of Reality', in *Break of Day*, trans. Mary Ann Caws and Mark Polizzotti (Lincoln: University of Nebraska Press, 1999), 3–20.

6 See Bertrand Schmitt, 'Detailed Biography with Commentary (I): 1934–1970', in *Jan Švankmajer: Dimensions of Dialogue; Between Film and Fine Art*, eds. František Dryje and Bertrand Schmitt (Prague: Arbor Vitae, 2013), 64.

7 For an exhaustive description of Švankmajer's early artistic trajectory, see Schmitt, 'Detailed Biography with Commentary (I)'.

8 See Ian Walker, 'Photo Analysis F: *J. S. Bach: Fantasia in G Minor*', in Krzysztof Fijalkowski, Michael Richardson and Ian Walker, *Surrealism and Photography in Czechoslovakia: On the Needles of Days* (Farnham: Ashgate, 2013), 149.

9 'After the Revolution the Shit!: Jan Švankmajer Talks to the Context', *The Context*, http://web.archive.org/web/20061120000017fw_/http://www.thecon-text.com/docs/3804.html/

10 Petr Král, 'Questions to Jan Švankmajer', *Afterimage*, 13 (1987): 22.

11 František Dryje, 'Vratislav Effenberger', *Analogon*, 40 (2004): xiv.

12 Král, 'Questions to Jan Švankmajer', 23.

13 See Bruno Solařík, ed., *Jan Švankmajer* (Prague: CPress, 2018), 12.

14 'Švankmajer on Alice', *Afterimage*, 13 (1987): 52.

15 See Bruno Solařík and František Dryje (eds), *Other Air: The Group of Czech-Slovak Surrealists 1990–2011* (Prague: Sdruzeni Analogonu, 2012), 71.

16 Král, 'Questions to Jan Švankmajer', 22.

17 Walker, *City Gorged with Dreams*, 28.

18 Walker, *City Gorged with Dreams*, 11; André Breton, *Surrealism and Painting*, trans. Simon Watson Taylor (Boston, MA: MFA Publications, 2002), 46.

19 Walker, *City Gorged with Dreams*, 11.

20 Walker, *City Gorged with Dreams*, 11.

21 For comprehensive discussions, see Krzysztof Fijalkowski, Michael Richardson and Ian Walker, *Surrealism and Photography in Czechoslovakia: On the Needles of Days* (Farnham: Ashgate, 2013).

22 Vratislav Effenberger, response to 'Enquiry on Surrealism', *Analogon*, 37 (2003): xii.

23 Effenberger, response to 'Enquiry on Surrealism', xii.

24 Krzysztof Fijalkowski, 'Objective Poetry: Post-War Czech Surrealist Photography and the Everyday', in Fijalkowski, Richardson and Walker, *Surrealism and Photography in Czechoslovakia*, 92.

25 Salvador Dalí, 'New General Considerations Regarding the Mechanism of the Paranoiac Phenomenon from the Surrealist Point of View', in *The Collected Writings of Salvador Dalí*, ed. and trans. Haim Finkelstein (Cambridge: Cambridge University Press, 1998), 258–9.

26 André Breton, *Arcanum 17*, trans. Zack Rogow (Los Angeles, CA: Green Integer, 2004), 107; for a more extensive discussion of concrete irrationality in Czechoslovak surrealism, see Kristoffer Noheden, *Surrealism, Cinema, and the Search for a New Myth* (Cham: Palgrave Macmillan, 2017), 166–8.

27 Vratislav Effenberger, 'The Raw Cruelty of Life and the Cynicism of Fantasy', in *Cross Currents: A Yearbook of Central European Culture*, vol. 6, ed. Ladislav Matejka (Ann Arbor: University of Michigan, 1987), 443.

28 See Fijalkowski, 'Objective Poetry', 89–101.

29 Fijalkowski, 'Objective Poetry', 97.

30 Effenberger, 'The Raw Cruelty of Life and the Cynicism of Fantasy', 439.

31 See Schmitt, 'Detailed Biography with Commentary (I)', 93.

32 See my discussion of surrealism and political film theory in Kristoffer Noheden, 'Against All Aristocracies: Surrealism, Anarchism, and Film', *Modernism/Modernity*, 27, no. 3 (2020): 567–82.

33 The film first entered production in 1973 but was only completed in 1979, due to Švankmajer suffering a multiyear ban from film-making.

34 Sigmund Freud, *The Uncanny*, trans. David McLintock (London: Penguin, 2003), 147.

35 Jan Švankmajer, 'Decalogue', in *The Cinema of Jan Švankmajer: Dark Alchemy*, ed. Peter Hames (London: Wallflower, 2008), 140–1.

36 See Jan Švankmajer, 'To Renounce the Leading Role', *Manticore/Surrealist Communication*, 2 (1997): [2].

37 Laura Mulvey, 'Visual Pleasure and Narrative Cinema', *Screen*, 16, no. 3 (1975): 6–18.

38 Jan Švankmajer, *Touching and Imagining: An Introduction to Tactile Art*, trans. Stanley Dalby, ed. Cathryn Vasseleu (London: I.B. Tauris, 2014), 149.

39 Švankmajer, *Touching and Imagining*, 151.

40 Švankmajer, *Touching and Imagining*, 149.

41 Edgar Allan Poe, *The Fall of the House of Usher and Other Writings*, ed. David Galloway (London: Penguin, 2003), 100.

42 For the vegetable soul, see Michael Marder, *Plant-Thinking: A Philosophy of Vegetal Life* (New York: Columbia University Press, 2013).

43 Solařík, *Jan Švankmajer*, 58–9.

44 David Skrbina, *Panpsychism in the West*, revised edn (Cambridge, MA: MIT Press, 2017), 25–7.

45 Solařík, *Jan Švankmajer*, 58–9.

46 Solařík, *Jan Švankmajer*, 219.

47 Švankmajer, ‘Decalogue’, 141.

PART THREE

A Living Art for Critical Re-enchantment: Contemporary Surrealism and Animation

Introduction to Part Three

Abigail Susik

In France and the United States, Robert Benayoun's 1961 book, *Le Dessin animé après Walt Disney*, discussed in the introduction to Part Two of this book, sparked a new wave of critical commentaries and surrealist imaginaries related to animation. First in line was a summer issue of the film journal *Positif* (nos. 54/55), 'L'Animation en 1963'. This special issue opened with Benayoun's important essay discussed in the general introduction to this volume, 'Le Phénix de l'animation', which was illustrated with diverse stills from films by Walerian Borowczyk, Vlado Kristl, Yōji Kuri and others. Also included in the animation issue of *Positif* was Benayoun's important interview with Chuck Jones, as well as an overview of the history of animation by surrealist associate Raymond Borde, along with other surrealist-centric content. This was around the time that French director Éric Duvivier was experimenting with claymation and kaleidoscopic animation sequences in psychedelic surrealist films such as *Images du monde visionnaire* (1963), made with poet Henri Michaux. Two years later, in 1965, a long and ambitious essay on animation as a favoured modality for screen-based surrealism by film critic Barthélémy Amengual appeared in the special double issue of *Études cinématographiques* devoted to surrealism and film.[1]

When the young Americans Franklin and Penelope Rosemont visited Paris in the winter of 1965–6, they stumbled into the *L'Écart absolu* surrealist exhibition at the Galerie de l'Œil in Paris, and soon became friendly with Benayoun and other surrealists.[2] After the Rosemonts returned to Chicago that summer, they formed the Chicago Surrealist group and made the indomitable character of Bugs Bunny their enduring symbol of countercultural revolt and anti-work resistance (contra the Elmer Fudds of the world).[3] The Chicago group would go on to make significant contributions to the surrealist discourse on animation in a range of publications since then, the most important of which was the series of articles devoted to animation in the special issue of *Cultural Correspondence* guest edited by Franklin Rosemont in the fall of 1979.[4] Together with the extensive filmography of surrealist Jan Švankmajer (in collaboration with Eva Švankmajerová) since the 1960s, which includes animation films and sequences achieved with the help of various collaborators, the Chicago surrealist interest in animation has pointed the way toward a contemporary discourse and practice devoted to surrealism and animation.

Benayoun himself remained at the forefront of this discourse, publishing numerous texts on the subject between the 1960s and the mid-1990s.[5] Following the debut of René Laloux and Roland Topor's legendary science fiction animation feature *Fantastic Planet* in 1973, a surrealist strain of animation was admired internationally.

dans notre pensée, à un gag authentique (1). Aujourd'hui, le gag peut se saisir d'une file indienne de cailloux affligés d'une tendance à la gigue et qui se recouvrent en pleine nature, de tatouages allègres à la Miro (comme c'est le cas dans *Stone Sonata* de Carmen d'Avino), il peut secouer d'un éclat de rire démoniaque un œuf qui se veut dur à cuire et qui attaque la caméra (*L'œuf à la coque*, de Marc Andrieux et Bernard Brévent), il peut en six ou sept images leit-motiv associées à des cris divers, ressusciter sur le mode hilarant certaines propositions du nô traditionnel, comme dans le film *Jardins humains* du Japonais Yoji Kuri. Il peut enfin se localiser dans une certaine rigidité de l'atroce et du grinçant, dans le déroulement mécanique et grandguignolesque d'un drame si schématique, si élémentaire, qu'il ressemble au pur dérèglement d'une arrière-pensée : ainsi en est-il dans *Le concert de Mr et Mme Kabal* de Walerian Borowczyk (*Ces quatre derniers films ont été, c'est justice, primés à Annecy* 63.).

Le gag est mis à la question par ses spécialistes incontestés. Chuck Jones, il vous l'expliquera plus loin, lui donne infatigablement dans son laboratoire personnel les coups de pied qui propulsent la vie. Dans un film comme *High note*, il veut lui donner toute la nudité d'une toile de Mondrian. Dans son tout dernier film *Now hear this*, qu'il co-réalisa avec son décorateur Maurice Noble, il lui donne des alibis d'évidence plastiques et remplace un gag sonore prometteur par le simple écriteau : EXPLOSION GIGANTESQUE.

Mais, soyons-en certains, le temps n'est pas encore venu où le gag lui-même sera remplacé par un écrivain GAG.

Robert BENAYOUN.

(1) Pour les non-initiés, ces différentes images apparaissent dans *Christopher Crumpet* de Robert Cannon. Rooty-Toot-Toot de John Hubley, et *Flebus* de Ernest Pintoff.

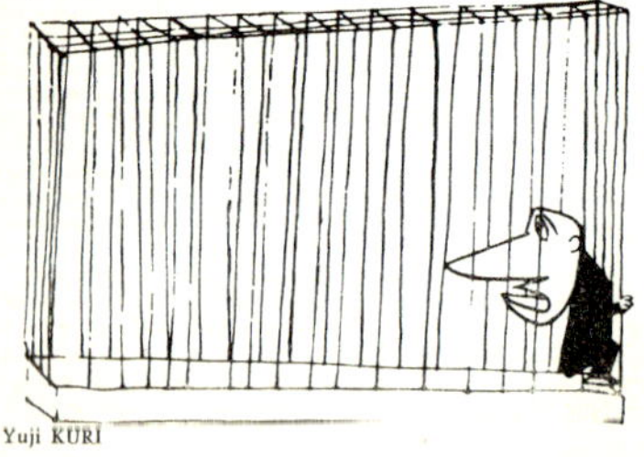

Yuji KURI

14

Paul TERRY

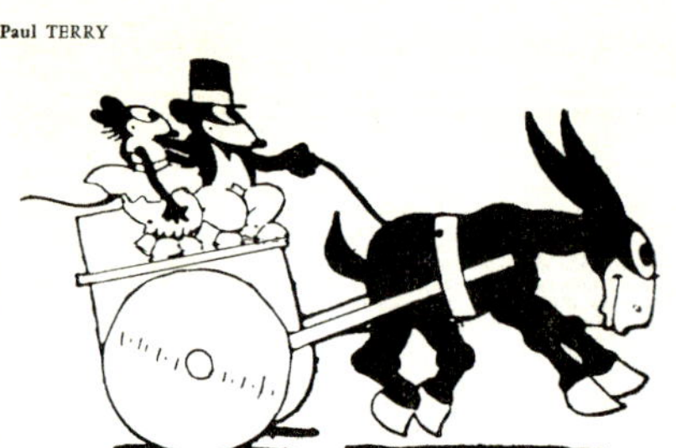

Notes sur l'histoire du dessin animé

L'Histoire du cinéma n'est pas tranchée. Elle comporte de larges zones d'ombre. Chaque époque a privilégié les films qui allaient dans le sens de ses goûts et ces hiérarchies périssables se sont transmises d'un historien à l'autre. Des milliers d'œuvres sont occultées, que le hasard des cinémathèques peut faire à chaque instant surgir de l'oubli.

Nous sommes donc tributaires d'une information partielle, suspecte et aléatoire, ce qui nous invite à la plus extrême disponibilité. Il n'y a qu'une façon d'aborder le cinéma : c'est de dévorer de la pellicule, de partir à la chasse des films inconnus, de ne tenir d'avance aucune valeur pour consacrée et de voir du même œil les programmes de la semaine et ceux de 1910.

En somme, nous prenons le contre-pied des méthodes de type répétitif qui ont ossifié l'Histoire de la littérature. Mais outre qu'il nous plaît d'avoir un regard neuf pour les fantômes de l'écran, nous estimons que cet état d'éveil, d'enthousiasme lucide, se justifie par les caractères propres au cinéma :

— Une sensibilité exceptionnelle aux phénomènes de vieillissement qui prennent ici un tour imprévisible et fracassant;

— En sens inverse, un pouvoir de révélation, un don de la surprise, qui n'ont pas fini de nous étonner.

Quand un film craque, il craque bien. Mais quand la cinémathèque projette quinze Keaton qui dormaient dans des boîtes entamées par la rouille, cela devient l'événement de l'année. Au cinéma, joue un facteur vitesse que nul ne semble avoir analysé. Les significations se modifient plus rapidement que dans les arts traditionnels, parce que la distance réalité-image est courte. Le film transpose moins que l'écriture ou le pinceau. Il est plus engagé, même s'il s'en défend, dans le magma de comportements, d'idées et de hantises qui détermine la sensibilité collective. Les significations sont amplifiées, mais elles acquièrent

15

Figure III.1 Double-page spread from *Positif*, nos. 54/55 ('L'animation en 1963'), July–August 1963, 14–15, including the last page of Robert Benayoun, 'Le Phénix de l'animation' (1–14) and the first page of Raymond Borde, 'Notes sur l'histoire du dessin animé' (15–23). Author's collection.

In 1971, surrealism scholar J. H. Matthews wrote that Benayoun's *Le Dessin animé après Walt Disney*, published a decade earlier, was so comprehensive that any further commentary on surrealism's relationship to cartoons and comedic animation was 'superfluous'.[6] This sentiment seems to reveal the field of Surrealism Studies' fears of redundancy, given the dearth of secondary material on this rich area of inquiry. Yet, even a cursory glimpse at surrealism's intersection with animation reveals that, in fact, there are myriad avenues awaiting exploration, far too many to encompass in a single volume such as this. In particular, there remains a dearth of Surrealism Studies scholarship devoted to the animation of Norman McLaren and René Laloux. Other important names related to the subject of surrealism and animation include Patrick Bokanowski, Leidy Chávez and Fernando Pareja, Terry Gilliam, Jean Giraud (Moebius), Jeff Keen, Jean-Jacques Lebel, Chris Marker, Bady Minck, Wangechi Mutu, Adnan Muyassar, Joseph Nechvatal, Yuri Norstein, Pat O'Neill, Wong Ping, Suzan Pitt, Brothers Quay, Carolee Schneemann, Julian Semilian, Martin Stejskal, Franciszka and Stefan Themerson, Stan VanDerBeek and Susana Wald. In their animation criticism alone, Kyrou and Benayoun together discuss an enormous range of topics in transnational animation. Contemporary surrealists gravitate toward Ralph Bakshi's work, while many animators today are exploring the connections between artificial intelligence and surrealism.

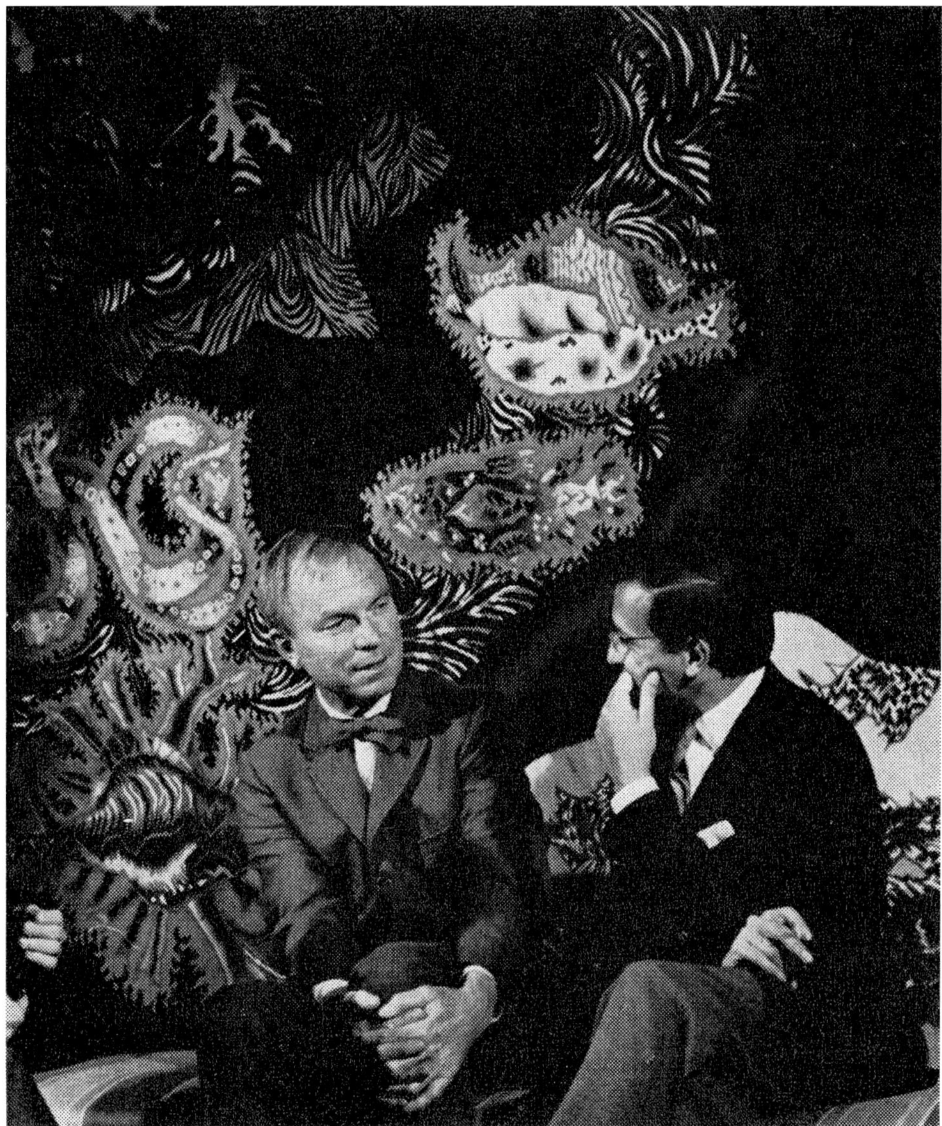

Figure III.2 Chuck Jones with Robert Benayoun at the Journées d'Annecy '63, from *Positif*, nos. 54/55 ('L'Animation en 1963'), July–August 1963. Author's collection.

Although, happily, our volume by no means exhausts this subject, the seven chapters in Part Three greatly expand our understanding of surrealism's relationship to and investment in animation. This final part questions how and why surrealist animation or animation discourse might still be relevant today, particularly in the light of what artist Penny Slinger calls 'critical re-enchantment', or a resistance to the instrumentalization of life under capitalism. Part Three features Ken Eisenstein's essay on structural film via Hollis Frampton and George Landow (with nods to Stan Brakhage and Kenneth Anger), while Ian Walker compares animated films by Jan Lenica, Geoff Dunbar and William Kentridge

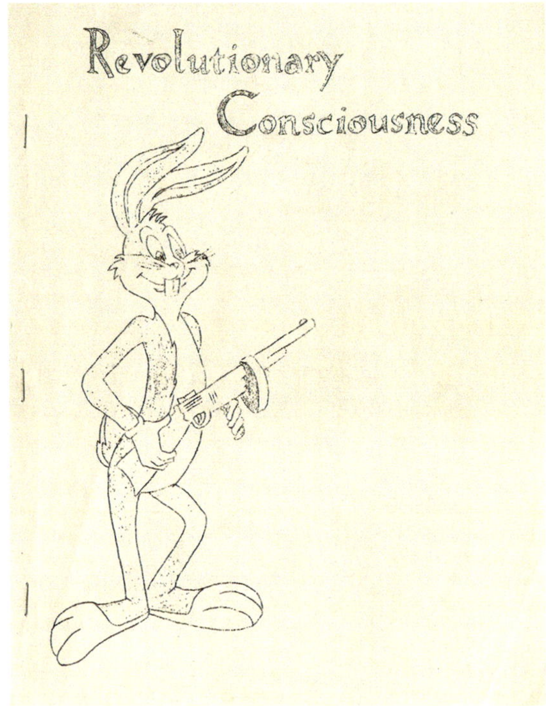

Figure III.3 Chicago Surrealist Group. Cover of 'Revolutionary Consciousness' pamphlet, 1966. Author's collection.

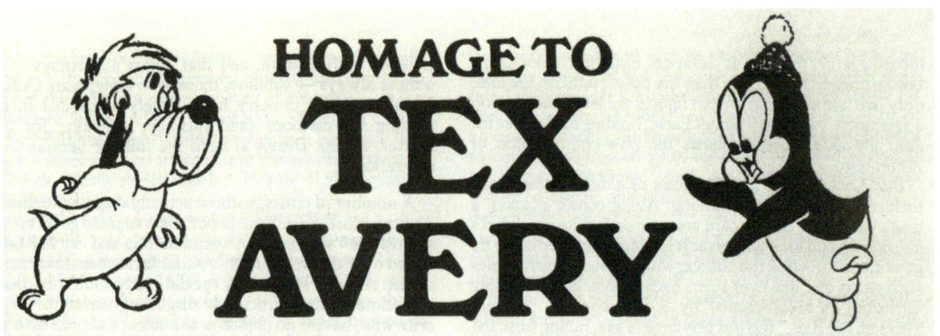

Figure III.4 Franklin Rosemont, 'Homage to Tex Avery', in 'Surrealism & its Popular Accomplices', guest edited by Franklin Rosemont, *Cultural Correspondence*, 10–11 (Fall 1979): 53. Author's collection.

based on Alfredy Jarry's 1896 play *Ubu Roi*. A trio of essays in Part Three highlight the work of transnational contemporary women artists. Paulina Caro Troncoso's chapter discusses the experimental film *Paracas* (1983) by renowned Chilean artist Cecilia Vicuña; Marie Arleth Skov delves into the innovative and transgressive clay animation of Nathalie Djurberg and Hans Berg; and Catriona McAra shows how artist Kim L. Pace engages animation as part of her dynamic mixed-media process. To highlight the sustained relevance of surrealism and animation today, two interviews with contemporary artists are also included here: Judith Noble in conversation with Penny Slinger, and myself in conversation with Jacolby Satterwhite. Satterwhite discusses the connections between surrealist automatism and animation, critiquing the use of artificial intelligence, while Slinger contemplates the process of digitally animating her photo-collages from 1969–77.

Throughout our collective engagement with surrealism and animation in this final part, key topics such as Indigeneity, gender diversity, ecofeminism and Black diasporic surrealisms arise, as do issues of colonialism, genocide, violence and racism. Together, these texts demonstrate that the reception and production of animation remained a key aspect of the surrealist movement's revolutionary horizons in recent decades.

Notes

1 Barthélémy Amengual, 'Le cinéma d'animation, expression privilégiée du surréalisme à l'écran', *Études cinématographiques*, 40–2 (Summer 1965): 209–45.

2 Abigail Susik, 'Direct Action Surrealism in Chicago', in *Surrealist Sabotage and the War on Work* (Manchester: Manchester University Press, 2021), 182–237.

3 Joanna Pawlik, *Remade in America: Transnational Surrealism 1940–1978* (Berkeley: University of California Press, 2021), 211–15, 263. Also see Joanna Pawlik, 'The Comic Book Conditions of Chicago Surrealism', in *Surrealism, Science Fiction and Comics*, ed. Gavin Parkinson (Liverpool: Liverpool University Press, 2015), 129–54. Franklin Rosemont, 'Bugs Bunny and the Philosopher's Carrot', in *Marvelous Freedom, Vigilance of Desire* (Chicago, IL: Gallery Black Swan, 1976), 13.

4 'Surrealism & its Popular Accomplices', guest edited by Franklin Rosemont, *Cultural Correspondence*, 10–11 (Fall 1979). Hal Rammel, 'Stop-Motion Marvelous', *Arsenal/Surrealist Subversion*, 4 (Winter 1989): 97.

5 See, for instance, Robert Benayoun, *Les dingues du nonsense: de Lewis Carroll à Woody Allen* (Paris: Balland, 1986), 295–315.

6 J. H. Matthews, *Surrealism and Film* (Ann Arbor: University of Michigan Press, 1971), 180, n. 23.

Chapter 13

Animating the Surreal Side of Structural Film

Ken Eisenstein

Disappearing acts aren't always deliberately performed. Nor must their cause be purposeful pressure. Sometimes such so-called mysteries are mundane, practical as parachutes. How the Belgian painter Paul Delvaux (1897–1994) slipped through the cracks in the indexing of the collected writings of Hollis Frampton (1936–1984) doesn't take too much figuring to straighten out, and it isn't anything anyone should be blamed for.[1] So many names and ideas are sprinkled throughout the photographer and film-maker's essays, the results of his activity at the 'trypewriter' (his term), that such misses were bound to occur.[2] The one in question here, Frampton's invocation of the canvas *The Echo* (1943), along with its creator, happens to sit within a passage that is itself about a 'vanishing'.[3] But before diving into the opening left by this gap, let us pair (or prepare) our plunge with some flotation, a bobber, another appearance Delvaux makes in the land of structural film, an echo.

In 2004, Mark Webber interviewed Owen Land (1944–2011) while preparing *Two Films By Owen Land* (2005) to accompany the touring package 'Reverence: The Films of Owen Land (formerly known as George Landow)'. The book's main focus is on the film-maker's two final 16-mm films – *Wide Angle Saxon* (1975; 22 minutes; United States) and *On the Marriage Broker Joke as Cited by Sigmund Freud in Wit and its Relation to the Unconscious or Can the Avant-Garde Artist Be Wholed?* (1978; 18 minutes; United States) – and it facilitated two other rebirths. But 'two final 16-mm films' is slightly inaccurate. First off, sandwiched between them were two reiterations of earlier ones: *New Improved Institutional Quality: In the Environment of Liquids and Nasals a Parasitic Vowel Sometimes Develops* (1976; 10 minutes; United States; hereafter *NIIQ*) from *Institutional Quality* (1969; 5 minutes; United States; hereafter *IQ*), and *Diploteratology* (1978; 7 minutes; United States) from *Bardo Follies* (1967; 45 minutes; United States) and/or *Diploteratology or Bardo Follies* (1971/74; 30 minutes/20 minutes; United States). Second, as the critics P. Adams Sitney and Paul Arthur have tracked, even films that Landow never formally remade were subject to tinkering, serving as direct reference points for later parody, or launch pads for hypothetical extension (being first parts of proposed series that never came to pass). 'Two final *starts in* 16-mm' might better capture the main catch of Webber's volume's web.

As the retrospective was making its rounds, Arthur covered the showcase for *Film Comment*. He emblematized Land's 'destabilizing tendencies of revision, non-closure, and fragmentary presentation' by turning to the artist's name as a site of flux because there had also been the short-lived intermediate, George Lando.[4] Sitney had concluded a 1981 pamphlet on the film-maker discussing these monikers. Once the 'w' was gone from Landow, the tail 'o' begged to become an originating orifice. As Sitney put it, the film-maker 'moved the "o" around from back to front; and scrambled the word "new." Owen Land is the name of the new, "improved" George Landow'.[5] Sitney read this reconfiguration as a parallel to the shift occurring in Land's medium of choice in those days (towards stage plays). Thirty years later, when it came to writing Land's obituary, Sitney began with 'Filmmaker George Landow'.[6] It was a call back to more than an art form and a signature. For if the 1981 appraisal startled with the claim that 'The most impressive avant-garde film-maker of the 1970s was George Landow', the 2011 farewell astonished with 'Our friendship predated our memory: We had been born in the same apartment building in New Haven, just thirty-two days apart.'[7]

Sitney attributed Land's digital movie-making, *Dialogues, or A Waist Is a Terrible Thing to Mind* (2009; 120 minutes; United States), to the energy generated by the renewed attention fostered by Webber. This is one of the resurrections I had in mind. The other is pretty peculiar. The twenty-first-century revisiting of Landow seems to have spawned a new way to talk about his films, both for the artist himself and for critics, if not for every single viewer. Early in Arthur's 2005 review, there is a litany of possible labels for Land. The second and third tags, 'Minimalist? Postmodern parodist?', fit with what had been written about Landow previously.[8] But Arthur's first term, 'Surrealist?', arises freshly out of the reflection he was covering. The word is used in some form in three of Land's anecdotes in Webber's book; one (related to Peter Saul) is cited in Arthur's essay, itself a reprise (the first major overview of Landow was Arthur's back in 1971).[9] Tellingly, the word surrealist did not appear then. To be fair, it is the major films of the mid and late 1970s that are most likely to spur such a categorization, what with *Wide Angle Saxon's* final line, 'Oh, it was a dream!', and *Broker Joke's* Freud. But *Remedial Reading Comprehension* (1970; 5 minutes; United States; hereafter *RRC*) had its own REM sleeper too,[10] and *IQ* contains a buried pleasure that this essay uncovers. And yet, even in David Ehrenstein's 1984 'Owen Land (George Landow)', 'wacky' is the closest that that surveyor gets to the word 'surreal'.[11]

The prime appearance of this newly aired association is the film-maker's 2004 reminiscence about a past interaction:

> When I was in Edinburgh [*c.* 1978], someone there in the audience was a filmmaker from Brussels who made documentaries on Magritte and Delvaux. He said that my films were the clearest examples of Surrealism that he had ever seen, which surprised me, but it makes sense. I think I see some influence in that film [*NIIQ*] from Magritte, in the oversized objects and the clear focus on common objects in a room.[12]

We too might be surprised. Not simply by the now lesser-known Delvaux's second cameo, but by the very thought of structural film, with its 'repudiation of psychology' jibing with surrealism. That characteristic was highlighted in a 1971 illustrated lecture that Sitney gave at MoMA between his initial formulation of structural film in 1969 (discussed below), and the arc he was to chart in *Visionary Film: The American Avant-Garde* (1974).[13] The presentation offered the book's main trajectory: from Buñuel and Dalí to Deren, from the trance film to the lyric, to the mythographic/mythopoeic, to the structural. Sitney saw the earlier forms as Freudian and Jungian; but structural film seemed to shed the psyche, being 'a cinema of meditation without the psychological intermediary'.[14] Looking for resurfacings of surrealism in *Visionary Film's* culminating category as I do here coincides with the way that Sitney's secondary concern with animation (part of later lectures that discuss Harry Smith, Jordan Belson, and Robert Breer) proves foundational for structural film.

Earlier, in 1976, Landow had mentioned the surrealists in an interview, but not in relation to one of his films (although his answer to a question about narrative in *Wide Angle Saxon* came close to their ideas). Instead, the movement comes up in response to a question about 'talking about [his own] work in front of an audience':

> I like it when someone asks me a specific question about the meaning of something, and I really don't know the answer. Then I have to spontaneously make one up. It's like some of the literary techniques of the surrealists. I have to use the question as part of the answer. I've tried coming up with the most far-fetched answers I could think of, and what usually happens is that they end up sounding perfectly reasonable. The reason seems to be that unconsciously I knew the answer all along.[15]

If surrealism provided Landow with a model for talking about films on the spot, why was it surprising that its influence was so legible to the perceptive 'filmmaker from Brussels'?[16]

Before picking up Landow's acceptance of Magritte, and before defining structural film further, let's return to Frampton's Delvaux to tap our other subterranean stream: animation. 'Incisions in History/Segments of Eternity' (1974) moves through so much in its dozen sections, is so richly illustrated by nineteenth- and twentieth-century photography, and contains so many allusions to earlier Frampton that it is difficult to summarize. Here are just the proper names that take the stage before Delvaux: Pound, Herodotus, Yeats, Aristotle, Zamenhof, Urquhart, Rabelais, Talbot, Piaget, Keats, Flaubert, Wordsworth, Beethoven, Buchner, Descartes and Praxiteles! A bare-bones set up for Delvaux's entrance could be sketched this way. After two epigraphs on time's power, a dialogue between Frampton and a female historian on 'just what history is, anyhow' kicks things off.[17] This occurs 'at an imaginary party' that, paradoxically, has been photographed. In the essay's second section, Frampton proposes the admittedly commonplace belief that art helps us survive by 'defen[ding] against the humiliating insistent pathos of our one utter certainty: that we are going to die'. Animals procreate as a way of prolonging their species; humans do too, but they also 'superimpos[e] upon animal sexuality the pursuit of art'. The third section analyses some of Talbot's language from *The Pencil of Nature* (1844). The fourth clarifies the third's distinction between two 'perceptual time[s]': '*historic*, and the other, *ecstatic*'.[18] The former is 'routine', but only 'retain[s] its credibility' if untested; 'I can believe in my own quotidian history', Frampton writes, by taking 'vague comfort' in 'the ordained tale of hours and days', in a ticking clock that seems to prove that 'something' must be happening despite 'my sad suspicion that most of life is remarkably unmemorable'.[19] And then comes:

> And when it comes to *your* history, I confess to utter skepticism. I can recall vivid encounters, and even whole ecstatic afternoons, that I've spent in your company, because they make up the warp of my *own* days … but as I watched you through my window, crossing into the park and vanishing among the beech trees, you ceased to breathe, you disintegrated … hastily reconstructing yourself, from a random shower of atoms, only seconds before we met, as design would have it, in the Museum, in front of Delvaux's painting, *The Echo*. The same thing happened to me.[20]

Whose history? And, if this meeting is also imaginary, why Delvaux?

Frampton's obsession with Marcel Duchamp may have played a role in the choice. An explicit reference in prior Frampton, Duchamp seems absent from 'Incisions'. As Thomas Singer puts it in a study that begins with a detailed look at Duchamp's photo collage *In the Manner of Delvaux* (1942), which distorts a nude from Delvaux's *Aurore* (1937), 'Duchamp was a magician in the economy of small gestures.'[21] So too Frampton. The

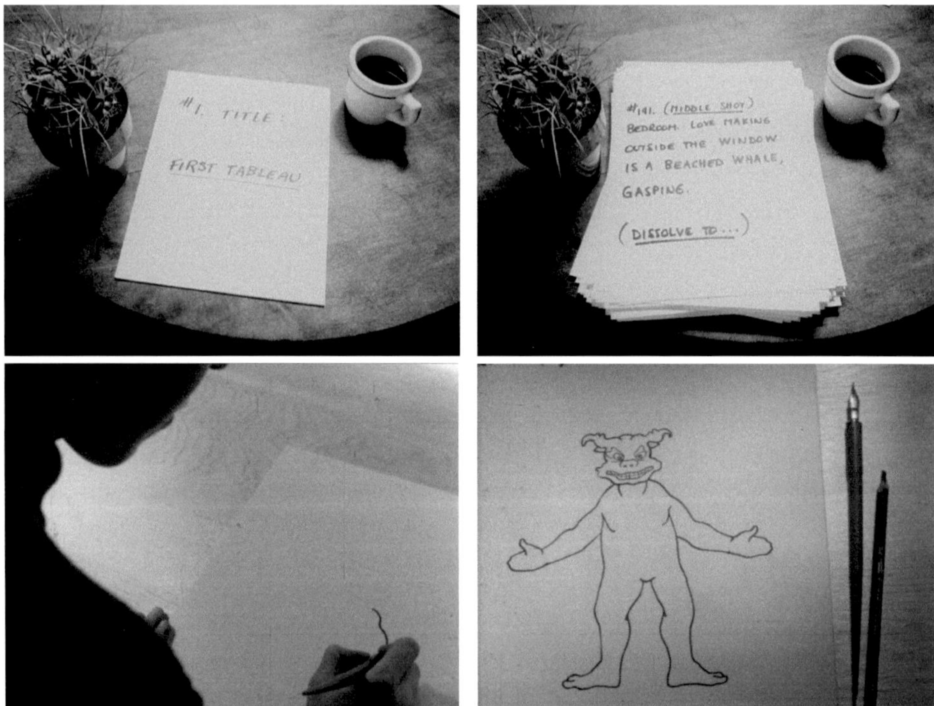

Figure 13.1 Two table tops for 'animation' in structural film. Top: Hollis Frampton, dir., *Poetic Justice*, 1972. Bottom: George Landow, dir., *The Film that Rises to the Surface of Clarified Butter*, 1968. (Opening shot and the first setup for the illusion of motion.)

almost last words of 'Incisions' are 'a veil of an aurora'.[22] *The Echo*, which depicts a nude woman's moonlit walk (her figure repeated three times in the same pose making a trailing path), helps to both cloak and mark Duchamp. The painting had also recently appeared in works germane to themes from 'Incisions': J. G. Ballard's short story 'The Day of Forever' (1967) and Martine Franck's photograph *Grand Palais. Paris. 1972*.[23]

'*Your* history' catches us off guard. Mine? As in … the reader's? Frampton had directly addressed us earlier, guessing at our preferences (by surmising that we 'wouldn't be interested in … a picture of my former wife and a friend, walking with a dog in the snow').[24] But this possibility dissipates with the specificity of the park's beech trees. Might the invocation of *Zorns Lemma* (1970; 60 minutes; United States) – whose finale shows Marcia Steinbrecher (a historian, and Frampton's wife from 1966 until their separation in 1971 and divorce in 1974), Bob Huot (painter and film-maker), and a dog traversing a field of snow to disappear into the woods (evergreens) – make the second person of the Delvaux paragraph Steinbrecher?[25] This play with pronouns brings another Frampton intertext into 'Incisions'. In fact, the essay's very first line, 'Here are some hand-tinted snapshots of myself', nearly mirrors one of the first shots from *Poetic Justice* (1972; 32 minutes; United States). As in animation, this film is made entirely from a single camera set up looking down. In this case, near the edge of a round table, pages of a screenplay pile up: '#6. (CLOSE-UP) / MY HAND PLACES A / HAND-TINTED PHOTO- / GRAPH OF YOUR FACE / ON A TABLE.'[26] The mount of 2D sheets that builds, shot after shot, is flanked by 3D objects: 'a potted cactus' on the left and 'a coffee cup' on the right, to quote descriptions in shot #4 (but the prop cup's liquid phases the phrase 'cupped coffee'). My face? Frampton's script has both his hand placing me (as viewer) and displacing my visage with one from 'the warp of [his] *own* days'. Mouthing the words as I watch *Poetic Justice*, might I internalize them and have my hand place a face from my now, or my yore? These sleights continue their morphing in the Delvaux story in 'Incisions'. Most shots from *Poetic Justice's* Third Tableaux bear the same top three lines, '(MIDDLE SHOT) / BEDROOM. LOVE MAKING. / OUTSIDE THE WINDOW /'. Two finish:

#137 – IS A PARK OF BAY / TREES.

#141 – IS A BEACHED WHALE, / GASPING.

Skip from 1972 to 1974: 'but as I watched you through my window, crossing into the park and vanishing among the beech trees, you ceased to breathe, you disintegrated'. Crossed indeed. The park trades its bays for beeches, and a different mammal is in need of air.

When *Poetic Justice's* bedroom window is envisioned as rectangular it mimics the sheets on its table. The string of phenomena outside it are all ostensibly filmable, just not as part of the same contiguous-to-the-window landscape. A spatial impossibility substitutes for the temporal fantasy of animation's drawings come to life. Frampton's pages are only roughly registered on their stand, their corners jabbing at flushness. No matter, the lines of words that they hold are not attempting the illusion of motion that a stack of traditional cels would aim for. Frampton's shooting technique also blasts continuity apart because the in-camera editing's disruptive white flash frames are left in as bumpers preventing fusion. Recognizing *Poetic Justice* as a critique of animation probably requires knowledge of an earlier comment of Frampton's. Speaking of *Heterodyne* (1967; 7 minutes; United

States), the only film he ever made without the photographic (unable to afford raw stock he used leaders), Frampton confessed:

> intend[ing] it to be a kind of revenge done with the bare hands against – first of all animation – or cell [*sic*] animation in particular and secondly against abstract films with a capital A … [*Heterodyne*] shares what I believe to be a major defect of nearly all animation: visual impoverishment within the frame.[27]

The riff in 'Incisions' on *Poetic Justice* helps point out a temporal destitution. Animation starts with atemporality. How can there be ecstasy in what is already out of the bounds of time?

Between *Heterodyne* and *Poetic Justice*, Frampton made a number of other films that messed with animation (e.g. stop motion in *Carrots and Peas* (1969; 5 minutes; United States), direct marking in *Artificial Light* (1969; 25 minutes; United States)), and he was not alone in this in the late 1960s. Michael Snow, whose very first film, *A to Z* (1956; 6 minutes; Canada), was a cut-out animation made while working at Toronto's Graphic Associates, later lagged time and cut-out motion in his distension of still photography, *One Second in Montreal* (1969; 26 minutes; United States). Joyce Wieland played with flatness/depth as well as repetition/looping in *Sailboat* (1967; 3 minutes; Canada). Ernie Gehr single-framed time exposures in *Wait* (1968; 7 minutes; United States) – to say nothing of the four frame alternations of *Serene Velocity* (1970; 23 minutes; United States), or the one, two, and three frame swaps in *Table* (1976; 16 minutes; United States). Finally, the flicker films of Tony Conrad and Paul Sharits exaggerated the one-frame-at-a-time basis of animation.

The above list deliberately includes every film-maker Sitney identified in 'Structural Film' (1969) but one, George Landow, who, as we will see, holds a special place in the formulation. The group (originally six, with Frampton added in the second version for *Film Culture Reader* (1970)) crystallized what Sitney saw as a break (in style only) from the avant-garde film of the late 1940s, 1950s and 1960s. The already established 'formal tendency' of Brakhage, Markopoulos, Kubelka, and Anger sought 'complex forms' of 'compact' '*conjunction*', cohering 'diverse strands' through their emphasis on editing and 'a tight nexus of content … [which] is, at root, a myth'.[28] The structural film's approach was '*apparently* in the opposite direction'; 'predetermin[ation]' of, rather than 'faith … in editing', meant that 'the shape of the whole film [was] … simplified' and became 'the primal impression'. But a deeper connection between the formal and the structural film is clarified by Andy Warhol, who, although a 'forefather' of the movement's techniques, 'is spiritually at the opposite pole' as in 'the difference between Pop and Minimal painting or sculpture'.[29] 'Mystical contemplation' is still in place in structural film, if more upon 'a portion of space' than a quest into the film-maker's subjectivity. That the methods of the fixed camera, flicker, loop printing, and (added in the second version) re-photography off of the screen are all related to animation's processes is interesting in relation to Sitney's idea that 'these [structural] film-makers wanted a new investigation of pure image and pure rhythm; or in other words, they sought to incorporate the aesthetics of painting and music (previously the domain of the animation film-makers)'. In running through other possible progenitors like Kubelka and Brakhage, Sitney surprisingly writes that 'if we are to seek a pioneer sensibility for the structural cinema it would be Robert Breer who literally founded the cinema of speed, single frame dominance'.[30] This animator's 'kinetic' quality seems to dialectically engender structural film's 'static quality'.

With all this gesturing toward animation, let's turn with Sitney to the only film he discusses in 'Structural Film' that depicts 'working animator[s]' and the results of their technique: George Landow's *The Film that Rises to the Surface of Clarified Butter* (1968; 9 minutes; United States).[31] It opens at a drafting table, looking over the shoulder of an artist inking a pencilled figure whose shoulder's curve, already completed, rhymes with the undulation of the illustrator's, and her turtleneck's collar, and, when she stretches for the inkwell, the ribbed shirt's bunching, as well as the grain of the wood visible to the left. Two dissolves speed the careful process of darkening the outline along; a jump cut brings us to detailing on the face. The next shot removes the animate. The paper, with its completed drawing, sits now to the left of the frame with pen and pencil resting to the right on bare wood. And then: the cartoon arms move, the smile expresses, the eyes blink in a graphic 2D illusion of motion alongside the photographic depiction of a 3D 'still' life. Unlike the pages on Frampton's tabletop, *Butter's* registration is orderly instead of ragged, giving the drawings a vitality that *Butter* also upsets with an offset. The screen is not filled with the illusion as it would be in regular animation. The pen to the right, which flexes and slips a little from being slightly jostled during the cycling of sheets, weighs down the fantasy. The film continues with a set of variations that include clumps of dust and hair gathering at the top of the frame/bottom of a rear projector's gate and a second animator and drawing (that dances beside a pencil only). Sitney, who stresses these ontological elements, gives a one-line summation of this particular example of Landow's 'simplistic', 'intellectual approach': the film creates 'the echo of an illusion'. Sitney sees such distillations in all of Landow, sharpening the glitter of his 'remarkable faculty … as maker of images … [they] are among the most radical, super-real, and haunting images the cinema has ever given us'. 'Super-real' is the closest 'Structural Film' gets to the word 'surreal'.

Sitney admitted that his 'Morphology' lecture was 'quite schematically' limned, and it wasn't too long before he added nuance. By 1977 he was pairing Frampton and Landow again (the two had closed out *Visionary Film*) in his 'Autobiography in Avant-Garde Film', published in *Millennium Film Journal's* première issue, the cover of which donned an image from Max Ernst's *Une Semaine de Bonté* (1934) to announce its main theme, 'Surrealism in Cinema', along with the subsidiary 'Autobiography/Diary'.[32] That Landow would keep rising to the top of the heap had already been foreseen. Sitney had named him 'the most devout' and 'perhaps the most sublime' of the pack in 'Structural Film', claiming that he may have 'actually invented' the form with his *Film in Which There Appear Edge Lettering, Dirt Particles, Sprocket Holes, Etc.* (1965/66; 4 minutes; United States).[33] Landow's 'sensibility … is the primary force in the structural film … a film-maker more than any other non-animator devoted to the flat screen cinema, the moving grain painting'.

There's animation again at the heart of 'Structural Film'. If surrealism was feeling forgotten, our return to Landow's Magritte in *NIIQ* helps us query this conjoined quarry of structural film's unconscious. The first truly oversized object in *NIIQ* comes when our main character begins to set foot 'in a room'. Yes, the objects in it are 'common' (a couch, an umbrella, a mirror, an end table, a lamp, a TV set, a framed picture, and a bowl of fruit), but Land's 'clear focus' on them clarifies just how uncommon things can seem at their seams. This inflection stems from the over-the-top surround of flowered 'wallpaper' clashing with the floral curtain and the fact that at least two of the props are clearly imitations. The couch is stiff plywood with painted fabric (flowers again). The television's speaker is brown paper beneath a screen made of white paper and a transparent plastic sheet (an overhead projector's?). But both are to scale.

Magritte painted unusual presences in rooms by type (a boulder by a balcony in *Invisible World* (1954)) and proportion (filling chambers with a gigantic apple or rose in *The Listening Room* (1952) and *The Tomb of the Wrestlers* (1960)).[34] The medley of stuff found in his *Personal Values* (1952), with its giant comb, match, glass, shaving brush, and lozenge (?), all of which overpower the regular (?) rugs, wardrobe and bed, provides a nice intertext. Landow only distorts the size of one thing in the initial scene inside his mock room, and it gets carried in by a man who enters nearly simultaneously via two different spots. Just as Magritte has the only visible window of his painting's bedroom appear as a reflection in the dressing mirror, Landow perfectly aligns his character's arrival beside the camera so it is reflected to us in a mirror. This precision allows an image of presence ahead of physical entrance. As the shot unfolds, our double vantage gives us a view from behind the left shoulder and empty left hand on the far right of the frame, along with a spectral view (frame right) of the chest and right hand, holding our object of interest. Due to the long shot framing and the diminution in the mirror's depths, we don't really sense that its scale is off until a swivel step allows us to see an extra-long and thick yellow pencil topped with silver band and pink eraser. This turns out to be an oversized disguise, a fabricated sheath wrapping the metallic tube of a permanent marker whose ink and tip will become easier to catch in closer views.

The original *IQ*, the film Landow released after *Butter*, is cut to a found soundtrack: 'an audio tape [Landow] had inherited from a former school teacher'.[35] On it, a female voice intones a set of prompts, testing pupils' abilities to follow directions. The opening shots depict a faux examiner, loosely lip-synching the words we hear. Then, with an exactness contradicting the mushy mouthing, there is a cut right after the words 'look at the picture' to a sedate living room, the backbone of the film. The proctor had told us that we had a picture on our desks. As film viewers, our looks diverge from the presumed downward glance. Landow has claimed, extratextually, another separation: while the sound was pre-existing, all of the imagery in the film is of his own devising (see Springer, 92). The proxy view of the room is alternated with diagrammatic images (a depth perception test, a film reel, etc.) first in an ABAB pattern, then by a longer stretch that flips the dynamic, making the final return to the room feel like an interruption. The gist is that the examiner is asking us to number things (e.g. 'Listen carefully. Dust the picture that is over the television. Put a number 9 on what you would touch.'). For four of the eight commands, we see a male hand write on the depicted object. Given the supplemental shots, complying with some tasks seems impossible.

The first time an object in the room gets acted upon our sense of the image before us adjusts as the depicted space enters an intermediary state. The shot of the room is now

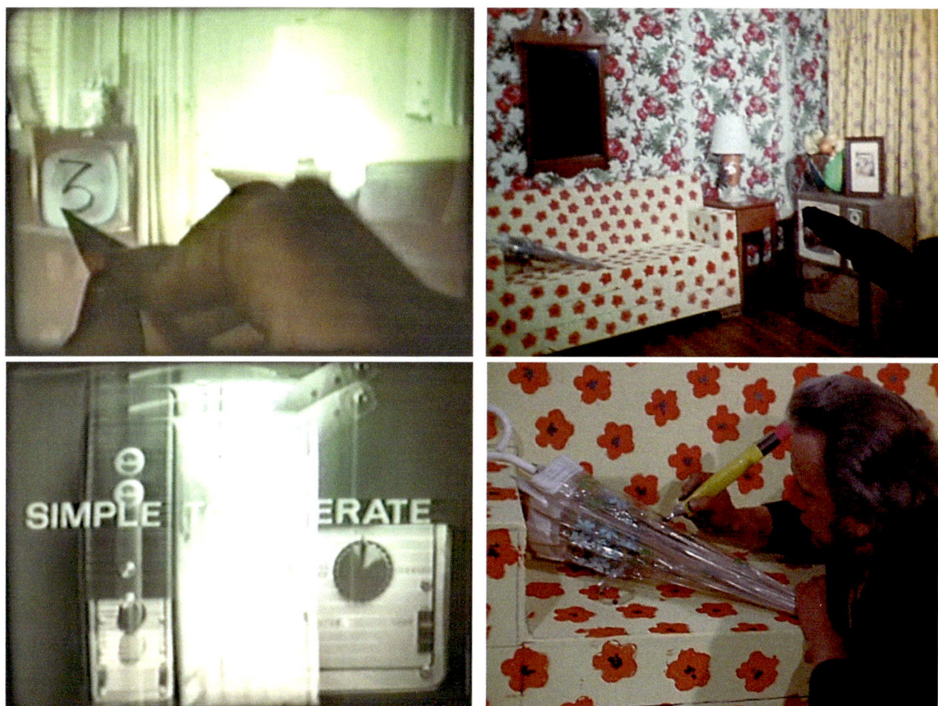

Figure 13.2 Left: George Landow, dir., *Institutional Quality*, 1969. Right: George Landow, dir., *New Improved Institutional Quality: In the Environment of Liquids and Nasals a Parasitic Vowel Sometimes Develops*, 1976.

being projected onto a sheet of paper hanging on the wall. A shift in the colour balance precedes the penetration of the intervening hand whose fingers manoeuvre a pencil as its knuckles obscure projection. In a very early essay of his, Tom Gunning takes up the pairing of Landow and Frampton that Sitney had used to conclude *Visionary Film*. In his discussion of *IQ*, Gunning latches on to the 'enormous hand fill[ing] the screen' in regard to the slippage around screen and desk that he had spotted: 'the gigantic hand … jolts us out of the imagined test situation and back into an awareness of being an audience watching a film … [unable to] respond to the [test] monitor's instructions'.[36] The largeness here is different from the remake's pencil (a ballooned prop), but both magnify thoughts on mark making.

'Listen. Have some fruit. Have some fruit. Put a number 19 on what you would touch' provides a ripe channel for comparing original and remake, which uses almost all of the soundtrack from the first version and then some. In *IQ*, #19 was heard over an insert of a woman's fingers adjusting switches and a knob on a projector. The 1976 film gorges on bananas, oranges, and apples held in a clamshell wastebasket-like bowl sitting atop the television next to a two-toned wooden picture frame (containing a China Girl colour test image). This whole complex is at the gaudy juncture of wallpaper and curtain, but this new and improved busyness, and 'correct' correspondence between sound and image, are not the only reasons we might get upcharged. We also have more soundtrack and, via the seed planted by the China Girl, the star of Landow's most infamous film (*Film in Which*), a package deal. *NIIQ* not only upgrades on all these fronts, it even concludes with two extensions of earlier films. *IQ* had ended with the words 'A RE-ENACTMENT' over a medium close-up of a woman loading a projector. Here we get a bringing to life of the just-mentioned photograph, and a re-enacting of part of *RRC* to boot.

When our test-taker in *NIIQ* was first prompted to mark his picture, he readied his pencil and looked down at the 'desk' below the bottom of the frame. A cut brought us to an eyeline match of his 'exam sheet'. Before walking into the room to comply in person, we/he saw an image of the room as a 2D 'transparency' to be written upon; then a dissolve takes us to the 3D entry described above. The comparison of this first marking shot to the ones in *IQ* is crucial. Instead of intercepting the projector's light, the fingers and writing tool in the remake's setup are backlit. What's more, compared to the pencil just seen, the instrument writes wrongly, trickling red ink. Another confusion emerges from the base 'holding' the image: scuffs show it to be moving. The easiest option for creating the shot would have been a still over a lightbox. Instead, Landow appears to have set up a rear projection loop (note identical splices) onto a vertical plastic (or plastic covered) surface. The wobble when the marker pushes off at the end of the shot gives it away with sway. Of course, no steadiness of support would allow writing on running film. Avoidance of smearing hangs on animation's intermittency and peg bar registration.

Why make so much of this shot? As a bridge between the opening view of our man, and his entrance into the room, it is an important building block of *NIIQ*. However, its inversion of the front projection setup from *IQ* raises it to keystone, intensifying an attention to writing and its orientations, urging the following of implements. Summarizing these: a pencil is used throughout the 1969 film; a pencil is cocked in the last seconds of the 1976 film's opening; *NIIQ's* next shot's silhouette is a red ink marker; that transformation is compounded when the main character enters the room to mark the physical television set with his oversized pencil cloaking a black marker. The first shots of *NIIQ* hold three different styluses. Things settle down for a little, but not without auxiliary problems (e.g. bed sheets). In the film's second half, we see the marker's bare tube before it turns back into the real pencil from the beginning. This then disappears in the testee's final exercises.

In 1974, Sitney referred to the original *IQ* as something 'reminiscent of childhood psychological perception tests and the television series *Winky Dink and You*'.[37] This 1950s CBS show invited viewers to use a 'magic window' over their sets for tracing. Although the concept of interacting with a transmitted image is in *IQ*, it wasn't until *NIIQ* that *Winky Dink's* orientation of rear rather than front delivery was literalized. The remake fuses these directionalities when an anomalous burn in superimposition of a white typeset '18' fades in as an 'overlay'. The number appears before its utterance on the soundtrack, returning us to the missed sync of the original's opening. That this special effect is reserved for an umbrella, a near-sacred object in the history of surrealism, whets the appetite. Two increasingly closer views reveal intrigues with its handle and the pattern on its clear (cel!) canopy.

If 18 marks a spot in *NIIQ*, it had really hit it in *IQ*. The call related to the umbrella there occurs as we are looking at an 8-mm projector after a sequence that includes a demonstration of the beta phenomenon with two blinking lights. As we hear the request to put a number 17 on a chair, there is a cut to a diagram of a projector with circled numbers indicating various parts. Sitney has rightly discussed this image as akin to the numbering of things in the room, but there is something more.[38] The digits in the diagram start in the bottom left with ‘1’ and end with ‘7’ on the right-hand side in a clockwise spread. Thus, a virtual 17 is produced if we yoke the actual ‘1’ and ‘7’ at left and right together. This is important training for the next command: ‘Put the umbrella away. Put the umbrella away. Put a number 18 on what you would touch.’ We see a contradiction. The words ‘SIMPLE TO OPERATE’ are superimposed over a rickety, vibrating view of the projector. The word ‘umbrella’ is delivered on the soundtrack against the textual image of the word ‘operate’ while a threading problem causes streaking. Umbrella, operate, thread: ‘as beautiful as the chance encounter of a sewing machine and an umbrella on an operating table’?[39] In Webber’s book, Land writes about ‘the early Surrealists notic[ing] that unrelated verbal images in Lautréamont’s *Les Chants de Maldoror* [1869] seemed to relate to one another in unexpected ways, simply through their juxtaposition’.[40] Yes, he is talking about a different film, but like the beta phenomena imagery that taught us how to stitch the separated ‘1’ and ‘7’ together, we can fuse again, conjuring Lautréamont’s line in relation to *IQ*. We are now in a better position to ask the father of structural film (Landow) what he thinks its midwife (Sitney) meant in calling his imagery ‘super-real’. Turns out, ‘unconsciously [Landow] knew the answer all along’.

Notes

1 Bruce Jenkins, ed., *On the Camera Arts and Consecutive Matters: The Writings of Hollis Frampton* (Cambridge, MA: MIT Press, 2009), 325. Delvaux would have appeared between Paul Delaroche and Maya Deren.

2 Frampton uses ‘trypewriter’ in a letter to Stan Brakhage, 18 September 1972 (see copies at Anthology Film Archives and University of Colorado Boulder Libraries, Rare and Distinctive Collections).

3 Hollis Frampton, ‘Incisions in History/Segments of Eternity’, *Artforum* (October 1974): 43.

4 Paul Arthur, ‘Joker at Play in a Sea of Holes: Owen Land’s (Non)Commodity Fetishism, or “The Size of the Jar Has Absolutely No Relation to the Number of Plums Contained Inside”’, *Film Comment* (September–October 2005): 43.

5 P. Adams Sitney, *George Landow* (St. Paul, MN: Film in the Cities, 1981), 17. Sitney’s line and Arthur’s discussion of ‘mouths’ and ‘openings’ and ‘the hole as a visual shape’ (43) inspired ‘originating orifice’. See p. 2 for Sitney on Landow ‘obsessively revis[ing] his films’ and the observation that a ‘second film-within’ *Broker Joke* is implied: ‘Landow has said that this will be a cartoon called *Noneuhemeristic Henotheism*.’

6 P. Adams Sitney, ‘Passages: Owen Land’, *Artforum* (November 2011): 63.

7 Sitney, *George Landow*, 1 and Sitney, ‘Passages’, 63.

8 Arthur, ‘Joker at Play’, 42.

9 Paul Arthur, ‘The Calisthenics of Vision: Open Instructions on the Films of George Landow’, *Artforum* (September 1971): 74–9.

10 J. D. Connor, 'What Becomes of Things on Film on Film: Adaptation in Owen Land (George Landow)', *Adaptation*, 2, no. 2 (2009): 161–76.

11 David Ehrenstein, *Film: The Front Line 1984* (Denver, CO: Arden Press, Inc., 1984), 47. One near exception proving the rule (depending on the original date of publication) is J. Hoberman's observation, used for the *Broker Joke* programme note at this 2011 memorial screening (https://www.sfcinematheque.org/wp-content/uploads/2011/08/PNLand_2012.pdf).

12 Mark Webber, ed., *Two Films by Owen Land* (London: LUX, 2005), 120.

13 A transcript was published as 'The Idea of Morphology: The First of Four Lectures on Avant-Garde Film Theory', *Film Culture*, nos. 53–54–55 (1972): 19 (both Sitney quotes in this paragraph).

14 Yet the very first question asked of Frampton's *(nostalgia)* (1971; 36 minutes; United States) at its world première was: 'Would I be right in thinking that you are a fan of the painter Max Ernst?' Frampton said sure, but didn't make much of it (50:05 of the track labelled Fv001 002 005 B Access https://records.cmoa.org/things/a7d71506-9a49-42ed-b802-168fb2cd2d9f/). On another occasion Frampton referred to himself as a 'reformed surrealist' (tape in the Harvard Film Archive's Frampton collection).

15 P. Gregory Springer, 'New Improved George Landow Interview (April 1976)', *Film Culture*, nos. 67–68–69 (1979): 93.

16 Jean Antoine (1930–2016)?

17 Jenkins, *Consecutive Matters*, 33 (then 33, 35 and 36).

18 Frampton, 'Incisions in History', 42.

19 Jenkins, *Consecutive Matters*, 40.

20 Frampton, 'Incisions in History', 43 (ellipses in original).

21 Thomas Singer, 'In the Manner of Duchamp, 1942–47: The Years of the "Mirrorical Return"', *The Art Bulletin*, 86, no. 2 (2004): 348.

22 Jenkins, *Consecutive Matters*, 50.

23 I first came across the Franck *and* Ballard's use of *The Echo* at Shiraz Randeria's tumblr site: https://fyishiraz.tumblr.com/post/29904256322/1-martine-franck-paris-1972-the-echo-by-paul/. Also see #11 at: https://archive.nytimes.com/lens.blogs.nytimes.com/2010/06/08/archive-18/.

24 Jenkins, *Consecutive Matters*, 34 (then 33 mid-paragraph).

25 For Steinbrecher's occupation and dates of marriage, separation and divorce see Bruce Jenkins and Susan Krane, *Hollis Frampton: Recollections/Recreations* (Cambridge, MA: The MIT Press, 1984), 112–13.

26 A copy of the text for the film was sent to Sally Dixon https://records.cmoa.org/things/d51a2fed-72a7-4bea-8e73-5c83244cc407/.

27 Hollis Frampton, 'Hollis Frampton Interviewed by Michael Snow', *Film Culture* 48–49 (1970): 8 + 12 (ellipsis mine).

28 P. Adams Sitney, 'Structural Film', *Film Culture*, 47 (1969): 1 (same for the next sentence). The second version of the essay is noted as 'revised, Winter, 1969' in *Film Culture Reader*, ed. P. Adams Sitney (New York: Praeger Publishers, 1970), 326–48.

29 Sitney, 'Structural Film', 2 (same for the next sentence), then 3.

30 Sitney, 'Structural Film', 2–3 (3 for the next sentence). Sitney mentions that Ken Kelman thinks Brakhage's stress on the visual is a major influence, but Sitney finds his 'rhythmic' sense antithetical to the 'static' (which solidifies shape?).

31 Sitney, 'Structural Film', 7. The same for the rest of this paragraph (ellipses mine). *Butter* was screened at the first Sitney MoMA lecture above.

32 For bibliographic information on the *Millennium* essay see note 38. The interest in surrealist film in the 1970s, especially Joseph Cornell's (which garnered major essays by Sitney and Annette Michelson, and a planned film by Frampton) fascinates here.

33 Sitney, 'Structural Film', 6 (same for the rest of the quotes in this paragraph, ellipses mine).

34 This preliminary list of relevant Magritte paintings is culled from Siegfried Gohr, *Magritte: Attempting the Impossible*, trans. John Gabriel and Donald Pistolesi (New York: Distributed Art Publishers, Inc., 2009).

35 Webber, *Two Films by Owen Land*, 118. Thanks to John Powers for supplying a study version (and, of course, to Abigail Susik and the press's readers and editors).

36 Tom Gunning, 'The Participatory Film', *American Film* (October 1975): 81 (ellipses mine).

37 P. Adams Sitney, *Visionary Film: The American Avant-Garde* (New York: Oxford University Press, 1974), 430.

38 P. Adams Sitney, 'Autobiography in Avant-Garde Film', *Millennium Film Journal*, 1 (1977–78): 95.

39 https://raunerlibrary.blogspot.com/2014/08/surrealists-inspired-by-lautreamont.html/

40 Owen Land, 'The Booth Bimbo and the Charismatic', in Webber, *Two Films by Owen Land*, 88.

Chapter 14
Ubu Animated: Jan Lenica, Geoff Dunbar and William Kentridge

Ian Walker

Ubu and surrealism

On the evening of 9 December 1896, the actor Firmin Génier stepped out on the stage of the Théâtre de l'Oeuvre, Paris, in the role of Père Ubu in Alfred Jarry's play *Ubu Roi*, and uttered the opening word: 'Merdre'. In the ensuing debacle, it seemed to many in the audience that theatre, literature, culture all had changed forever and indeed Ubu would go on to stomp through the coming century.[1]

There are no photographs of Génier in that first performance, but our image of what Ubu looks like is not solely based on his appearance on stage. For, as well as writing the words that came out of Ubu's mouth, Jarry created pictures of him that he published in books, journals and on posters.[2] He also constructed marionette figures, with which he would perform a puppet-theatre version of *Ubu Roi*. Together, these images and objects established templates from which later artists would develop their own versions of Père Ubu.[3]

Jarry died in 1907, but his influence was carried forward by those who had known him late in life. Foremost was Guillaume Apollinaire, who passed on the myth of Ubu to the young writers who would form the Parisian dada movement and later the surrealist group. When André Breton published a text on Jarry in 1919, he wrote that, after the scandal of 1896, Jarry 'no longer owned his big marionette' and quoted the comment of Jarry's friend Rachilde: 'the puppet called Ubu began to walk all alone'.[4]

Surrealism would adopt Ubu as one of its presiding magus-figures; when, in Marseilles in 1940, members of the group devised their own pack of playing cards, Ubu was designated as the Joker. Many variations on the image of Ubu were made by surrealist artists. In 1923, Max Ernst had painted *Ubu Imperator*, in which the abundant flesh of Ubu was transformed into a rigid metal casing, and he was shown balanced like a spinning top in a desert landscape.[5] In 1937, Ernst designed the decor for Sylvaine Itkine's staging of Jarry's sequel, *Ubu enchaîné*. Several other surrealist artists contributed pictures of Ubu to the programme for which Breton wrote an introduction.[6] Another important reworking was Dora Maar's 1936 photograph *Portrait of Ubu*, picturing what is most likely an armadillo foetus,[7] whereas, after the Second

World War, artists such as Joan Miró, Roberto Matta and Enrico Baj also created powerful images of Ubu.[8]

Although Jean-Pierre Lassalle has suggested that the fastidious Breton may have been uncomfortable with 'the triviality of the ubuesque "Merdre"', there is no doubt that, for Breton, Jarry was above all influential in his deployment of 'black humour'.[9] This key concept is important for later depictions of Ubu and we need to consider its history and its implications. Breton first proposed an *Anthologie de l'humour noir* in the mid-1930s and, after passing through the hands of several publishers, it appeared in June 1940; however, with the German invasion, the book was promptly suppressed. It did not re-emerge until 1945, when the postwar intellectual milieu found 'black humour' inadequate as a response to the recent horrors. One criticism was from Raymond Queneau, who, in the words of Dawn Ades, argued that the 'only way to fight Nazism ... was with machine guns and bombs'.[10]

Yet slowly the influence of the *Anthologie de l'humour noir* grew. When a 'definitive edition' of the *Anthologie* appeared in 1966, just months before Breton's death, he remarked that the concept 'remains full of effervescence'.[11] As he noted, it had by then spread through both popular culture and contemporary literature, as exemplified in the work of figures such as Eugène Ionesco, Joe Orton, Joseph Heller and Kurt Vonnegut. But was this 'black humour' still indebted to Breton's formulation, or had it become a different and looser element in the wider culture? It is a question that is related to the broader issue of the place of surrealism as it spread in the second half of the twentieth century.

Perhaps, though, it was already significant that Breton himself did not characterize black humour as specifically surrealist and it is rather the fact that he was himself a (the) leading surrealist that makes the reader think of the texts in that way. Moreover, he emphasized the partiality of his selection, and later writers have argued that there are also other sorts of surrealist humour.[12]

Breton was careful not to give a definition of black humour, but rather, by choosing the form of an anthology, he offered a range of differing exemplars by forty-five writers. Each was prefaced by a short text and, presenting Jarry, Breton wrote, 'it is easy to see in the character of Ubu the magisterial incarnation of the Nietzschean–Freudian *id* that designates the totality of unknown, unconscious, repressed energies, of which the *ego* is but the sanctioned emanation, dictated by prudence'.[13] In examining the presence of Ubu through the rest of the century, we will inevitably recall that evocation of the *id* and its revelation through black humour.

By the postwar period, then, the figure of Ubu was thoroughly embedded in surrealism and surrealism had become integral to the understanding of Ubu. This history was complex, but I want to concentrate here on three animated film versions of Ubu, two from the 1970s and one from the 1990s, each reflecting their distinctive national contexts. None of the film-makers was a surrealist, yet their films obliquely demonstrate the continuing presence of surrealist ideas during this period as well as the continuing relevance of Ubu himself. Moreover, black humour is important in all the films, although the context of each one was markedly different.

Jan Lenica and Ubu in Poland

It was inevitable that Ubu would come to occupy an established if unsettled place within Polish culture.[14] After all, Jarry himself, introducing the play at its première, had announced: 'The action, which is about to begin, takes place in Poland, in other words: Nowhere.'[15] And, indeed, at that point in time, this was true; only in 1918 did Poland achieve the status of a nation.

Ubu's presence in Polish culture continued after the Second World War, although inevitably it often circulated underground. It is striking that two of the most important versions by Polish artists were made in exile: Franciszka Themerson's variations were produced in London between 1951 and 1970, whereas Jan Lenica's 1979 film *Ubu et la grande gidouille* was made in Paris. (Both will be discussed below.) The leading composer Krzysztof Penderecki had long wanted to stage an operatic version of Ubu but knew it would not be acceptable to the communist authorities. Only in 1990 was his *Ubu Rex* produced in Munich, with a Polish version finally being performed in 2003.

For perhaps related reasons, there was never a formal surrealist movement in Poland (unlike neighbouring Czechoslovakia), but the influence of surrealism was nevertheless pervasive.[16] Nowhere was this more so than within the new Polish cinema of the 1950s, with young directors like Andrej Wadja and Roman Polanski acknowledging its presence in their work.[17] Polanski, for example, later said, 'I owe my apprenticeship to surrealism. For ten years, even when I made my first films, I viewed things solely by its light.'[18] (His short *Two Men and a Wardrobe* of 1958 is an instructive example here.)

An adjacent context where social critique could be masked by humour was in animation. This was important across Eastern Europe and, in Poland, was best represented by the collaborative films made by Walerian Borowczyk and Jan Lenica in the late 1950s. Their work together reached its culmination with *Dom* (The House; 1958; 12 minutes; Poland), which had a wide international circulation. It is deliberately fragmented, juxtaposing scenes from various rooms in a single building; the segments are also stylistically different. A sequence where a blonde female wig climbs onto a table and consumes or wrecks all the objects on it could have easily found a place in one of Jan Švankmajer's films from a few years later. Ado Kyrou, in his book *Le Surréalisme au cinéma*, described the sequence as 'merveilleusement lautréamonesque'.[19]

After *Dom*, Borowczyk and Lenica parted company (apparently in some acrimony), and soon both left to work in France. This is not the place to give details on Borowczyk's subsequent trajectory, with further celebrated short films leading into features and a late career laced with transgressive eroticism; Michael Richardson has subtly discussed his work from a surrealist perspective.[20]

Meanwhile, Lenica continued with his major artistic activity as a designer of posters. These were mostly for plays, film screenings, and operas and produced for a wide clientele across Europe, including back in Poland. He developed a bold graphic style that had elements of Pop Art while remaining unsettling and subversive. The poster he made for a production of *Wozzeck* in Warsaw in 1964 is a well-known example: swirling forms in shades of red out of which emerges a screaming mouth.[21]

In addition he made short films (also often on commission). There were some ten substantial animations produced between 1959 and 1974 and they often share a common visual style, a mix of collage with the rough drawing technique familiar from his posters. Typically, they centre on a male protagonist threatened by the anonymous brutality of society. The hero of his condensed version of Eugène Ionesco's absurdist play *Rhinocéros* (Rhinoceros; 1963; 11 minutes; France) finds himself surrounded by friends and colleagues turning into the eponymous pachyderm. Perhaps the most extraordinary of all these films was *Labyrinthe* (Labyrinth; 1962; 15 minutes; France), in which a moustachioed gentlemen flies on a pair of giant wings into a nineteenth-century city, where he encounters a range of hybrid monsters collaged out of old engravings. In both its style and oneiric atmosphere, it inevitably recalls Max Ernst's collage novel *Une Semaine de Bonté* of 1934. Writing of *Labyrinth* in the surrealist journal *La Brèche*, Robert Benayoun called Lenica 'a bold, acrobatic creator … His films, strident and anguished … are marked with the seal of the most restless, the most enigmatic surrealism'.[22]

Lenica was nearing fifty when, in the mid-1970s, he started work on his film of *Ubu*. It was a work of maturity, although still with a subversive and unnerving edge. Writing again on Lenica's work in 1980, Benayoun remarked that he 'threw himself on Ubu with a savage joy as if on a long-lost friend who had been finally rediscovered'.[23] Here, Lenica's affinity with Jarry's play came together with his relationship with both the country of his birth and the country of his habitation.

The project began with a commission from West German television to make a film of *Ubu Roi*. This was completed in 1977,[24] but was soon superseded when Lenica decided to extend it by adding material adapted from the two later plays, *Ubu Cocu* and *Ubu enchaîné*.[25] The final film was released in 1979, with the title *Ubu et la grande Gidoulle* (1979; 80 minutes; France). ('Gidoulle' is the name given to the spiral that adorns Ubu's corpulent belly.)

Lenica deliberately kept his technique minimal, even crude. Whereas his posters often exploited vibrant colour, here the tones were restricted to heavy washes of brown, blue and a dirty green. There was little attempt to make either characters or scenery three-dimensional and all the action clearly takes place on the flat surface of a table top. An arm might be raised or a head turned, but the rest of the body (and the scene around it) remains still and flat. But if the animation was simple, the design of the characters was not, and Lenica pushed the thickened black outlines of his graphic work to new excesses.

The monstrous Ubus are reptilian in their physiognomies, although his body is rotund and hers angular. This bestiality was something that Jarry had himself emphasized, writing: 'If he [Ubu] resembles an animal, he particularly has a porcine face, a nose similar to the crocodile's upper jaw, and the totality of his cardboard caparison makes him overall brother to the most aesthetically horrible of all marine beasts, the sea louse.'[26] The first shots of the film show a snoring Ubu swallow a fly, which then emerges out of his eye socket; there is evidently little inside his head to prevent its passage. A little later, as Mère Ubu tries to persuade her husband to kill the king, she turns into a giant insect descending from above to confront him. The other characters are drawn with equally grotesque precision; Prince Bougrelas is a pinched and petulant midget, whereas Ubu's skeletal co-conspirator Captain Bordure is first discovered having intimate relations behind a bush with a cow possessing remarkably human breasts.

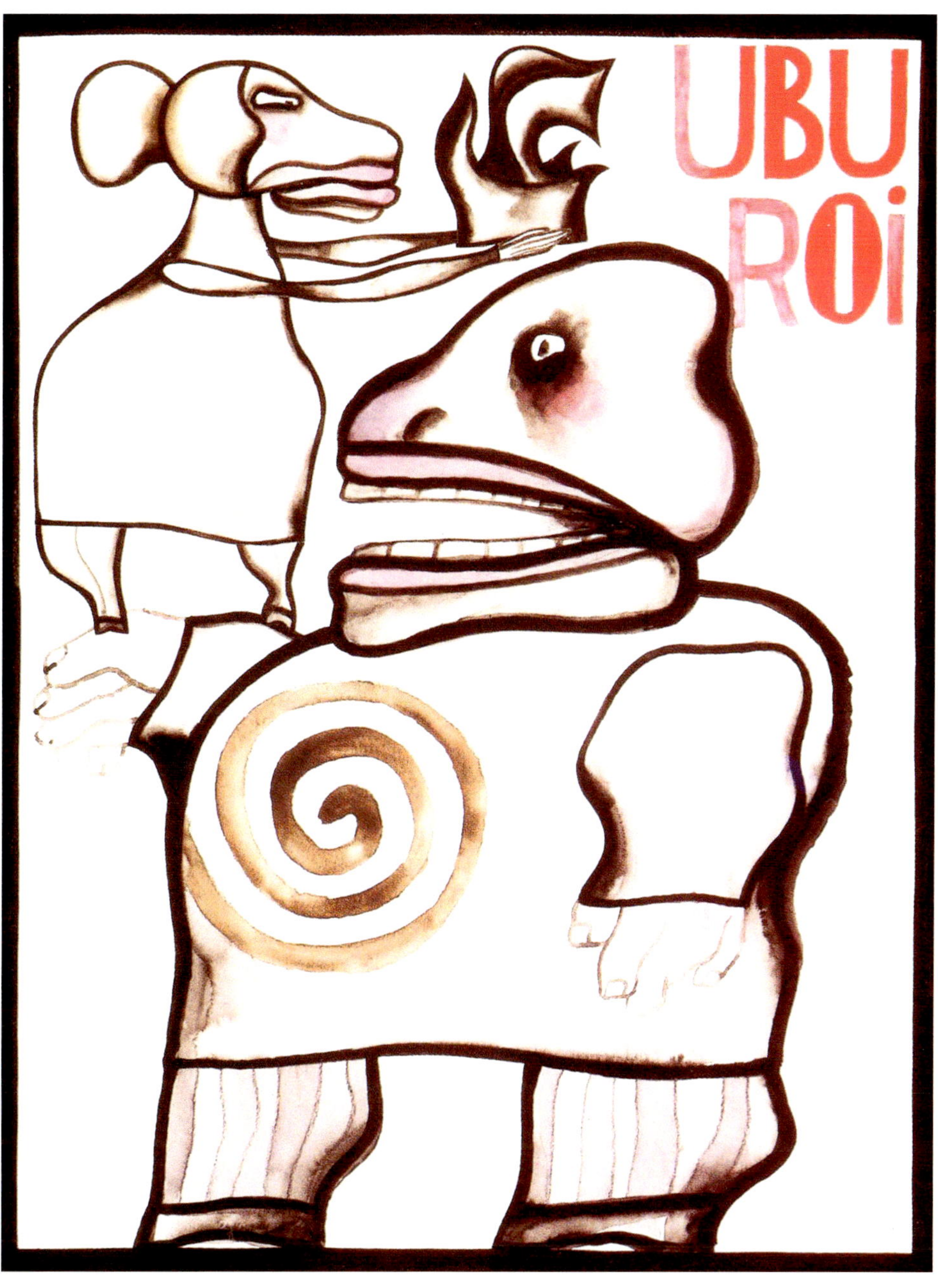

Figure 14.1 Jan Lenica, dir., *Ubu et la Grande Gidoulle*, 1979. Film Poster. © ADAGP, Paris and DACS, London 2024.

This is set within an endless landscape painted with broad washes of dull colour. Benayoun compared it to the way that Yves Tanguy placed amorphous forms in a wide and empty environment. However, whereas Tanguy's pictures have the pearly luminescence of his native Brittany, Lenica's landscapes are heavy and monotonous, evoking the flat plains of northern Europe as well as the dreariness of totalitarianism. The humour of the film is also brutal. Lenica introduces a character that is not in Jarry's original, a gnarled peasant who digs out of the ground an alarmingly humanoid root. Climbing the steps to the palace, the peasant is confronted by guards who demand pay-offs from what he has found in the fields. When he has nothing for the last one, he is kicked back down the steps.

All this happens in the first few minutes of the film. The rest of *Ubu Roi* has a similar thrust and energy, a high point being when the Ubus dance frenetically to Tchaikovsky's 'Russian Dance' from *The Nutcracker*; for a while, even Père Ubu defies gravity. The battle scenes are also full of knockabout and caustic sarcasm. However, the audience are probably by this point feeling rather battered, as much by the film's eccentric excess as by its harshness. At the end of *Ubu Roi*, when the Ubus make their escape and sail away to France, we are 43 minutes through the film, just over half way. One might well feel that the film should have ended there, as the first version had done. In general, animation works best as a short form and animation that is visually and intellectually challenging punches hardest when it is brusque and to the point.

The second half of *Ubu et la grande Gidoulle* takes us through the other two Ubu plays at greater speed than we have moved so far, and Lenica edits and rearranges their content with such freedom that the narrative gets rather lost. (The titles have told us that the film is 'inspiré trés librement des oeuvres d'Alfred Jarry'.) There are, though, marvellous scenes – when Ubu sets up a 'debraining' salon where he replaces a customer's brain with scrunched up newspaper, when Mère Ubu cuckolds her spouse with the sinister Memnon inside a grand piano, when a fashionable soirée is disrupted by Ubu's vulgar interruptions, allowing Lenica some satirical comments on the fashionable Paris he himself now inhabited. These may not altogether justify Lenica's extension of his first Ubu film, but they do provide deliciously dark pleasures. Lenica's Ubu remains memorable precisely because he can't be pinned down. Emerging out of nightmares, he hovers in the darkness, that *id* that is ever present and threatening.

A retrospective exhibition of Jan Lenica's work was mounted at the Centre Pompidou in 1980, but in the following decade, he was mainly based in Germany, having been appointed the first professor of animation at the University of Kassel. He died in Berlin in 2001, shortly after completing his final film *Wyspa R.O.* (Island R.O.; 2001; 31 minutes; Poland). Bringing together live action and special effects, it has not stood the test of time so well, but nevertheless it is a reminder of the constant process of invention in Lenica's work, from his posters to his films, from *Labyrinth* to *Ubu et la grande Gidoulle*.

Geoff Dunbar and Ubu in Britain

In the postwar years, surrealism in Britain lay largely dormant despite the continuing work of a number of individuals. However, in 1967, a committed surrealist group was formed, its prime movers being John Lyle and Conroy Maddox; with others, they established a new journal, *Transformaction*. (Parenthetically, one of my favourite surrealist Ubus appeared there in 1977; it is a drawing by Anthony Earnshaw, in which Ubu regards an outline of the state of Oklahoma and recognizes in it his own profile, with his eye just where the town of Enid is. This makes him have 'second thoughts about a trip to America'.[27])

Outside this committed activity, though, surrealism came to represent something broader and looser. A fracture occurred in the *Transformaction* group when Maddox objected to a supplement entitled 'Blue Food', which he considered 'a title yielding too obviously to dominant hippie, psychedelic fashion'.[28] This indicates something of the promiscuous interflow between surrealism and the larger counterculture of the time. There were major works which made something memorable out of this interaction, but of course there was also much that was ersatz.

The case of animation is interesting here. The most ambitious animated film of the period was *Yellow Submarine* (1968; 88 minutes; UK), directed by George Dunning. It was very much a product of the time of its inception, the previous summer of psychedelia (the Blue Meanies ate 'blue food', presumably). Its whimsicality and relentless jolliness can be hard to take now, though the surrealist-derived elements, if lightweight, are also consistently inventive. The animated sequences that Terry Gilliam made for *Monty Python's Flying Circus* (starting in 1969) were much less technically ambitious, making a virtue of their DIY quality. Prams gobbled up old ladies, a giant cat menaced London, and strands of spaghetti turned into the flyaway hair of Botticelli's *Venus*. Again, the surrealism was lightly worn, as much descended from *MAD* magazine as anything more highbrow. Indeed, Gilliam claimed that he hadn't heard of Max Ernst until George Melly made the comparison in a review. Perhaps, but he must surely have seen that intermediary film, Lenica's *Labyrinth*, which is so similar in technique and the use of Victorian apparatus.

By now Ubu was well established in the British avant-garde and making his way into popular culture. The first English version of *Ubu Roi* had been in 1951, when Barbara Wright published her translation with the Gabberbochus Press, set up by Stefan and Franciszka Themerson after their exile from Poland.[29] On each page, Wright's handwritten text intermingled with Franciszka's drawings. The latter would continue in the succeeding years to produce versions of Ubu in a range of media. She made masks for a reading of *Ubu Roi* at the ICA in 1952, and in 1963, designed a production in Stockholm. Finally, in 1970 she published a comic book version of the play, to which we will return.[30]

In 1965, the *Selected Works of Alfred Jarry* was published, an invaluable compendium of translations containing further Ubu material as well as the seminal *Exploits and Opinions of Doctor Faustroll Pataphysician*.[31] Across the British art and literary scenes of the sixties and seventies, one would come across many Ubu-esque moments. To give just one example, the Liverpool poet Adrian Henri wrote poems about the city, peopling it with an eclectic mix of American bebop jazzmen, abstract expressionists, pop singers and masters of the European avant-garde. In one, he declared, 'I have seen Père Ubu walking across Lime St / And Alfred Jarry cycling down Elliott Street.'[32]

Another Liverpool artist was also entranced by Ubu and Jarry. On the evening of 10 January 1966, Paul McCartney was driving back to Liverpool when he tuned his car radio into a production of *Ubu Cocu*. He subsequently tracked down what he could find about

Jarry and indeed worked pataphysics into his song 'Maxwell's Silver Hammer'.[33] This was McCartney's own attempt at black humour, though, unfortunately, it was also one of those teeth-grindingly jaunty songs that he regularly turned out.

Later in 1966, McCartney was in the audience at the Royal Court Theatre to see an epochal production of *Ubu Roi*. This was mainly memorable for two aspects. One was the stage and costume designs by David Hockney. His faux-naif drawings now look a little thin, although photographs of the production suggest they had a more robust presence on stage. The other noteworthy aspect was the casting of Max Wall as Père Ubu. Wall was a comedian with a background in the music hall; he had a flexible and grotesque face and body, which would have suited the comedy of the role if not so much its savagery.

Also in the audience for *Ubu Roi* in 1966 was a young animator named Geoff Dunbar, who would a decade later make his own version of the play: 'I thought at the time, if I ever got the chance to do it, *Ubu* would just be the most natural animated picture.'[34] Born in Oxfordshire in 1944, Dunbar worked during the 1960s in a number of commercial studios before forming Dragon Productions with colleagues. His first individual work was *Lautrec* (1975; 5 minutes; UK), which, through a number of brief vignettes, evoked the life and work of Henri Toulouse-Lautrec. The main visual element was a delicate use of a soft pencil to create tender reworkings of Lautrec's images. *Lautrec* won the Palme d'Or at the Cannes Film Festival and its success encouraged Dunbar to return to his desire to make a film of *Ubu*, although the gentleness of *Lautrec* did not presage what came next: 'I've always been of a mind to try something different each time … Each subject demands a certain treatment.'[35]

Dunbar's version of *Ubu* (1978; 19 minutes; UK) was half funded by the Arts Council of Great Britain and half by his commercial work. Although the film was admired and won festival prizes, it also shocked many of its first audiences.[36] Using very different techniques to Jan Lenica (whose film Dunbar only came across later), it was just as faithful to the savage humour of its source. It was much more compact than Lenica's version, with the action regularly interrupted by titles proclaiming Act One, Act Two, etc. (This serves also to emphasize the Shakespearean references, most obviously to *Macbeth*.)

The dominant visual feature of Dunbar's *Ubu* is the extravagant flung ink technique, which splatters and dribbles across the blank space of the screen. 'I would take a bottle of ink with those plunger things, just squeeze it, and then just whack it right across it, and you'd just let the blobs go.'[37] It is instructive to compare this with Franciszka Themerson's *Ubu Comic*, published in 1970.[38] (Dunbar did not know Themerson's work at the time, but a recent viewing led him to call it 'magnificent and inspiring'.[39]) Themerson and Dunbar share a loose, dynamic and semi-automatic drawing style to evoke Ubu's anarchic presence, but there are also important differences. Themerson's linear gestures are exuberant and playful where Dunbar's are messier and more uncomfortable, the flung paint and ink suggesting the splattering of unnamed bodily fluids around the space.

The grotesque characters inhabit this messy environment with a raw energy. According to Dunbar, this involved unlearning the conventions of animation: 'Sometimes we'd be sitting there looking at it, and I'd say this looks a bit too good, isn't it a bit smooth – let's just bang it up a bit.'[40] Ubu himself is a large blob, although his face has a range of expression that Lenica did not attempt, shifting constantly from rapacious low cunning

Figure 14.2 Geoff Dunbar, dir., *Ubu*, 1978. Courtesy Geoff Dunbar.

to savagery through a glint in the eye. Ma Ubu is an even more extraordinary figure, her head encased in a structure inspired by an Indian mask and her mobile breasts capped with large nipples that constantly point like machine guns in the direction of her attention.

The interaction of the two figures often degenerates into a violence that is just as savage as that they inflict on others. And that violence remains extreme, most notably towards the end of the film when Ubu confronts a large bear, tears its legs off and stuffs its bloody innards in his mouth. The shock of that scene is then succeeded by the tranquil image of Pa and Ma afloat in their canoe, relaxing and sipping cocktails. This final scene is held and the tranquillity is just as disturbing as the violence that preceded it.

The alien strangeness of the characters is underlined by a brilliant coup with the dialogue. This initially came out of budgetary constraints. Dunbar couldn't afford to hire actors to do the voices, so he and the sound designer Terry Brown came up with the idea of using treated animal noises. The sounds coming from the Ubus are harsh and guttural, a bestial subhuman language; the actual words are then 'translated' in speech bubbles that emerge from their mouths. This aural effect is as visceral as the visuals, with grinding sound effects merging with stirring martial music composed by Laurie Scott Baker. (Dunbar was working with a small creative team, each adding crucial inputs. One of them, Annabel Jankel, credited here with 'inking', would go on to make significant work of her own in the 1980s.)

If the sharp, nervous pen drawing and splattered colour is used in scenes involving the Ubus, other techniques emerge elsewhere in an appropriately anarchic manner. The background scenery also changes; when Captain Drubbish (as Bordure is here named) calls on the Ubus, one of Seurat's pointillist paintings of the Seine is in the background. (A generalized Poland is suddenly Paris.)

When the Polish army marches past Ubu in a grand parade, the drawing style is much looser and basic. According to Dunbar, this was also due to the restricted budget, but 'it was a bonus in many ways. It helped the irreverence of it.'[41] Likewise, when Ubu rides into battle, it is on a horse drawn as if by a child, propelled by creaky wheels rather than hooves. The ensuing battle scenes are different yet again, full of sound and fury (and yet more dismembered bodies). Describing these scenes, the Argentinian animator Oscar Grillo evoked other operatic visions of war: 'In the battle of *Ubu*, which is to my view one of the most powerful, violent sequences in the history of European film, I think only you could find things that is in Japanese films [*sic*], live action films.'[42] Grillo was presumably thinking here of Kurosawa, with perhaps echoes also of Eisenstein's *Alexander Nevsky*. This feels at one with the ironic, self-aware nature of the film, which uses shifts of tone and style to unsettle its audience.

Between the time it was conceived and when it was completed, the cultural context changed around Dunbar's film. When he began it, it was situated in the counterculture of the mid-1970s. By the time the film appeared in 1978, it was inevitably viewed in the framework of punk. This was, perhaps, coincidental, but also fortuitous in that it gave an added edge to the film (and brought it to other audiences). Moreover, although punk may have projected itself as a clean slate, *Ubu* also provided a connection into a history of avant-garde provocation, back from punk to dada, a lineage traced by Greil Marcus in his 1990 book *Lipstick Traces*.[43] In 2005, the theatre director Dominic Dromgoole, in the course of a generally dismissive article on the crudeness of *Ubu Roi*, had to admit: 'Simply forcing the door open into the modern, and being the first to walk in new rooms, creates an energy. Ubu is full of that delirious freedom. The punk desire to howl the House down shouldn't create anything enduring, but it does.'[44]

After *Ubu*, Geoff Dunbar's career took another, very different turn. Paul McCartney much admired the film and commissioned Dunbar to create the animation to accompany his 'Rupert and the Frog Song' (1984; 13 minutes; UK). (Note for non-British readers, Rupert is a comic-strip talking bear who wears tartan trousers. For boys like McCartney and Dunbar growing up after the war, he was a staple of their childhood.) 'I was delighted', Dunbar commented, 'I didn't want to make another film like *Ubu*.'[45] The resulting film was charming, clever, and, as with some of McCartney's other work, a touch too cheery.

Dunbar's later films were a mix of commercial work – like his version of Beatrix Potter's *Peter Rabbit* (1993–4) – with more personal and ambitious projects. *Daumier's Law* (1992; 15 minutes; UK) reworked the drawings of Honoré Daumier with real force, whereas his visualization of Janáček's opera *The Cunning Little Vixen* (2003; 75 minutes; UK), was imbued with a feel for sweeping landscape. Yet good-humoured and indeed moving as *The Cunning Little Vixen* was, one can understand Geoff Brown's summation that 'if Dunbar's Pa Ubu saw the film, let alone *Rupert* or *Peter Rabbit*, he would probably let loose with rude noises and an expletive'.[46] But then, perhaps *Ubu* is all the more memorable and powerful because it is unique.

William Kentridge and Ubu in South Africa

The two very different animations by Lenica and Dunbar occupy the centre of this essay, but there is a third film which is also significant: *Ubu Tells the Truth* (1997; 7 minutes; South Africa), made by William Kentridge, in which Ubu became the embodiment of the brutality of Apartheid.

Ubu Tells the Truth first appeared in 1996 (the centenary of Jarry's play) as a suite of eight etchings in which rough line drawings of Ubu were laid over Kentridge's own naked and heavy body; 'I'm going to take responsibility for that character as myself', he said.[47] The following year, Kentridge directed a stage performance, *Ubu and the Truth Commission*, which he developed with the writer Jane Taylor and the Handspring Puppet Company. (The title referenced the Truth and Reconciliation Commission set up in 1995 by Bishop Desmond Tutu.) Pa and Ma Ubu were here played by actors (Pa dressed in singlet and Y-fronts), the other characters were large puppets, and the staged action was intercut with Kentridge's animations projected on a screen above the actors.[48] Those short vignettes were then stitched together to form the film *Ubu Tells the Truth.*

Unlike the films of Lenica and Dunbar, *Ubu Tells the Truth* is not a narrative retelling of Jarry's play, but rather a montage of images through which the figure of Ubu moves. Moreover, its most likely viewing space is not a cinema but an art gallery. (In the darkened room devoted to *Ubu* in Kentridge's 2022 exhibition at the Royal Academy in London, the film was looped and shown on a large screen across one corner, surrounded by related wall drawings. The sound was loud and aggressive.) In the words of Kate McCrickard, *Ubu Tells the Truth* is 'violent, electric, rough-cut and vertiginous'.[49] Kentridge's dynamic drawing style – white line on a black background – is mixed with collaged elements and sudden inserts of found footage, piling up and changing before one can process their significance.

Kentridge's relationship with previous art is complex. Questioned by Carolyn Christov-Bakargiev about the way he mixed art-historical references, he talked about his early years in the 1970s, when he felt distanced both geographically and temperamentally from the contemporary avant-garde: 'The art that seemed most immediate and local dated from the early twentieth century, when there still seemed to be hope for political struggle rather than a world exhausted by war and failure.'[50] Of these earlier art movements, the most important for Kentridge were Expressionism in his drawing style and Russian Constructivism in some of his film work (the close-up eye that appears in *Ubu Tells the Truth* could have come from Vertov).

As far as I am aware, Kentridge has never claimed any relationship with surrealism and critics' use of the term 'surreal' to describe certain works has been rather generalized. Yet such connections need not be only to surrealism as an historical movement but also to an allied spirit and tactic which is not explicitly named. There is an image in *Ubu Tells the*

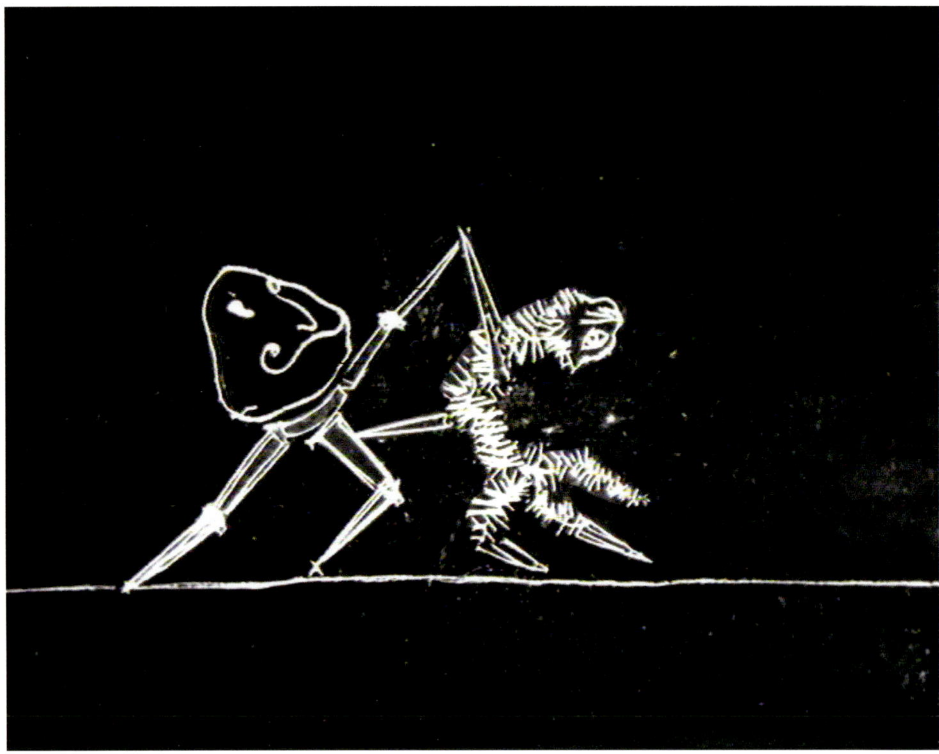

Figure 14.3 William Kentridge, dir., *Ubu Tells the Truth*, 1997. Courtesy the artist and Goodman Gallery.

Truth of a pig's head wearing a Walkman that explodes. Its visceral impact on the viewer is partly because it is not explained; as Kentridge remarked, 'Many viewers don't know that this is based on South African police photographs of experiments testing a Walkman booby trap on a pig's head.' Behind the strange, striking image, then, there existed an equally strange actuality. And it not only imparts a direct physical impact, it also carries weight as a symbol of a political system losing its grip on reality. In Kentridge's own words, 'If you stick closely enough to specifics – which are usually stranger than fiction – somehow that authenticity will convince an audience, bring them along with you.'[51] One need not call this example 'surrealist' for it to operate – both imaginatively and politically – like a surrealist image.

The power of *Ubu Tells the Truth*, though, rests not only in such individual moments, but in the staccato way the film jumps from one image to another, exploiting the power of animated forms to metamorphose and create new meanings. There is, for example, a sequence where Ubu takes off his head and unzips his body to reveal a camera on a tripod, which then upends itself and becomes a helicopter with its rotors whirling. This happens very quickly, one form changing into another to dizzying effect and without any obvious rationale. The process of metamorphosis in *Ubu Tells the Truth* is extreme, but it is also present in the other films discussed here – one might remember Ma Ubu as the descending insect in Lenica's *Ubu et la grande Gidoulle* or Pa Ubu's ricketty horse in Dunbar's *Ubu*. This shape-shifting is a powerful aspect of animation and a significant element in making each of the films both unsettled and unsettling.

Conclusion

In a 1988 television interview, Geoff Dunbar remarked, 'It seems to me that all the animation I have ever seen has been surreal.'[52] Recently, he elaborated on this with an example: 'ducks wearing jackets, carousing with a couple of mice who own a dog and eat turkey for dinner. I mean – where did all that come from?'[53] This is a reference to popular forms of animation – the early films of Disney – where the evocation of 'surrealism' is at its loosest and yet also where it might be most apt. However, this applies just as much to the art-animation represented in different ways by Kentridge, Lenica and Dunbar.

We have to be careful in using the term 'surrealism' not to claim too much of a link or to dilute the central core of the surrealist proposition. At the same time, surrealism has had a pervasive presence throughout the wider culture, resulting in major works that are at the same time surrealist and not surrealist. That ambiguity can be a strength. After all, Ubu himself has never been subsumed under any one heading – Dadaist, surrealist or absurdist – yet is a vital figure in all of them. (And 'black humour' is a thread that links them together.)

Moreover, despite Ubu's widespread presence on stage, in paintings, drawings and prints, it is, I think, altogether possible to argue that animation is his ideal medium. Live-action performance can descend into burlesque as one is only too aware that we are watching actual humans in fancy dress. An animation, though, can create a world, which we know is made up (and indeed often has a wilful exaggeration that would not be possible on stage) yet where the characters move, speak and occupy space just as they might in reality. We almost believe the illusion at the same time that we know it is indeed an illusion. In their different ways, the films of Jan Lenica, Geoff Dunbar and William Kentridge exploit this paradox to make the world of Ubu altogether palpable and much too uncomfortable.

Notes

1 See Alastair Brotchie, *Alfred Jarry: A Pataphysical Life* (Cambridge, MA: MIT Press, 2011), and Jill Fell, *Alfred Jarry* (London: Reaktion, 2010).

2 See Michel Arrivé, *Peintures, gravures et dessins d'Alfred Jarry* (Paris: Collège de 'Pataphysique et Cercle Français du Livre, 1968).

3 For collections of Ubu portraits, see Marie-Claire Adès and Jean-Hugues Piettre, *Ubu Cent Ans de Règne* (Paris: Musée-Galerie de la Seita, 1989), and Christine van Schoonbeck, *Les Portraits d'Ubu* (Paris: Séguier, 1997).

4 Written in 1918, Breton's text was reprinted in *Les Ecrits nouveaux*, January 1919. André Breton, *The Lost Steps* [1924], trans. Mark Polizzotti (Lincoln: University of Nebraska, 1996). 31.

5 Max Ernst's *Ubu Imperator* (1923) is in the collection of the Centre Pompidou, Paris.

6 For images of Ubu by Man Ray, Tanguy, Roger Blin, Maurice Henry, Magritte and Picasso, see van Schoonbeck, *Les Portraits d'Ubu*, 89–93. Breton's essay was reprinted in *La Clé de champs* (Paris: Éditions du Sagittaire, 1953) and translated by Michel Parmentier and Jacqueline d'Amboise as 'Alfred Jarry as Precursor and Initiator', *Free Rein* (Lincoln: University of Nebraska Press, 1995), 247–56.

7 See Ian Walker, 'Ubu in London: Between Surrealism and Documentary', in *Dora Maar*, eds. Karolina Ziebinska-Lewandowska, Damarice Amao and Amanda Maddox (London: Tate Modern and Los Angeles, CA: J. Paul Getty Museum, 2019), 124–7.

8 See Renée Riese Hubert, '*Ubu Roi* and the surrealist *livre de peintre*', *Word & Image*, 3, no.4 (October–December, 1987): 259–78.

9 Jean-Pierre Lassalle, 'Alfred Jarry', in *The International Encyclopedia of Surrealism*, vol. I, ed. Michael Richardson (London: Bloomsbury, 2019), 590.

10 Dawn Ades, 'Humor', in *The International Encyclopedia of Surrealism*, vol. 1, 224.

11 André Breton, *Anthology of Black Humour*, trans. Mark Polizzotti (London and Berkeley, CA: Telegram, 2009), 17–18.

12 As well as Ades, 'Humor', see Michael Richardson, 'Black Humour', in *Surrealism: Key Concepts*, eds. Krzysztof Fijalkowski and Michael Richardson (London: Routledge, 2016), 207–16.

13 Breton, *Anthology of Black Humour*, 258–9.

14 This section is indebted to Mikołaj Gliński, 'Kings with No Nation: Polish Adaptations of Ubu Roi', online at https://culture.pl/en/article/ubu-roi-polish-adaptations/

15 Quoted in Brotchie, *Alfred Jarry*, 161.

16 See Piotr Piotrowski, *In the Shadow of Yalta: Art and the Avant-garde in Eastern Europe* (London: Reaktion, 2009).

17 See *Dzieie grzechu: surrealism w kinie polskim / A Story of Sin: Surrealism in Polish Cinema*, eds. Kamila Wielebska and Kuba Mikurda (Kraków: Korporacja Ha!art (*sic*), 2010).

18 Translated by Michael Richardson, *Surrealism and Cinema* (Oxford: Berg, 2006), 146, from 'Surréalisme et cinéma', special issue of *Études cinématographiques*, 41/42 (1965): 171.

19 Ado Kyrou, *Le Surréalisme au cinéma*, 2nd edn (Paris: Le Terrain Vague, 1963), 203.

20 Richardson, 'Walerian Borowczyk and the Touch of Desire', *Surrealism and Cinema*, 107–20.

21 See *Jan Lenica*, ed. Jean-Loup Passak (Paris: Centre Georges Pompidou, 1980), 32.

22 R. B., 'L'anthropométrie fantastique de Lenica', *La Brèche*, 4 (February 1963), 17 (author's translation).

23 Robert Benayoun, 'L'anthropométrie fantastique de Lenica', in *Jan Lenica*, ed. Passak, 24 (author's translation). This essay has the same title as Benayoun's 1963 review, but is considerably expanded.

24 I have not been able to view Lenica's first Ubu film and have assumed that it is largely the same as the first section of *Ubu et la grande Gidoulle*.

25 The histories of these two latter plays is complex. *Ubu Cocu* was left unfinished by Jarry and not published until 1944. *Ubu enchaîné* was published in 1900, but not performed until Itkine's staging in 1937. The three plays were first published together in English as *The Ubu Plays*, trans. Cyril Connolly and Simon Watson Taylor (London: Methuen, 1968).

26 This was in Jarry's text 'Les Paralipomènes d'Ubu', published in *La Revue Blanche*, 1 December 1896. This translation by Mark Polizzotti in Breton, *The Lost Steps*, 28–9.

27 This and another Earnshaw drawing of Ubu were placed on the inside covers of the journal *Transformaction*, 8 (1977) and reprinted in Anthony Earnshaw, *Flick Knives & Forks* (Harpford, Devon: Transformaction, 1981), 16 and 40.

28 Michel Remy, 'Transformaction', in *The International Encyclopedia of Surrealism*, vol. I, ed. Richardson, 482. Also see Remy, *Surrealism in Britain* (Aldershot: Ashgate, 1999).

29 Alfred Jarry, *Ubu Roi*, trans. Barbara Wright with illustrations by Franciszka Themerson (London: Gabberbochus Press, 1951).

30 See Jaisa Reichardt, *Franciszka Themerson & UBU* (London: Richard Saltoun, 2017).

31 *Selected Works of Alfred Jarry*, eds. Roger Shattuck and Simon Watson Taylor (London: Methuen, 1965).

32 Adrian Henri, 'Liverpool Poems', in *Penguin Modern Poets 10: 'The Mersey Sound': Adrian Henri, Roger McGough, Brian Patten* (Harmondsworth: Penguin, 1969), 15.

33 The line was 'Joan was quizzical, studied pataphysical science in the home'.

34 Geoff Dunbar, speaking in the 4mations documentary *Dunbar's Lore*, quoted on the website *The Lost Continent: Exploring the Art and History of British Film*, http://ukanimation.blogspot.com/2011/06/geoff-dunbars-ubu.html/

35 Geoff Dunbar, video interview with author, 7 August 2022.

36 Ubu won the Golden Bear prize at the Berlin Film Festival, and a Grand Prix at the Ottawa International Animation Festival.

37 Dunbar, in *Dunbar's Lore*.

38 Franciszka Themerson, *Ubu Comic* (Indianapolis, IN: Bobb-Merrill, 1970). See Barnaby Dicker, 'Franciszka Themerson's *Ubu Comic Strip*: Autography, Caricature, and the Avant-Garde', in *The Popular Avant-Garde*, ed. Renée E. Silverman (Leiden: Brill, 2010), 227–49.

39 Email from Geoff Dunbar to the author, 7 August 2022.

40 Dunbar, video interview.

41 Dunbar, video interview.

42 Oscar Grillo, in *Dunbar's Lore*.

43 Greil Marcus, *Lipstick Traces: A Secret History of the Twentieth Century* (Cambridge, MA: Harvard University Press, 1990).

44 Dominic Dromgoole, 'Rebel without a Clue', *The Guardian*, 16 November 2005, 20.

45 Dunbar, video interview.

46 Geoff Brown, 'Geoff Dunbar (1944–)', *BFI Screenonline*, http://www.screenonline. org.uk/people/id/858602/index.html/

47 Quoted by Kate McCrickard, *WK – William Kentridge* (London: Tate, 2012), 77, n. 58.

48 A recording of *Ubu and the Truth Commission* is on YouTube.

49 McCrickard, *WK*, 47.

50 Interview with Carolyn Christov-Bakargiev, in Dan Cameron et al., *William Kentridge* (London: Phaidon, 1999), 10.

51 Christov-Bakargiev, 35.

52 Geoff Dunbar in conversation with Magenta De Vine, *Animation Week*, Channel 4, 6 September 1988, now on YouTube.

53 Dunbar, video interview.

Chapter 15

Surrealism, Animation and Ecological Consciousness in Cecilia Vicuña's *Paracas* (1983)

Paulina Caro Troncoso

The distinctive imagery created by Chilean artist, film-maker, poet, and activist Cecilia Vicuña (b. 1948) in her oeuvre offers new perspectives on the legacies of surrealism in contemporary art. Across different media, Vicuña has developed a poetics of resistance addressing complex issues related to colonialism, Indigenous knowledge restoration, and the environmental crisis. Since the beginning of her artistic trajectory in the 1960s, surrealism has provided a reference for her understanding of art and poetry, her use of automatism in writing, and the dreamlike fusion of elements in her figurative painting. The influence of surrealism has also been evident in the artist's experimentation with animation techniques in her only animated work, *Paracas* (1983), a 16-mm film that revives the harvest traditions of the Paracas people (800 to 200 BCE) in the south coast of Peru. In this project, Vicuña finds inspiration in the so-called Paracas Textile, a nearly 2,000-year-old mantle discovered in the Paracas Necropolis, to offer a unique interpretation of the pre-Columbian world. Vicuña's exploration of the decorative elements of this cloth reflects her commitment to reclaiming ancestral knowledge and traditions. The artist's understanding of the Paracas culture also illuminates her proximity to surrealism, specifically to the work of British artist Leonora Carrington, whom the artist met during a trip to Mexico in 1969. This chapter provides an overview of the influence of surrealism in Vicuña's trajectory and explores how the artist uses animation to delve into the hidden stories of this Andean textile, prompting us to reconsider ancient cultures as a valuable source for rethinking our relationship with nature and imagining a new ecological consciousness.[1]

Reanimating the Pre-Columbian world

Paracas is often described as a visual and sound poem. In this 18-minute film, Vicuña evokes the relationship of the Paracas people with nature and invites the modern viewer to rediscover the textile's rich and colourful iconography depicting the Andean flora, wildlife, and god-like creatures engaged in a ritual battle and procession to celebrate the harvest. Vicuña's creative process involved photographing some of the characters embroidered on this cloth to incorporate them onto a 3D stage with handcrafted small objects designed by the Chilean artist. Using stop motion, Vicuña brings these figures to life, compellingly portraying the Paracas traditions. The artist decodes and activates the knowledge embedded in this mantle, creating a fictional reconstruction of the environment where this ceremonial object was created. In doing so, Vicuña not only captivates viewers with a unique recreation of the Andean landscape and rituals of the Paracas people, whose culture is well-known for their textiles, ceramics and advanced irrigation system, but also introduces them to the cosmovision of the mantle's weavers, who, as one of the film captions reads, 'spoke to the dead by weaving'.

The theme of ancestral knowledge explored in *Paracas* is central to Vicuña's artistic practice. Since the 1960s, the artist has developed a body of work that reflects on the individual's relationship with nature and on the significance of the beliefs and traditions of Indigenous communities. From her assembled objects created with debris, known as the *precarios* (precarious) or *basuritas* (bits of garbage), to her exploration of the *quipus* – an accounting system of knotted strings used by the ancient Andean peoples – and textile installations, Vicuña has configured a decolonial perspective in which art, nature and collective histories interweave to communicate with the present. According to Lucy Lippard, 'If the *precarios* are the common formal thread, the act of weaving itself is the aesthetic and spiritual thread that runs through all of Vicuña's cultural production.'[2] In her

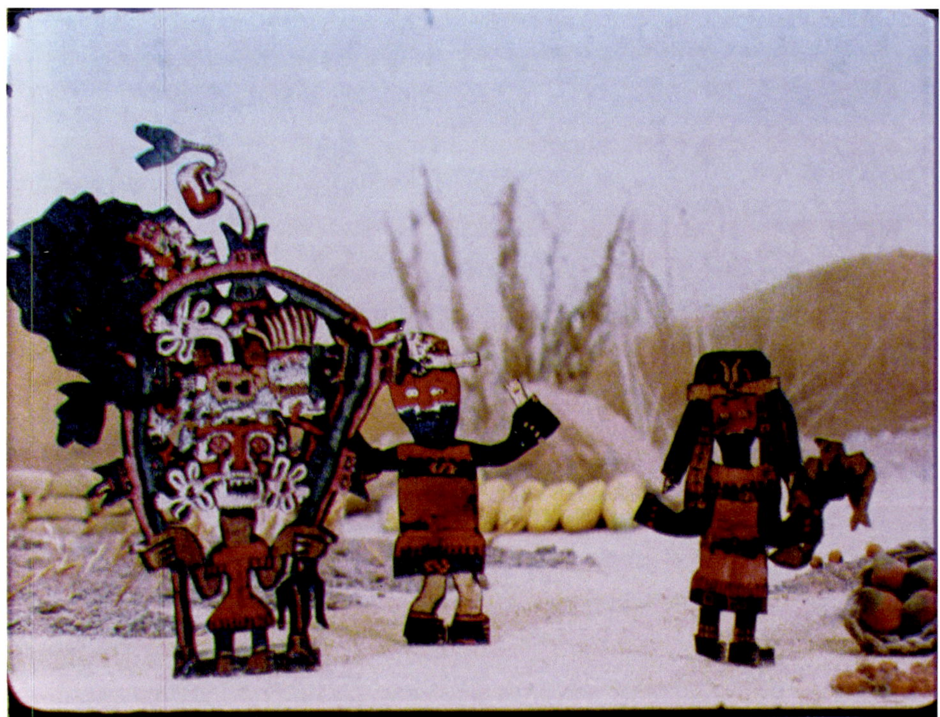

Figure 15.1 Cecilia Vicuña, *PARACAS*, 1983. 16mm film on video. Courtesy the artist and Electronic Arts Intermix (EAI). © 2024 Cecilia Vicuña/Artists Rights Society (ARS), New York. Courtesy the artist and Lehmann Maupin, New York, Hong Kong, Seoul and London.

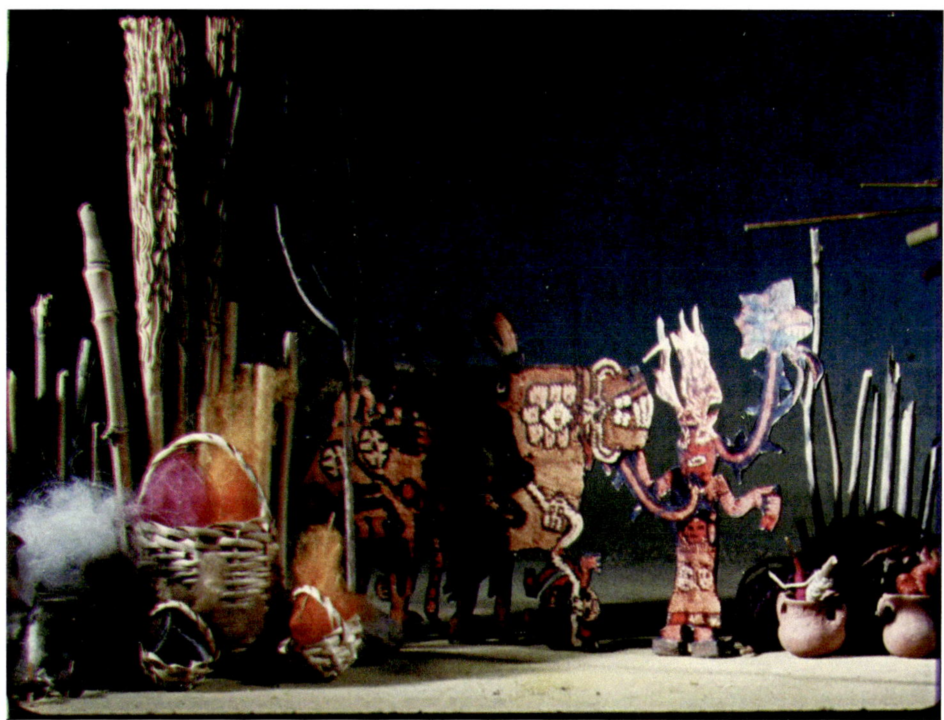

Figure 15.2 Cecilia Vicuña, *PARACAS*, 1983. 16mm film on video. Courtesy the artist and Electronic Arts Intermix (EAI). © 2024 Cecilia Vicuña/Artists Rights Society (ARS), New York. Courtesy the artist and Lehmann Maupin, New York, Hong Kong, Seoul and London.

work with textiles, Vicuña investigates materiality while delving deeper into this process to reclaim the knowledge involved in this activity widely practised by Indigenous peoples across the Americas. For Vicuña, weaving operates as a language that speaks about the stories of those who have been silenced, including women and Indigenous peoples.[3] Arguably, in works such as *Paracas*, weaving also serves as a metaphor for thinking about how the past can inform a more conscious relationship with the natural world, which will enable us to protect our ecosystem in the light of an imminent ecological catastrophe.

In the early 1970s, Vicuña continued developing a unique approach in her visual and poetic work while responding to social, cultural and political concerns in Chile. In this context, Vicuña was among the group of artists and intellectuals who played an influential role in a process of cultural transition that began in 1970 with the election of socialist candidate Salvador Allende and the left-wing political coalition known as *Unidad Popular* (Popular Unity). Art institutions also responded to the local cultural landscape, as exemplified in the work of Chilean artist Nemesio Antúnez during his period as director of the Museo Nacional de Bellas Artes (National Museum of Fine Arts) between 1969 and 1973. Antúnez's vision sought to 'transform a museum-mausoleum into a living and dynamic museum, following the needs of students and the people who demand art, the best art, to be available to all'.[4] One of the works from this period that possibly better reflects Vicuña's revolutionary view is *Otoño* (Autumn) of 1971, a performance where Vicuña, assisted by her family, friends and workers, gathered dead leaves from the streets of Santiago de Chile and placed them inside the museum's galleries. Vicuña has referred to this intervention as 'coming from the complete freedom of [her] Indigenous side'[5] and described it as 'an art of dissolution as renewal, the core of my precarious work'.[6] Indeed, through this poetic gesture, Vicuña reveals how she has focused on the collective to develop a praxis around nature since her early artistic practice.

At the age of twenty-four, with the support of a British Council Scholarship, Vicuña moved to the UK to study art at the Slade School of Fine Art. The artist was in London when Allende was overthrown by a military coup on 11 September 1973. Vicuña immediately reacted to the violent events in the country, capturing her memory in *La muerte de Allende* (The Death of Allende) (1973), a canvas that depicts a drop of blood similar to a red-coloured cloud falling into an abyss. A few months later, in May 1974, Vicuña participated, along with US artist John Dugger, Filipino artist David Medalla, and English art critic and curator Guy Brett, in Artists for Democracy, a collective initiative of artistic solidarity with the Chilean people that promoted the defence of democracy.[7] Following her experience in the UK, Vicuña returned to Latin America for a few years before relocating to New York, where she currently lives and works.

During her time in Bogota, from 1975 to 1980, Vicuña worked on several projects. The artist participated in an art workshop for the Guambiano Indigenous community of Cauca, created stage designs for a theatre group, and directed her first 16-mm film entitled *¿Qué es para usted la poesía?* (What is Poetry to You?) (1980). This work demonstrates how the artist's experimentation with poetry and language evolved over the years. In this 23-minute documentary, Vicuña surveys the role of poetry in everyday life through a series of interviews with artists, sex workers, police officers and children. In the film, Vicuña mentions the concept of *palabrarmas*, a neologism in Spanish formed by combining the terms 'words' and 'weapons', which the artist developed in the 1960s and has become central to her artistic practice. Through *palabrarmas*, Vicuña has sought to activate the multiple meanings of words revealed by deconstructing their structure. Sound is another key element in *¿Qué es para usted la poesía?*, and so it is in *Paracas*. In the former, Vicuña further explores the revolutionary potential of language using audiovisual resources, highlighting the sound component of poetry. On the other hand, the constellation of sounds included in *Paracas* – a combination of chants and nature sounds – enhances and enlivens her surrealist-like recreation of the traditions of this Andean culture.[8]

As the work of Vicuña lies at the crossroads of art and poetry, it is important to consider in more detail how surrealism has informed her practice as a committed artist. According to Lippard,

> Despite her impassioned activism, Vicuña followed a more unorthodox path in her poetry and art than was expected of 'political artists.' Her work has ranged from surrealistic portraits to trance-like poetry performances, often in natural sites, to large scale museum installations evoking ancient rituals. She has always moved easily between the present and the distant past.[9]

Vicuña's artistic view and the political dimension of her work resonate with surrealism's revolutionary aspirations and ideals, prompting us to reassess her contribution to surrealist traditions and the movement's significance today.

Vicuña has stated on several occasions that the work of surrealist artists and poets has been a significant reference in her art.[10] Vicuña's early encounters with surrealism can be traced back to 1964, when, at the age of sixteen, the artist read the influential account of the surrealist movement, *Antología de la poesía surrealista*, edited by Argentine poet and art critic Aldo Pellegrini and published in Buenos Aires in 1961. This experience was a turning point for Vicuña, describing it as follows: 'I believe my poetry grew out of that encounter, of the doors it opened for me.'[11] From 1967 to 1972, the artist was part of the experimental collective Tribu No (No tribe), formed by artists and poets who shared a common interest in the subversive dimension of everyday life and collective work.[12] The group's activity was diverse and included art actions, a public appearance at the 1969 Encuentro Latinoamericano de Escritores (Meeting of Latin American Writers) – where they distributed their manifesto *Los hijos deben enseñarles a sus padres* (Children Must Teach Parents) – and the publication of the anthology of poetry *Deliciosas criaturas perfumadas* (Delicious Perfumed Creatures) in 1972. Vicuña also contributed to the Tribu No with a manifesto that traces a lineage of the group's influences, including John Coltrane, Arthur Rimbaud, and André Breton,[13] possibly mirroring the writing style of other avant-garde manifestos.[14]

During her time at Tribu No, Vicuña was able to publish her poetry in international publications. While working on the manuscript of *Diario estúpido* (Stupid Diary) – a daily creative exercise that the artist practised between 1966 to 1971 – Vicuña began to correspond with Mexican poet Sergio Mondragón, who, along with American poet, photographer and activist Margaret Randall, co-edited the Mexican counterculture periodical *El corno emplumado* (The Plumed Horn) from 1962 to 1969. Vicuña's poetry was issued in the journal between 1967 and 1968. As the editors had to leave Mexico after publishing an article in response to the 1968 Tlatelolco student massacre, the journal activity was soon suspended. Yet Vicuña maintained her correspondence with Mondragón, who began working on the publishing of a Latin American poetry series at Indiana University. The artist was invited to collaborate on this project and, in 1969, embarked on a trip to the United States. On her journey back to Chile, Vicuña visited Mexico and had the opportunity to meet surrealist artist Leonora Carrington. The encounter between the two artists was brief yet significant for the Chilean artist. Vicuña stayed at Carrington's house for three days, an experience that, as she has recalled, was 'enough to influence my painting for the rest of my life'.[15]

Comparing the works of Carrington and Vicuña provides a different perspective on the presence of surrealist aesthetics in *Paracas*. Like Vicuña's film, Carrington explored in her painting an interest in ancient knowledge and traditions, as seen in *El mundo mágico de los mayas* (The Magical World of the Maya) (1963–4), a four-metre-long mural that the National Museum of Anthropology in Mexico commissioned to the artist in 1963. The mural presents a surrealist-like view of the pre-Columbian world, depicting human, animal and god-like figures coexisting in a dreamlike landscape. In this work, Carrington proposes a whimsical interpretation of Mayan civilization and synthesizes her characteristic pictorial style with the knowledge the artist acquired through the study of ancient Maya mythology and her experiences with Indigenous communities in Mexico, where, invited by Swiss anthropologist Gertrude Blom, she was able to attend traditional healing ceremonies of the Chiapas people.

Drawing a connection between Carrington's most representative painting of her exploration of the pre-Columbian world and Vicuña's interpretation of the Paracas' traditions demonstrates how surrealist ideas and aesthetics have been a fertile reference for the Chilean artist.[16] As Karen Eckersley has argued, by delving into Mexico's Indigenous past from a surrealist perspective, Carrington interrogates Eurocentric humanism and 'maps a future for both her and the country itself, one no longer caught within a Eurocentric orbit that dictates Humanism as the ruling principle'.[17] This idea can also be extrapolated to Vicuña's approach to the Paracas world.

Vicuña, like Carrington, proposes her interpretation informed by the surrealists' creative and ludic approach to reality. In *Paracas*, Vicuña showcases a poetic experiment in which animation transforms into an effective tool to revive the imagery of an ancient mantle and the stories contained in its material dimension. In this way, Vicuña's visual and sound poem invites the modern viewer to look differently at the cultural memory of ancient Indigenous peoples and to see it as a source of inspiration for awakening a new ecological consciousness.

Notes

1 I thank Jessica Gordon-Burroughs for the insightful discussions we have had regarding Cecilia Vicuña's work and the intersections between surrealism and animation in the work of Latin American artists. See Gordon-Burroughs, 'Shamanic Double Vision: Cecilia Vicuña's *Paracas*', in *Foreign Elements: Latin American Cinematic Experiments in Dis-placement*, forthcoming; and Gordon-Burroughs, *Poli Marichal: In-Between Aesthetic*, Dada and Surrealism Research Group's talks, University of Edinburgh, 23 February 2021, online.

2 Lucy Lippard, 'Spinning the Common Thread', in exhibition catalogue *Cecilia Vicuña. Veroír el fracaso iluminado/Seehearing the Enlightened Failure* (MUAC, Museo Universitario Arte Contemporáneo. UNAM, Universidad Nacional Autónoma de México, Mexico City, 2020), 58.

3 Juliet Lynd, 'Precarious Resistance: Weaving Opposition in the Poetry of Cecilia Vicuña', *PMLA*, 120, no. 5 (2005): 1590.

4 Amalia Cross, 'El museo en tiempos de revolución', in exhibition catalogue *Nemesio Antúnez, Centenario* (Santiago: Museo Nacional de Bellas Artes, 2019), 37. Original quote: 'Convertir un museo-mausoleo en un museo vivo y dinámico, que estuviera "de acuerdo con las necesidades de los estudiantes y del pueblo que exigen que el arte, el mejor arte, esté al alcance de todos."' Quoted in Nemesio Antúnez, 'Nemesio Antúnez, el hombre corcho', *Punto Final* (Santiago, 11 de mayo de 1971), 28.

5 Cecilia Vicuña and Tatiana Flores, 'In Conversation with Cecilia Vicuña. An Interview by Tatiana Flores', in exhibition catalogue *Cecilia Vicuña: Water Writing: Anthological Exhibit 1966–2009* (New Brunswick, NJ: Rutgers University, 2009), 5.

6 Vicuña and Flores, 'In Conversation with Cecilia Vicuña', 5.

7 See Lucy Lippard, 'Cecilia Vicuña: The Persistence of Joy', in exhibition catalogue *Artists for Democracy: Archivo de Cecilia Vicuña* (Santiago: Museo de la Memoria y los Derechos Humanos and Museo Nacional de Bellas Artes, 2014), n.p.

8 In response to a question concerning her Indigenous knowledge, Vicuña recounts details from her childhood but acknowledges that art also played a role in mediating it: 'I remember as a little girl seeing cowboy films and I knew in my heart that I was an Indian. Later, when I started seeing wonderful art books about the revolution in the arts of the late 19th and early 20th centuries in Europe, the discovery of so-called "primitive" art, I knew that that was the future.' Vicuña quoted in Flores, 7.

9 Lippard, 'Cecilia Vicuña: The Persistence of Joy', n.p.

10 In Vicuña's words: 'I discovered Taoism as a teenager, and that philosophy increased my passion for Indigenous thinking, which in time I expanded to include Dada and Surrealism, which always brought me back to ancient knowledge.' Cecilia Vicuña quoted in Lucy Lippard, 'Floating between Past and Future: The Indigenization of Environmental Politics', in *Cecilia Vicuña. About to Happen* (Catskill, NY: Siglio, 2019), 134.

11 Cecilia Vicuña quoted in Dawn Ades, 'Cecilia Vicuña's Calcomanías', in exhibition catalogue *Cecilia Vicuña* (London: England & Co. Gallery, 2013). http://www.ceciliavicuna.com/ (accessed 11 January 2024).

12 Members of Tribu No included Cecilia Vicuña, Claudio Bertoni, Coca Roccatagliata, Francisco Rivera, Sonia Jara and Marcelo Charlín.

13 Cecilia Vicuña, *No manifiesto de la Tribu No*, in *Cecilia Vicuña. Veroír el fracaso iluminado/ Seehearing the Enlightened Failure*, 194.

14 For further information about the Tribu No, see Magda Sepúlveda, 'Cecilia Vicuña: La Subjetividad Poética como una Operación Contracanónica', *Revista Chilena de Literatura*, 57 (2000): 111–26.

15 Cecilia Vicuña, 'On My Relation to Leonora', in *Cecilia Vicuña. Veroír el fracaso iluminado/ Seehearing the Enlightened Failure*, 85.

16 For the artist's appreciation of her early painting, see Cecilia Vicuña, 'Pain Things & Explanations', in *Saborami* (Oakland, CA and Philadelphia, PA: ChainLinks, 2011), 70–1.

17 Karen Eckersley, 'Posthuman Destinations: Indigenous Cultures in Leonora Carrington's Mexican Oeuvre', *Romance Studies: A Journal of the University of Wales*, 41, no. 1 (2023: 30–40), 38. See also Jonathan P. Eburne, 'Leonora Carrington, Mexico, and the Culture of Death', *Journal of Surrealism and the Americas*, 5, no. 1–2 (2011): 19–32.

Chapter 16

A Feminist–Surrealist Metamorphosis: The Charged Objects of Kim L. Pace

Catriona McAra

Surrealism supercharged objects, endowing them with energy, autonomy and life.

ESTHER LESLIE (2002)[1]

Merry-making

Throwing clay is a process of animation, of using an existing ground of mineral matter to mould, knead and conjure ideas into being. Ceramics are ancient and versatile, close to the earth and crafted by hand, ampules and entities that are capable of summoning alternative material realities. But how does an object become activated? Where does the image stop and the imagination take over? At what point does ceramic vessel tip into wild beast? And how does a glaze congeal into a haunted spectre? Kim L. Pace, a self-confessed 'merry-maker', is among the few contemporary artists currently engaged in these very questions, working through a backdrop of a feminist–surrealist lore.

Her distinctive, multimedia oeuvre offers an illuminating glimpse into the position of the surrealist-fantastic, marvellous or uncanny within the ever-expanding domain of the contemporary arts.[2] Pace lives and works in her studio in St Leonards-on-Sea, a promenade town and seaside resort on the southern English coast, but identifies closely with her Czech family heritage, particularly its combination of folk culture, children's picture-book illustration, avant-garde puppetry and mask-making traditions. She is intrigued by the uses of stop-motion animation to critique the status quo and recalls her Czech father's puppet theatre and the profound impact that it had on her childhood imagination. This is true too of the comics industry, especially *Rupert*, *The Beano* and *MAD* magazine, which she describes as formative encounters.[3] Mexican archaeology and

Catriona thanks Kim for her correspondence and support and the editor and peer reviewers for their thoughtful suggestions.

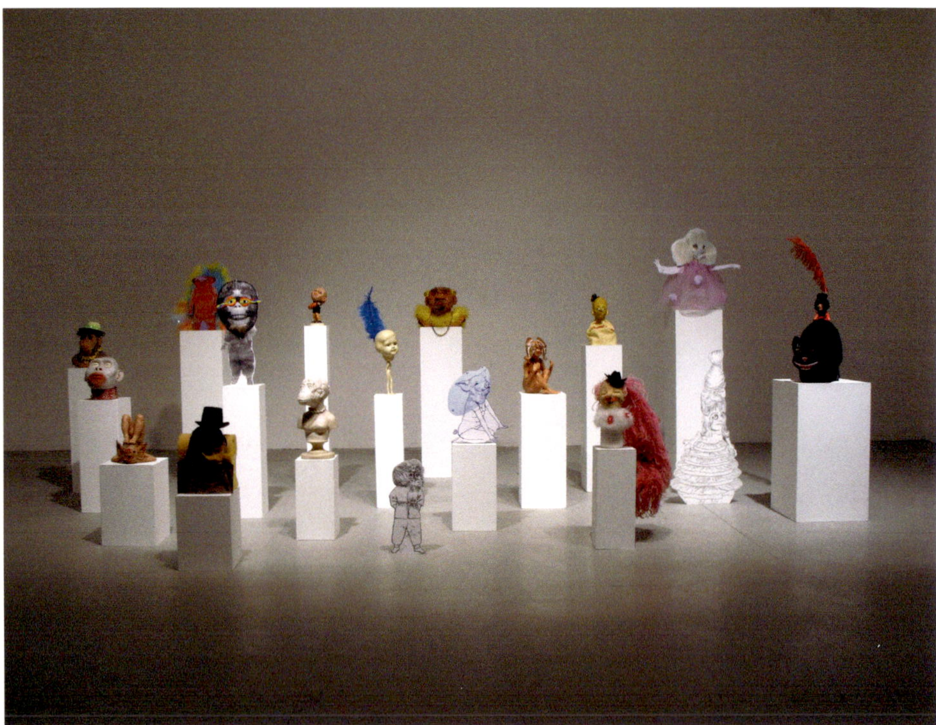

Figure 16.1 Kim L. Pace, *A Company of Strangers*, 2012–13. Clay, fabric, paper, fur, feathers, paint. Installation, 18 of 26 elements. Courtesy the artist.

the Day of the Dead are further traditions that have informed Pace's art-making, with the artist citing the exhibition *Skeleton at the Feast* (1992), as a foundational experience which has become integral to her aesthetic. Given this intriguing combination of Czech, Mexican and pop cultural interests, it is perhaps no surprise that surrealist-associated artists have become primary touchstones for Pace. She describes them as 'bewitching'.[4]

Since the 1990s, Pace has been engaging with the visual narrative legacies of an explicitly feminist surrealism, both the imagery by the women of surrealism as well as the revisionary scholarly landscape.[5] Such ingredients enable us to position Pace as apprentice to Angela Carter (1940–92), particularly Pace's installation *A Company of Strangers* (2012–13) and filmed watercolour sequence *Fabulous Beings and Comic Bodies* (2017), which is a direct homage to Carter. Although a generation apart, Carter and Pace share a high baroque, circus style which draws on theories of the carnivalesque, the hybrid and the grotesque.[6] In 2016, Pace interviewed the Brothers Quay (b.1947), an encounter based on long-term knowledge of their stop-motion puppet films which has further shaped and honed her own perspectives on animation. As a result of such extensive dialogues and artistic research, a range of dreamlike, eclectic characters have come to populate Pace's visual and tactile playground. Pace now works predominantly in ceramics and watercolours, due to their malleable properties, pursuing a practice of metamorphosis which offers a unique dialogue with the history of surrealist animation.

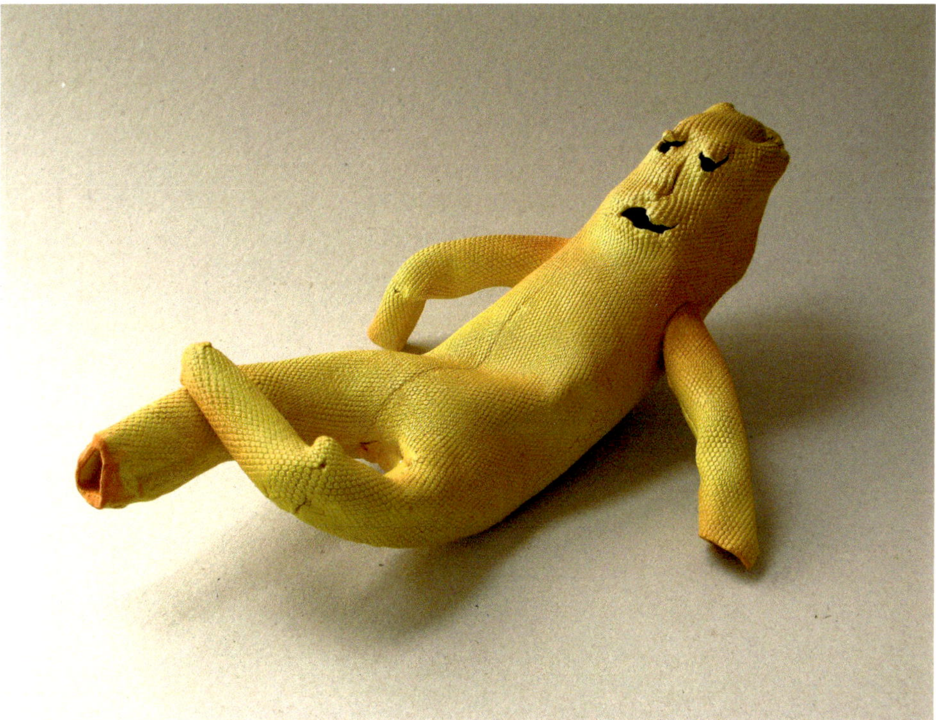

Figure 16.2 Kim L. Pace, *Cultivar Horizontalis*, 2018. Glazed ceramic. Courtesy the artist.

'Esoteric art is certainly having a cultural moment', writes Amy Hale, which she believes is 'clearly linked to the continuing reconsideration of women's art'.[7] Indeed, recent curatorial reappraisals of art by the women of surrealism, especially the Venice Biennale *Milk of Dreams* curated by Cecilia Alemani (2022), which Pace visited, have already come to be seen as representing a major sea change in contemporary art world collecting, curating and critical interests. Working through a unique constellation of media, including claymation, installation and works on paper, it is arguably only now that a vocabulary and critical framework for such peculiar appropriation, thoughtful eccentricity and complex array of reference points can even begin to be approached, for the work of Pace presents a much-needed alternative to existing aesthetic ecologies and medium specificities. Her interdisciplinary work, I would suggest, unhinges the very experience of exhibition viewing too.

This chapter seeks to comprehend the compound occurrence of the animator–ceramicist and what this hybrid practice might reveal about a history of surrealism and its relevance to contemporary art. Pareidolia, animism, automata, and the anthropomorphic are recurrent terms when it comes to discussing the visionary spectrum and epistemologies present in Pace's work. Such intricate terminologies and iconographies propose a subcultural mood board on which to anchor them. With reference to specific surrealist exemplars, I argue that Pace's work offers a suspended animation of surrealist history.[8]

Grace of clay

Pace is known for a substantial portfolio of moving image work and stop-motion sequences (2008–17), many of them involving clay as her chief medium. Indeed, the roots of her current ceramic practice can be found in her earlier use of claymation (stop-motion animations that predominantly rely on characters made of clay or, in other cases, plasticine). These include monochromatic character studies such as *Tabby-Tha* (2008; 1 minute; United Kingdom), *Changeling* (2009; 1 minute, 34 seconds; United Kingdom) and *Let It Out* (2011; 2 minutes, 38 seconds; United Kingdom), as well as the marine-like *Depth Wish* (2009; 6 minutes, 37 seconds; United Kingdom) and the prehistorical self-help guide *À la Recherche du Temps Perdu* (In search of lost time; 2011; 3 minutes, 34 seconds, United Kingdom). These are intricate, labour-intensive projects, the latter two involving complex dioramas, each taking several months to bring to completion. Pace often uses a regular stoneware clay with wire armature to create a miniature skeleton for ease of manipulation between camera shots. She has also utilized a special brand of animation clay that she found in an art supply store in Berlin – this is flesh-coloured and infused with oil to keep her puppets wet and thus malleable for longer.

The genesis of this body of work can be found in the experimental animation Pace saw during the time she was at art school in the late 1980s. One might consider her resulting works decades later as the next branch of a family tree that includes Jan Švankmajer (b.1934) and the Brothers Quay.[9] Švankmajer's *Možnosti dialogu* (Dimensions of dialogue; 1982; 14 minutes) offers a demonstrative precursor for Pace's *Changeling*. In Švankmajer's claymation, faces and busts self-consume and metamorphose, from a recognizably surrealist iconography to an unclassifiable *informe* (more of an amorphous verb than a tidy noun) associated with Georges Bataille.[10] Interestingly, the phantasmatic potential of abjection was being theorized concurrently with Pace's initial exposure to experimental animation suggesting a potential correlation in her early thinking.[11] Such massing and moulding of references not only stresses the malleable materiality and 'self-awareness' of the clay but also its grotesque ability to mimic, channel or even engulf other art forms. Pace's *Changeling* adopts a similar rhythm to Švankmajer's *Dimensions*, morphing like quicksilver from incubus-to-phallus-to-nose-to-arms-to-man-in-the-moon-face. Indeed, her long-term preoccupation with pareidolia (an ability to find or 'see the faces in things') in her ceramics can be traced back to stop-motion investigations like *Changeling*. In both *Dimensions* and *Changeling*, the soundscapes (and, in Pace's case, shadow play) contribute to the ominous moods. Meanwhile, the manipulation of clay bodies (as well as detritus and vegetable puppetry in Švankmajer's case) are enabled through the fidgety and pleasingly jittery movements effected via the stop-motion sequences. Such sculptural transformations can only be achieved to this desired effect through this hybrid medium. *Changeling* extracts further power from the folkloric associations of its subject matter, another recursive element which Pace found in Švankmajer; a changeling itself is the offspring of a magical creature that came before.

Similarly, the intertextual register of the Brothers Quay has become a potent source and attitude for Pace. Suzanne Buchan describes the Quays' puppet animations 'as a kind of palimpsest of Surrealism', noting that their work draws extensively on a European pantheon of Romantic fantasy literature including E. T. A. Hoffmann and Heinrich von Kleist.[12] Hoffmann's 'The Sandman' (1816) is a well-known surrealist citation, informing the Freudian uncanny through the notorious image of eyes being torn out.[13] One thinks of the eyeless dolls and tailor pins in the Quays' *The Cabinet of Jan Švankmajer* (1984; 14 minutes) and *Street of Crocodiles* (1986; 21 minutes), an uncanny sensibility that has subsequently informed Pace. She too is a keen reader of pre-animation philosophy, admiring von Kleist's discourse on the superior agility of marionettes (1810): 'Grace appears most purely in that human form which either has no consciousness or an infinite consciousness. That is, in the puppet or in the god.'[14]

The pre-human or humanoid characters of Pace's *Depth Wish* and *À la Recherche du Temps Perdu* offer interesting views on the 'grace' of such de-anthropocentricism. The former takes the perspective of a foetus-like mer-person exploring the microclimates that occur around shipwrecks and the alien-looking creatures of the deep. The latter considers a neanderthal and the animal depictions of cave paintings now widely believed to be the making of female hands.[15] The feeling towards knowledge in both is represented through their very making (both the mer-person and the neanderthal are handmade clay puppets).[16] Such interests are further mirrored in the tricycle character and non-human behaviour of Quays' *This Unnameable Little Broom* (1985; 11 minutes), a puppet animation that holds strong appeal for Pace. She describes the startling effect of seeing this animation as if being transported to another world.[17]

Although Pace's more recent ceramic engagements increasingly result in more colourful and organic outcomes than the tool-box contraptions of the Quays, they share interests in tactility, ludic devices and analogies as well as the expressive, secretive and sentient potential of puppets. Buchan argues compellingly for the empathic textures of the Quays' practice, their ability to imbue matter with emotion, and how this is achieved through the mechanics of animation, with the camera often operating as a 'third puppet'.[18] Such textured emotion is followed through by Pace in the caricatured cat-woman of *Tabby-Tha* or the tearful golem of *Let it Out*. In the former, a personified feline reclines like a statue and croons before instinct takes over and she swallows a tiny mouse that has emerged from her skirt. In the latter, a self-help voiceover coaxes the golem to release its inner feelings, again a self-reflexive nod to the wet clay from which this golem is modelled.

Over time, the uncanny inevitably took hold. While Pace was 'casting' which of her characters were to star in her claymations, she became starkly aware of the physicality of her puppets. Her suggestion is that the experimental paraphernalia or raw materials that feature in her stop-motion animations might be just as interesting *in their own right* as the final projected sequence. This realization has led to a new dimension of her practice, which has taken her characters off-screen and into a more grounded uncanny presence.

Suspension of disbelief

The material ingredients of Pace's feminist grotesquery have developed into her more recent ceramic output (2016–present), which offers a further layer of excavation of surrealist precursors. One of Pace's major accomplishments has been her repositioning of concept art and creature design (the very 'stuff' of animation) within a curatorial arena. She combines this shift with a playful take on the grotesque (traditionally assigned to an underground aesthetics and now frequently designated as a feminist aesthetic trope due to its subcultural values) using the visual, sculptural and curatorial language of contemporary art. Pace describes herself as a 'fan of the grotesque', and her work provides insight into the potentially lively ground between surrealism and the grotesque.[19] Frances S. Connelly defines the grotesque in relation to the etymology of the grotto as: 'earthy and material, a cave, an open mouth that invites our descent into other worlds. It is a space where the monsters and marvels of our imagination are conceived [...] fusing humor with horror, wit with transgression, repulsion with desire'.[20] Feminist surrealism is a similarly elastic, open notion associated with a next generation of perspectives on the surrealist movement from Angela Carter to Penny Slinger (b.1947).[21] The term also offers a way of understanding how output by the women of surrealism might have differed from or revised that of their male counterparts, what Susan R. Suleiman has termed a 'double allegiance', a simultaneous acknowledgement and critique of historical surrealist formats

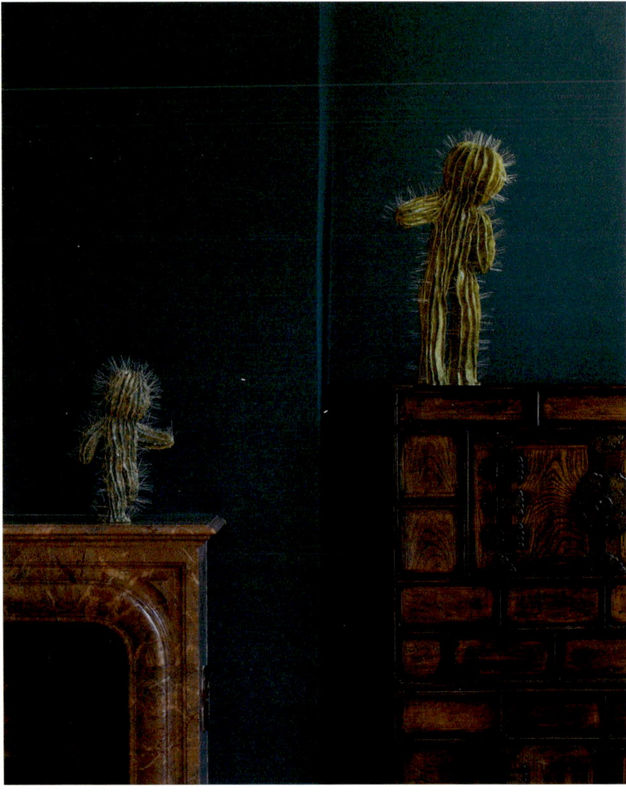

Figure 16.3 Detail from Kim L. Pace, *A Fantastic Fermentation of Matter*, 2018, featuring *Cactaceae 1* (left, 2016) and *Cactaceae 2* (right, 2017). Glazed ceramic with bristles. Courtesy the artist and Danielle Arnaud, London. Photo by Oskar Proctor.

and techniques.[22] The possibility of a feminist grotesque and a feminist surrealism are the conjoined, twin-thinking which has informed Pace's thinking too.

In terms of how such theories and visual stylistics manifest in Pace's ceramic animations, we might consider their very exhibition as a form of critically invested encounter. Rather than using a projected moving image, Pace has tended to use the platforms or spaces of the gallery and the pages of the artist's book to single out her characters and throw emphasis onto their transpositions. Her work functions at its most effective when exhibited in former residential spaces of Georgian or Victorian architectural interiors. In this respect, Pace closely aligns with a surrealist insistence on the outmoded and the anachronistic, even a ghostly or haunted sensibility.[23] This has to do with Pace's aforementioned ambition for the uncanny that she seeks to invoke. Marina Warner further unpacks Freud's *unheimlich* as follows: 'the feeling arises when a figure or an image stirs a memory of something familiar that has been mislaid, or lost – hence the shivery or uncanny feel of *déjà vu*, or the prickly sensation excited by feeling that someone is in the room when there turns out to be nobody there'.[24] This 'prickly sensation' of uncanny haunting was highly prized by the surrealists and continues to be sought after by Pace. She endows static, handmade objects, from her *Cactaceae* (2016–18) to her *Masks* (2019–22), with a seemingly infinite array of expressive gestures and characterization, an effect she describes as 'charged'.[25]

Meret Oppenheim (1913–85) touches on such uncanny, charged tactility with her surrealist objects of the mid-1930s such as *Object* (*Breakfast in Fur*) and *Ma gouvernante, My Nurse, Mein Kindermädchen* (both 1936). Warner writes of their appeal to surrealist humour and how Oppenheim 'makes visible, with quite remarkable economy, the problematic presence of the wild in the civilised, the place of the animal in society, and the containment and ordering of female sexuality'.[26] The gift of such rectified *objets trouvés* is how the unusual combination of material factors enables ostensibly static things to metamorphose within the imagination. The unlikely association of cup with fur being matter out of place simply but effectively summons an array of possible meanings. Although Oppenheim was not an animator, her value to a contemporary animator like Pace is substantial. Oppenheim's fur-covered tea set and trussed shoes evoke the etymology of 'animation' as tied to animal motion and the anima (what Carl Jung discusses as the inner feminine archetype).[27] Pace, too, allows us to see a furry-feminine side to ceramics, as well as their scaly, leafy and shell-like sides. Such subversion of traditional art materials and lofty classical antiquities through black humour and kitsch embellishments forms the dislocating strategy of the feminist grotesque.[28]

This reanimation of inert materials has become a lively preoccupation for Pace. Dwelling on puppet animation further, Buchan points out: 'The animated object is a category of "being" that is rooted in a material, empirical existence in the extant world we live in.'[29] Aligning with surrealist principles, the chance encounter of what might become manifest is a crucial aspect of Pace's practice. For example, Pace allows mouths and other orifices to pucker expressively and somewhat automatically into shape as if summoned by the ritual of modelling. Another of Pace's methods of conjuring an uncanny animation and of channelling a surrealist grotesque is in the technical prowess of her glazes, particularly the dexterity of her contrasting colour palette (of electric blues segueing into acidic yellows in *Boulder Girls*, 2021) to create the effect of vibrant shadow play, and her intricate, *trompe l'oeil* textures as forms of mimicry. Ceramic surfaces are glazed, flocked and treated, chameleon-like, as if brought to life. They shimmer. In Pace's hands, this illusionism constitutes a compelling form of animation with static ceramic objects whose sophisticated surface detail enables viewers to suspend their disbelief in these being living organisms and haunted spectacles.

Such narrativization of the still-life genre has at least a century-long history. Esther Leslie alerts us to the integrity of surface within the history of animation, with early characters such as Ko-Ko the Clown literally made of ink blots in Max Fleischer's *Out of the Inkwell* (1918).[30] Leslie further suggests that early animation obliterated the high/low dichotomy that characterized some of the perceived tensions between the avant-garde and mass culture in the 1930s and 1940s, the height of surrealist production. Leslie singles out American art critic Clement Greenberg and his trope towards painterly flatness as a self-reflexive antidote to what he perceived as surrealist kitsch and a grotesque confusion of media.[31] Pace's attention to surface texture as an animation-formation could be said to offer the opposite, mimicking the effects of other representational surfaces, gleefully embracing or extracting pop culture from the mantelpiece ornament to the crystal collector's guidebook. Indeed, the boundaries between craft and fine art have long since crumbled, with ceramicist Alison Britton (b.1948) emphasizing the representational nature of clay pots. Britton notes a ghostly 'double presence' of function and poetics in contemporary ceramics in her famous essay of 1982: 'The objects in the middle, my main concern, are about life and still-life at once.'[32] A similar hybrid occurs in the work of Pace, especially in her own recent return to making vessels that are also simultaneously representations of flourishing tree stumps or creatures associated with evolution.

To bring in a narrative perspective, Warner claims that such '[s]hape-shifting is one of fairy tale's dominant and characteristic wonders', an idea at the root of Pace's animations.[33] For Leslie, as for Walter Benjamin, the fairy tale is a form of political resistance, and '[t]he cartoon offers a moment's freedom, a quick break for the psyche. And it most often does this by offering displaced identification, mostly animals in place of people, or animals substituting for other animals'.[34] Pace imaginatively reforms the genres of the fairy tale and cartoon through the secret language of clay, imitating their façades yet providing a fresh response that combines creature design, emoji languages and artisan techniques of dry glazes and flocking. Consider the weathering and surface 'patina' of Pace's masks and stone circles (2019–22). Many of her recent ceramic masks and monumental maidens mimic the hues, patterns, and textures of the crystalline minerals, iridescent amphibians and botanical specimens. Pace also musters the extraterrestrial behaviour of insects, for example in *Mask 30* (*Pollinator*, 2019), and prehistoric existence of geological formations, such as *Mask 21* (*Uluru*, 2019), in defining and differentiating her genus of disguise. Such attributes suggest an otherworldly evolution akin to the surrealists' own intrigue in entomology and natural history, whether in the transformational potential of a moth's chrysalis or the capricious behaviour of the praying mantis, and hint at an ability to transpose at will. Pace speaks of her working method for her ceramic animations, of 'allowing the clay to have an active role' and that 'the character will tell you what it needs'.[35]

Tableau vivant

The notion of a living picture is paramount to obtaining the uncanny. Pace has revealed a long-term affinity with the diminutive paintings and soft sculptural characters of Dorothea Tanning (1910–2012). Tanning's paintings, *Tableau vivant* (*Living Picture*, 1954) and *Les Trois Garces* (*The Three Bitches*, 1953), serve as feminist–surrealist talismans for Pace.[36] Here the caricaturing of Tanning's pet or spirit animal, Kachina, is championed by Pace not only for its 'animated' visual narrative properties but for its close association with Native American prayer dolls. Moreover, Tanning's mid-twentieth-century painterly intrigue in revising and debasing art-historical traditions of the high-art nude suggests a hybridity of skin and fur, human and animal, that has been adopted from the surrealist pastime of the exquisite corpse or game of consequences, a practice in turn inherited by the imaginative juxtapositions of Pace. In *The Three Bitches*, Tanning subverts Canova's highbrow neoclassical marble sculpture *The Three Graces* (1815–17), a gesture which appeals to Pace's own impish sensibility and offers intertextuality as a method of cultural collation for working through a wealth of feminist-surrealist imagery.[37] Tanning becomes a powerful representative of such an anti-taxonomic stance in Pace's artist-histories.[38] Pace's *Night Monkey Princesses* (2007–08), featuring tiny nocturnal primates with enormous eyes and women's bodies dressed in nightclub gear, or even her frocked feline of *Tabby-Tha*, might be compared fruitfully with Tanning's *Three Bitches*. Primates appear elsewhere in Tanning's oeuvre too, for instance in *Messages* (1989), a series of playful pastels of gorillas with bicycles not to mention Tanning's inaugural self-portrait *Birthday* (1942), in which Tanning wears an extravagant costume and is flanked by a winged lemur. Pace's *Night Parade* (2013–16), a series of meticulous drawings, also presents a contemporary response to and embodiment of such hybrid dualities through cosplay and a cast of revellers in an assortment of fancy dress. These are thought-forms that converge even more seamlessly through Pace's three-dimensional ceramic animations from *A Company of Strangers* (2012–13) and beyond. Tanning's *Tableau vivant* draws on a combination of existing fairy tales, such as Hans Christian Andersen's saucer-eyed pooch in 'Tinderbox' (1835), as well as commercial illustration and pulp fiction from the early 1950s.[39]

Tanning's anthropomorphic soft sculptures of the early 1970s are also of interest to Pace who was struck by Tanning's installation *Hôtel du Pavot, Chambre 202* (*Poppy Hotel, Room 202*, 1970–3) as early as 1993 in the Camden Arts Centre as well as the more recent Tanning survey show at Tate Modern (2019). The idea of a liminal space that is haunted, with bodies bursting out of the walls and with furniture in the process of coming to life, complements Pace's own curatorial approach to the matter of animation. Tanning's individual soft sculptures are also of importance to Pace, both their material qualities and frisky behaviour: *Verbe* (1970) presents an inverted comma or quotation mark, an open mouth full of jigsaw teeth that borrow from a Vermeer reproduction; *Emma* (1970) is a pregnant bump wearing a lacey skirt; while *Étreinte* (*Embrace*, 1969) comprises two beings in a somersault configuration. As with Pace's work, the animative qualities of this three-dimensional facet of Tanning's oeuvre are enhanced when exhibited on antique furniture (as for example in Tanning's sculptural debut at Galerie Le Point Cardinal in 1970)

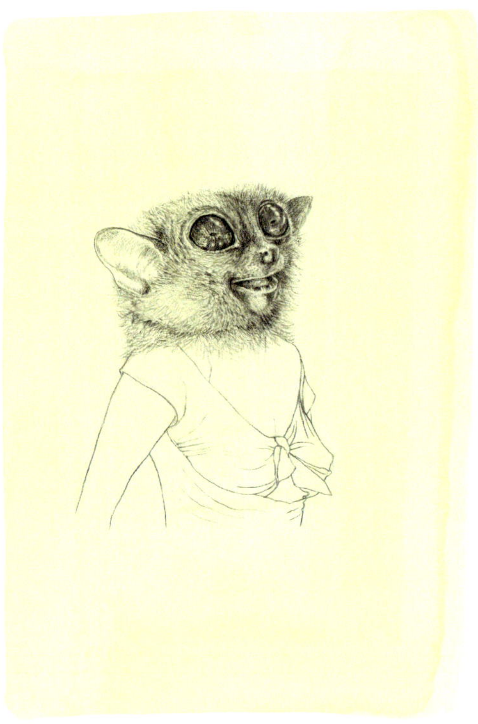

Figure 16.4 Kim L. Pace, *Night Monkey Princess*, 2008. Pencil and watercolour on paper. Courtesy the artist.

or in similarly non-clinical space, for instance, when animated and tumbling down the staircase in Peter Schamoni's filmic portrait, *Insomnias* (1978; 15 minutes).

Concurrently, the stitched bodies, tapestry heads, fabric towers, and latex experiments of Louise Bourgeois (1911–2010) have much to offer this discussion of Pace's ceramic animations, particularly Pace's doll-headed *Totem* (2022), which plays on such matriarchal genealogies. Bourgeois' patched, voodoo-like characters in *Seven in a Bed* (2001) and *Oedipus* (2003) offer a miniature puppet show or *tableau vivant* of the psychoanalytic fairy tales so key to surrealism's self-articulation (one recalls the playful appendages in Pace's *Changeling*). Again, static figures are imbued with the suggestion of animation through the handmade. Both artists demonstrate a light-heartedness combined with a sincerity of material purpose, and both are intrigued in animating the edges of the psyche as a mode of archaeology. Writing on Bourgeois' 'ancestor totems' and 'animistic oeuvre', Lucy Lippard prefigures Pace's work 40–50 years prior: 'Much tribal art is made to ensure continued contact with natural forces, to ward off evil, encourage good, and to deal with fear. Bourgeois' animism serves similar functions', as does Pace's.[40] Again, Pace taps into a feminist surrealism as amulet, compass or disorganizing principle as a device for disruption.

Frida Kahlo (1907–54) is another non-conformist admired by Pace for her transformative identity and thematic use of metamorphosis within her self-portraits. Kahlo's *Girl with Death Mask* (1938), for instance, pre-empts Pace's interest in fancy dress and Day of the Dead sugar skulls as *memento mori*. Here, the figure of a young girl self-presents in a skull mask although it could be a depiction of her true, inner appearance. Meanwhile, another toothy beast headdress rests at her feet. The picture suggests a 'trying on' of multiple identities, of the monstrous id beneath the polite veneer. Again, Kahlo's clout lies in her witty combination of feminist–surrealist–grotesque metamorphosis.[41] Writing on the grotesque as a chief characteristic of carnival, Susan Stewart tells us: 'the mask, the costume, and the disguise find their proper context in carnival and festivity [...] where hierarchy is overturned'.[42] The mask is a performance object, a conduit that imbues the wearer with the power to channel magical transformations, which is why they are so often used in rituals and rites. The mask is yet another uncanny object. When we don a mask, and peep through its eye-holes, we become me/not-me, animating the object through interaction with it. In some ancient cultures, especially across Mesoamerica, masks are worn to adopt the attributes of the creature represented. Again, for Pace, such ideas are animated through clay and set in motion. Pace details an interest in the spirit realm

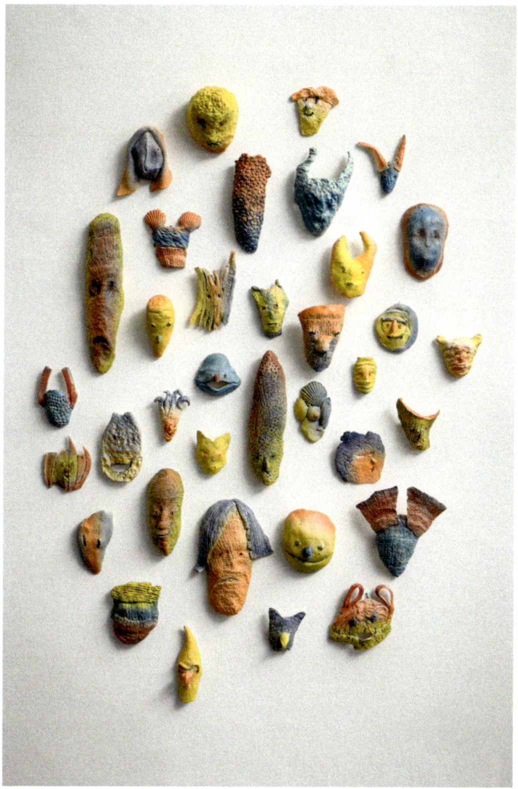

Figure 16.5 Kim L. Pace, *Constellation*, 2022. Glazed ceramic, 36 elements. Courtesy the artist and Arusha Gallery, Edinburgh. Photo by ZACandZAC.

that is an ever-moving afterlife, far from a static or comatose interpretation of death. While her fluorescent watercolours have captured a range of glowing *Spectres* (2019–22) on paper, her ability to sculpt a ghost in clay relies on her ability to animate through texture, colour, expression and position.

Pace's multifaceted ability to present a collective set of animated characters finds another visual precursor in Leonora Carrington's (1917–2011) paintings, especially those of the 1970s. Carrington's surrealist paintings of many figures in flux include the lively menagerie of mythological creatures in *Sanctuary for Furies* (1974) and the collected oddities in *Warning to a Mother* (1973). The latter includes a shamrock-printed feline, diminutive jack-in-the-box jesters, matryoshka dolls, domestic *domoviye* and a nebulous blue incubus floating above. Such descriptive curiosities and strange juxtapositions occur within narrative scenes that behave like theatre sets; one can imagine the characters in motion and their activities extending beyond the contours of the picture plane. Again, such compositional arrangement is vital to the success of Pace's ceramic animations, and her study of Carrington's picture-book domains, animal familiars and toy-like transitions of scale serve as useful reference material in this respect. Pace's *Constellation* (2022) is a family tree of thirty-six relief faces, a vibrant convergence of unique physiognomies. No two are alike morphologically, yet these like-minded beings cohabit in one communal space. Pace's *Constellation* represents a beachcombing of the imagination, surrealist found objects chanced upon in a dreamscape. Like Carrington's bestiaries, *Constellation* is a cacophony or chorus in which each constituent appears to be pulling faces, mouthing and uttering. Here, the ceramic animation is achieved through multiplicity and de-hierarchy. The eye can never quite settle.

Little Otik

Familial themes and textures can be found elsewhere in Pace's recent oeuvre. The mandrake root holds a privileged position in the aesthetic universe of Pace, as one of her longest-term preoccupations and as a chief exemplar of the metamorphosing grotesque. Pace holds a sustained interest in Karel Erben's folk tale 'Otesánek' ('The Wooden Baby', 1865), which provided the source for Švankmajer's stop-motion horror-film adaptation *Otesánek* (Little Otik; 2000; 132 minutes; Czech Republic). The changeling at the kernel of the story serves as a persistent totem for her. The tale concerns a couple who cannot conceive and so adopt a surrogate tree root that resembles a newborn in scale. Their performative care, attention, and investment in this twiggy 'offspring' brings it to life, but, as the root grows, it disturbingly develops teeth and an insatiable appetite, consuming the postal worker, the social worker, and, eventually, even its parents. This dark tale has frequently been interpreted as a parable or moral for the Czech Republic's immersion into capitalist ideology after the Velvet Revolution, although one might also read it as an allegory for animation itself in bringing inert matter to life.[43] Pace's art is more implicit in its political commentary, although her topsy-turvy ceramic animations suggest a desire to overturn societal convention and to rethink the magic in the everyday.

The appeal of *Little Otik* for animators is surely its folkloric and anthropomorphic associations of mandrake root and baby as well as the evolutionary and pseudo-ecclesiastical themes of fertility and immaculate conception; the allegory of bringing inert matter to life. The unpredictability of such raw materials (be they roots or clay) hewn from underground, not to mention the paradoxical nature of carnivorous plants, add further layers of psychic complexity. In Švankmajer's disturbing vision, recurrent imagery of vegetable stews and inert dolls comingle with hallucinations of sentient babies cradled inside watermelons and being netted at a fishing market. The use of such recurrent motifs is carried forward by Pace, and the animated tree root, metonymic textures, and inclusion of toy dolls in Švankmajer offers Pace an abundant ecosystem of visual and tactile source

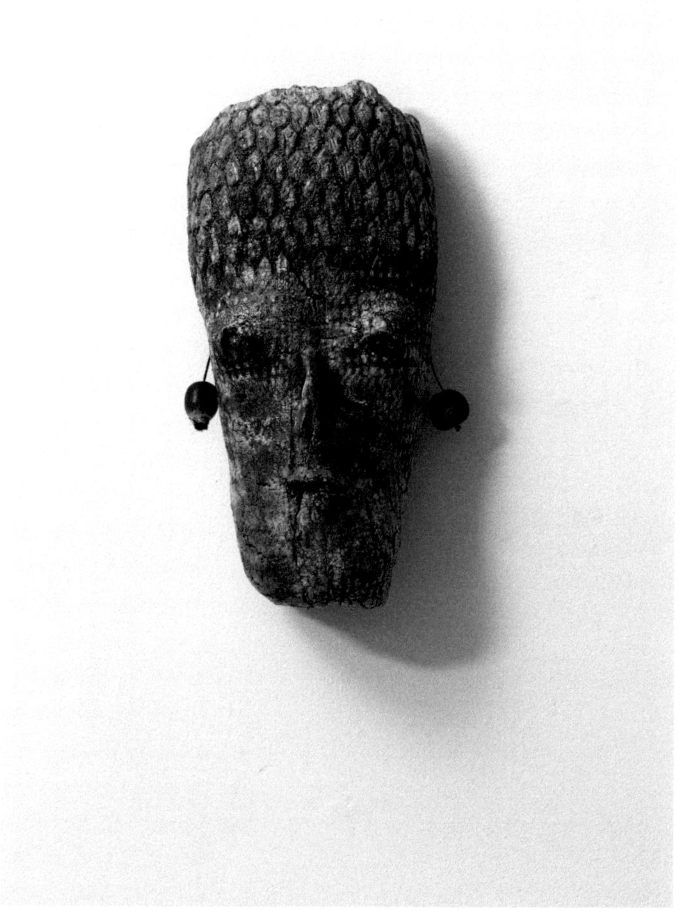

Figure 16.6 Kim L. Pace, *Tree Sprite (Cherries)*, 2021. Glazed ceramic. Courtesy the artist. Photo by Alex Brattell.

material for her ceramic creatures. Pace's *Tree Sprites* (2019–21) uncannily evoke gnarled and peeling bark on their surfaces. One might compare them with turquoise mosaic Aztec masks, suggesting artefacts that animate the histories of ancient cultures. Her *Cactaceae Ballet* (2015) and *Cactus Garden* (2016–18) similarly borrow from the botany of elsewhere, reprising *Little Otik* with puppet-like saguaro performing the human figure, ready to walk off the plinth or paper.[44] Personification runs riot throughout her oeuvre.

Conclusion: boundary creatures

Kim L. Pace is a maker of charged objects, an animator of mirages. This chapter has explored how her use of clay has evolved throughout her career to date, from experimental stop-motion animations informed by Švankmajer and the Brothers Quay towards reanimating a feminist-surrealist dynamic with her ceramics. How to best encapsulate this transition and particular set of interests? Pace's treatment of *Otik*, and other surrealist hybrids, from Tanning's *Three Bitches* to Carrington's *Furies*, and from Oppenheim's cup to Kahlo's mask, can all be said to evoke Donna J. Haraway's notion of the 'boundary creature': the anomalous cyborgs, mermaids and alternative women who inhabit Haraway's writing.[45] This uncanny boundary creature is a slippery, metamorphic entity that has been further embedded into the feminist grotesque by Frances S. Connelly as 'something that creates meaning by prying open a gap, pulling us into unfamiliar, contested terrain'.[46] This pull or forcefield is the animating spectre at work in Pace's ceramics, the uncanny, declassifying sprite which Pace pursues across her practice.

Pace's ceramic animations are beings hewn from a different imagination having found their gestation and calling through the lessons and legacies of surrealism. Within a vast array of reference points, from the archaeological to the cartoon, surrealism provides a provocative methodology for Pace precisely because of its ability to facilitate hybridity and beckon the marvellous.[47] As I have argued, her ceramic output also proposes a redefinition of surrealist animation, as something ontologically static that can summon uncanny sensations, even imitating motion, through a highly imaginative and skilled manipulation of matter and make-belief. Through utilizing the iconography of surrealist visual narratives, Pace effectively animates them into the very fabric of reality, thereby offering a compelling revision of a feminist-surrealist art history through clay.

Notes

1 Esther Leslie, *Hollywood Flatlands: Animation, Critical Theory and the Avant-Garde* (London and New York: Verso, 2002), 90–1.

2 Kim L. Pace, 'The Greatest Show on Earth', in *Cult Fiction* (London: Hayward Gallery Publishing, 2007), backmatter.

3 In 2007, Pace curated 'Cult Fiction' at the Hayward Gallery in London, an exhibition that aimed to demonstrate the close ties between comics and fine art, already detailing her interest in hybrid genres, 'Curatorial Preface', *Cult Fiction*, 9.

4 Kim L. Pace cited in Catriona McAra, *The Medium of Leonora Carrington: A Feminist Haunting in the Contemporary Arts* (Manchester: Manchester University Press, 2022), 190.

5 Pace cites Whitney Chadwick's *Women Artists and Surrealism* (London: Thames & Hudson, 1985) as a formative text, in conversation with the artist (18 November 2022).

6 For an exploration of the Bakhtinian carnivalesque, see Susan Stewart, *On Longing*: *Narratives of the Miniature, the Gigantic, the Souvenir, the Collection* (Durham, NC: Duke University Press, 1993), 20.

7 Amy Hale, 'Communist Witches and Cyborg Magic: The Emergence of Queer, Feminist, Esoteric Futurism', *Burlington Contemporary* (June 2022): https://contemporary.burlington.org.uk/journal/journal/communist-witches-and-cyborg-magic-the-emergence-of-queer-feminist-esoteric-futurism (accessed 19 December 2022).

8 The 'image thinking' and anachronism of Mieke Bal are operating in the background here, *Quoting Caravaggio: Contemporary Art, Preposterous History* (Chicago, IL and London: The University of Chicago Press, 1999), 8.

9 Much of this was possible in the 1980s due to what Pace and others have called the 'golden age' of funding for experimental animation under the auspices of Channel Four, see Suzanne Buchan, *The Quay Brothers into a Metaphysical Playroom* (Minneapolis: University of Minnesota Press, 2011), 24.

10 Such surrealist iconography might include René Magritte's *The Lovers* (1928), Salvador Dalí's *Autumnal Cannibalism* (1936), and Maria Martins' *The Impossible III* (1946).

11 Rosalind Krauss and Yve-Alain Bois, *Formless: A User's Guide* (Cambridge and New York: Zone Books, 2000), 237.

12 Buchan, *The Quay Brothers*, 50–1, 53.

13 Sigmund Freud, 'The Uncanny', *Writings on Art and Literature: Sigmund Freud*, ed. Neil Hertz (Stanford, CA: Stanford University Press, 1997), 193–233. See also E. T. A. Hoffmann, 'The Sandman', in *The Golden Pot and Other Tales*, ed. Ritchie Robertson (Oxford: Oxford University Press, 2008), 87.

14 Heinrich von Kleist, 'On Marionette Theatre', trans. Idris Parry, *Southern Cross Review*, issue 9 (2001): https://southerncrossreview.org/9/kleist.htm (accessed 5 June 2023).

15 Kim L. Pace in conversation with the author (31 May 2023).

16 Jiří Trnka's *The Hand* (1965; 18 minutes) is championed by Pace in this respect.

17 Kim L. Pace, unpublished interview with the Brothers Quay (2016).

18 Buchan, *The Quay Brothers*, 120, 144.

19 Kim L. Pace cited in Bob Chaundy 'Kim Pace, Multi-Media Artist', *Considering Art Podcast* (29 April 2022): https://consideringart.com/2022/04/29/considering-art-podcast-kim-pace-multi-media-artist/#more-4562 (accessed 28 December 2022).

20 Frances S. Connelly, *The Grotesque in Western Art and Culture: The Image at Play* (Cambridge: Cambridge University Press, 2012), 1.

21 Anna Watz, *Angela Carter and Surrealism: 'A Feminist Libertarian Aesthetic'* (New York: Routledge, 2016), 4.

22 Susan Rubin Suleiman, *Subversive Intent: Gender, Politics, and the Avant-Garde* (Cambridge, MA and London: Harvard University Press, 1990), 162.

23 Hal Foster, *Compulsive Beauty* (Cambridge, MA and London: The MIT Press, 1995), xvii, 176; Katharine Conley, *Surrealist Ghostliness* (Lincoln: University of Nebraska Press, 2013), 18.

24 Marina Warner, *Phantasmagoria: Spirit Visions, Metaphors and Media into the Twenty-first Century* (Oxford: Oxford University Press, 2006), 54. See also Freud, 'The Uncanny', 195.

25 See for example the artist's personal website, Kim L. Pace, 'About' (2022): https://kimpace.co.uk/about (accessed 4 January 2023).

26 Marina Warner, *From the Beast to the Blonde*: *On Fairy Tales and Their Tellers* (London: Chatto & Windus Ltd, Random House, 1994), 385.

27 Suzanne Buchan reminds us of the 'prevalent Aristotelian concept of the anima in animation studies', 'A Cinema of Apprehension: A Third Entelechy of the Vitalist Machine', *Pervasive Animation*, ed. Suzanne Buchan (New York: Routledge, 2013), 146; see also Leslie, *Hollywood Flatlands*, 235.

28 Connelly, *The Grotesque*, 2.

29 Buchan, 'A Cinema of Apprehension', 147.

30 Leslie, *Hollywood Flatlands*, 13.

31 Leslie, *Hollywood Flatlands*, 132. See also Clement Greenberg, 'Avant-Garde and Kitsch', *Clement Greenberg, The Collected Essays and Criticism: Perceptions and Judgments, 1939–1944*, vol. 1, ed. John O'Brian (Chicago, IL: University of Chicago Press, 1986), 5–22.

32 Alison Britton, 'Essay', *The Maker's Eye* (London: Crafts Council, 1982), 16.

33 Warner, *From the Beast to the Blonde*, xv.

34 Leslie, *Hollywood Flatlands*, 119, 234. See also Walter Benjamin, 'The Storyteller', *Illuminations*, ed. Hannah Arendt (London: Fontana Press, 1992), 101.

35 Kim L. Pace in conversation with the author (18 November 2022).

36 A *tableau vivant* is typically a scene from a famous painting or narrative performed by costumed actors or models in freeze-frame. The genre peaked in popularity between 1830 and 1920, concurrent with the development of photography and animation.

37 Suleiman on 'feminist intertextuality', *Subversive Intent*, 142.

38 Dorothea Tanning cited in Chadwick, *Women Artists and the Surrealist Movement*, 12.

39 Alison Rowley, 'Lapses of Taste: On Dorothea Tanning', *Woman's Art Journal*, 66 (1995): 18.

40 Lucy Lippard, 'Louise Bourgeois: From the Inside Out', *From the Center: Feminist Essays on Women's Art* (Toronto and Vancouver: Clarke, Irwin and Co. Ltd, 1976), 238–40.

41 This is despite Frida Kahlo's own admission that she was only 'surrealist' by affiliation.

42 Stewart, *On Longing*, 107.

43 Adam Whybray, *The Art of Czech Animation: A History of Political Dissent and Allegory* (London: Bloomsbury Academic, 2020), 94, 157–8. See also Keith Leslie Johnson, *Jan Švankmajer* (Chicago: University of Illinois Press, 2017), 113, 135.

44 Angela Kingston, *Kim L. Pace*: *A Fantastic Fermentation of Matter* (London: Danielle Arnaud, 2018).

45 Donna J. Haraway, *Simians, Cyborgs, and Women: The Reinvention of Nature* (New York: Routledge, 1991), 4.

46 Connelly, *The Grotesque*, 8.

47 Mieke Bal, *Louise Bourgeois' Spider: The Architecture of Art Writing* (Chicago, IL: Chicago University Press, 2001), 29.

Chapter 17

Sweet Horror Claymation: Nathalie Djurberg and Hans Berg's Neo-neo-surrealism

Marie Arleth Skov

A tiger licks a girl's butt, and she likes it. Two daughters compete for their father's sexual attention and are spanked by him until they kill him. In the dream of a young girl, all her children's toys engage in an orgy, and she joins in. The Claymation films of Nathalie Djurberg open a view into a world of seduction, shame and sadism. The short and often erratic stories, filmed with stop-motion techniques, are accompanied by the hypnotizing tunes of Djurberg's partner, Hans Berg – a techno musician who sometimes uses a barrel organ sound, emphasizing the old-fashioned childish atmosphere of Djurberg's inventions. As a viewer, it becomes almost impossible to divert your eyes – and ears! – from this enchanting universe of violence and weirdness.

Both Djurberg and Berg were born in Sweden, but they met in Berlin in 2003. Djurberg was already working on her clay and plasticine animations and was making the music tracks herself. In an interview from 2017, they talk about the beginning of their work together, and Djurberg recounts:

> We met here in Berlin through a mutual friend, and she suggested that he make music for me. Beforehand, I had tried to make music on my own, which is now laughable. Initially, I gave him a finished animation and said: 'OK, see what you can do with this.' What he did changed it completely. It added another layer; it changed the film. It was what I had wanted to do, but hadn't been able to make on my own.[1]

Berg adds: 'It's the combination of images and music that makes it so great because it is emotional, but also starts an intellectual thought process.'[2] The emotional component is key here. Often, visual and emotional *senses* take over in our response to these films. As Pernille Fonnesbech writes of Djurberg's plots: 'Her stories conjure up repressed or taboo topics and emotions, and thus create a connection to twentieth-century Surrealist art.'[3] With all the spellbinding magic of puppet theatre and the colourful cuteness of Play-Doh, we are lured into watching explicitly brutal and vulgar acts. As viewers, we seemingly accidentally come upon predatory excesses, moral transgressions and painful vulnerability and are left in a dilemma of feeling fascinated and disgusted.

The excess of kitsch, violence, and sex as well as the absurd and irrational features in Djurberg and Berg's collaborations have often engendered comparisons with surrealism. Like surrealist films, Djurberg's storylines deprive us of easily legible narratives, often subverting our expectation of what we think is about to happen with weird, illogical turns. 'This follows all good surrealist projects of setting out a deliberate path and then suddenly subverting that path in order to disgust and seduce', MacCormack writes.[4] As Luis Buñuel and Salvador Dalí did in their films, Djurberg and Berg juxtapose unexpected elements, lure us into watching, and then confront us with delightful and disgusting horrors, including our own voyeuristic fascination.

There are other connections too. The places where the films take place (woods, caves, closed chambers) often mirror the places depicted in surrealist art, bound as they are to psychological primal loci. Djurberg fills her films, as Massimilano Gioni notices, with 'archetypical and oneiric images'.[5] The Claymation technique in itself – built upon the very surrealist principle of creation and destruction – links to a childish perspective, an effect that was also used by surrealist film-maker Jan Švankmajer. The film figures, which Nathalie Djurberg forms out of modelling clay, textile, and artificial hair, bring to mind the dolls and mannequins that frequently appear in surrealist art in the work of artists such as Hans Bellmer and Salvador Dalí.

'Surrealism's exploration of irrational drives and compositions of different and absurd realities were based on a grotesque tradition that Nathalie Djurberg and Hans Berg are also related to',[6] Lena Essling points out, thus expanding this tradition beyond surrealism, towards Hieronymus Bosch or contemporary art by Jake and Dinos Chapman. The black, violent humour of the latter duo certainly ties in both with surrealism and with Djurberg and Berg's work.

This chapter examines three aspects that underscore Djurberg and Berg's connection to surrealism: the first section analyses the concept of dispersed, undirected desire, especially in children, drawing on concepts described by Gilles Deleuze and Félix Guattari. The second deals with nature in Djurberg and Berg's films in comparison with surrealism (while also touching upon Charles Baudelaire). Third, in 'Bataille and Bodies', the notions of 'formlessness' (Georges Bataille) and 'abjection' (Julia Kristeva) are applied in relation to the figures formed and deformed by Nathalie Djurberg. These topics tie together to show us the role of transgression in Djurberg and Berg's films: a transgression that is not about breaking rules, but about exploring what our (inner) world might produce without them. In so doing, Djurberg and Berg reveal a twenty-first-century visualization of the expansive potentials of desire and instinct – what we might understand as a renewal, even as an update, of the surrealist tradition.

Desire machines and kinky toys

'I remember sexual dreams and fantasies from when I was very little, and they did not have a target. They were absurd'[7] (as Djurberg says about making *Delights of an Undirected Mind*, 2016). In this short film, we see a young girl in her room, lying in her bed. All around her, children's toys, from a Little Red Riding Hood doll to My Little Pony, start engaging in diverse sexual acts building to a veritable plaything orgy. An animated and horny soft toy wolf fellates the udder of a plush textile cow. A bullfighter doll dressed up in sparkling gold and ice cream blue sparks a bulging erection in his pants. All colours are heightened, from the intensely pink room to the striking green crocodile. The film shows the young girl watching and then engaging in the kinky debauchery of her lustful toys.

The use of Claymation situates the film in a child's world, and the setting in a young girl's bedroom underlines that ambiance. Not unlike Jan Švankmajer's films, created in the perspective of the child, *Delights of an Undirected Mind* delves into surreal and absurd viewpoints of sexuality. 'Sex is something that connects all humans and animals', Djurberg stated, 'I am really channeling what I see as basic human needs and desires, and visualizing every aspect of those desires – even those that could potentially be considered shameful or violent.'[8]

Djurberg's figures often allude to fairy tales, only to then go wildly off script. As viewers of today, we might primarily associate animated movies with anthropomorphic toys or animals with a fairytale plot with the Disney universe. However, the friendliness and romance of Disney toys and animals, often amiably assisting the leading human characters of the film, stand in stark contrast to the reckless and predatorial behaviour of the animated toys and animals in Djurberg's filmic cosmos.

The behavioural differences between Disney's animations and Djurberg's thus become a burning lens for the nature of human conduct. The animalistic actions of the figures in Djurberg's films are performed equally by all creatures. Furthermore, because these films are shown in exhibitions, where they are, during opening hours, looped again and again, it seems these creatures neurotically repeat themselves. 'Why do I have this urge to do these things over and over again?' as the young naked girl in Djurberg and Berg's breakthrough film, *Tiger Licking Girl's Butt* (2004), wonders, as she lets herself be licked by a tiger.

Small girls tend to turn sexual and violent in Djurberg's narratives. One particularly brutal example of this is in her film *Florentin* (2004), in which two daughters are molested by their father, revealing the insipid sadism of the Oedipal family. It is all very Freudian, with a twist at the end. We see a dollhouse-style room, with a black-and-white chequered pattern floor and red wallpaper. A father is playing with his girls, throwing them up in the air and catching them – but each time, his hand moves a little closer to their underwear. He puts them on his shoulders, rather like he is 'wearing' them, as a fox fur, and their crotches right next to his face begin to feel wrong. The skirt of one daughter covers the father's head. Each daughter seems both wanting of the attention, jealous of the other, and at the same time disgusted by the father. As a viewer, one is kept on alert, spellbound by the underlying yet obvious tension of it all. Then, things turn violent: The father spanks one of the girls, knickers down – but the victims become perpetrators: the girls attack their father, throwing him to the floor, where they begin to jump on him, using him as a trampoline, as he cries until he lies still; it is unclear if they have killed him. 'And in great surrealist style, tears and suffering lead to laughter and joy (from them, anyway)', MacCormack writes.[9]

We might conceive the characters in Djurberg's films as *desiring machines*, in the sense of Gilles Deleuze and Félix Guattari, that is: as libidinally dispersed, rather than as

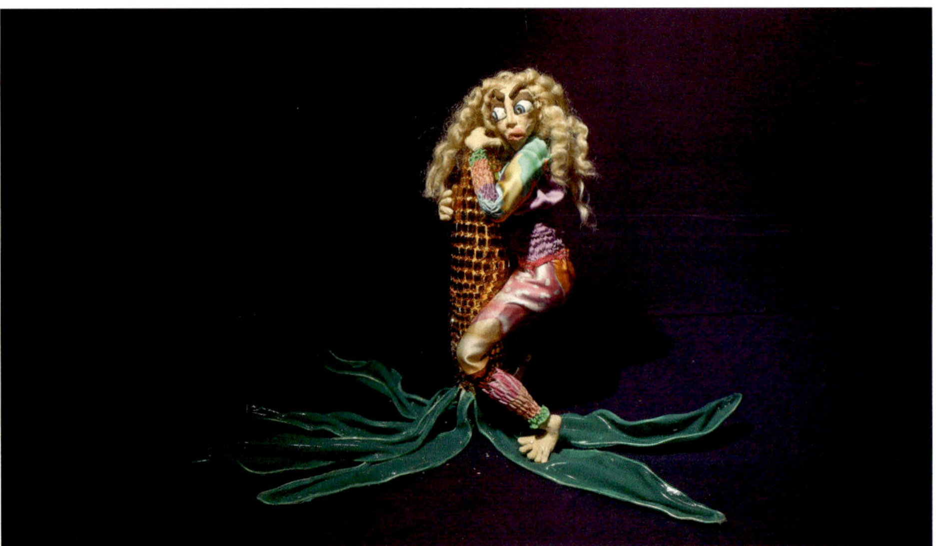

Figure 17.1 Nathalie Djurberg and Hans Berg, *Worship*, 2016. Clay animation, digital video, stereo audio, 8:06 min. © Nathalie Djurberg and Hans Berg. Courtesy Lisson Gallery.

purely ego-driven or focused (Deleuze and Guattari, *Capitalisme et schizophrénie. L'anti-Œdipe* (*Anti-Oedipus: Capitalism and Schizophrenia*, 1972)). Desire is all over the place in Djurberg's films, especially when it comes to young girls. Indeed: 'Female children are the most germinal of desiring machines', MacCormack argues.[10] Desiring machines, as developed by Guattari and Deleuze, are not systematic or directed. Lust then is neither intentional nor imagined, but instead extensive and creative. This scattered sexuality messes with the traditional syntax of filmic storytelling. There is no restraint, nothing to be overcome, nothing to suppress.

An example from the world of grown-ups is *Worship*, likewise from 2016, the same year as *Delights of an Undirected Mind*. The two films are similar in their depiction of a space in which all things are desired, although here we have moved from the child's bedroom to a sweaty night club, completed with a pulsating beat by Hans Berg. '*Worship* is about exposing the superficiality of the world today; scraping away at it and exposing its underbelly', Nathalie Djurberg explains. 'What happens when I peel away the layers of division between desire, sexuality, and worship.'[11] *Worship* is rife with all things shiny, shallow, and sexual: fornication with phallic golden corn, fingering cream cake, grinding on gold motorcycles, humping massive eggplant cars. The grotesque humour of these exaggerated and kitschy references and the obvious sexual innuendo of the symbols likewise allude to surrealism. All the tropes and stereotypes of pornography are there: latex, whips and huge phallic objects.

Not unlike how Max Ernst attacked the outdated narrative models of the Victorian novel in his *Hundred Headless Women* (1929), Djurberg plays with the hidden tensions and libidinal drives in pop culture entertainment, such as boastful music videos, while also subverting Disneyfied storytelling. In Djurberg and Berg's films, childhood is no place of innocence. And neither, as we shall see, is nature …

Evil flowers, dancing bones and macabre cycles

We cannot flee Djurberg's cosmos. Even outside, the setting is claustrophobic: the dark impenetrable forest, the mysterious archaic cave. Nature only emphasizes our vices and is vividly merciless: *Fleurs du Mal* and animal predators, rot, decay, death. In the installation *The Experiment* (2009), which won Nathalie Djurberg and Hans Berg the Silver Lion in Venice, visitors walk through a wicked kind of garden to reach the films. Human-sized flora in fluorescent orange, bright pink, vein-ish blue and faeces brown. Plants shaped like male and female genitalia. Flowers slick and hard like lollipops. 'I smell Sex and Candy,' as the Marcy Playground song goes (Universal, 1997). The oversized menacing flowers and plants might speak to our fear of being overcome by an uncontrollable nature. Furthermore, this kind of immersive installation is distinctively surrealist, carnivalesque too. Enter the grotto, enter the chamber of horrors, enter the tunnel of love.

Flowers: there are few other symbols in the history of art that so directly take the shape of labia, clitoris or glans penis. (Just ask Robert Mapplethorpe or Linder Sterling.) Aside from a more dulcet, domesticated and innocently pretty flower-and-vase kind of flower painting, the *sujet* of flowers – especially in paintings by women surrealists – likewise then stands for a liberated (often queer or female) sexuality.[12] Surrealism scholar David Lomas points out that botanical science describes floral reproduction as sexuality, 'that resembles in its freedom from constraints Freud's account of the polymorphously perverse character of human sexuality'.[13] This is part of what Charles Baudelaire was getting at in 'The Flowers of Evil' (1857) when he cast the floral as beautiful and malicious. Baudelaire pointed to the dreadfully frail surface of alleged cultivation we have put on top of a deep sea of natural (wicked) behaviour.

Djurberg, in her depiction of flowers, certainly leans on the vanitas tradition in European still-life paintings, but in her flowers, the cyclical aspect is even more pronounced than the ephemeral. Flowers do not just wither and die; they recycle, they come back anew. Dying is requisite. Tina Teufel notices how Baudelaire describes flowers and nature as reprobate, but so much more interesting than the 'civilization' in human cities.[14] Instead, the flower world offers sex, taboo, pain and death without mercy. Teufel quotes Charles Baudelaire: 'In fact, I have always believed that there is something sad, hard, cruel, almost shameless about nature when it blooms, when it renews itself.'[15] This shamelessness and cruelty of nature's renewal is on show in Djurberg and Berg's *Turn into Me* (2008).

In this film, nature (in the form of diverse fauna and a bit of flora) devours and dismembers a young woman. The title, *Turn into Me*, sounds like a spell cast by nature. The film begins with a female figure walking naked and alone through the woods (as one does). The scene conjures up associations of the dark and enchanted forest. In Djurberg's film, the young woman suddenly and inexplicably dies and falls down. We see strange creatures, soft tissue, and shiny soil. Her pale naked body lies on the ground.

The image of her white flesh lying on the dark green forest ground has a fairy-tale mood: think of *The Sleeping Beauty in the Woods* or *Snow White*. The image likewise evokes symbolist paintings, such as *Sleeping Diana, Spied on by Two Fauns* (1877) by

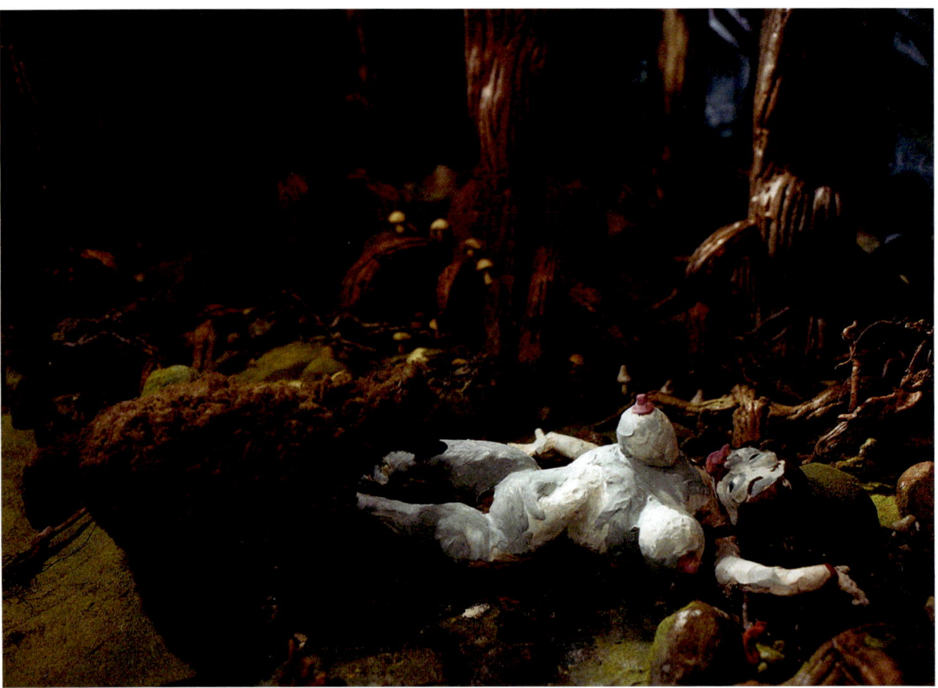

Figure 17.2 Nathalie Djurberg and Hans Berg, *Turn Into Me*, 2008. Clay animation, digital video, stereo audio, 7:10 min. © Nathalie Djurberg and Hans Berg. Courtesy Lisson Gallery.

Arnold Böcklin or *Death of Ophelia* (1852) by John Everett Millais. In the case of Böcklin's *Diana*, the animalistic fauns lustfully eye her as she lies there slumbering and virtuous. In Millais' painting, suicidal and beautiful *Ophelia* lies in the deep, dark waters, surrounded by flowers. In Shakespeare's play, Ophelia expresses her sorrow after Hamlet has killed her father by giving out flowers to the court, seemingly in a state of madness.

But in *Turn into Me*, we see no fetish of the unsoiled, passive woman. Like most of Djurberg's female bodies, this one is endowed with exaggeratedly large breasts and voluptuous lips. Her dead body is overcome by worms, maggots and vegetation, seemingly lustfully overtaking and consuming her flesh and guts to expose the skeleton. Worms and maggots crawl around in all her holes. A cute, curious raccoon and a soft, blind mole live in the dead body. The corpse is thus restored to life; the skeleton body wakes up again and resumes walking, starts dancing. MacCormack describes it as 'a jubilant ecosophy'.[16]

The dead woman's body thus becomes a place of consummation, transformation and interchange. The insects evoke Salvador Dalí's artworks, for example his *Retrospective Bust of a Woman* (1933) – a white porcelain torso of a naked woman, fragile and fine, onto which Dalí painted small black ants crawling over her face. Or the wound on the hand swarming with ants in his film collaboration with Luis Buñuel, *Un Chien andalou* (*An Andalusian Dog*, 1929). Ants are reminiscent of rot and an uncomfortable tingling sensation, which links Dalí's tickling ants to the small creatures consuming the body in Djurberg's film. In *Turn into Me*, the revitalized corpse seems to celebrate metamorphosis, to celebrate the cycle of life and death; indeed, to celebrate death and desire as equal.

Rather than the Christian ashes to ashes, dust to dust, this is rather dirt to dirt, predator to prey. Human demise is not all that important, Djurberg seems to be stating. Nothing lasts. The nature of humanity is violence. The nature of nature is death. In another film by Djurberg and Berg from 2008, *Putting Down the Prey*, we see a fur-clad Inuit woman killing and skinning a seal, climbing into its fur, then diving into the icy water, becoming animal. Seals are fierce, aggressive predators; they attack and eat their own species, and male seals have been found to rape both female seals and penguins.[17] No noble nature, no noble humanism, and no noble 'primitive' cliché is to be seen here. No pretence of a beautiful balance between nature and humans either. In Djurberg and Berg's films, no one is innocent.

In one of the most recent works by Djurberg and Berg, *A Pancake Moon* from 2022, we see an anthropomorphized egg, round, white, full, with spindly arms and big buttocks, prancing around in the woods to the tune of a single flute. However, danger lurks for the female-connoted egg: a gator-wolf and a boar with huge jaws and a long red tongue emerge. The two creatures eye the egg with lust and hunger. She tries to escape, transforms into a round and pale moon with pink cheeks and rises to the sky. The egg turned moon, however, is not safe for long: she starts bloating, descends, lands as a deflated pancake on the ground. Now, the pancake moon is dismissed by the boar, who doesn't even bother eating her. The animation closes with a new egg: the prospect of a new life. This new film touches both on the cyclical element and metamorphosis topic in Djurberg's work and it leads us into the next subchapter via the egg that is much like the eye.

Bataille and bodies

In the Claymation films of Djurberg and Berg, the body is (literally) squeezed and deformed. The material itself underlines the stretchiness of the human body. The bodies Djurberg gives form to are often exaggerated, especially the female bodies, with extreme curves and full lips, like pornographic caricatures of human bodies. The figures in these films are often too close for comfort, entangled into one another, even literally attached to one another, unable to escape. Bodies are often hurt, intoxicated, wounded, attacked. Moreover, bodies constantly change in Djurberg's hands; they lose their shape and find new ones. Metamorphosis is the 'fundamental trait' of Djurberg's figures, as Massimiliano Gioni writes.[18] From dead to alive and back, from calm to excess. The metamorphosis not only concerns the bodies, but the roles of the figures in the films too: perpetrators become victims and victims become perpetrators, sadists turn into masochists, and vice versa, in a salute to the Marquis de Sade. This being in flux stands in contrast to the stop-motion technique: inexorably, the gradual change is halted, then resumed, halted, resumed.

In the filmic cosmos of Djurberg and Berg, suffering takes place all the time. But this suffering is base here, even clownish, not spiritual, not distinguished, but accompanied by sweat, excrements and rowdy laughter. The suffering is raw and physical, despite the Play-Doh material. In their merciless depiction, in their sordid misery, and in their sheer physicality, Djurberg's bodies resemble those painted by Francis Bacon. As Gioni points out, ‘Djurberg’s characters are immune to the sometimes cloying mysticism of surrealism and its dissidents.’[19] If, in these films, nature evades romanticism and childhood evades innocence, suffering similarly evades sublimation.

The criticism of Georges Bataille, surrealism’s self-described ‘old enemy from within’, thus echoes in Djurberg’s work. Bataille famously ended his comradeship with the surrealists with the words ‘too many bloody idealists’.[20] He criticized the aestheticization of violence, sacrifice and seduction – the surrealists, in his view, only flirted with transgression. Bataille’s publication *Documents* transgressed in a more sadistic manner – although, and this links it to Djurberg, with a sense of parody and humour too.

Djurberg’s depiction of bodies connects with the rendering of bodies in surrealism in several ways. Her main figures are puppets: the fragmented dolls of Hans Bellmer immediately spring to mind. The abject also plays a role – all that Julia Kristeva describes in her seminal *Powers of Horror: An Essay on Abjection* (1982). Kristeva’s study focuses on the feeling of abjection and taboo experienced in the confrontation with bodily functions, especially those of the female body, which are hidden away and deemed impure or indecent. In Djurberg’s films, as in surrealism, all that is bloody or seedy is effusively shown, even celebrated.

Furthermore, the eye is emphasized in Djurberg’s clay figures. Often the clay figures’ eyes are oversized, and the camera often zooms in on an eye, expressing surprise, lust or fear. In the film *Untitled (Acid)* from 2010, for example, the bulging eyeballs of a woman’s face are dramatically highlighted, the hairless eyelids seemingly only barely preventing the protruding orbs from falling out. This focus on the eye in Djurberg and Berg’s films relates back to *Un Chien andalou* (1929) and the famous scene in which we see a close-up of a woman’s eye and later the eye of an animal being sliced with a razor. The eye was a significant *sujet* in surrealist poetry, film and visual art, as it symbolized the verge between the external world and the inner self. The ‘Eye’ as substitute and as symbol of its homophone ‘I’ (singular, first person), used for example in the horror tales of Edgar Allan Poe, could also be a reference.

The eye creates a specific link to the viewer, who is emotionally drawn into Djurberg’s films, (unwillingly) becoming a voyeur or possibly a witness. In Georges Bataille’s *L’Histoire de l’œil* (*Story of the Eye*, 1928), the tears of eyes are metaphorically interchangeable with cat’s milk, egg yolks, urine, blood and sperm, as Roland Barthes notices in his essay ‘The Metaphor of the Eye’ (1962).[21] Going back to Julia Kristeva’s concept of abjection, the eye (and by extension, the ‘I’) thus becomes an equally tabooed body part, by association as ‘impure’ or ‘indecent’ as genitalia. The egg and the eye metaphorically and visually overlap in Bataille’s novella, as Roland Barthes describes: ‘It is a double variation, affecting both form (*oeil* and *oeuf* share one sound and vary in the other) and content.’[22] If for a moment we think back to the film mentioned before, *A Pancake Moon* (2022), Djurberg similarly plays on the triple metaphor of the egg, the eye, and the ‘I’.

Indeed, Djurberg has often cited Georges Bataille as an influence, as Pernille Fonnesbech, Lena Essling and Massimiliano Gioni indicate. Apart from the use of the eye metaphor, this connection to Bataille manifests in two aspects: the first is the overlap of death and sex, pleasure and pain. ‘With Bataille in mind, one might describe her work as a new kind of “death by a thousand cuts,” to borrow an image from the final page of

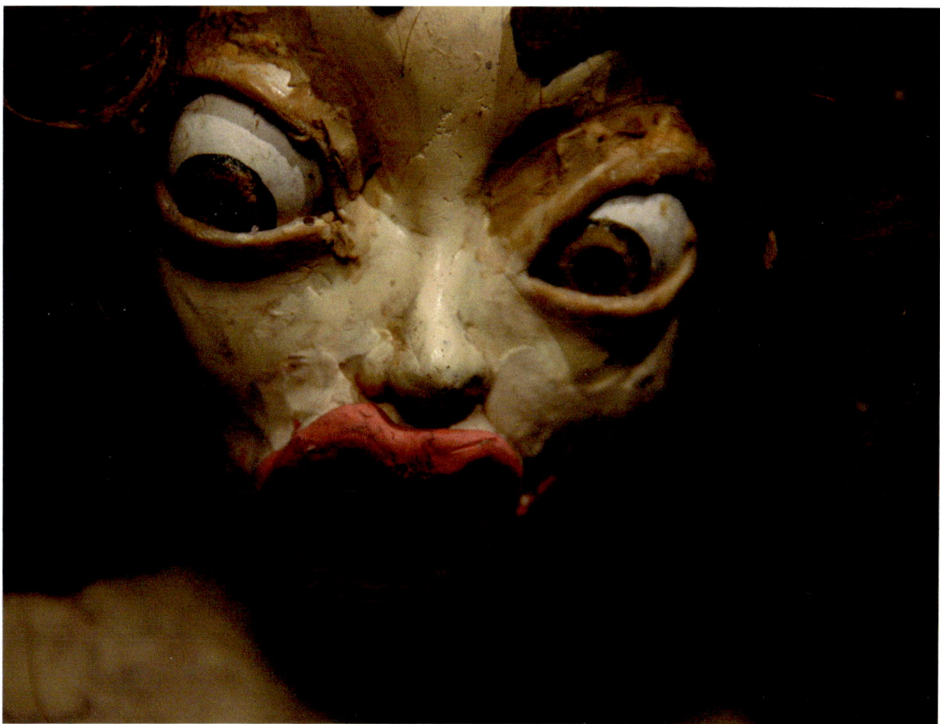

Figure 17.3 Nathalie Djurberg and Hans Berg, *Untitled (Acid)*, 2010. Clay animation, digital video, stereo audio, 6:05 min. © Nathalie Djurberg and Hans Berg. Courtesy Lisson Gallery.

the French writer's *Tears of Eros*: a ritual in which pleasure is mingled with pain, yielding a new ecstasy', writes Gioni.[23] Indeed, Susan Sontag's observation about *The Story of the Eye* – 'What Bataille exposes in extreme erotic experience is its subterranean connection with death'[24] – could just as well be applied to Djurberg's wicked and erotic stories that so often end in slaughter. Eros and Thanatos reunite.

The second is the notion of the *informe* (the formless), as Essling writes of Djurberg and Berg's playful approach to desire, excess, and ache: 'It is here, in the rebelliously Dionysian, that the experience of *l'informe* in their work is primarily located.'[25] *L'informe* for Bataille is a dissolvent of form and content, *l'informe* as destabilizer, as destruction of categories. Formlessness stands for irrationality; for Bataille it is 'the epitome of what eludes classification'.[26] In his artist journal *Documents*, which he published from 1929 to 1931, the French writer and his associates examined various phenomena (factory chimneys, Buster Keaton, etc.), mostly through photo essays with original literary texts. In the final issue of 1929, Bataille writes about *l'informe* in the 'Critical Dictionary' of the journal: 'Thus formless is not only an adjective having a given meaning, but a term that serves to bring things down in the world, generally requiring that each thing have its form. What it designates has no rights in any sense and gets itself squashed everywhere, like a spider or an earthworm.' Bataille notices how 'academic men' long to give shape to what is formless, even the universe, attempting to tame formlessness with 'a mathematical frock coat'.[27]

Next to the formlessness of the universe, the formlessness of the human body is equally angst-inducing. A shapeless, undefined body makes the viewer uneasy. Essling mentions Marcel Duchamp's *Étant donnés* (1946–66) as an example of a formless body, 'a form of parody reminiscent of Bataille's'.[28] The same kind of amorphousness characterizes Djurberg's Play-Doh and clay bodies – deformed, bendable, somehow too much meat and too little structure. Hans Bellmer and Francis Bacon, both mentioned above, or Cindy Sherman's *Sex Pictures* (1992) and *Broken Doll* (1999) series, likewise come to mind.

In viewing these artworks, fear and fascination become entwined. The art represents a transgression both for the artist and the viewer. However, the transgression in these artworks is not edifying. 'Art's relational affect is found not in the dialectic between art and spectator but in the mucosal intimacy between them. Here is also where we find true transgression, forsaking "edgy" content that relies on the rules it breaks to be transgressive.'[29] MacCormack's use of the word *intimacy* here fits the work of Djurberg and Berg. Arguably, intimacy also tallies in the case of *Étant donnés*, where Duchamp forces us, the viewers, to peek through two small holes to see the horror. The films of Djurberg and Berg we likewise watch alone with only our own conscience (or lack thereof). What we experience in viewing these films is not the breaking of rules, but a world without rules. These films are not just about acts of overstepping, but about a much more encompassing shapeless transgression and undirected transmutation. These films are about what happens in a world without limits, an existence of formless Dionysiac flow.

Conclusion

We see in the work of Djurberg and Berg the whole spectrum of human, animal and posthuman creatures going through primal states of vulnerability, fear, innocence, aggression and arousal, accompanied by carnival music and throbbing beats. Djurberg sets the scene in archaic primeval sites, in closed claustrophobic homes, or before the backdrop of decadent club culture, MDMA dreams, and sick overflow. The viewing experience is comic, grotesque, and somehow at the same time invasive and liberating. If we think of late twentieth-century artists and film-makers of the American West Coast, like Mike Kelly, Paul McCarthy and David Lynch as neo-surreal in their approach, then Djurberg and Berg's films propose a neo-neo-surrealist take on the twenty-first century. Like their American counterparts, Djurberg and Berg work with low culture and pitch-black humour. However, the brevity and anti-epic idiosyncrasy of Djurberg and Berg's films give them a contemporary feel.

We experience physical discomfort watching Djurberg and Berg's sick tales. A warm rush of shame, a hand to protect the eyes, a need to physically turn away – but do we turn away? These films are not here to educate us, but to shock. We could thus situate Djurberg and Berg's films as a continuation of the more de-sublimated strain of the surrealist tradition (Bellmer, Buñuel, Bataille). As MacCormack emphasizes: 'In these films, Djurberg uses textures, movements, and media, as well as lugubrious images and actions, to critique these structuring systems.'[30] Both in form and in content, Djurberg and Berg's films constitute a criticism of structuring regulations.

The circumstance that we are, the whole time, watching dolls and Play-Doh figures fortifies the transgressive effect. Especially for small girls, dolls have always been a teaching instrument too; showing small misses how to emulate role models of perfect wives and mothers. The unhinged behaviour of Djurberg's Claymation figures thus symbolizes a loosening of restricting norms. Dolls are surrogates, fetish and projection objects, in which ideals, fears and wishes are mirrored. To let the dolls loose ('who let the dolls out?!') in this manner thus exemplifies the release of oppressed energy and creativity.

The artistic potential of formlessness makes the connection to Georges Bataille especially clear. Susan Sontag identified the project of both Georges Bataille and the Marquis de Sade: 'to explore the scope of transgression'.[31] This is what interests Nathalie Djurberg too. Both technically and substantially, she disregards the parameters and rules. Her aesthetics and storylines, together with the sound by Hans Berg, thus update the surrealist approach to our times.

Notes

1 Djurberg Louisa Elderton, 'The Delights of Undirected Minds: Nathalie Djurberg and Hans Berg. Interview', *Elephant*, 33 (Winter 2017): 170.

2 Berg Elderton, 'The Delights of Undirected Minds', 171.

3 Pernille Fonnesbech, 'A Beautiful, Lewd and Gruesome Garden: The Experiment', in *Snake Knows Its Yoga*, ed. Kristin Schrader (Nürnberg: Verlag für Moderne Kunst, 2010), 111.

4 Patricia MacCormack, 'Joy is the Core of Horror', in *A Journey through Mud and Confusion with Small Glimpses of Air*, ed. Lena Essling (Berlin: Hatje Cantz, 2018), 107.

5 Massimiliano Gioni, 'Morphologies of the Folk Tale', in Esseling, *A Journey through Mud and Confusion with Small Glimpses of Air*, 226.

6 Lena Essling: 'Across the Stage and into the Trees: Place and Memory in the Work of Nathalie Djurberg and Hans Berg', in Esseling, *A Journey through Mud and Confusion with Small Glimpses of Air*, 28.

7 Djurberg in Hettie Judah, 'Once Upon a Bondage Crocodile', in *The Guardian*, 29 March 2017.

8 Djurberg in Elderton, 'The Delights of Undirected Minds', 167.

9 MacCormack, 'Joy is the Core of Horror', 108.

10 MacCormack, 'Joy is the Core of Horror', 108.

11 Djurberg in Elderton, 'The Delights of Undirected Minds', 167.

12 See Marie Arleth Skov, 'Shady Plants, Ecstatic Trees, and Vulva Seashells: Symbols of Erotic Nature in the Surrealist Work of Rita Kernn-Larsen and Elsa Thoresen', in *Modern Women Artists in the Nordic Countries, 1900–1960*, ed. Kerry Greaves (London: Routledge, 2021).

13 David Lomas, 'A Language of Flowers: Surrealism, Psychoanalysis, and the Botanical Imaginary', talk at the conference *Surrealism & Psychoanalysis: Conquest of the Irrational?* Freud Museum, London, 27 January 2019.

14 Teufel: 'Les Fleurs du Mal', 202.

15 In a letter of dedication to C. F. Denecourt quoted in Tina Teufel: 'Les Fleurs du Mal. Über Sein und Schein', in *Flowers & Mushrooms*, ed. Toni Stars (Munich: Hirmer, 2013), 208. Author's translation.

16 MacCormack, 'Joy is the Core of Horror', 111.

17 See e.g. S. Rohner, K. Hülskötter, Gross et al. 'Male Grey Seal Commits Fatal Sexual Interaction with Adult Female Harbour Seals in the German Wadden Sea', *Scientific Reports*, 10, no. 1 (2020): 13679.

18 Gioni, 'Morphologies of the Folk Tale', 225.

19 Gioni, 'Morphologies of the Folk Tale', 227.

20 Both quotes in Simon Baker, 'A Corpse', in *Undercover Surrealism: Georges Bataille and* Documents, eds. Dawn Ades and Simon Baker (London: Hayward Gallery, 2006), 82.

21 Roland Barthes, 'The Metaphor of the Eye' (1962), printed in Georges Bataille, *Story of the Eye* (London: Penguin Classics, 2001), 121.

22 Barthes, 'The Metaphor of the Eye', 121.

23 Gioni, 'Morphologies of the Folk Tale', 227.

24 Susan Sontag, 'The Pornographic Imagination', 107.

25 Essling, 'Across the Stage and into the Trees', 28.

26 Michael Richardson, 'Dictionary', in Ades and Baker (eds,), *Undercover Surrealism*, 92.

27 'Formless' by Georges Bataille, *Documents* 7, Paris, 1929. Translated from the French by Dominic Faccini, *October*, 60, (Spring 1992). Quoted in: Michael Richardson, 'Dictionary', 92.

28 Essling, 'Across the Stage and into the Trees', 28.

29 MacCormack, 'Joy is the Core of Horror', 109.

30 MacCormack, 'Joy is the Core of Horror', 106.

31 Sontag, 'The Pornographic Imagination', 107–08.

Interviews

Chapter 18

'We Are All Surrealists': in Conversation with Jacolby Satterwhite

Abigail Susik

Jacolby Satterwhite (b.1986) is a widely known contemporary artist who incorporates lavishly detailed 3D animations into a multimedia practice that includes installation, painting, sculpture, photography, live action, performance and original music. The lush visual panoramas of his work and their engagement with themes of mythology, memory and desire have inspired many descriptions of the surreal quality of his oeuvre. In this interview, art historian Abigail Susik talks with Satterwhite about the influence of surrealism upon his art, with a focus on the connections between surrealism, 3D animation, live action, CGI (computer-generated imagery), software, artificial intelligence and stop motion.

Abigail Susik: How has surrealism been an influence on your work?

Jacolby Satterwhite: Surrealism has been important to me since I was a teenager. Eventually, I started to have a deeper understanding of where those influences aligned politically and personally for me. When I was studying fine art in my boarding school, during my undergraduate and graduate studies, and during many residencies after that, I continued to think about Fluxus, dada, and surrealism. The reason why they were created was a reaction to the propagandistic properties of painting history and its association with war and adverse political themes that were happening at the time.

Growing up in a postmodern world as an African American queer minority, there was a limitation to my voice in the institution because my professors and peers were often trying to place and understand me or contextualize me and use my identity as a vessel or platform for a propagandistic function. When I was making objects, they would try to steer me towards using the colour of my identity to represent something, tokenizing me as an artist for what I represent instead of just seeing me as an artist. So that forced me to find alignment with dada, surrealism, and Fluxus because I constantly wanted to give a middle finger to what I was expected to do.

When I went back home, one Christmas, and I saw my mother, Patricia Satterwhite, still drawing these schematic diagrams that she had been drawing since I was a child, I noticed that what she was doing was surrealism. Her drawings were also like dada and Fluxus scores. They had written instructions, prayers, and sonnets. They were visions

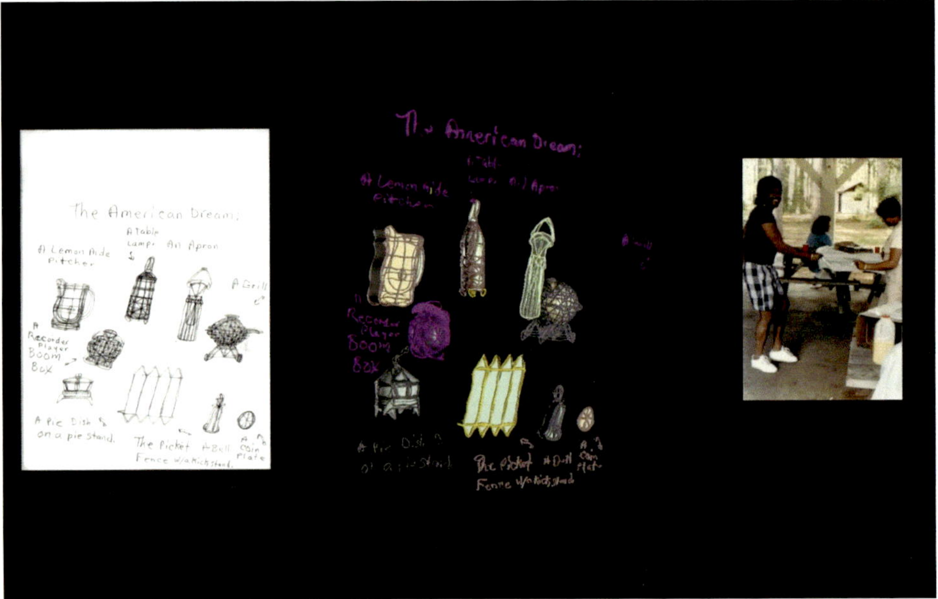

Figure 18.1 Jacolby Satterwhite, *The Matriarch's Rhapsody*, 2012. HD colour video and 3D animation with sound, 43:47 min. © Jacolby Satterwhite. Courtesy of the artist and Mitchell-Innes & Nash, New York.

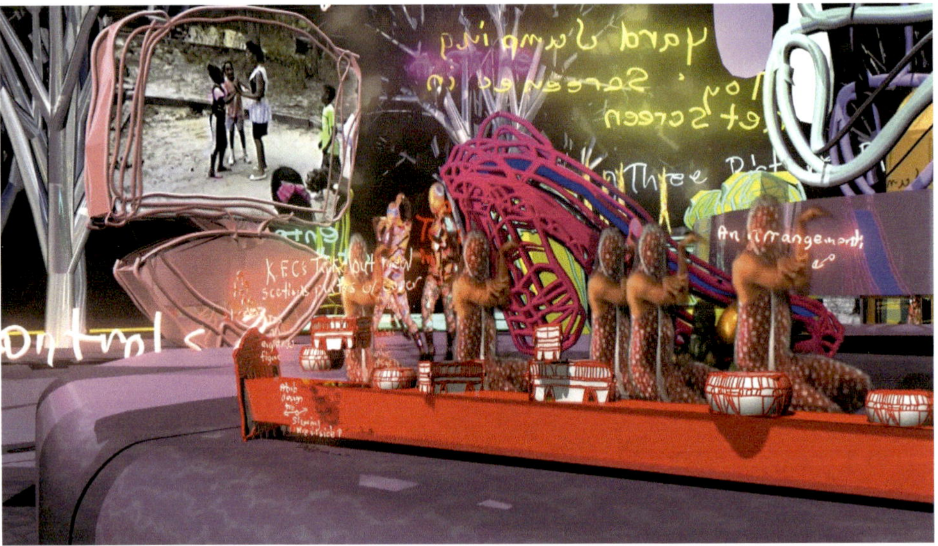

Figure 18.2 Jacolby Satterwhite, *Country Ball 1989–2012*, 2012. 3D animation and video, 12:38 min. © Jacolby Satterwhite. Courtesy of the artist and Mitchell-Innes & Nash, New York.

for absurd objects. They had all the principal characteristics of the Surrealist movement, and they felt like an heirloom, or an inheritance, or a blueprint for how I should think about moving forward in my own life. My mother's drawings were what influenced me to become an artist.

I started to align my private life with my public life. I was using my private archive to figure out how to regenerate my practice, allowing this heirloom from a schizophrenic woman, her clairvoyant eye, to be a surrealistic vessel for me. Her drawings helped me learn how to innovate. Every time I reproduced one of those drawings it was not necessarily a literal action. It was akin to surrealism, dada, or Fluxus because it was reacting to the absurd with absurd. These drawings could emerge in any medium – in a provisional performance, a painting, a CGI film, and it extrapolated from there for twelve years.

I started to expand the practice to different communities. Instead of using my mother's drawings, I would go to dilapidated, sickly communities in the Midwest and ask them to find something within the darkness. I would say, 'What do you look at to find utopia?' and ask them to make a drawing about that and build a world around it. I started to use that strategy in different communities, workshops, and psychiatric wards.

That's my story about surrealism being the backbone of my practice.

AS: How did you initially learn about surrealism?

JS: I grew up in Columbia, South Carolina and my dad would take me to the Columbia Art Museum. They had a lot of Suprematist and Constructivist art. But I also remember when I would go to Walden bookstores and Barnes & Noble, there were books on Salvador Dalí, Max Ernst, and El Greco, who was a proto-surrealist. Books on Hieronymus Bosch were important, too.

AS: Does your animation work relate specifically at all to surrealist interests or techniques?

JS: I'm doing a much more spherical version of the exquisite corpse, in which the disparateness of archive and genre bridge together to make one form. That is the exquisite corpse game that I'm playing. I like taking things that have an abrasive connection with each other and forcing them to match. To bring those incongruent forms together and find a way to force congruency between them is a surrealistic practice. That's what makes it have that tension. The negative space is my action and my action is the nuance that makes it individual and unique. It is my attempt to force these drawings and family photographs into this computer software, or through these contemporary performers; it's like the gumbo of it all to make to the idea of collaging these psychic spaces together to create something poetic and uniform.

Some of these pieces were generated in 1992 and never knew they were going to find a home in work made in 2020. Sometimes I'll have something dormant in my hard drive from 2009, and then the pandemic happens, and people are protesting, and I'm shooting the protests in my phone, and there's some kind of strange mirroring between this piece and that piece. As a digital artist, I'm dealing with twenty-five terabytes of data that I'm connecting schizophrenically and trying to find form with. That is what the surrealists wanted to do, but they didn't have the technology. I mean, literally, we all are surrealists.

AS: Do Afrosurrealism or Afrofuturism interest you as an artist?

JS: Before I even knew what those words were, I used those strategies from a real place by default. The whole thing about Sun Ra was that it was in the 1970s, right after the civil rights movement, and the hellscape of Black America was on Earth. In order to find

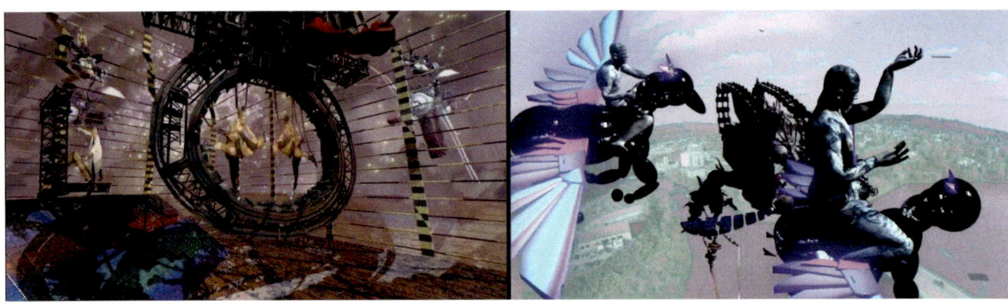

Figure 18.3 Jacolby Satterwhite, *Blessed Avenue (Jade Edition)*, 2018. Two-channel HD colour video and 3D animation with sound, 19:18 min. © Jacolby Satterwhite. Courtesy of the artist and Mitchell-Innes & Nash, New York.

autonomy of free expression, it was necessary to simulate a vision of being in outer space, without context. This was a kind of phenomenology: what does it mean to have the body oriented around another object? What does that look like and what does it express? As long as you're in America, your Black body being adjacent to a chair signifies something. The semiotics between the Black body and an object are loaded, no matter what object on earth we are talking about, and so to place the Black body in outer space, gives it autonomy to take on another meaning.

Afrofuturism is about coming from a bad place, a horrible place, an adverse place, and using futurist ideas and aesthetics to offer possibilities for new forms and solutions. For me, coming from a broken home with a schizophrenic mom, and coming from a queer background, and coming from all these really weird, strange places, I was using futuristic mediums and sci-fi aesthetics to rearrange the codifications of those things at their roots, repurposing them to be gentle and poetic.

AS: Do you feel like you're playing exquisite corpse with different parts of yourself, or is your mom there in the game as a consciousness?

JS: Everybody I've worked with in my practice, whether it's a vocalist or a stylist, affects me. I've spent a significant amount of time tracing the touches of other people who influenced me, and their spirits show up because I'm attentive. So, yeah, subconsciously, I know what her intentions were with the drawings. I knew her very well, I sat with her making those drawings for years in South Carolina, where's there's nothing else to do. So, I'm inheriting the spirit of her intention, but bringing in my own interpretation of the contemporary world with it. She's just a gesso. It's not a tribute. I barely work with her content anymore. The only thing she shows up in now is her vocals and even with that, I used an artificial intelligence program to learn her voice. I'm quoting Buddhist prayers and vocalizing with her voice.

AS: Are you using artificial intelligence (AI) in any other aspects of your work?

JS: I'm using artificial intelligence to learn my rendering style, so I can render things in another software. The hard part is learning how to tell it what to do, how to phrase it. That's a new art form in itself, which is crazy. For me to learn the language to tell an AI to generate my work would result in something that contains all the things I hate about

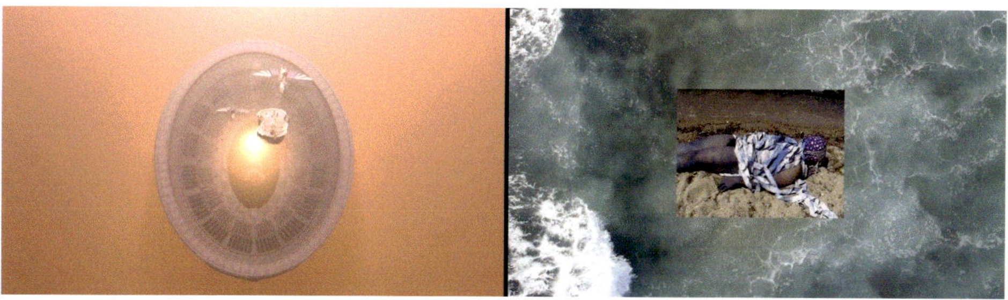

Figure 18.4 Jacolby Satterwhite, *Birds in Paradise*, 2019. Two-channel HD colour video and 3D animation with sound, 18:20 min. © Jacolby Satterwhite. Courtesy of the artist and Mitchell-Innes & Nash, New York.

myself, it would be an embarrassing dystopia, you know? AI is taking all the bad parts about art and exploding them. I don't know why people are so impressed. When I look at Midjourney and DALL-E, I want to die and throw up. They are stealing my art. They are making the good parts of art obsolete and ugly. I'm not moved by it at all. Honestly, if it was up to me, I wish my skill set was using Kodak film from 1979. I'm trying to get away from AI as much as possible, but the reason why I use CGI is because it is a more fluid way to explore themes without the rigour and the labour of doing it on the physical ground. I can cover more territory at a more rapid pace because my mind moves really fast.

If I had the economy of using live action only, I would probably do that. But I know that my sensibility is not there yet. As I get older, I just want to reduce, reduce, reduce, reduce. Painting has come back into my practice extensively. I've done forty paintings in the last couple of years, and I've shown paintings at PS1 and in Basel, Switzerland. Painting is my primary medium. I'm a formalist. I couldn't do film without painting. I didn't study film; I didn't study 3D animation. I graduated with a full ride in graduate school for painting, and then I discovered film, video, 3D animation, and performance afterwards. I did twelve residencies to learn these other media privately, staying in bunkers and cabins alone. My foundation for learning those tools is using the principles of painting and drawing, so at the end of the day, my talent lies in my mind and in my hand, not some fucking stupid software. It's all about getting to the bare bones.

AS: Is the medium of animation something that is essential for the realization of your vision, and if so how does it relate to the notion of the extended frame, or animation's ability to go beyond the limitations of 2D and 3D art?

JS: I love game engines and making video games. Everything's a tool. But they all inform one another. Practising all of them at once makes them inform one another. When I make a painting, I modulate and build that object in a secular way. The commitment to this still object and the rumination over it allows me to relax my mind and expand on complex ideas. Sitting at a computer and looking at a screen or digital media is very mentally taxing and paralysing. It's sort of like how I use Transcendental Meditation to reset and to clear my mind and focus my ideas. Painting is a form of meditation using colour and stillness as a mantra to figure out the core concepts of what to do in the actual moving image. All my paintings are footnotes to or the almanac of what is happening in the digital arena, the digital space. That was how the function of the C-prints worked. Some people think that the paintings can be an anomaly for me, but they're not. If you look at *The Matriarch's Rhapsody* (2012), and you saw those family photographs on the right, and you saw the drawings in the middle and 3D objects on the right, the family photographs are the stillness that I was ruminating on to find the core concepts of what I was doing in the surrealist space. But when I do it as a painting, it explodes things ten times larger because I'm spending seventy-five hours using colour, texture, space, light, and everything about that image. I'm using the image as a mantra, meditating, until it becomes nothing, and nothing, and nothing. And then I find what the true spirit in the meaning of that piece is.

AS: Is there a relationship between animation as a medium and your body?

JS: I've always wanted to do bad, bad things. Like when I was in graduate school, someone was like, 'Why are you making a video game? That's not art. His queer Black body against a white wall is so singular and so special. I don't know why he doesn't just do that …' I'm like, uh, 'You are racist.'

The reason why my body was such a central object is that I was too lazy to trust myself to put another person's body at risk for my experiments. I was trying to understand how to home in on those radical experiments. Also, the purpose of my body was not about it being me but having some kind of physical form act as a font, or some kind of gesticulated angle in the animation, because I was just building composition. When you look at Renaissance paintings, the curvilinear, dancing movement helped create the angles that made the perfect composition. Using modern dance phrasing in my body that was based on object orientation allowed me to build narrative that was non-linear using

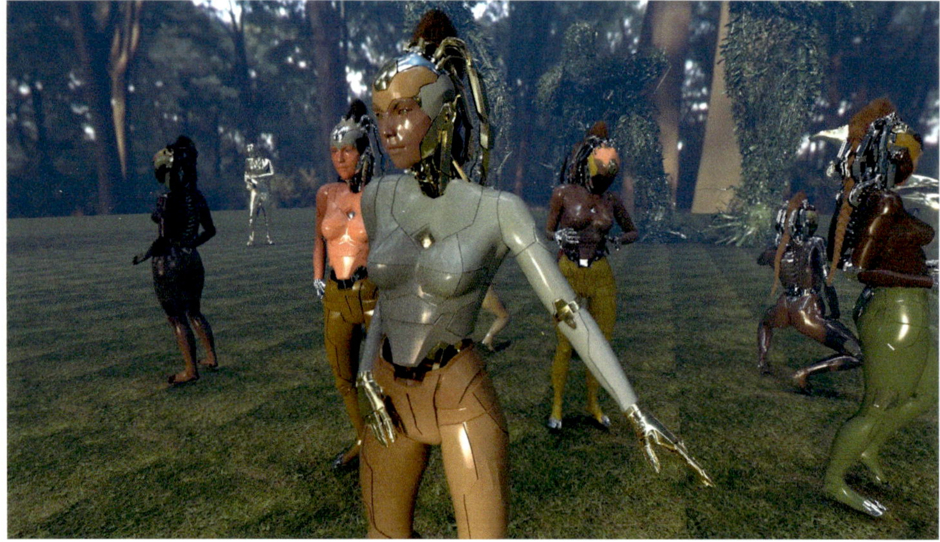

Figure 18.5 Jacolby Satterwhite, *We Are In Hell When We Hurt Each Other*, 2020. HD colour video and 3D animation with sound, 24:22 min. © Jacolby Satterwhite. Courtesy of the artist and Mitchell-Innes & Nash, New York.

movement and utilitarian objects. I began to use my body more symbolically and more politically over time.

I love modern dance and movement, and I love my body as a modernist tool. I love Bruce Nauman, Joseph Beuys, and Matthew Barney, and the idea of the body as a mythic vessel in space. I'm obsessed with the idea of Leonardo da Vinci's Vitruvian Man; the man is the measure of all things; using a toe and a thumb to create a column and an arch. With Bruce Nauman, he would use his name as a form of measurement, like with the neon pieces, or measure the negative space underneath his chair to make a work. He turned his body and the space around him into this mythic being. That gave me permission to think about my own studio practice as being in my own body, and having that immediate access to be the measurement for all things that scale my work. It's not that there is something special about my body. It's just cheap. I don't have to sign a licence of agreement with it; I don't have to sign a confidentiality clause. I can sexually harass my own body.

AS: Are you interested in stop-motion animation?

JS: I love stop-motion animation. Nathalie Djurberg is one of my favourite contemporary visual artists, and she uses stop motion. I think she's so cool, bold, free, and dope.

My work technically is stop-motion animation. I record my movement on a green screen or someone else's movement on the green screen, and then I take that footage onto After Effects and key it out. Then I export it as a PNG image sequence. I take out certain movement phrases in that and I loop it. I import the image sequence and paste it onto a 2D plane in Maya. It is work frame by frame by frame, like in stop-motion animation. I have to go in frame by frame and manipulate each frame … like 10,000 frames. With *Blessed Avenue* (2018), I had to, frame by frame, cut and paste a polygonal object into that 2D space. Especially in the earlier works, whenever you saw a 2D figure interacting with 3D form, that was pretty much stop-motion animation. I would sculpt frame one, and then move the object next to the outer frame, and then the next frame, and the next frame, and so on. I would spend six months on that. I took six to ten Adderall a day. People will never know what I went through.

AI will never sync with the clumsiness and rawness of my work because it will try to make it polished. I think the bare-bones tactility of some of my animations will become

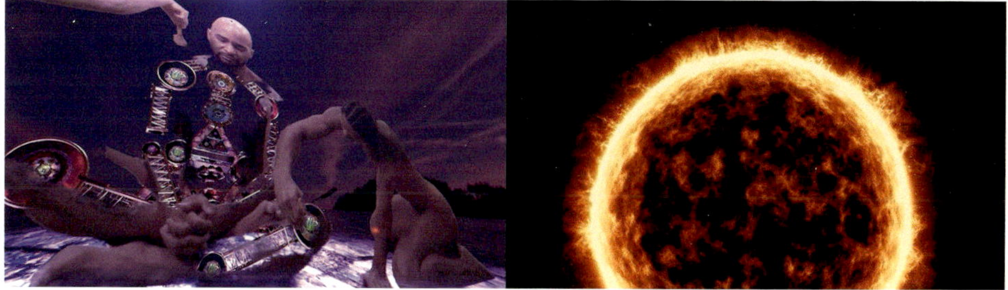

Figure 18.6 Jacolby Satterwhite, *Reifying Desire 7 – Dawn*, 2022. Two-channel HD colour video and 3D animation with sound, 27:25 min. © Jacolby Satterwhite. Courtesy of the artist and Mitchell-Innes & Nash, New York.

more special, because artificial intelligence will never want to make those weird, abrasive mistakes. My work is so handmade that it cannot be regenerated by AI. I never wanted to polish. There had to be evidence of my hand. That's what I like about using Maya. It was the closest thing to making a painting, how you scrape the palette knife against the canvas, and the tooth of the canvas makes the colour raw and like a form of light. You're not rendering, you're allowing the material to use its own language to express the sentiment of something in real life.

Chapter 19
'An Exorcism and Liberation': in Conversation with Penny Slinger

Judith Noble

Penny Slinger (b.1947) began exhibiting her work in 1969. She had a successful career as an artist working in collage, sculpture, and text and image and also worked in experimental theatre and performance. She is recognized both as a surrealist and as one of the first feminist artists to emerge at the end of the 1960s. In the late 1970s she walked away from an art world that she found sexist and repressive and began making work based on more spiritual concerns, including a series of works based on Tantra.

Judith Noble (nee Higginbottom, b.1955) was one of a number of feminist artists in the UK in the late 1970s and early 1980s making work in which her own psyche and body were the subjects. After making a series of widely exhibited installations and films (*Water Into Wine*, *Sea Dreams*, *Mysteries*), she found her increasing concern with spirituality and feminism was at odds with the materialist art world. She too walked away and made work in more private contexts.

In recent years, the 're-enchantment' of the art world and an increasing recognition of women artists has seen Slinger and Noble both return to making work in a more public context. This conversation ranges across surrealism, animation, their experience of the art world, a feminism that explores the psyche and spirituality, and eroticism.

JN: When you were a student at Chelsea, Roland Penrose saw your work and recognized its surrealist elements. This led to your meeting with Max Ernst in Paris, and also to your participation in the *Young and Fantastic* show at the ICA in 1969. How did you integrate surrealist techniques into your work?

PS: When I discovered Ernst's collage books, that was like a light being switched on. When I saw *Une Semaine de Bonté*, I understood how he used collage to explore the psyche and dive into a dream, and to create these seamless visionary interiors that became a new reality in themselves. You can make new worlds and this gives you licence to explore unknown realms, but also to bring in pieces of the real world, because you are using actual found objects. Ernst used engravings; in my case I decided to use photography because it was more of the moment, and it allowed me to incorporate things that were very of the now, as well as archetypal and universal elements. I thought, this is a bag of tricks you can shake up, delve into, and assemble whatever kind of dreamscape you want. It was a technique that seemed to have limitless possibilities. When I discovered

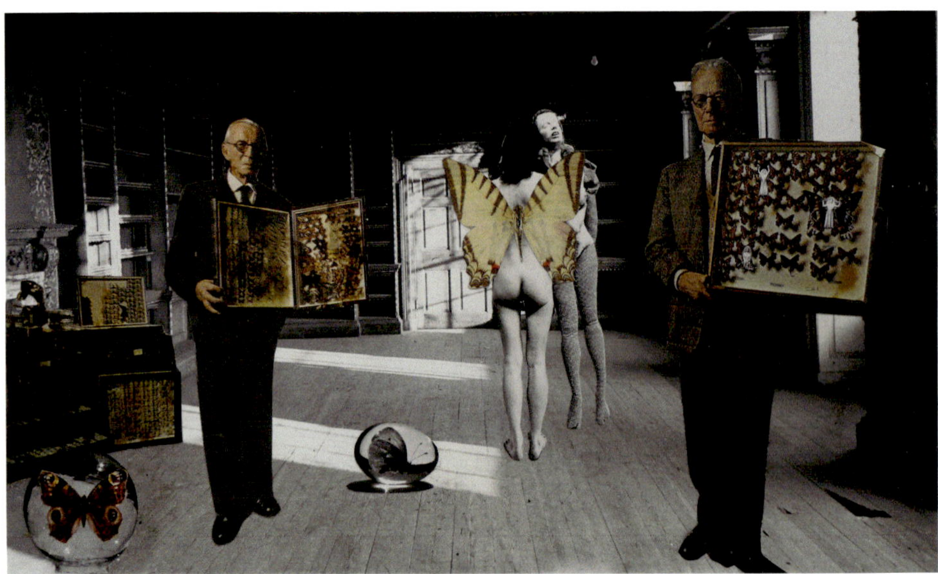

Figure 19.1 Penny Slinger, *Butterfly Collection*, photo collage from *An Exorcism*, 1969–77. 20 × 13.5 in. © Penny Slinger.

Ernst's work, I thought the best way of paying tribute was to use these techniques myself and the inspiration he gave me to explore femininity and my own interior landscape. Throughout the history of art, most of the language had come from the male side of things. I needed to be self-reflective and find a way of describing the interface between the inner and outer worlds; to explore how women are perceived as well as the way we perceive ourselves. This was why I wanted to get into surrealism and being above realism. I was never very interested in representation per se, because it does not give you much depth, or show you much of the invisible, which is what I am interested in.

JN: You are best known today for the photo-collage works you made in the late 1960s and 1970s (*50% The Visible Woman* and *An Exorcism*), but some of the earliest works you made were on film and contained a mix of live action and collaged animation.

PS: When I was a student at Chelsea School of Art, they didn't have a movie camera and I had to borrow a 16-millimetre camera from the nearby tech institute. I basically had to teach myself film-making; I just dove in and experimented and did a lot of in-camera compositing and editing. I made a number of short films and part of my thesis was an animated film of Max Ernst's collage work *Une Semaine de Bonté.* I filmed the actual images in Ernst's book and added live-action imagery of my own, for example filming lions in the zoo, and montaged all of this together. From the beginning I incorporated collage in the film work; I didn't see it as separate from the rest of my work in photography and sculpture. I discovered stop-motion animation effects, and in one of my other films called *Rhythm of Two Figures* I montaged my drawings together with live action. I was an avid visitor to the British Film Institute at that time and watched a lot of European films. I particularly liked *Last Year in Marienbad* because it went beyond linear time and linear

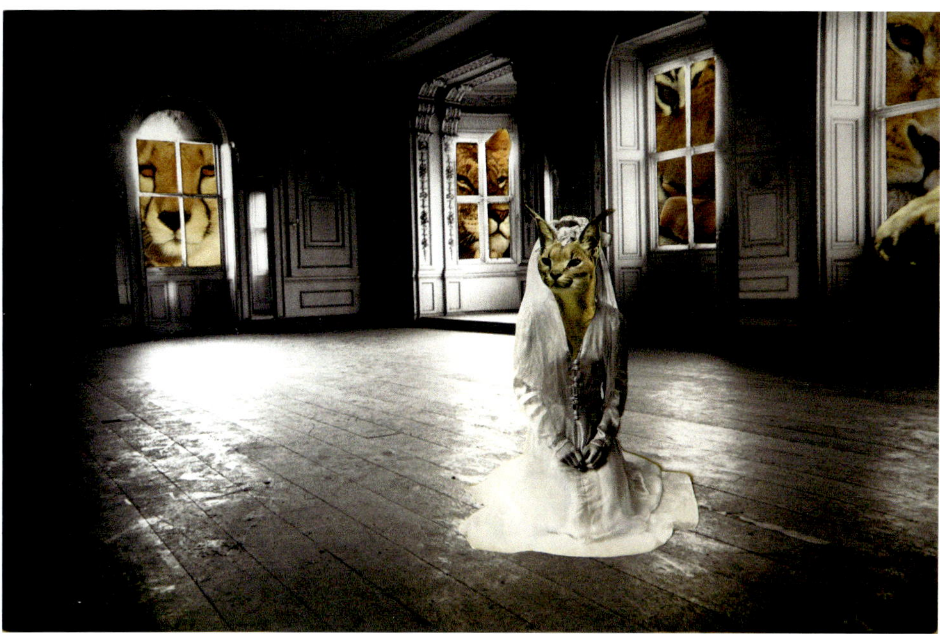

Figure 19.2 Penny Slinger, *Call of the Wild, The Bride*, photo collage from *An Exorcism*, 1969–77. 19 × 12.5 in. © Penny Slinger.

structures and arrived at a kind of timelessness. Surrealist films (Dalí, Buñuel, Cocteau) were also a source of inspiration. In a way, I found films more inspirational than the other plastic arts. I was accepted to study film-making at the Royal College of Art but didn't take up the place because I met Peter Whitehead and began working with him in film outside the academic field.

From the time of my Pre-Diploma course at Farnham School of Art (prior to coming to Chelsea) I chose to mix media in dynamic ways. As my work developed, it was the concern with collage that became more and more important. I was combining sculptural objects and body casts with photographic images in my *Mummy Case* and *The Bride in the Bath* (both of which formed part of *50% The Visible Woman*) and it was the interplay between the two- and three-dimensional that was important, as well as collage as a way of examining the self and the psyche.

JN: You completed the most recent iteration of *An Exorcism* in 2019, working with Dhiren Dasu. You went back to the original still images shot with Peter Whitehead at Lilford Hall in the early 1970s and reinvented the piece as a digital animation.

PS: It was a very healing thing for me to be able to realize it in this way now. One of the big motivating factors for me doing *An Exorcism* originally was that I needed to reclaim that journey of death and rebirth that was depicted in the images. I tried to find myself and leave behind the ghosts of Penny's past. Only about half the original images were used in the 1977 book and I was able to bring many more into the film. My partner, Dhiren Dasu, did the animation for me, and it was wonderful to be able to work with him.

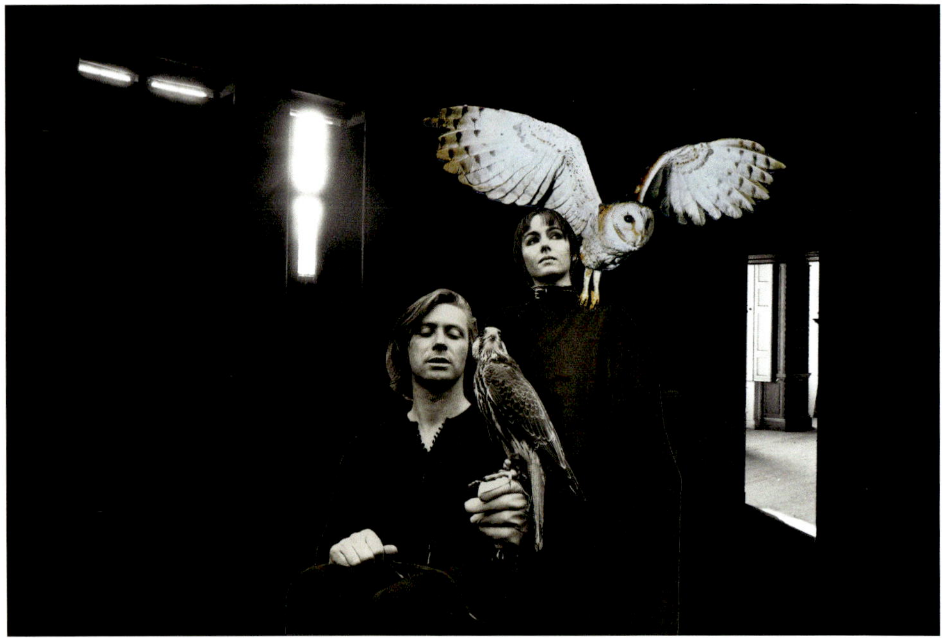

Figure 19.3 Penny Slinger, *His and Hers*, photo collage from *An Exorcism*, 1969–77. 19 × 12.5 in. © Penny Slinger. Courtesy of the artist and Richard Saltoun Gallery.

JN: The pace and the sense of physical movement through the narrative work in an extremely effective way. I read that you had intended to make a film at Lilford Hall when you shot the original images, but the material filmed at the time did not evolve in the way you and Peter had envisioned and was abandoned, so the work evolved as a photographic piece, organized in a series of chapters, and was published as a book in 1977.

PS: I still had all the negatives that were used to create the backgrounds of the images in the book, plus many more, so I was able to put those onto the computer, and deconstruct and reconstruct all the elements of the collages so that we were able to create the sequence of the journey through the house, which is also my own interior journey.

JN: Even with digital technology, this must have been an incredibly labour-intensive process?

PS: It was. Then in the film we tried to keep the processes as simple as possible, so that the attention is always concentrated on the images themselves and the movement through a series of doorways, each one beginning a chapter, rather than being distracted by technique or effects. Organizing the camera moves was central. It allows you to feel the energy of the different chapters.

JN: There is a tremendous sense of inexorable movement through the spaces of the house which is an alchemical descent, dissolution and rebirth, and also through time.

PS: It's like music; it has an intrinsic rhythm and cadence, like a song. We took the film to our friend David Kobza in San Diego and created the music together with him. I told him the essence of what I was trying to get, so again there was a strong collaborative process. My vocal track, the poetry was done live, in one take; it was not edited.

JN: Would you describe yourself as being in a kind of trance state when you 'wrote' that?

PS: You can't be in the ego; you just have to lose everything and see what comes from the spirit of the moment, allow something else to speak through you. So for me, as a surrealist, this is absolutely fundamental.

JN: At the beginning the protagonist is contained by the house; imprisoned within it. At the end of the film, it is the woman who contains the house. She has not only freed herself, but she is now in control.

In some ways, the erotic sequences reverse conventional gender roles. The male figure, 'played' by Peter Whitehead, allows himself to be very vulnerable, and objectified and humiliated.

PS: Reflecting on it recently, I thought it was quite outstanding that, even though we were no longer together, Peter continued to allow me to photograph him in that way, because he believed in my art. He saw my art (*Young and Fantastic*, ICA, 1969) before he met me and wanted to meet me because of the art. He responded to it and allowed himself to be my muse in that sense, which was in itself very radical. I have always been interested in being able to treat myself as both subject and object, and I think I did the same with Peter. In terms of the eroticism, one time a young man said to me, I love *An Exorcism*; it's my favourite book to masturbate to, and I was quite put out. Okay, I shouldn't feel bad about that; it's a sort of natural response, but I felt that maybe he did not understand my commentary on these situations and just took them at face value.

JN: I was part of the group of women that founded Circles, the UK women's film distribution cooperative in the 1980s. American artist Carolee Schneemann had the experience of her feminist erotic film *Fuses* being distributed by a porno cinema chain, which was the wrong context for it entirely. We wanted women to be able to control the context in which their work was seen, and to deal with eroticism in a way that did not just equal titillation.

PS: Exactly. I felt affronted because that was not how I was presenting the work. I did deliberately put my work in men's magazines in the 1970s and sometimes appeared nude with it, but I made sure that the text that went with it was extremely confrontational. I thought, I am going to deliver a lot more than the male audience is expecting and make them have to step back and realize this is not an object for my pleasure; this is a subject we are looking at here. I have to question what I am feeling and see beyond the surface value of objectifying this woman. I wanted to break barriers in terms of how women were seen by men. Definitely *An Exorcism* is dealing with many erotic scenarios from a psychological point of view, because the film takes place in a psychic space, not a physical one.

JN: The editing and structure of the film contribute a lot to its success. The viewer is forced to go on a horrendous alchemical descent into the depths of degradation and despair.

PS: I tried not to be myself looking back at how I was then or recreate that. Rather, it is the sum of all my responses. When we get to the end I just channel what I felt in the moment as we finished the film; what came through then.

JN: Something that fascinates me about your work, and especially *An Exorcism*, is how the spiritual aspects of it are perceived, or ignored. I had very similar reactions to my own early works (*Water Into Wine*, *Mysteries*). People described them as a rebellion against the patriarchy; a feminist descent into difficult areas of the psyche, and very political (which they were), but for me the main purpose of them was entirely spiritual, and this tended to be ignored.

PS: I have always had this spiritual underbelly. It has been something right from when I was young. When I was a teenager, I read various esoteric writings and at one point went to a convent school because I felt it was going to be a mystical experience, but unfortunately that was not the case. That is why, when I discovered Tantra, I left behind the career that I had built in order to follow that spiritual path. Now I feel I practise Tantra not as people see it as a religion, or sex, but in the sense of being the way to weave together your whole interdimensional self between spirit and matter.

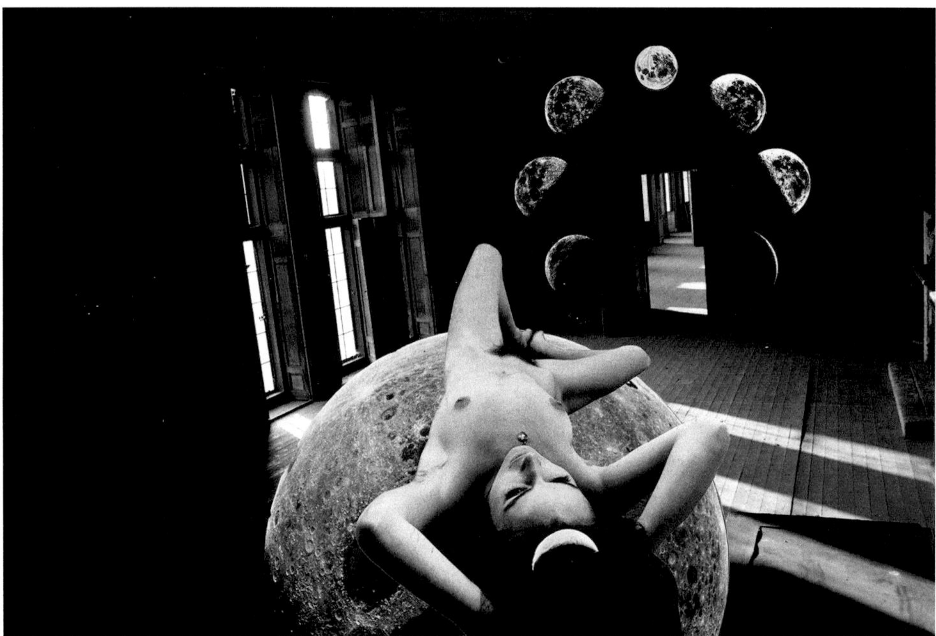

Figure 19.4 Penny Slinger, *Lunar Mansion*, photo collage from *An Exorcism*, 1969–77. 19 × 12.5 in. © Penny Slinger.

JN: That concern with a personal spirituality was something that came through very much in the work of the earlier generation of women surrealists: Leonora Carrington, Remedios Varo, and Leonor Fini, for example.

PS: We have had to do that. Recently there has been something of a dawning and an opening up, which has been great. It was only a few years ago that I had to take my website down because my gallery said you are talking about the goddess and the divine feminine too much and it's putting off our clients. The spiritual side has always been a little at odds with the fine art world. I have always seen a way to integrate it all, and I am hoping that we are moving toward an understanding of that integration now.

JN: I think the art world has changed enormously in the last few years. My own 'walking away' happened some years after yours. It was related to the way that spirituality and acknowledgement of the divine feminine was incompatible with the art world at that time. Like you, I experienced the sexism, but it was the continual denial and denigration of the spiritual that became too much, so I thought I will keep making this work but I won't call it art.

PS: I had my first show in 1969 and a major show in London in 1977 and showed in New York, but I was bitterly disappointed with the reaction. Only a select few people could understand what I was doing, and those who did understand the more psychological aspects could not accept the radical stuff. It just wasn't understood in London. In New York, I had a number of men who wanted to buy work, but they were all convinced that, because the work was erotic, I went with it, and I wasn't prepared to play that game. Then I met my partner. I became involved in Tantra and we moved to the Caribbean and I stopped making work for London and New York. Instead, I wanted to use my talents and my gifts to try and interface with the culture that I was living in at the time. Along with Tantra, that period of my work was concerned with the way Indigenous people live and the need to change in the face of climate crisis.

JN: In your latest work, *The 64 Dakini Oracle*, for example, you embrace digital collage technologies.

PS: In the 1990s I taught myself Photoshop. The concerns of my work remain the same. Instead of refuting and kicking out all the Indigenous ways and dominating them with our sensibilities, we need to embrace them and integrate them with the new technologies.

JN: You have been quoted as saying, 'My life and art are interwoven.'

PS: I have never been one for putting things in separate boxes; they should be integrated. I took that on as a challenge and I totally believe that artists, their lives and their artwork should be one thing. What I like about surrealism is that it's not just the life you see, but the life in the head and the psyche as well; the superconscious and the subconscious, and we are in the middle interfacing between all these things and hopefully expressing all of it. My recent work has involved using myself as a naked muse, challenging the ageism of the art world.

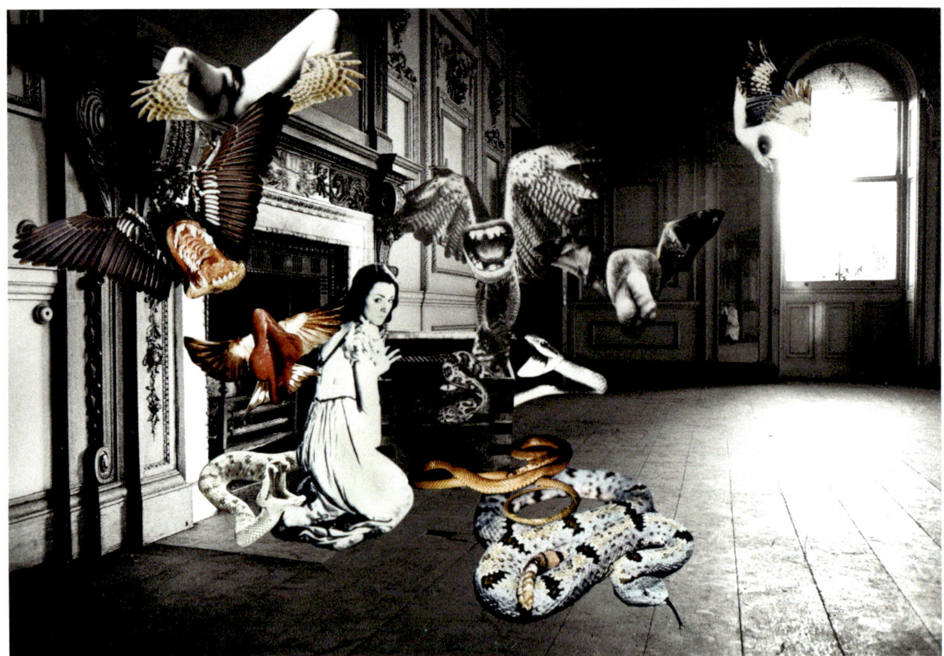

Figure 19.5 Penny Slinger, *Pandora's Box, version 2*, photo collage from *An Exorcism*, 1969–77. © Penny Slinger.

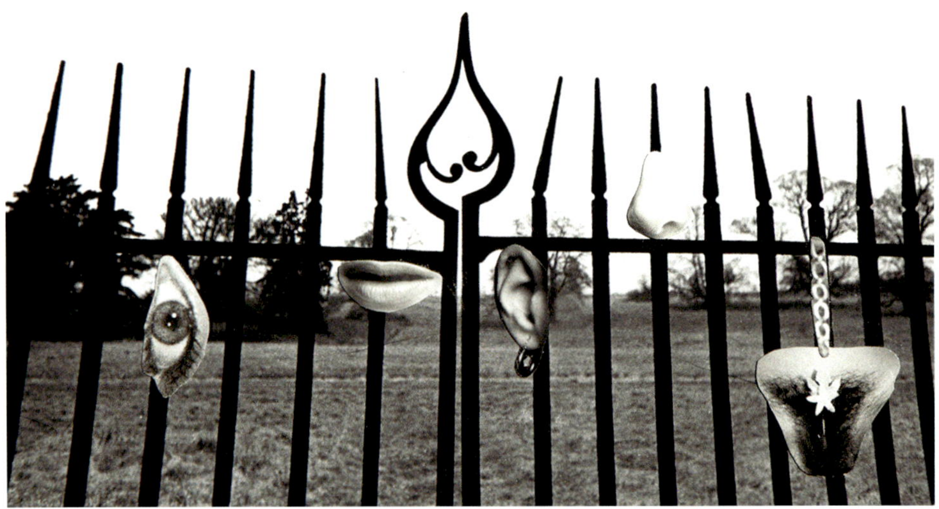

Figure 19.6 Penny Slinger, *Shrine*, photo collage from *An Exorcism*, 1969–77. 9.57 × 7.5 in. © Penny Slinger. Courtesy of the artist and Richard Saltoun Gallery.

Index

Note page numbers followed by *f* refer to figures.